Digital Marketing

Second Edition

Digital Marketing: A practical approach second edition is a step-by-step guide to marketing using the Internet. Concentrating on the operational and functional aspects of this dynamic subject, the book is packed with tactical advice and real-life examples from those leading the field to help you succeed.

Written as an accessible guide to equip you for the digital element of any contemporary marketing role, *Digital Marketing* covers all the key topics including search engine optimization and social media marketing. With real-world case studies to illustrate digital marketing in practice and exercises to help you analyse, plan and execute effective strategies within the workplace, this practical resource will prepare you to undertake digital marketing across a variety of organizations.

More than just a book, this complete package features an associated website at alancharlesworth.eu/DigitalMarketing which hosts the case studies for the book, offers further tips and advice and provides access to a wealth of extra material such as up-to-date references and web links.

This new, second edition builds on the first edition's success by addressing the key recent developments in digital marketing, including an expanded section on social media marketing and an appreciation of the impact of mobile devices. Moreover, it has been thoroughly updated throughout, with brand-new case studies and examples with an international range, all of which encourage the reader to quickly learn the practical applicability of the theory and practice of e-marketing.

Alan Charlesworth, a Senior Lecturer in Marketing and Digital Marketing, has been involved in online marketing as a practitioner, consultant, trainer, researcher, educator and author since 1996.

Digital Marketing

A practical approach

Second Edition

Alan Charlesworth

Routledge
Taylor & Francis Group

LONDON AND NEW YORK

First published 2014
by Routledge
2 Park Square, Milton Park, Abingdon, Oxon OX14 4RN

and by Routledge
711 Third Avenue, New York, NY 10017

Routledge is an imprint of the Taylor & Francis Group, an informa business

British Library Cataloguing in Publication Data
A catalogue record for this book is available from the British Library

Library of Congress Cataloging-in-Publication Data
  Charlesworth, Alan, 1956–
  [Internet marketing]
  Digital marketing: a practical approach / Alan Charlesworth. — 2nd edition.
     pages cm
  Revised edition of: Internet marketing: a practical approach, published in 2009 by Butterworth-Heinemann.
  Includes bibliographical references and index.
  1. Internet marketing.   I. Title.
  HF5415.1265.C488 2014
  658.8′72—dc23

                                                        2013032727

ISBN: 978–0–415–83482–7 (hbk)
ISBN: 978–0–415–83483–4 (pbk)
ISBN: 978–0–203–49371–7 (ebk)

Typeset in IowanOldStyle
by RefineCatch Limited, Bungay, Suffolk

To those who meet up in the Vaults of a Sunday evening. Gentlemen: for the banter and laughs . . . you have been dedicationed.

Contents

List of figures   x

Acknowledgements   xii

Preface   xiii

Chapter 1   The online environment   1

1.1   Introduction   1
1.2   A background to the Internet   2
1.3   The impact of the Internet on society   6
1.4   The impact of the Internet on business   13
1.5   The impact of the Internet on not-for-profit organizations   19
1.6   Online buying behaviour   22
1.7   The Internet goes mobile   29
1.8   Online marketing objectives   32
1.9   Legal considerations   37

Chapter 2   Getting started online   41

2.1   Introduction   41
2.2   Domain names   42
2.3   Website hosting   52
2.4   Who 'owns' the web presence?   54
2.5   Website analytics and e-metrics   57
2.6   The Internet as a tool for market research   66

Chapter 3   Developing the online presence   74

3.1   Introduction   74
3.2   Web presence management and development   79
3.3   The basics   87
3.4   Online credibility   105
3.5   Content development   108
3.6   The global web presence   125

Chapter 4   The B2C online presence   **132**

4.1   Introduction   132
4.2   Multi-channel retailing   137
4.3   The retail website   141
4.4   The checkout process   150
4.5   Fulfilment   154
4.6   e-marketplaces and comparison shopping sites   162
4.7   Third-party retail websites   165

Chapter 5   The B2B online presence   **169**

5.1   Introduction   169
5.2   B2B buying practices   170
5.3   The B2B website   174
5.4   Lead generation   177
5.5   E-marketplaces   180
5.6   Online auctions and tendering   183

Chapter 6   Search engine optimization (SEO)   **188**

6.1   Introduction   188
6.2   How search engines work   193
6.3   Keyword selection   198
6.4   On-site optimization   203
6.5   Off-site optimization   209
6.6   Strategic SEO   215

Chapter 7   Online advertising   **222**

7.1   Introduction   222
7.2   Objectives and management   225
7.3   Where to advertise online?   231
7.4   Online ad formats   236
7.5   Search engine advertising   242
7.6   Network advertising   252
7.7   Affiliate programmes   258
7.8   Landing pages   261

Chapter 8   Permission marketing   **265**

8.1   Introduction   265
8.2   Personalization   268
8.3   Email as a medium for direct marketing   273
8.4   Email as a medium for marketing messages   284
8.5   Newsletters   288

Chapter 9   Social media marketing   **291**

9.1   Introduction   291
9.2   Consumer generated content   297
9.3   Social networks and online communities   304
9.4   Blogging   310
9.5   Viral marketing   314
9.6   Online public relations and reputation management   320
9.7   Strategic social media marketing   329

Chapter 10   Epilogue   **336**

Index   339

List of Figures

0.1   The author's website, alancharlesworth.eu   xxii

0.2   The author's *when you're inside the bottle, you can't read the label* blog   xxii

1.1   World Internet users, June 2012   10

1.2   World Internet usage and population statistics, June 2012   10

1.3   World Internet penetration rates, June 2012   11

1.4   The Internet's potential impact on the buying cycle   24

1.5   The basic AIDA sales funnel   25

1.6   A contemporary sales funnel   25

2.1   How a domain name is constructed   45

2.2   A small section of a log file   63

2.3   The interpretation of part of a line from the log file   63

2.4   Visit details of the most popular pages of the site   64

2.5   How the 700 visitors to the site over a seven-day period came to be on the site   64

2.6   Which mobile devices were most popular for accessing the site over a seven-day period   65

2.7   Where in the world visitors were located when they visited the site   65

2.8   A simple yes/no response form   70

2.9   The home page of SurveyMonkey   72

3.1   Four pages from the author's websites which use templates provided by the sites' hosts   85

3.2   The home page of gov.uk   88

3.3   The home pages of alancharlesworth.eu and of this book's first edition   98

3.4   A page from nffcblog.com   114

3.5   Website content   119

3.6   Examples of commonly used widgets   124

4.1   A helpful delivery text   158

5.1   An example of a B2B buying process   173
6.1   SERP heat map   196
6.2   The long tail of keywords   201
7.1   Common types of banner ads   239
7.2   Keyword matching options   249
7.3   PPC network advertising in action – a Google ad on one of the
      author's web pages   254
9.1   The four levels of content control on the web   293
9.2   The AIDAT model – Attention, Interest, Desire, Action, *Tell*   295
9.3   A page from my own blog   311
9.4   The reputation management process   324
9.5   Four types of engagement profile   331

Acknowledgements

All at Routledge who helped make this publication possible – thanks.

All the students, trainees and audiences at any event at which I have spoken – if you hadn't asked the questions, I would not have had to find the answers.

All those practitioners, writers, bloggers and researchers who do the work that keeps people like me informed.

All those organizations that have asked me to monitor or participate in their digital marketing efforts – you learn more in an hour at the sharp end than you do in days of reading the theory.

All those individuals and organizations that gave me permission to use content or images that are copyrighted to them.

Those colleagues who have supported and encouraged me in writing this book – and others. It is a constant grievance of mine that academia values papers read by only a few over texts that help educate thousands.

Preface

In theory, there is no difference between theory and practice. But in practice, there is.

Yogi Berra

Before telling you about this book, let me tell you a little about its title – perhaps the problematic aspect of both this and its first edition.

I'll come to the subtitle – 'A practical approach' – in a moment, but it was the main title that was undecided right up to the final manuscript of the first edition being submitted, and it was changed for this one. The problem was, and still is, what is the book about? Is it: *Internet Marketing, e-Marketing, Online Marketing, Digital Marketing* or even *New Media Marketing*? I must admit, in the classroom I have used 'e-marketing' – but I think that is a combination of habit and laziness (of the options, it is the quickest to say). The book I co-authored with Richard Gay and Rita Esen uses 'online marketing'. My book in the Essential Managers series is called *The Digital Revolution*. Despite this, for the first edition, I was drawn to what I eventually opted for – Internet marketing – because it actually tells potential readers what the book is about. That is, marketing using the Internet. The *actual* subject was the problem I had with the term that eventually came second in the contest – digital marketing. When I asked them, many within the industry advised me that 'digital' was the term that was in vogue in the boardrooms and at conference discussions. However, I felt it might be rather 'faddish' – a term that is trendy when people talk about something they don't really know about – and it would go the same way as 'new media' as a populist term. I was, of course, wrong. Over the last four years, 'digital marketing' has become the accepted term for the subject I teach, practise and write about – so this book now has that title.

In reality, however, I don't suppose it really matters.

The subtitle is, I think, self-explanatory. It was always my intention that the book's ethos would be to get down in the e-marketing trenches rather than standing back and taking a strategic point of view on the subject. Whilst strategic issues are included where appropriate, this book is designed to be more practical in nature – addressing tactics, operational and functional issues in detail. This is in contrast to many other academic texts on the subject of online marketing, which tend to concentrate on the strategy itself, rather than how that strategy is implemented at the virtual coalface.

After reading this book – and completing the exercises within it – the reader will be equipped to undertake any digital marketing role within a variety of organizations. The practical case-study exercises – based on theory and recognized good practice – will ensure that readers will be able to analyse situations within the workplace, identify the most appropriate course of action and implement the strategies and tactics that will help the organization meet its online objectives. Which leads me to the final point in this introduction. Although this book is primarily aimed at an academic market, the practical nature of the content and its presentation mean that it will be equally useful in both training and self-learning scenarios.

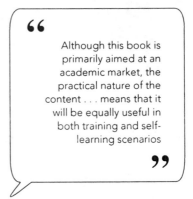

" Although this book is primarily aimed at an academic market, the practical nature of the content . . . means that it will be equally useful in both training and self-learning scenarios "

THE SUBJECT

This is a book on digital marketing – it is not a book on marketing *per se*. To get the best from this book the reader should be aware of – though not necessarily an expert in – common marketing theories, strategies and tactics. To spend time explaining aspects of marketing – segmentation, for example – within this book would be to diminish the focus on its titular subject area. The content is, therefore, driven by digital marketing applications rather than elements of traditional marketing – though naturally there is some commonality.

Nevertheless, it is inevitable that each chapter will integrate elements of marketing within its subject area. For example, facets of the marketing mix are a constant throughout the book – as are issues associated with buyer behaviour, product/service, customer/consumer and market orientation. Other more strategic elements of marketing permeate the book. Relationship marketing, for example, is an inherent component – or objective – of many aspects of online marketing.

Any book that has pretensions as an academic text must have appropriate academic underpinnings, which this book has. There are, however, three addenda to this:

1. The practical nature of the content means that there are also significant 'practical' underpinnings – that is, there are also references to the work of practitioners who have proved themselves at the coalface of digital marketing.
2. References are also made to statistics or research findings from commercial organizations. Although there may be an element of bias in some of these, they are up to date and represent real-world issues.
3. The academic research in the subject area is limited, outdated or – in some cases – of dubious quality.

Considering the third point in greater detail, a comment taken from one of the better pieces of academic work is worth noting. Doherty and Ellis-Chadwick (2006) make the point that: 'Much of the discussion of the internet's potential has been conducted at a conceptual level, and there have been rather fewer contributions that have empirically explored the actual benefits delivered via the internet, or the wider organizational impacts that it might engender.' Although this particular comment refers to literature about Internet *retailing*, I find it to be equally applicable to most digital marketing-related academic articles. Other criticisms I would make of academic research include that:

- Whilst some findings pass the test of time, many conclusions do not. For example, any comments with regard to social media marketing made in 2000 – a time when Facebook and Twitter did not exist – are not necessarily true for Internet users now.

- A continuation from the previous comment is that some later work uses the findings of earlier research without question, making subsequent conclusions potentially flawed.

- A surprising amount of the research is conducted only on university campuses, with respondents being either (a) academics, or (b) students. Whilst this might be acceptable in *some* research, when looking at anything Internet related this sample is not a reasonable representation of the population as these two groups are experienced uses of the web and, in the case of students, representatives of the first Internet generation.

- I also find that the results of a great deal of academic research actually tell us nothing new. Or rather, they tell practitioners nothing they have not already discovered by trial and error. For example, a special issue of the *European Journal of Marketing* published in 2013 featured an article entitled 'The Impact of Online User Reviews on Cameras Sales' by Zhang *et al.* (2013). Its abstract includes the following:

> Practical implications – This research indicates that the retailers should provide channels for and encourage customer online reviews for search goods to improve sales. It is also beneficial for online retailers to provide detailed product attributes to help their customers make the purchase decision. Carefully designed and executed price promotions could also be effective ways to improve sales of searchable goods.

> Originality/value – This study is one of the first attempts to investigate the impact of online user reviews on sales of search goods.

Now, I do not doubt or question the integrity of the article's authors, but – in my non-academic-research opinion – Amazon and a thousand other online retailers knew the first element of the 'practical implications' back in the last century (*I* certainly did) and, by definition, a *search good* is a product that is easily appraised before purchase and so is subject to price competition – and so nothing new there.

As for the 'originality/value', Amazon – and its contemporaries – will have been, and are still, running real-time research on *the impact of online user reviews on sales of search goods,* again since the last century. This might well be one of the first academic studies of its kind – but it does not tell us anything new.

My scepticism toward *academic* research is not, however, absolute. Of course there are papers out there which challenge conventional thinking and so inspire marketers to reconsider practices. One which springs to my mind is 'A New Marketing Paradigm for Electronic Commerce' by Donna Hoffman and Thomas Novak. Published in 1996 – and so written at least a year earlier – this paper predicts (almost) exactly what impact the Internet has had on *digital marketing* in the years since that time. It's available online – take a look and see what you think.

Also with regard to academic research, I find there is confusion in the crossover between computing and business subject areas – with examples of both disciplines making basic errors when they stray out of their own field. This includes marketers making 'technical' statements that are flawed as well as IT writers who – without the qualification or experience in the subject – make erroneous comments about business applications or, of specific relevance to this book, about marketing. The language used by the two can also cause problems for students. For example, Maulana and Eckhardt (2007) make the point that in an IT environment, research into 'connectedness' concentrates on physical dimensions, whilst in a social setting the concentration is on the emotional interpretation. Naturally, there are exceptions to this edict. There are a number of subject specialists – academics and practitioners – in both business and IT who have successfully crossed over and can now be considered to be experts in both. These are however – in my experience – rare. And in case you are wondering, though I have a smattering of IT knowledge, any expertise I may have is firmly in the *marketing* side of digital marketing.

Anything related to digital marketing is bound to be a very dynamic subject. Online marketing is no different. For example, the book I co-wrote with Richard Gay and Rita Esen – *Online Marketing: A Customer-Led Approach* – was published in March 2007. In that book, I wrote the content that included 'social media marketing' – and it warranted a small section within a chapter that also covered several other aspects of online marketing. In the first edition of this book, not only did social media marketing get its own chapter, but it was one of the longest chapters. Not only is the subject also the longest chapter in this edition, but I have also written an entire book on the subject.

CHAPTER STRUCTURE

Each chapter is divided into a number of sections that address specific aspects of the chapter's subject area, and each of these elements is split into two parts. The first part examines the background to the subject, whilst the second part, called 'Decision time', identifies the issues about which the online marketer must make an evaluation of how they might impact on their organization, brand or product. At the end of each section, readers are presented with a challenge – 'You decide' – where a case study-based question is posed. The following sample is from Section 4.7:

YOU DECIDE

Advise Robert Terwilliger on the advantages and drawbacks of using a third-party website to sell the Modeller's Stand (case study 9).

Alternatively, conduct the same exercise on your organization or that of your employer.

Throughout the book you will come across a number of content boxes, each with a specific function. They are:

RESEARCH SNAPSHOT

These are snippets of information taken from published research – sometimes academic, but often the information has commercial origins.

MINI CASE

As the name suggests, these are short examples that illustrate a concept or model. They are often examples of good practice in that concept.

PRACTICAL INSIGHT

These give readers an insight into how elements of Internet marketing are practised in real life – with many serving as 'tips' for students when they might become practitioners.

GO ONLINE

From these boxes, readers are directed toward the book's website. There, links are provided that take them to information, articles or comments on the subject being discussed in that section that will supplement the content of the book.

The case studies are designed to make clear how the impact of each online application varies between organizations and markets. For each section, I have tried to select a case study that is pertinent to that section – although you are welcome to switch case studies for each question if you so wish. Alternatively, if you are employed or run your own business, you can ask that question of your – or your employer's – organization. A similar format is followed at the end of each chapter, but at this time you are invited to advise one of the case-study organizations on all aspects of digital marketing covered in that chapter. The following sample is from Chapter 9:

CHAPTER EXERCISE

Giving justifications for all your decisions, advise the board of the Matthew Humberstone Foundation Hospital (case study 6) on all aspects of social media marketing covered in this chapter. This includes taking a look at the 'dummy' blog that can be found by following the link from the chapter's web page.

Alternatively, conduct the same exercise for your organization or that of your employer.

THE CASE STUDIES

Throughout the book case studies are used as both examples of how theory might be practised and as exercises for readers to complete. Although the case studies are fictional, they all characterize real-life situations. The cases are not intended to be comprehensive or exhaustive – merely a snapshot of a particular state of affairs within what is normally a complex environment. The case studies have been compiled in such a way that all aspects of digital marketing can be addressed, with each element of the chapters having its own case-related question, with one case being presented as an end-of-chapter exercise.

The case studies are:

1. The Rockridge Museum – a not-for-profit organization with a mix of public and private funding.
2. Clough & Taylor Engineering – a small engineering company that makes bespoke products.
3. The Gilded Truffle Hotel – a new boutique hotel opening soon in a prime city-centre location.
4. Cleethorpes Visitors Association – a publicly funded tourism centre.
5. BethSoft – a small business that sells a range of specialist software to the engineering industry.
6. Matthew Humberstone Foundation Hospital – a private medical facility with hospitals and clinics around the world.
7. 22 Catches Fish Products – a consumer packaged-goods manufacturer.
8. Hill Street Motorist Shop – a chain of retail outlets with a limited online presence.
9. The Modeller's Stand – a single product sold in a niche market.
10. Huxley University – a small academic institution.
11. Two Cities Manufacturing Ltd – a medium-sized manufacturer and distributor of commercial and private grass-cutting appliances.
12. Lindsey Naegle Consulting – a sole trader who works as a consultant in Internet marketing.
13. Phelps Online Department Store – a pure play online retailer that sells women's clothes and accessories.

Note that all of the above are UK based, but their geographic location could be changed to suit readers' needs.

I have not included the actual case studies within the book – rather, online on the book's website, where they can be printed off. Although I accept that might cause you a small inconvenience, I have made this decision for a very good reason. If the cases were within this text I would not be able to change them – at least not until the next edition of the book is published! Online, however, it is relatively simple for me to change, add or delete any element of each case. This means that as the Internet, the way it is used by the public and how it is adopted by organizations change, I can adapt the scenarios to suit the environment in which those case-study organizations operate.

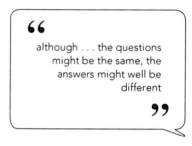

> **66**
> although . . . the questions might be the same, the answers might well be different
> **99**

I have left the case-study *subjects* the same. I hope this will help with continuity for teachers using the book for their modules, programmes or courses. However, times change and digital marketing is constantly changing; therefore, although the case studies and the questions might be the same – the answers might well be different. (I acknowledge that when quizzed by a student with regard to an exam question being the same as the previous year, Albert Einstein is said to have replied that the questions are the same, but this year the answers are different.) I have also made the conscious decision not to offer any answers to the case studies. The key reasons for this are fourfold:

1. As with all marketing – there is no single answer that can be considered to be unambiguously 'right'.
2. Such is the nature of not only the web's development, but the global environment in which it exists, that the answers might actually change on a monthly basis.
3. As teaching staff may choose to use the case studies for summative assessment, I do not want sample answers in the public domain where misguided students might be able to get hold of them and present them as their own work.
4. The objective is that you should work to develop the answers yourself. If I put suggested answers in the book, too many students would succumb to the temptation to read them rather than do the work necessary to understand the subject.

MULTIPLE-CHOICE QUESTIONS

New to this edition is a set of multiple-choice questions for each chapter. These can be used by readers to test themselves or by teaching staff as part of formative assessment and feedback. The questions are split into two categories: (1) generic questions on the chapter's subject area, and (2) questions based on the chapter's case studies. The second of these is designed to test understanding of the subject by looking for the application of theory and concept to real-life scenarios in much the same way as the section exercises do.

As with the case studies, these are available on the website – rather than within the pages of this book – in order that they can be amended or replaced as necessary throughout the lifetime of the text.

TERMS OF REFERENCE

Throughout the book I occasionally refer to 'companies' or 'firms', but in the main I use the term 'organization'. This is deliberately vague. Whenever you see the word 'organization' feel free to replace it with any other term that you feel is more relevant to the context or your own circumstances. As well as 'company' and 'firm', other examples might include 'government department', 'university', 'hospital', 'foundation', 'school', 'society', 'not-for-profit', 'business', 'association', 'college', 'religious body', 'charity', 'club' or any other entity – including 'individual'.

In a similar vein, it is common for marketers to use the term 'customer' to describe anyone who uses or partakes of the service on offer – not just the person who pays for a tangible product. In some cases the customer has their own descriptor – opticians have patients, universities have students, political parties have voters, sports teams have supporters, churches have members and so on. Likewise – and this is particularly relevant online – the objective is not always to have the target customer *buy* something. It could just as easily be to elicit a donation, a subscription, an order, an application or to have someone become a member. Again, please use whichever term you feel is most relevant wherever you see the word 'customer' or 'buyer' within this text.

Wherever possible, I have avoided any promotion of specific brands or products within the text. This is particularly the case where digital marketing tools, services or technologies are concerned – naming a particular website hosting company or software that helps with search engine optimization, for example. This is deliberate for two primary reasons: (1) I have not used all of the applications/companies and so am not in a position to rank one above another, and (2) to name one and omit another would appear to show favouritism which may be construed as prejudice. There are instances, however, when *not* to name names would be to the detriment of the content – for example, some aspects of the ubiquitous Google empire have become common terms to describe elements of online marketing and so are difficult to replace with a generic description. Indeed, to 'Google' something is now recognized as the generic term for using a search engine. Note that it is also the case that for many of the tasks described within the text there are software applications that *claim* to do the job for you. As I have used very few of these I am not in a position either to recommend them or otherwise. I am sure some work, just as I am certain that some do not. I have deliberately not mentioned the availability, or suppliers, of any such software – effectively, this book is about the *manual* way of doing online marketing. A slight deviation to this rule comes where I have used organizations as examples to illustrate a subject, concept or practice – often with an accompanying image. This is not meant to promote any organization, brand or product; it is simply that these are examples I have come across as I surf around the web.

ONLINE SUPPORT

As well as the online elements of the case-study exercises, this book makes extensive use of the Internet as a source of information. This includes the book's own website (alancharlesworth.eu/DigitalMarketing), features of which include:

- Each chapter having its own page that includes references to websites that provide more details on subjects covered within the text and links to information that will enhance the book's content.
- All case studies in pdf format.
- Multiple-choice questions for each chapter.
- Tips and advice for lecturers and trainers – including 'what to look for' in the answers to the case-study questions.

In addition, the dynamic nature of the subject is acknowledged by there being – where appropriate – chapter 'updates'. Whilst it is not feasible to produce complete rewrites of chapters, on occasion it might be prudent to add to or amend elements or sections in accordance with changes in contemporary practice. Whilst I cannot predict the future, before a third edition of this book might be published it is pretty certain that there will be (for example) changes in how search engine algorithms work. Similarly, any future mergers between key players in the industry would have a significant impact on the digital marketing environment.

Figure 0.1 The author's website, alancharlesworth.eu

Figure 0.2 The author's *when you're inside the bottle, you can't read the label* blog

In addition to the book's website, I also maintain my own website, which – amongst other things – has sections on digital marketing-related articles and practical tips, hints and advice. Judging by the visitor numbers around assignment time, this is already a popular site with students. Updates and additions to the website are just two features of my Facebook page, with all Facebook entries repeated on my Twitter account. My blog – *when you're inside the bottle, you can't read the label* – is a personal view on examples of good and bad digital marketing practices that I have come across.

My website is on alancharlesworth.eu and my blog address is alansinternetmarketingblog. com.

Finally, whether you are a student, trainee, lecturer, trainer or practitioner, I hope you find this book *useful*. Note that I have refrained from wishing that you *enjoy* reading it. Although I have tried to make it easily readable, you should *enjoy* a John Grisham mystery or a Robert Ludlum adventure whilst relaxing in a comfy chair or on a sun lounger. I have written this book not to entertain but to help you achieve a professional or educational objective. Of course, if you do get pleasure from it, that is a bonus.

Alan Charlesworth, Sunderland, UK
email@alancharlesworth.eu

References

Doherty, N.F. and Ellis-Chadwick, F.E. (2006) New perspectives in Internet retailing: a review and strategic critique of the field. *International Journal of Retail and Distribution Management.* Volume 34, number 4/5, pp. 411–428.

Hoffman, D.L. and Novak, T.P. (1996) A new marketing paradigm for electronic commerce. *The Information Society.* Volume 13 (special issue on electronic commerce), pp. 43–54.

Maulana, A.E. and Eckhardt, G.M. (2007) Just friends, good acquaintances or soul mates? An exploration of website connectedness. *Qualitative Market Research: An International Journal.* Volume 10, number 3, pp. 227–242.

Zhang, L., Ma, B. and Cartwright, D.K. (2013) The impact of online user reviews on camera sales. *European Journal of Marketing.* Volume 47, number 7, pp. 1115–1128.

Chapter **1**

The online environment

> *The future ain't what it used to be.*
>
> *Yogi Berra*

Chapter at a glance

1.1 Introduction
1.2 A background to the Internet
1.3 The impact of the Internet on society
1.4 The impact of the Internet on business
1.5 The impact of the Internet on not-for-profit organizations
1.6 Online buying behaviour
1.7 The Internet goes mobile
1.8 Online marketing objectives
1.9 Legal considerations

1.1 INTRODUCTION

In the early days of the commercialized Internet, an article in the *Journal of the Academy of Marketing Sciences* (Peterson *et al.*, 1997) made the point that 'No one can predict with certainty what the ultimate impact of the Internet will be on consumer marketing. There is virtually no information on how, or to what extent, consumers will use the Internet in the context of marketing or what new marketing paradigms will prove viable.' No matter the year that you are reading this, I suggest we have some idea of that impact, but so dynamic are the technologies, the practitioners and the environment in which it is used

66

we are still unsure of what the future will bring to digital marketing

99

that we are still unsure of what the future will bring to digital marketing in both consumer (B2C) and industrial (B2B) trading as well as the not-for-profit and public sector environments. Furthermore, we are equally unsure as to how much *more* the Internet will change society – for change it has. For marketers, this is significant as it is society that makes up our customers. Back in the mid-1990s, predictions of how the Internet would change the way we do business were manifold – and they were largely ignored by those businesses that would be affected by that change. Opinions, however, have softened over the years and the use of digital media is now accepted by business leaders. As we will see in subsequent chapters, whether it is practised effectively by a significant number of organizations is still open to debate.

1.2 A BACKGROUND TO THE INTERNET

Although it is not necessary for practitioners of online marketing to be given a full history lesson on the development of the Internet, a basic introduction to its history and how it works will help the new online marketer to implement a digital marketing plan. Contrary to common misconception, the Internet was borne of military – not academic – parents. Although many universities took up use of the fledgling technology at the end of the 1960s, research into what became the Internet had begun a decade earlier when Cold War era American leaders, fearing that a limited nuclear attack on the USA would disable conventional communications systems, instigated the ARPANet (Advanced Research Projects Agency Network) project. The system's development as a simple medium of character-only communication continued throughout the 1970s until an Englishman, (now Sir) Tim Berners-Lee, developed his 'rules for the World Wide Web' in 1980. Further technical advances were made in the 1980s, including the development of the Transfer Control Protocol (TCP), the Internet Protocol (IP) and the Domain Name System (DNS) – all of which are cornerstones of what we now know as the Internet. Still academia-centric throughout this period, it was not until the early 1990s that the technology moved into a more commercial environment – not least with the 1991 release of the World Wide Web – and some business leaders began to recognize the potential of the new medium of communications.

PRACTICAL INSIGHT

The web, email and the Internet – misconceptions

In both technical and practical terms the Internet is the parent of the other two. In other words, the Internet is made up of the World Wide Web and email. The World Wide Web and the Internet are not the same thing. Email is not part of the World Wide Web. The Internet is not an element of either the World Wide Web or email.

The 1993 launch of the first web browser – Mosaic – meant that the general public now had easy access to the web. Although a number of commercial websites appeared during this time, few really appreciated the web – indeed, scepticism ruled the day, with many condemning the Internet simply as a fad that would go away. In the opinion of many – myself included – the real birth of the commercial web was in October 1994 when *Wired* magazine's online edition, Hotwired.com, featured the first online banner advertisement (for AT&T). While 1995 and 1996 saw great commercial steps forward for the Internet in the USA (Amazon.com was launched in 1995), the rest of the world was slower in its uptake. Although the northern Europeans – including Scandinavia – were at the forefront of outside-USA adoption, it was 1997 before businesses – and, significantly, governments and the EU – really took it seriously. Even then there was a long tail of uncertainty, with some major brands and household names not even having a website until closer to the end of the 1990s. The end of the old century and the beginning of the new millennium saw a kind of 'Internet fever', with every news medium featuring web-related stories of some kind in every bulletin or edition. This culminated in the frenzy of ill-conceived investments in 'dot-com' businesses – and their inevitable failure, the so-called 'dot-bomb' era. But despite the highly publicized crashes of web-based ventures, the value of the Internet was obvious, and the doom mongers' predictions of its demise were well off the mark.

As with the history of the Internet, it is not necessary for the online marketer to know all the scientific and technical aspects of the medium. However, if only to prevent programmers and other techies baffling them with science, the marketer should at least have an inkling of how the thing works.

PRACTICAL INSIGHT

It's in the numbers

'Everything we encounter online and everything we produce is ultimately a series of numbers, packaged together, sent through a series of routers located around the world, then reassembled at the other end.'

Google's Executive Chairman Eric Schmidt and
Director Jared Cohen, 2013

What follows is a very rudimentary version of what happens when you go online.

1. The website is hosted on a computer (server) that holds it in the form of a program code until it is *requested* by a user.

2. When the user either types a URL into a browser or clicks on a hyperlink, a request is sent from their computer – via an Internet service provider (ISP) – for the files that make up that website to be delivered.

3. The elements that make up the website are sent – in 'packets' – to the requesting computer. Note that it was the 'packets' element of the communication system that satisfied the ARPENet military requirements. Essentially – and this is still the reason why the Internet rarely fails and delivers quickly – the transmitted message is broken down into its component parts and each is tasked with finding its own way to the destination. The Cold War scenario was that standard single-line methods of communication could be easily broken by an atomic explosion. With the Internet, there is no single line, so if a packet hits a blockage it simply keeps looking until a clear route is found.

4. The packets arrive at the destination where they are re-formed to make the complete message, which users see on their screens as a web page.

Of course – despite its complexity – online, this all happens in a fraction of a second.

> ## GO ONLINE
>
> For an excellent pictorial demonstration of how the web works, follow the links from the chapter's web page to the BBC's 'SuperPower: Visualising the internet'.

Throughout this book I make reference to 'techies' and 'creatives'. These are meant as terms of endearment rather than being derogatory. Although very rare exceptions exist, in general those involved in the technical aspects of the Internet and web presences, and the designers – those who *create* them – do not have marketing experience or qualifications. Of course, the reverse is also true, with few marketers having either technical or creative skills.

Therefore, I use 'techies' as a non-abusive term bestowed on people whose work is primarily the development – or operation – of technical aspects of the Internet in particular or computing in general. I am happy to admit that although I know the *very* basics of how the Internet works, I have no skills as a *techie* – indeed, computer science is well beyond my comprehension. Similarly, I have no training or education in design skills, let alone the use of digital technology in the development of those designs. However, both techies and creatives would do well to return me the same compliment – having a rudimentary knowledge of the 4Ps does not constitute an understanding of marketing. (Incidentally, if you are a techie or a creative seeking to advance your online marketing understanding and skills by reading this book, I applaud your endeavours. Sadly, few marketers will take programming courses.)

This issue is addressed predominantly in Sections 2.4 and 3.2 – who 'owns' the web presence and web presence management and development, respectively.

GO ONLINE

Internet history

A number of websites include 'a history of the Internet'. One of the best is Hobbes's *Internet Timeline*, which will give you a sound background to the Internet. For a view of how banner ads have developed since AT&T's first one, Toronto web designer Tari Akpodiete has a website chronicling their history. Follow the links from the chapter's web page for both sites.

In concluding this section, it is worth mentioning two web-delivery issues that may impact online marketers in the future. Although both seem to frequently rise up the agenda only to drop back down again, 'net neutrality' and 'Internet overload' do not seem to want to go away – and that they are both closely related is significant.

Like any highway, the 'Information Superhighway' (a term made popular by the (then) US Vice-President Al Gore) has a limit to the amount of traffic it can carry. Despite advances in pertinent technology, the capacity of the Internet is finite – and that capacity is being severely tested by 'new media', such as streaming video. In 2013, network solutions provider Sandvine looked at downstream access to the Internet in North America and found that videos are eating up bandwidth, with Netflix and YouTube accounting for nearly 50 per cent of that bandwith. As more and more applications are moved online, so the system is struggling to cope, with some experts predicting the whole system will grind to a halt as we all try to watch the latest blockbuster movie or play the latest video game online. To get around this impending gridlock, the service providers have – repeatedly – put forward a solution. This entails a split in website availability – effectively a fast and a slow lane. In the fast-download-easily-available lane would be the websites of those organizations that can afford to pay for the faster service. The rest, it is feared, would disappear on the slow-dirt-track-to-nowhere – essentially creating a situation that blocks (or at least hinders) free competition. Although at the time of writing congressional action (in the USA) has prevented the introduction of a two-tier Internet, many commentators feel the issue has not gone forever.

YOU DECIDE

It is likely that the majority of people who use this book will be aged under twenty-five, meaning that they have grown up as part of the first 'digital generation'. For those readers, the following question will require some imagination; for the others (like me), it is a test of memory.

In the following sections of this chapter we look at the impact that the Internet has had on both society and business – but before doing that consider how different your lives would be if the Internet did not exist. I'll start you off by saying that doing assignments at college or university would be a *lot* harder!

1.3 THE IMPACT OF THE INTERNET ON SOCIETY

While a book of this nature cannot ignore the impact of the Internet on society in general, that could be the subject of a social-science focused book in its own right. For example, how in traditional societies – where the elders are revered and respected for their accumulated knowledge – has the availability of knowledge online usurped their prestige and caused. Or can online gambling sites increase addiction? In this section, therefore, we will concentrate only on where societal issues interact with the organization – in particular the commercial organization. It is difficult, however, to differentiate between the socially relevant and the not-relevant. The influence on buyer behaviour, for example, is pretty straightforward. But whilst the impact on society might not be overtly commercial, it is rare that there is none. Political parties could be described as commercial in that they practise marketing; or if the 'societal' aspect is the content of a news item then the medium carrying the news might be doing so as a business model.

RESEARCH SNAPSHOT

When online is not online

Staff at Forrester Research were a little confused when they were analysing the findings of research they had conducted into Internet use. It seemed that the respondents' average time online had declined from 2011 to 2012. The solution came in observing users rather than simply accepting what they say they do. It would seem that some people now see the Internet as such an integral part of their lives that they do not register its use as 'being online'. Checking Facebook, for example, is identified as being on Facebook – not being on the Internet.

Source: 'Understanding the changing needs of consumers' at forrester.com

Although in its early commercial days, the Internet was described – by, for example, Butler and Peppard (1998) – as a substitute for traditional business channels in three ways: distribution, transaction and communication, the first two have only limited application. Distribution is restricted to products that can be digitalized (music, word files and computer software, for example) and despite the hype, online is far from the preferred option for making

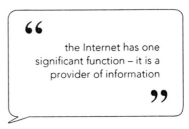

> the Internet has one significant function – it is a provider of information

purchases (see Section 4.2). Essentially, for most users, the Internet is a medium of communication. Certainly it has unique characteristics and facilitates types of communication – particularly interactive – that other media lack, but it is first and foremost a medium of communication, full stop. As such, the Internet has one significant function – it is a provider of information. This is the reason for search engines being so powerful – they help people find information. That information could be commercial (how much is product X and where can I buy it?), non-commercial (when was the Battle of the River Plate?) or a mix of the two (what is killing my tomato plants, and what can I buy to stop it?). Naturally, a marketer might reinterpret this and see the Internet as the source of solutions to people's problems, so it has the potential to help sell products or services that help solve those problems.

PRACTICAL INSIGHT

You can't have the good and not the bad

Because this book is primarily about commercial use of the web, I have chosen not to include a section on the misuse of the Internet for illegal or nefarious purposes. In societal terms this mainly entails the use of the Internet for the dissemination of material deemed unacceptable by society – and in much the same way as the web is lauded for its ability to spread the *good* word, so it is efficient in spreading the *bad*.

Note, however, I do appreciate that there is an *adult* industry that is legal – and so can benefit from the legitimate marketing practices covered in this book. Indeed, because it was one of very few industries that made a profit from online activities in the early days of the web, the adult industry is responsible for many of the marketing-related technical innovations that are now commonplace on websites. Pornography, legal or otherwise, is also – according to Businessinsider.com – responsible for 36 per cent of Internet content and one in four of all search engine queries, and it makes around $3,000 every second.

However, I would be naive to disregard the impact of easy access to the websites of a sexual nature that children and teenagers now *enjoy* – and its impact on society.

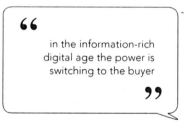
> in the information-rich digital age the power is switching to the buyer

In commercial terms, it is the provision of high-quality, well-developed, relevant, product-related information in a manner that is easy to access so that it best meets the needs of the customer that is the primary use of the Internet. Commenting on their research into the uptake of the Internet, Papacharissi and Rubin (2000) suggested that people will only use media because of the utility they derive from the medium – the subsequent success of the web would indicate that users do indeed derive a benefit from it. I – and others – would contend that the benefit gained is the availability of information – and that information is changing the way that customers shop. Sir Francis Bacon's axiom that 'knowledge is power' holds true in business – and in the information-rich digital age the power is switching to the buyer. The concept that marketers are losing control of their brand is covered in more detail in Chapter 9.

In previous eras of business, a marketing text would concentrate on how the organization might use a medium to interact with its market. Any social interaction would be either beyond its control or so informal as to be insignificant in any strategic planning. Certainly, in some industries – entertainment, for example – word of mouth (the so-called 'water-cooler' effect) might have played a part in a product's promotion, but for most any such benefits were ad hoc rather than formal and – importantly – not accountable.

However, the Internet has brought a way for society to interact with itself. No longer is the public media governed by an elite few that may limit its views to that of its owners, a particular political persuasion or the demands of its advertisers. We now have the *social* media – which is open to anyone with the ability to access the Internet. Although we cover marketing in the social media in Chapter 9, the social phenomenon is worth considering within the context of the impact of the Internet on society.

PRACTICAL INSIGHT

Who are you on online?

It would appear that social media has created a paradoxical online environment where people embellish their 'boring' lives in order to match the more exciting posts of others. This is hardly surprising when one-third of Facebook users leave the site feeling worse because they are envious of others' lives. Feelings of inadequacy when comparing yourself against the *domestic perfection* presented on the female-dominated social network has even spawned its own name: Pinterest stress.

Women exaggerate what they're doing for the benefit of their Facebook friends, fibbing about being on wild nights out when they were actually at home alone, or exaggerating in stories about holidays or work. Men are just as dishonest when 'microblagging'. However, it would seem that their primary motivation is presenting a 'cool online persona' and impressing their workplace colleagues.

Although this information is interesting and belongs in the social sciences department, there is an impact on advertisers who pay for the delivery of ads that are matched to users' personalities and stated demographics. So delivering an ad targeted at a single person is a waste of time and money if that person is, in fact, married.

Sources: Today.com, OnePoll and Barclaycard Bespoke offers

Although there are myriad reasons why someone might visit a social media website, there are four primary purposes:

1. As part of their *social* life – that is, chatting with friends or acquaintances in much the same way as their ancestors might have passed time by gossiping about nothing specific. Essentially, this is the social conversation that has always existed – and marketers should be aware that the technology-driven communication medium that is the Internet can spread an opinion – or rumour – in a way only imagined previously. Twenty years ago the early adopter who was the first to see a new movie might pass a glowing review to only a few close friends and workmates. Now – with the power of social networks' 'friends' facilities – hundreds might read that review, and in turn pass it on to hundreds of their 'friends'.

2. Using the web as a medium to engage in an existing and/or offline pastime or hobby. This can range from supporting a particular football team, through arts and culture via cult TV shows or pop stars, to growing particular types of flower. As is the case with (1) above, such chat can be monitored by marketers as research into how products might be perceived by the public.

3. Joining a particular social group to gain benefit from their combined knowledge – self-help and support groups linked to illness and/or disease, for example. Although there may be an element of chatting to like-minded individuals, this interaction is information based – 'can anyone help with this problem?' to 'where can I buy this product?' Once again, this can have commercial implications and so is pertinent to the online marketer.

4. Employment, career or industry related. As with the previous listings, there will be an element of gossip about these sites, but they are primarily about networking with individuals or groups that may help further an individual's work or income stream. Though such sites might be considered as *commercial* media (rather than *social*), they differ in that they are inhabited by individuals rather than organizations, with commercial media sites more likely to be the industry portals or marketplaces that are covered in Section 5.5.

PRACTICAL INSIGHT

Digital multi-tasking

The days of sitting and looking at one screen – traditionally, watching the TV – are, it seems, over. Research from Microsoft suggests it is now commonplace for us to 'multi-screen' using multiple devices, including televisions, PCs, laptops, tablets and smartphones. The study identified four different behaviours that consumers typically exhibit:

1. Content Grazing: Practised by 68 per cent of consumers, this is when two or more screens are used simultaneously to access unrelated content, such as watching a TV programme and at the same time checking your email or texting on your mobile phone.
2. Investigative Spider-Webbing: 57 per cent of consumers fit in this category where they seek content across several devices at the same time – for example, watching a movie on the TV and looking up the other movies the actors have been in on a tablet or smartphone.
3. Quantum Journey: This is where multiple screens are used independently to achieve a goal – for example, taking a photo of a product on a mobile phone and then looking for reviews on a PC at home. Forty-six per cent of consumers fit this category.
4. Social Spider-Webbing: The least common multi-screening category with 39 per cent of consumers, this group are extroverted and focused on sharing content and connecting with others across devices.

Source: 'Cross-screen engagement' at microsoft.com

Given the *why* of people going online, let's now consider *who* is going online. Although the USA cannot be held as an absolute exemplar of Internet use – it is a reasonable benchmark for 'mature' Internet adoption. Research from the Pew Research Center's Internet and American Life Project (2012) suggests that around 80 per cent of Americans are online – a figure which has remained fairly static since the same organization published similar statistics in 2005 (in 2000 it was 47 per cent). However, 95 per cent of teenagers but only 41 per cent of over sixty-fives are online. It would be reasonable to expect that the teenagers of this decade will not dispense with the Internet, so we should see Internet adoption getting close to 100 per cent as that age group ages. Statistics from other Internet-mature countries (e.g. northern Europe and Scandinavia) suggest the American figures will be mirrored in these areas. Other regions of the world lag behind – China being the obvious example – and web marketers should take this into account if they are seeking to appeal to a global market. Figures 1.1, 1.2 and 1.3 give a snapshot of Internet usage statistics. The website (internetworldstats.com) also includes regional breakdowns for these figures. It is worth visiting this site on a regular basis as it is frequently updated. Similarly, the BBC provides an interesting interactive map which tracks the rise of the Internet around the world. Links to both can be found on the chapter's web page.

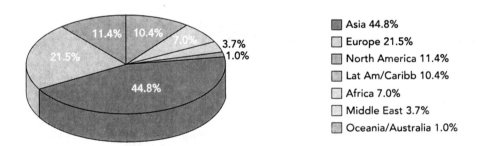

Figure 1.1 World Internet users, June 2012

Source: www.internetworldstats.com. Copyright © 2001–2013, Miniwatts Marketing Group. All rights reserved worldwide.

World Regions	Population (2012 Est.)	Internet Users Dec. 31, 2000	Internet Users Dec. 31, 2000	Penetration (% Population)	Growth 2000–2012	Users % of Table
Africa	1,073,380,925	4,514,400	167,335,676	15.6%	3,606.7%	7.0%
Asia	3,922,066,987	114,304,000	1,076,681,059	27.5%	841.9%	44.8%
Europe	820,918,446	105,096,093	518,512,109	63.2%	393.4%	21.5%
Middle East	223,608,203	3,284,800	90,000,455	40.2%	2,639.9%	3.7%
North America	348,280,154	108,096,800	273,785,413	78.6%	153.3%	11.4%
Latin America/Caribbean	593,688,638	18,068,919	254,915,745	42.9%	1,310.8%	10.6%
Oceania/Australia	35,903,569	7,620,480	24,287,919	67.6%	218.7%	1.0%
WORLD TOTAL	7,017,846,922	360,985,492	2,405,518,376	34.3%	566.4%	100.0%

Figure 1.2 World Internet usage and population statistics, June 2012

Source: www.internetworldstats.com. Copyright © 2001–2013, Miniwatts Marketing Group. All rights reserved worldwide.

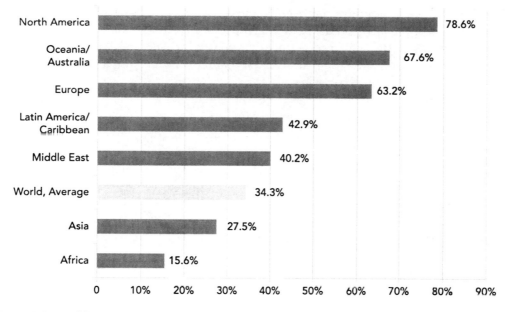

Figure 1.3 World Internet penetration rates, June 2012

RESEARCH SNAPSHOT

Internet use in the UK

According to Internet analytics provider comScore, in the UK in December 2012:

- Of the population of around 63.2 million, 44.8 million used the internet.
- Brits spend more time online than any other European country.
- Nine out of ten UK Internet users have visited retail sites.
- One in five Brits have used their smartphone to make an online purchase.
- Sixty-four per cent of mobile users have a smartphone. However, as 82 per cent of new phones sold in December 2012 were smartphones, this figure has already risen.

Source: 'UK digital future in focus' at comScore.com

In concluding this section it is necessary to point out that not all people have access to the Internet. The previously mentioned Pew Internet and American Life Project (2012) puts this figure at around 20 per cent of people in the USA. Of that group, half don't go online because they don't think the Internet is relevant to them. Only a fifth of this group cited cost as a reason for not going online – a significant drop from years gone by. This drop has a number of causes, not least that many governments have subsidized public Internet access in the more deprived areas of their countries (in schools and libraries, for example) because they have recognized a scenario where 'haves' have access to information that will improve their lives (through access to education or cheaper products, for example) whereas 'have-nots' do not – a situation often referred to as the 'digital divide' – and so the have-nots will fall still further behind the haves. It is also the case that groups that have traditionally been on the 'wrong' side of the digital divide in basic Internet access are using wireless connections to go online, in particular via smartphones. Only six per cent of American 'non-users' (in the Pew research) said that they did not access the web because of technical difficulties. However, it is doubtful that the same can be said of 'non-users' in other parts of the world, where wi-fi access is not as complete as it is in the USA. However, as previously mentioned, the rise of mobile access is changing the story. This is particularly the case in some developing countries where populations have jumped from no Internet access to mobile access – missing out the stage of 'wired' access through which early adopting countries passed at great expense to users and suppliers.

RESEARCH SNAPSHOT

The Internet: right or privilege?

Research conducted by GlobeScan (globescan.com) in 2011 on behalf of the BBC's World Service found that 79 per cent of respondents believe that Internet access is a basic human right and not a privilege. Furthermore, they thought that a country's technological infrastructure was as important as more traditional utilities, such as roads and water.

This contrasts starkly with the stance of the new Chinese leadership, led by Xi Jinping, which was installed in November 2012 by the ruling Communist Party. China has tightened its rules on Internet usage to enforce a previous requirement that users fully identify themselves to service providers – a move reported to have been instigated as part of a package of measures to protect personal information. Critics, however, believe the government is trying to limit freedom of speech. The Chinese authorities are known to closely monitor internet content that crosses its borders closely and regularly block sensitive information through use of what has become known as the Great Firewall of China.

DECISION TIME

Right up to the end of the last century, many organizations refused to accept that the Internet was anything more than a fad that would appeal to only the computer geeks in society. Similarly, a percentage of the public thought that the Internet was not for them, with computer-phobia the most common reason. However, it is now the case that the majority of organizations and the public not only accept its presence, but have access to it and, indeed, depend on it as a way of life.

PRACTICAL INSIGHT

Location, location, location, Internet connection

Research from Rootmetrics and the Halifax Building Society, respectively, suggests that 54 per cent of potential buyers would be put off from buying a house if its broadband coverage was poor, and 22 per cent of buyers would pay up to 10 per cent more for a house with a fast Internet connection.

Source: *Sunday Times*, 3 March 2013

Significant, however, are the figures from the United States where the public's web access seems to have levelled out at around 80 per cent. This means that there is a significant minority that will not use the Internet in (1) any buying decision or actual purchase, or (2) seeking any information that might improve their quality of life. For the business, it is likely that their product will appeal to either a segment that *does* or *does not* use the web – and so this can be taken into account in any marketing expenditure. However, non-commercial organizations – particularly those in the public sector – must continue to cater for any segment of their public that cannot, or will not, access the Internet.

YOU DECIDE

Consider the (continuing) impact of the Internet on society and, in particular, on those who cannot afford access.

1. How might continuing non-access have a significant *negative* impact on their lives?
2. Does the government have an obligation to deliver free or subsidized access, or is the Internet simply another commodity that people can take or leave?

1.4 THE IMPACT OF THE INTERNET ON BUSINESS

Although it may seem to the reader as puzzling for an online marketer to admit it – not all businesses will benefit from having a presence on the Internet. Some will continue as they have done for centuries. The independent local greengrocer, for example, does not need a website. Nor will they ever sell online – and their procurement will be conducted locally, and in person. Similarly, a local service provider might have such a good reputation that repeat business or recommendations provide all the business they can handle. In the small business B2B environment, although digital does play a role in new customer acquisition, the top three tactics are traditional face-to-face methods, with personal relationships and networking, trade shows and industry events, and in-person events ranking as the most popular (Forrester Consulting, 2012).

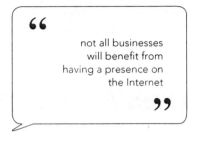

> not all businesses will benefit from having a presence on the Internet

However, I do have five caveats to this declaration.

1. If the web is a source of information for those who have access to it (see previous section), then a customer of the aforementioned greengrocer may have been online to research the nutritional values of a certain fruit, for example. However, that information is unlikely to drive the customer away from their *local* fruit shop.

2. Things change. If it has not yet arrived, we will soon be at the stage where people go online before they reach for the printed Yellow Pages (or similar – in the USA in particular, YELP is seen as a first point of search for a local product or supplier). In this case a basic web presence is necessary – although this may not be a website. An entry in an online local business directory will be necessary for most businesses (though don't forget that not all of the population is online).

3. An extension to the previous point is the matter of online search/offline purchase. This is where the customer uses a search engine to select and source a product or service they know they will purchase offline. As well as the online directories, a presence on the likes of *Google Places* might be deemed necessary. A restaurant or pub might have limited purpose for a website, for example, but visitors to an area might be looking for somewhere local. The use of mobile devices has moved this forward significantly.

4. If we believe research from the likes of Facebook – though my own research does not concur with it – consumers now use social media sites as a search facility – and so, in some markets, a social media presence might be deemed a necessity.

5. I accept that a manufacturer's digital promotion for a consumer packaged good (CPG) may drive a customer to the small store – but it has always been the case that various media beyond the control of the shopkeeper have been used by manufacturers.

A caveat to these points is that they will normally apply to small businesses and so the temptation to make a half-hearted effort – in budget and time – will be great. It is in such cases that we see the *amateur* website developer make an appearance (see Section 3.2) – with all the associated problems that can be the result.

> **MINI CASE**
>
> **Selling and sold**
>
> One thing that I find causes a problem for students is something that is basic to all marketing – the word 'sell'. The problem comes from its two main meanings, namely: (1) to exchange goods for money, and (2) to promote the benefits of something. In the second, an *exchange* may take place some time after I have *sold* you on a product. For the digital marketer, the issue is that we normally refer to *online sales* as being when a credit card is used to make a purchase online. However, this is a narrow definition – a customer might, for example, read about a product on a company's website and be *sold* on the product, then jump in her car, drive to one of the same firm's outlets, and purchase it. If this is the case, where did the *sale* take place? And which element of the organization's marketing should take the credit – the website or the physical store? The answer is important when the allocation of budgets is considered. Add to this scenario that the content of company A's website might *sell* the product, but the customer buys it from company B, and the problem becomes a significant issue for online sellers.
>
> This interpretation of 'sell' is a constant throughout both off- and online marketing – and it is also a recurring issue in this book.

Whilst statistics on overall Internet usage are widely available, less common are any guides to how much the Internet is used in a *business* context. For the business, we must consider it as both the seller – which uses the Internet as part of its marketing effort – and the buyer, which may use the web as part of its procurement plan. A third consideration is where the business uses the Internet as part of a wider e-business strategy. Let's consider these three in turn.

The business as the seller

Although the following content covers a number of specific issues, essentially the impact of the Internet on business is directly related to its impact on society covered in the previous section. As any good marketer knows, we should be looking to satisfy customers' needs and wants – and if digital technology has affected the ways in which those needs and wants are expressed, we should respond to them. Perhaps the most significant aspect of this notion is in how consumers now see their relationship with marketing. In an extensive review of social networking (TNS, TRU and Marketing Evolution, 2007) it was found that users consistently expressed their desire for brands and organizations to treat them less like *customers* . . . and more like *friends*. The days of marketers pushing a message at a mass audience and expecting them to comply with it have been numbered for a while – the Internet has hastened their demise at an accelerated rate. That organizations have responded via social media suggests that they have recognized their customers' needs, but the poor standard of some of the social media marketing in evidence suggests that those organizations are paying lip service to those needs rather than changing the culture of the organization to one that is customer-centric.

Commenting on how this phenomenon has impacted on marketing management at both strategic and operational levels, Hughes (2007) identified that organizations that had previously either dealt with customers in outlets or delegated customer contact to intermediaries now have to handle direct contact via the website. Similarly, where previously divisional silos each 'owned' groups of customers, those customers were now bypassing divisional communication channels and going to the head office via the Internet. For many companies who were unused to direct contact with customers, this has come as something of a shock. It has also meant that in markets where information could be restricted to a specific target demographic any such segmentation is now problematic. Given that it would be an unusual Internet user who never used the web to gather product information – even if they never made purchases online – it would be reasonable to suggest that all web users are *potential* recipients of a marketing message. Furthermore, the conversation between consumer and organization is often now conducted in the public forum that is social media. Those organizations that respond well in a timely fashion gain kudos in the eyes of the digital public. Those paying only lip service to the new media effectively wash their dirty linen in public – with a significant negative effect on the value of the brand, product or organization.

It is also the case that some companies perceive digital media as a panacea to poor communications (or marketing). This is not the case; it is simply another medium for good communicators to use. This is evident in those organizations that have been successful online and those that have not.

> " some companies perceive digital media as a panacea to poor communications (or marketing). This is not the case; it is simply another medium for good communicators to use. "

Despite the increase in online sales and the opportunities the web gives to *some* sellers, it is still – and probably always will be – the case that online represents only a small – if significant – proportion of all sales. It is not, therefore, the ability to conduct an exchange online that is the significant impact of the Internet – it is the capability to disseminate information that will aid the purchaser to make their buying decision.

RESEARCH SNAPSHOT

Tangible still outsells digital

Despite 2012 being the first year in which UK consumers spent more than £1 billion on digital music, videos and games, this still represented only a quarter of total sales – the majority of buyers preferring the tangibility of a physical product.

Source: Entertainment Retailers Association (eraltd.org)

> **❝**
> marketing has moved from 'helping the seller to sell' to 'helping the buyer to buy'
> **❞**

This leads us to another concept that has been augmented by the popularity of the Internet, and that is: 'helping the buyer to buy'. As digital marketing authority Gerry McGovern (2011) says, 'old-school marketing is about getting customers to do things. Web marketing is about helping customers do things.' Traditional advertising and promotion was mainly geared towards 'helping the seller to sell', where ads for a product would promote it in such a way that it inevitably drive the customer to a shop, and so help the retailer to sell the goods to the end user. Market-orientated organizations have long since realized that by providing the customer with the information for them to make an educated buying decision they are more likely to meet the needs of that customer and so develop a lasting relationship. For those customer-centric companies the Internet was simply a new – and more effective – way of getting their 'decision' material out to a wider public.

PRACTICAL INSIGHT

Is your organization web-compatible?

Writing on econsultancy.com, digital strategist Paul Boag reckons most websites lack focus and offer inconsistent user experience and tone of voice – no wonder then that he declares, 'the nature of organisations is not compatible with the web'. He goes on to say that 'most organisations pre-date the web and so are not equipped to handle the changes that digital has introduced' and that the web is never going to fulfil its potential in an organization that attempts to force the web into their current business model. Boag's reasoning for this is that:

- Most organizations work in departmental silos, while the web is cross-disciplined.
- Organizations are often internally focused while the web demands that we are user-centric.
- Organizations like projects with fixed budgets and specific end points. The web, on the other hand, is an ongoing investment.
- The majority of organizations' approach to marketing is to broadcast their message. However, the web is about a dialogue with users.
- Many organizations have thorough decision-making processes to avoid mistakes, while the web demands quick, agile and iterative decision-making.

Source: Boag (2013)

The business as the buyer

Although we should not dwell on this subject for too long – this book is about selling, not buying – all marketers should be aware of their customers' buyer behaviour.

The nature of B2B exchanges gives us something of a paradox in online B2B trading. On the one hand, not only do we have the issue that the very nature of many products makes them unsuitable for online purchase (e.g. bespoke or made to order) but there is also the significant issue that few B2B sales are conducted on a 'pay-on-order' basis. The vast majority follow the standard practice of order ⇨ delivery ⇨ invoice ⇨ pay. In such cases, it is the *order* that might be made online – not the actual *purchase*. Indeed, the majority of products being purchased online by businesses are 'consumable' – in effect, they are more B2C in nature than they are B2B. An example of this would be stationery – where a business can easily access a suitable website, select items on their description, and as the final bill is unlikely to be high a purchase can be made using a (company) credit card or charged to a pre-arranged account. Any generic items could be purchased in this way, but it is highly unlikely that a business seeking, for example, a part that is critical to the product they are manufacturing would order it online without some discussion over tolerances, delivery schedules, prices and credit arrangements.

It is the case, therefore, that we have a situation in which, although they are not buying online, businesses are using the web in a similar way to what happens in consumer markets, with firms using the Internet as an information source in their purchasing process.

Another important development that digital technology has brought to the B2B purchasing environment is the automation of traditional models such as bid tendering and both standard and reverse auctions, as well as the use of the web to produce e-marketplaces, where multiple sellers can be introduced to multiple buyers. Whilst these models have all existed for many years, the Internet has opened them up geographically and made them available to far greater numbers than previous offline incarnations because of the convenience and simplicity presented by having them online. (Note that e-marketplaces and online auctions are covered in Chapter 5.)

As part of an e-business strategy

Although what is accepted as 'e-business' is still open to discussion, many businesses rely on the Internet as an integral element of both strategic and operational planning – and so are seen to practise 'e-business'. Where digital technology is incorporated as a fundamental aspect of the business – purchasing with stock holding and logistics further down the supply chain, for example – it is unusual for any organization to practise sell-side e-commerce and still ignore the buy-side adoption. This is significant for the marketer in that they must be aware of their (potential) customers' business practices and procedures in order to best meet their needs. For example, a company that has integrated e-technology into its operations will require any supplier to be able to fit seamlessly with that technology, particularly if any kind of *just-in-time* system is being practised. Similarly, if the buying organization wants to diffuse its buying down to individual staff or departments, then they may insist on some kind of online shopping facility being available.

Finally a point that is alluded to earlier in the section, but is so important it should be addressed specifically. The Internet is a *pull* medium. Other media *push* the marketing

> ❝
> The Internet is a pull medium. Other media push the marketing message at . . . recipients.
> ❞

message at – often reluctant – recipients. TV ads would be the best example of this, where for the vast majority of viewers the ads interrupt the shows (hence the alternative title of *interruption* marketing). Similarly, as with any advert in the public domain – be it on public transport or billboards – there is no choice about seeing it because it is *pushed* at you. Online, however, for a web page to appear in a user's browser window they must have *chosen* to see it by requesting the page (typing in the URL or clicking on a link) – so they have *pulled* the content to them. It is this notion that has resulted in some aspects of online marketing being dubbed 'consumer-initiated marketing'. This concept should be remembered when developing web content – that is, a message that is requested should be delivered in a very different way from one that is being imposed on someone.

Note that some web pages include ads – but these can be ignored by users whilst they are reading the sought-for content. I also appreciate that some web pages or ads use technology to *force* themselves on the user without prompt – though such tactics are generally recognized as having limited useful application, are normally associated with *adult* products, and should not be considered by reputable organizations or brands. Before any such ads are triggered, however, you must have requested the web page in the first place.

DECISION TIME

Although it is unusual for a business not to benefit from the web in some way – even if it has no direct involvement or influence – in many industries an effective online presence is absolutely essential if an organization is to compete in that marketplace. Whether the Internet is important to the organization as an integral element of a much wider business strategy, part of its procurement process or a valuable marketing tool, is a decision each organization must consider in the context of the environment in which it does business.

YOU DECIDE

Advise Milo at 22 Catches Fish Products (case study 7) on how much influence the Internet has, will or might have on the environment in which the company trades.

Alternatively, conduct the same exercise for your organization or that of your employer.

1.5 THE IMPACT OF THE INTERNET ON NOT-FOR-PROFIT ORGANIZATIONS

Whilst any section on the societal impact of the web could include the thousands of clubs, societies and interest groups, we will concentrate on those organizations that exist as entities beyond informal collections of individuals. Essentially, then, we will consider the following:

1. The public sector, including national and local governments, health, fire and police services.
2. Funded institutions, such as religious organizations and political parties.
3. Charities, including self-help and support groups as well as brands such as Save the Children and Oxfam.

Often misguidedly considered a 'Cinderella' occupation as far as practitioners are concerned, marketing in the not-for-profit and public sectors is arguably amongst the more difficult undertakings for the profession. This is because not only is the standard marketing mix difficult to apply (there is rarely a tangible product, for example), but such organizations are seldom market – or marketing – orientated.

A significant further problem is that of stakeholder satisfaction. In the commercial model, stakeholders are normally satisfied by steady profits, security, reasonable working conditions and a healthy attitude towards the environment. In not-for-profit, however, the stakeholders can demand more marketing attention than the actual consumers. Take a public museum, for example, where marketing efforts must be directed towards all potential sources of funding – each of which has a different agenda and needs. Such is the nature of this type of marketing that the consumer – who gets the service at no direct charge – is often well down the marketing priorities list. This is reflected in many not-for-profit websites that – by necessity – are more geared towards ticking funding-criteria boxes than improving the service to the consumer.

PRACTICAL INSIGHT

Information as a product

Not confined to the online environment, but given greater prominence because of the Internet's ability to deliver it, is the issue of information being a product. Throughout history information has been a valuable commodity, with those who have (1) gathered the information, or (2) have the skills to develop or decipher it being able to sell it on to willing buyers. Such information provision could range from maps to legal advice – and was traditionally made available either verbally or in print. The Internet, however, offers a more convenient and cheaper medium to communicate the *information product* over a wider geographical area to a more diverse market.

In this section the *information product* concept increases in complexity in that not-for-profit organizations often have a duty to make certain information freely available to the public. Unlike the solicitor therefore, who can sell her advice directly to a *customer* in a commercial exchange, the local government officer cannot charge directly for the information product he is responsible for, but nevertheless must distribute it appropriately.

Any government body has a remit of making services available to the general public that – through its taxes – pays for those services. An inherent aspect of the provision of those services is that the public must be made aware of them – in marketing terms, the services must be promoted. Once again, we return to the notion that the best application of the Internet is in the dissemination of information.

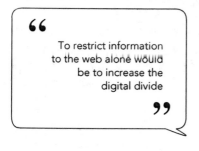

> **"**
>
> To restrict information to the web alone would be to increase the digital divide
>
> **"**

The introduction of the Internet has caused questions to be raised about a number of issues related to contemporary marketing – and one that arises in the digital marketing of public services is a distinction between *product* – or more specifically, *service* – and *promotion*. If, for example, a government body has a role that is to make available certain information – let's say with regard to environmental issues – if that information is put online, is that web page a promotion of the service, or is it the service itself? The question arises because never before has a medium been available that allows the full range of data to be made available to the general public. Prior to the Internet, the information might have been in printed format, with any promotion being to make society aware of the printed publication – the *product* – and how it was available. Now, however, the promotion (the website) is also the product (the information). Pedantic perhaps, but for the marketer knowing where something fits in the marketing mix is important for any strategic decision, if only to determine from which budget its costs are met.

This example emphasizes an irony of the web which impacts on the non-profit organization (which must meet the needs of *all* of its customers) more than the commercial company (which can adapt its product to suit only its target market) in that the government or not-for-profit body concerned must still produce printed versions of the information to meet the needs of non-web users. In this case, therefore, the advent of the Internet as a disseminator of information is actually increasing the workload and costs (costs per unit will be higher because of reverse economies of scale) for the organization concerned. To restrict information to the web alone would be to increase the digital divide mentioned in Section 1.3.

For each of the three groups identified earlier – the public sector, funded institutions and charities – there is also the potential for the Internet to be used to distribute actual products. The UK government, for example, has made it possible for car tax to be paid online – with the display disc being sent out by post. Churches – particularly in the USA – have websites on which their congregation can download podcasts or videos of sermons. Charities can not only present the results of their activities online, but can also accept donations and sell goods. A caveat to these, however, is the potential impact on society. Churches need real people in them, not virtual visitor statistics. Charities need to continue to make their particular issues real. And online car tax means fewer visitors to post offices, which may then close – at great loss to each one's community.

DECISION TIME

For the not-for-profit organization, the decision is not so much whether to go online, but how best to use the digital medium. Compared with other media, the Internet is an extremely cost-effective way of getting a message across to a wide audience in a way that would have been only a dream in pre-Internet days. Indeed, for the smaller organization, it is often easy to negotiate provision of a *free* web presence with service providers, website design companies or educational establishments. That said, many local not-for-profits over-estimate the power of the web. Local charities, for example, will benefit little from launching a website – getting out into the community being a much better way to get the message across (though a limited web presence may reinforce offline communications efforts).

Essentially, the decision is one that is also faced by commercial organizations: is the Internet to be used for marketing communications (i.e. dissemination of information) or e-commerce (or should that be e-non-commerce)? For charities, online credit-card dona-tions are relatively easy to sanction and online sales can be arranged if there are physical products to sell. Similarly, funded organizations can use the web to accept donations or distribute associated products. However, neither of these groups can rely exclusively on the Internet for their communications or fundraising efforts and so it should be seen as part of an integrated marketing strategy – with online often playing a relatively minor role.

For government and other institutions, there is the issue of reaching *all* of their constitu-ents. A business can make a commercial decision to ignore certain sectors of society because they do not represent potential customers for their products. This is not the case for public sector organizations that must cater to the lowest common denominator. So whilst putting the majority – if not all – of its services online would be an economically advantage, this can only be practised if 100 per cent of its market has access to the Internet. An online appointment-making facility at a doctor's surgery, for example, would disenfranchise any patient without access to the web in their home – and in societal terms it is that group that is most likely to need the services on offer at the surgery.

YOU DECIDE

Advise Howard Johnson at the Rockridge Museum (case study 1) on the impact of a significant minority of the public having limited access to the Internet, and the effect that might have on the museum's marketing efforts.

Alternatively, conduct the same exercise for your organization or that of your employer.

1.6 ONLINE BUYING BEHAVIOUR

Although students and practitioners of marketing should have no problem with the notion, it is important that all readers understand that, in marketing terms, *buying* a product does not always refer to a transaction where a good is exchanged for a sum of money. Indeed, in a wider context, we are looking at an *exchange* being the result of marketing activities. Customer behaviour, therefore, refers not only to a financial transaction, but also to when or where the *customer* agrees an action in return for a commitment on their part. It is often the case that use of the term 'customer' is not appropriate to the *selling* organization. Universities prefer 'students', hospitals 'patients' and churches 'worshippers', for example – but essentially each of these groups will demonstrate customer-behavioural traits in choosing the provider of their education, treatment or religion.

Rather than covering the myriad theories that exist in the social science that is customer behaviour, in this section we will briefly consider how people behave *online* and how that behaviour can best be exploited by the digital marketer. One way to do this is to take one of the most common models in the subject and consider how it might be applied online. Before doing that, however, it is worth adding that buyer behaviour is inherent in many (if not most) aspects of marketing – for that reason the subject re-emerges throughout subsequent chapters of this book. Successful website development (Chapter 3), for example, is dependent on the visitor being able to interact with the site (their behaviour), and in Section 2.5 we consider website analytics – much of which revolves around tracking users' online behaviour.

Perhaps the most commonly used model of buyer behaviour is that which considers the purchase process as a cycle, taking the customer in the following series of steps: problem recognition ➪ information search ➪ evaluation of alternatives ➪ purchase decision ➪ post-purchase behaviour. Normally presented as a flow chart, Figure 1.4 shows how the Internet can impact on that cycle.

A further consideration is the length of time that the potential customer takes to progress from problem recognition to purchase. For some products, the decision-making process is swift, with all stages taking place almost instantaneously. For other products, the decision is swift by necessity – a distress purchase, perhaps. Other product purchase cycles, however, might be much longer – a new car would be an example of this, where the buyer might take months, or even years, in coming to a decision.

GO ONLINE

In this section – on online buyer behaviour – I mention the buying cycle, AIDA and the sales funnel, all of which are standard marketing concepts. Also straight from the sales and marketing environment is Bryan Eisenberg's list of 'What makes people buy? 20 reasons why'. Most are fairly obvious (and should not be new to marketing students or retailers), but the reason I have included a reference to this article is so that you can consider how people would make these purchases online – and more importantly, how the online marketer meets their expectations in making those purchases.

The aforementioned buying cycle (see Figure 1.4) is a development from the AIDA concept – which has been around since the 1890s. Introduced by salesman St Elmo Lewis and given even greater prominence when E.K. Strong included it in his 1925 book *The Psychology of*

Stages of the buying cycle   Potential role played by the Internet

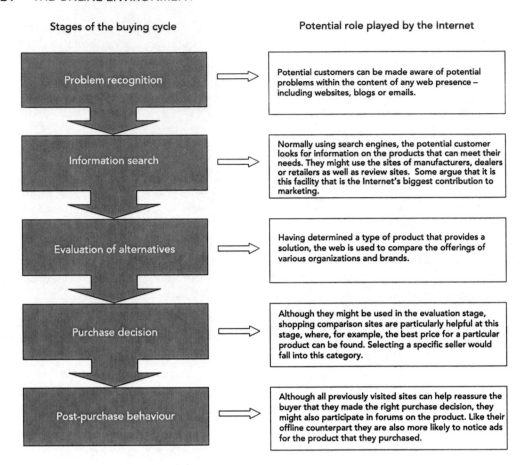

Problem recognition

Potential customers can be made aware of potential problems within the content of any web presence – including websites, blogs or emails.

Information search

Normally using search engines, the potential customer looks for information on the products that can meet their needs. They might use the sites of manufacturers, dealers or retailers as well as review sites. Some argue that it is this facility that is the Internet's biggest contribution to marketing.

Evaluation of alternatives

Having determined a type of product that provides a solution, the web is used to compare the offerings of various organizations and brands.

Purchase decision

Although they might be used in the evaluation stage, shopping comparison sites are particularly helpful at this stage, where, for example, the best price for a particular product can be found. Selecting a specific seller would fall into this category.

Post-purchase behaviour

Although all previously visited sites can help reassure the buyer that they made the right purchase decision, they might also participate in forums on the product. Like their offline counterpart they are also more likely to notice ads for the product that they purchased.

Figure 1.4 The Internet's potential impact on the buying cycle

Selling, the AIDA (Attention, Interest, Desire, Action) model requires the marketer to ask: 'Did the ad: grab *attention,* arouse an *interest,* stimulate *desire* and provide a call for *action?*' Naturally, the flip side to this model is that it mirrors the buyer's behaviour in making a purchase – their attention is drawn to a problem which then sparks their interest, creates a desire and they then take action to meet that desire. More contemporary models such as the sales, or conversion, funnel, are also based on the AIDA principle and – like all research into buyer behaviour – are used to help develop marketing strategies (see Figure 1.5). Although the funnel concept can be adapted for many similar purposes – brand adoption, for example – in *online* marketing it is most frequently used in developing or assessing websites – where the top of the funnel is the home or entry page and the exit represents the site's objective being achieved. The funnel model can be seen as a useful aid to marketers in that it (unlike the buying cycle which is more linear) represents the fact that people leave the buying cycle at various stages – hence the funnel narrows as it progresses to the 'sale'.

A further extension of the AIDA/cycle/funnel concept is to combine them so that customer retention is taken into account – and so the process becomes circular, that is the

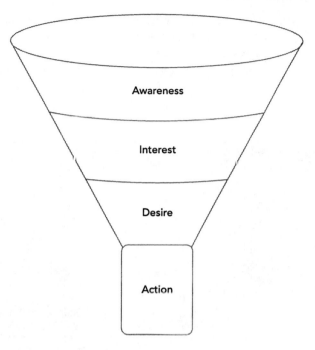

Figure 1.5 The basic AIDA sales funnel

last stage of one purchase leads directly into the first stage of the next. Commonly recognized as 'relationship marketing', this is the concept that sales should not be considered as isolated events and that customers should be encouraged to develop a relationship with the supplier – so increasing the opportunities for repeat purchases from the organization or brand. This is reflected in Figure 1.6, which shows a contemporary sales funnel.

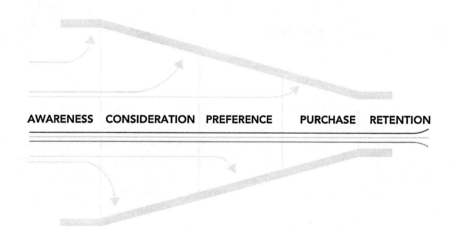

Figure 1.6 A contemporary sales funnel (the arrows indicate that potential customers can leave the funnel at any time)

Beyond considering the relevance of traditional models in online buyer behaviour, we can also look at *behavioural* traits of people when they are online – though it should be noted that we have already addressed many of these issues in the earlier sections on how the Internet has impacted on society, businesses and non-commercial organizations.

RESEARCH INSIGHT

The influence of the Internet

Based on research from the Nielsen organization, the Internet plays a significant role in influencing consumers who are interested in purchasing new products in a variety of categories such as: electronics (81%), appliances (77%), books (70%), new clothing (69%), music (69%) and cars (68%). Although it was not always the case, consumer goods are now included in the list of products whose purchase is affected by digital information, including: food and beverages (62%), personal hygiene (62%), personal health/over-the-counter medicines (61%) and hair care (60%).

Just where online that influence is strongest comes from research by Technorati Media who found that the top five online services most likely to influence a purchase were: retail sites (56%), brand sites (34%), blogs (31.1%), Facebook (30.8%) and groups/forums (28%).

Digging deeper into what digital marketing influences buyers most, Forrester Research identified: brand or product recommendations (USA 70% / Europe 61%), professionally written online reviews (55%/33%), consumer written online reviews (46%/38%), natural search engine results (43%/37%), information on company or brand websites (32%/23%), search engine adverts (27%/24%) and emails from companies or brands (18%/11%) as the top influencers.

Sources: 'Nielsen global survey of new product purchase sentiment, 2013' at nielsen.com; 'Digital influence report, 2013' at technoratimedia.com; Stokes *et al.* (2013)

A number of authors have attempted to segregate online shoppers, but rather than some of the theoretical academic proposals, I prefer the more pragmatic submission from practitioner and writer Gerry McGovern (2002), whose suggestion has stood the test of time. It is that there are four types of user that might arrive on a website, and he presents his list of users in the context of web designers needing to cater for each. It reflects his commercial outlook that he considers all but one of the groups to be potential customers – in marketing terms, *prospects*. They are:

- Perfect prospects – those people who know what they want and so may well take an action that helps the site meet its objectives – a purchase, for example.

- Prospects who 'sort of' know what they want, but are not sure.
- Prospects who aren't even sure if they want anything, but would buy something if the right product came along.
- The only one not made up of prospects – and that is because its members have arrived on your website by mistake. It is the only group that can be ignored when developing a website.

Also of concern to the e-marketer are issues of how and why Internet users behave as they do when they are online. As with offline buyer behaviour – on which much is written – the key elements revolve around psychological and social factors, though the concept of *benefits sought* is also a key consideration, particularly for e-tailers looking to make online sales.

Research into the purpose behind people's visits to the web strongly suggests that it is a search for information that drives them online. As we covered in the earlier sections of this chapter, that information need not be commercial in nature – but it would appear that even with commercial intent the web is used primarily to gather information. Furthermore, the product-related information gathering is not limited to high-value items. Although facilities to easily compare selling prices for products is something the web has brought to the homes of users, price is not the single driver of online sales. As we will see in this and subsequent chapters – although the web is used to find low prices, it is for an *offline* purchase. Indeed, when considering online purchases, price is not a key determinant – convenience having the most positive impact on their purchase behaviour.

MINI CASE

At four pounds an hour, it's a bargain

In 1997, I worked on a project to develop a website selling a series of 'past times' books that featured photo-histories of UK towns and cities. Books featuring specific towns or cities were readily available in local bookshops, but our target market was ex-pats who wanted to revisit their past, but could not physically return to their hometowns. The first subject city was our own – Sunderland. The office sweepstake for the country of origin for the first order had Canada and Australia as joint favourites. So it was something of a disappointment when the first online order came in from the village of Whitburn, a couple of miles up the coast from Sunderland's city centre. Contact was made with the buyer. Why had he paid full retail price plus postage for a book he could have purchased at a discounted price in a city centre shop?

On reflection, his reason was obvious – and many others in the still-emerging practice of e-commerce were soon to realize it, too. Our customer – who ran his own business – worked 7 a.m. until 7 p.m., Monday to Friday. On Saturdays he played golf. Sunday was his family day. To travel to the city centre on a weekend, park his car, walk to the shop, buy the book and return home would take at least an hour, nearer two on busy days. To this gentleman, ordering online during the evening and paying an extra £4 or so to have the book delivered to his house was a bargain. He valued his leisure time at well over £4 an hour.

Fast forward sixteen years, and while I was writing this book I needed something from IKEA which only that retailer sells. The cost of the product was £15; I paid an extra £5 for delivery. Why? The nearest IKEA to me is sixteen miles away. In my car, the return trip would cost me more than that in petrol. And at least an hour of my time – like my customer above, I value my time.

And for those of you who might dismiss this notion – note that a survey by Verdict Research in 2013 found that leading the way with 70 per cent, the main reason shoppers in the UK bought groceries on line was ... *convenience*.

Source: verdictretail.com

A further consideration is that segment of the market for which visiting bricks-and-mortar shops is physically problematic. This applies not only to those who are disabled, but those who might have family obligations that tie them to their homes – be that caring for elderly or infirm family members or a growing family. For others, shopping is simply seen as being a chore – something to be avoided if at all possible. Zinkhan (2005) makes the point that many online buyers revel in the fact that they can complete a transaction without having to go through a third party – in other words, by completing their buying cycle online, the hassle of dealing with pushy, ill-informed – or just poor – sales staff is eliminated. Could this be another significant factor in the rise of online grocery shopping?

DECISION TIME

In their efforts to develop a marketing mix that best meets the needs of their customers, marketers have long used the science of psychology to address why buyers behave the way they do in relation to the purchase of their products. Not only has the Internet added to the *why* aspect of buyer behaviour, but it has also intensified the issue of *how* they practise that behaviour. Although the issue of *why* raises new problems – and solutions – for the marketer, it is the aspect of *how* that impacts most on them. Most significant is customers' use of the web to seek information on which they base their buying decision. For the contemporary marketer, simply putting product instructions and information on the packaging is not enough, they need to find out where the customer expects to find information – and then make sure it is there for them to access – in whatever digital format that might be.

YOU DECIDE

Advise Frank and his management team at Hill Street Motorist Shops (case study 8) on how they should adapt their communications mix so as best to suit their potential market.

Alternatively, conduct the same exercise for your organization or that of your employer.

1.7 THE INTERNET GOES MOBILE

> "
> Technology doesn't change behaviour – technology enables behaviour to change
> "

If there is one aspect of digital marketing that has changed most since the first edition of this book it is that we now access all aspects of the Internet on mobile devices, that is outside the home or office. However, I recall that even as I was writing the content of that first edition 'experts' were predicting – as they had done every year of the new decade – 'next year will be the year of the mobile'. Well, somewhere between that edition and this, that *year* certainly happened. In reality, however, the explosion in mobile access exceeded the expectations of its most ardent supporters. Proliferation of mobile devices – when the first edition of this book was written, tablets were something you swallowed for a headache – and the availability of affordable 3G or 4G and wifi brought on by a combination of advances in technology and competition in the supplier market obviously played roles, but more significant is the way we now expect to be online 24/7/365 – whether we are in our home, at work, on a train, in a shop, pub or coffee bar or just on the street. This gives us a 'chicken and egg' consideration: was the rise of the mobile Internet a result of consumer behaviour, or was consumer behaviour changed by the technology? Digital marketing practitioner and writer Gord Hotchkiss is more succinct. He says (2010), 'Technology doesn't change behaviour – technology enables behaviour to change.' Research from the Pew Research Center's Internet and American Life Project (2009) suggests that once people have a wireless device, they become much more active in how they use the Internet: they go online not just to find information but to share what they find and even to create new content much more than they did before. This would account for the simultaneous rise of social media and the adoption of mobile devices over the years since that research was conducted.

As a footnote, I am one of those who questions the societal impact of the 'always on' phenomenon – but that is the subject of a social science book. This book is about how marketers can take advantage of the 24/7/365 generation.

PRACTICAL INSIGHT

Showrooming

If you are in a physical store and use your mobile device to check other suppliers' prices for the item you are looking at, then you are 'showrooming'.

However, the impact of this on offline shops is open to debate. Research from the Interactive Advertising Bureau in 2013 found that 65 per cent of shoppers who use their mobile device in-store said it made them more likely to buy the product and 42 per cent indicated that they completed their purchases online, not offline. Thirty per cent went on to complete their purchase in the store. However, shoppers who used a mobile device generally spent more than non-showroomers, suggesting that showroomers – like all buyers – can be segmented into the price sensitive and not so price sensitive.

Ultimately, however, perhaps showroomers – like nearly all shoppers – have already checked online before they enter the store in the first place, therefore retailers should just accept the practice as a part of contemporary multi-channel retailing.

This section serves as an introduction to the subject of accessing the web on the move; throughout the book, where relevant, the issue of use of mobile devices is addressed within each section. The use of search engines while *mobile*, for example, differs from PC-based searches, and viewing on a small screen must be considered by website designers. However, this section would not be complete without consideration of some of the statistics available on the subject at this time. I wonder how they will compare with a similar section for a third edition of this book – or will *all* web access be on devices other than PCs by then? Research that emphasizes the impact of *mobile* includes:

- December 2012 saw page views from non-PCs reach an all-time high with nearly a third of all UK page views being on smartphones and tablets (comScore.com, 2013).
- 46 per cent of search traffic on Christmas Day 2012 was on tablets and mobiles (econsultancy.com, 2013).
- In the run-up to Christmas 2012, smartphones and tablets accounted for 28 per cent of clicks on retail paid search ads (Kenshoo, 2013).
- 34 per cent of US consumers own a tablet computer (Pew Research Center's Internet and American Life Project, May 2013)
- Nearly 40 per cent of all Internet time is now spent on mobile devices (comScore.com, 2013).
- Around 70 per cent of takeaway food ordered online is done so using a smartphone or tablet (Interactive Advertising Bureau, 2013)
- Twitter says that 60 per cent of its active user base accesses the service via mobile devices.

- 78 per cent of people check email on their smartphones, compared to 73 per cent who browse websites and 70 per cent who access Facebook (IDC, 2013).

GO ONLINE

For an excellent collection of updated statistics on mobile phone use, follow the link on the chapter's web page.

DECISION TIME

If a solution to your customers' problems, needs or wants can be addressed on a mobile device out of the home (though, of course, mobile devices can be used in the home or place of work), then the organization should meet that requirement. Although the increasing use of mobile devices has made on-mobile branding a potential mobile-centric objective, it is income generation and service that are the two key objectives for this element of digital marketing. As with my comments on the Internet in general earlier in this chapter, providing a mobile service for customers is not essential – or even necessary – for all organizations.

This leaves the digital marketer with the consideration of whether to (1) integrate mobile marketing within the existing offering (a website that is equally accessible on a smartphone and a PC, for example), (2) develop a standalone web presence for mobile devices (in addition to the *standard* website), or (3) develop an app for mobile users to download onto their own device. An app is a piece of *application software* which is downloaded onto a computer to perform a specific task, unlike system software which manages a computer's capabilities. A popular example would be the eBay app, which facilitates the user accessing all of the auction site's functions on a mobile device without the negative user experience of using the conventional website – aspects of which may not run or be easily useable on a hand-held device with limited functions (e.g. very small screen and no mouse). Note that thousands of other apps exist for mobile devices, but in the context of this book these would be considered to be products rather than elements of digital marketing – a torch app, for example. That said, apps can be used as branding giveaways in the same way that more tangible, physical items have been over the years. The torch app might be available free from a battery manufacturer – with the brand name being prominent on the mobile's screen before, during and after the device is used to find your way in the dark using the app.

YOU DECIDE

Advise Syd and Charlie at Two Cities Manufacturing Ltd (case study 11) on how they might use the mobile Internet – now or in the future – in their marketing.

Alternatively, conduct the same exercise for your organization or that of your employer.

1.8 ONLINE MARKETING OBJECTIVES

Without specific objectives the likelihood of any venture succeeding diminishes significantly – and this is equally true for digital marketing – and yet perhaps the biggest failing when organizations go online is that they fail to determine their objectives for doing so. As John Blackmore, Senior Manager for Web Demand Generation at IBM, said in 2011: 'I think deciding what our website was meant to do was the first and most important step to achieving results.'

there is a lack of joined-up thinking between off- and online marketing efforts

The reasons for any lack of strategic direction are many, though IT departments' 'ownership' of the web presence was certainly a significant factor in the mid- to late 1990s. So too was a lack in understanding of what the new medium of communication had to offer. While these reasons are (sadly) still in evidence today, another problem has moved to the fore – a lack of joined-up thinking between:

- Off- and online marketing efforts, where too often online is considered to be separate from other marketig activities – and so is treated as such in strategic planning;

but perhaps worse for those studying this subject . . .

- The various elements of digital marketing – particularly where different aspects are 'owned' by separate departments, PR, social media and sales, for example.

GO ONLINE

Throughout this book, references to the work of Gerry McGovern outnumber those to any other single source and his view of online strategy, 'How online is changing the game and the playing field for strategy development', is available online. Follow the link from the chapter's website to read it in full.

In marketing terms, there are three objectives for any Internet presence or activity. They are:

1. Brand development – where the online presence complements and enhances the offline branding efforts of the organization.
2. Revenue generation – where the online presence increases revenue into the organization by direct sales, lead generation or direct marketing.
3. Customer service/support – where the web is used to enhance the service and support offered to customers – and potential customers.

(Note that I developed the 'three objectives' concept around 1997, and it was first published in a book I co-authored – Gay *et al.* (2007) *Online Marketing – a customer-led approach*).

However, such is the nature of the web that (1) it is possible for a single website or presence to address one, two or all three of these objectives, and (2) it is rare that a

> **"**
>
> In all aspects of digital marketing any marketing action with a specific objective will also influence the other objectives as a spin-off advantage.
>
> **"**

web presence addresses only one. Given this second point, perhaps it would be more accurate to describe the site's *leading* or *primary* objective, expressed as a percentage. For example, an online-only retailer might have income generation at 85 per cent (if they don't sell anything, they will go out of business), with 5 per cent for branding and 10 per cent for service.

Online marketing guru Gerry McGovern (2011), who has declared that 'support is the new marketing!', argues that effective after-sales services such as installation guides serve to increase the brand of the organization – and I would agree that he has a point. If the product can be purchased on the same site, this means that not only are all three objectives being met but any might be the primary objective. Whichever that is, if it is practised effectively then there is a *spin-off* advantage to the other objectives. And this is an important point. In all aspects of digital marketing any marketing action with a specific objective will also influence the other objectives as a spin-off advantage. In my earlier online-only retailer example, any efforts to establish the validity of the organization in order to encourage an immediate sale will also help build the brand in the perception of the customer. Similarly an excellent returns policy – again, highlighted in sales copy to elicit a purchase – will also act as an after-sales service should the customer wish to return the goods.

Although specific objectives are necessary in order to develop effective strategies, having distinct objectives is also essential to the digital marketer in (1) determining whether or not the site – or online activity – has been successful, and (2) assessing any return on investment (ROI) for online operations. As is true for much of marketing – strategic and operational – establishing ROI for digital marketing is difficult, and despite there being a plethora of metrics with which to track online activity (see Section 2.5) effective qualitative or quantitative of digital marketing ROI are still problematic. Certainly some objectives can be tangible – sales, for example – and so total costs can be calculated against direct income (i.e. cost of sales), but others, such as branding and after-sales service, are intangibles that are difficult to translate into monetary benefits. It is also the case that some quantitative metrics do not reflect overall marketing objectives. For example, in the same way that the best restaurants might promote exclusivity by making it difficult to get a table, so website visitor numbers are not everything – with strategies for building online volume being potentially counter-productive in building customer relationships.

Although the first two of my proposed objectives are – I believe – self-explanatory, when I wrote the first edition of this book I had a particular view on the third. Unfortunately I didn't express my opinion in such a way that it was obvious what my intentions were. It is rather ironic, therefore, that since I wrote that edition the use of the web presence as a service to support existing customers has been recognized and increased to such an extent that it is now common practice. Significant in this is the rise of social media – with an increasing number of people turning first to a social media presence when they experience a problem, rather than a website. Indeed, research from Nielsen (2012) found that one in three users prefer to contact brands using social media rather than the telephone.

However, that is not the end of this particular story in that *we* – that is writers and practitioners – have differing views on what denotes online 'service and support'. If a customer is the *person who buys*, then what is the definition of 'buy'? There is a temptation for marketers to refer to the target market of their goods or services as 'customers', and this is taken up as a criticism of marketing by people who do not fully understand the discipline (although some, including me, would debate just what marketing is – but that is an argument for another book). For example, academics dislike using the term 'customers' for their students, and the same applies for doctors and their patients. Yet, in marketing terms, they are *customers* of the service. The discussion expands when we also consider the marketing of ideas and ideals. Are voters the *customers* of political parties or congregations the *customers* of religions? Marketing theory says yes – but there are obvious difficulties in justifying this to the non-marketer.

It is too easy to divorce objectives two and three and say one is where a sale takes place and the service is for the non-profit organization. A council website, for example, tells council tax payers (their *customers*) things like when their bins will be emptied and how to apply for planning permission to extend their house. There is no specific online payment for that information; it is just part of the service paid for in the council tax. However, on a revenue-generation site, a potential customer might use the 'support' content to help solve a problem (a forum discussing a PC software issue, for example) before paying to download a fix to the problem.

Unfortunately, there is no finite answer to this issue. But then such is the nature of marketing that few – if any – of its problems have a finite answer. And that in turn is why digital marketing should be practised by marketers and not computer scientists. Effective marketing requires the marketers to make a decision on what is right for their customers – whatever term those customers might be known by.

“
that . . . is why digital marketing should be practised by marketers and not computer scientists.
”

Worth mentioning at this point – though it is a theme throughout the entirety of this book – is that the market or industry in which the organization operates will have a profound influence on how that organization might use the Internet in its marketing. As you will find in the chapters to come, the key factors of Internet adoption are whether: (1) the organization trades only from bricks-and-mortar locations – i.e. it does not facilitate online sales, (2) it trades both off- and online clicks and mortar – i.e. it facilitates online sales/orders – or (3) it trades online only – so-called 'pure play'.

As digital marketing has matured, a further consideration comes into the objectives equation – that of different elements of the Internet having different strategic objectives. Normally, elements of the digital marketing mix would be used to achieve an overall strategic objective – online advertising or search engine optimization being geared towards driving potential customers to a retail site where they will make a purchase, for example. However, as we have seen in the last section, access to the web via mobile devices has increased exponentially – and so perhaps the website might have an objective of lead generation, whilst the mobile application has one of service. For the pure play online business, the online strategy is, in effect, *the* strategy – and although we will return to pure play marketing throughout the book, the objectives of such an organization are worth considering here, in isolation from the other two models.

The pure – online organization

Whilst it is a popular pastime to list *types* of website, less common are attempts to identify the business models of pure online businesses. One concept that has stood the test of time comes from David Rappa. His 1998 list of *online trading business models* does not attempt to describe types of website, but what income models are available to the online-only business. Rappa's models are:

- The Brokerage Model – buyers and sellers are brought together in an online environment. Income is from fees charged for each transaction.
- The Advertising Model – the website provides content that attracts readers. Income is from the sale of ads on the site.
- The Infomediary Model – the website is used to collect data on visitors. Income is from the sale of that data to third parties.
- The Merchant Model – the website is a retail or wholesale outlet. Income is from the sale of goods or services.
- The Manufacturer Model – income is generated by selling goods direct to the end user, so reducing the dependence on channels of distribution.
- The Affiliate Model – visitors are encouraged to purchase goods or services from businesses to which the website is affiliated. Income is from fixed fees or a percentage of each sale.
- The Subscription Model – income is generated by charging for access to the site. This model requires high value-added content to attract subscribers.
- The Utility Model – online services that are accessed from the site are offered for a fee.
- The Community Model – a model that relies on income generated through affiliates, ads or subscription, but where the content is community orientated. Because of the visitor's investment in both time and emotion in the site's subject, community sites are ideal for targeted marketing.

Such is the nature of the web that whilst a model can be used in isolation, it is common practice for several to be employed within one website.

While it is worth noting that – like all aspects of online marketing – all of these models existed in other media or industries prior to the development of the new digital media, I wonder if David Rappa could have imagined just how those models would be presented online some 15 years later.

A final point in this section is also one which permeates the entire book – that of the role of digital technology as an integral part of the product, rather than the marketing of that product. This book is about the latter, but there is an argument that as product is one of the 4Ps (or 7Ps if you are so inclined), then digital technology in products should be covered as part of the subject. I disagree.

That new cars may have DAB radios and access to the Internet in their dashboards is not part of marketing, neither is having a home CCTV linked to the house's wifi so that the picture can be accessed by the homeowner from anywhere in the world.

The case is less clear cut, however, when the product is a service. Is using digital communications platforms to meet a 'service' objective part of the product or part of the marketing? There are, obviously, grey areas, but I would argue that contacting an organization via Facebook or accessing an installation diagram on a website is not part of the product, but part of the service that adds to the overall relationship that is developing between the customer and the brand, product or organization. And as the name suggests, that is part of relationship *marketing*.

DECISION TIME

Although many would consider it to be an essential element of any organization's strategic planning, setting objectives for any digital marketing endeavours is not something that all organizations practise. For the pure play business, determining key objectives for the online presence is pretty straightforward – in essence, whatever it is that generates income. For example, in Rappa's advertising model the strategy must be built around driving the maximum number of visitors to the website, or for the merchant model generating online sales is the goal.

For both offline only and off- and online organizations, the marketing objectives must go beyond online sales generation – and should complement, enhance or be integrated with the organization's overall strategic marketing and business aims. Ultimately, of course, the marketing objective of any Internet presence must be to meet the needs of the target visitor. If you do not achieve that goal no organizational objectives will ever be met.

> **YOU DECIDE**
>
> Advise the marketers at the Matthew Humberstone Foundation Hospital (case study 6) on what their key online objective might be.
>
> Alternatively, conduct the same exercise for your organization or that of your employer.

1.9 LEGAL CONSIDERATIONS

Because the legal aspects of any organization are best left to experts in that discipline, in this book we will not consider legal aspects of online marketing in great detail. However, as a basic guide – and so that e-marketers are aware of when they should seek professional legal advice – the following should be considered for any website:

1. A copyright statement that makes it clear that you own the content on your website and that no other parties have the right to reproduce it without your permission. Note that by the same token, if you publish content from another source (perhaps comments in a blog, or from another website) that owner's copyright should be acknowledged and the source identified.

2. Terms and conditions should outline the conditions for using your website.

3. A privacy statement explaining your commitment to keeping users' data private. This must comply with any data protection laws of the seller's home country (in the UK, the Data Protection Act, 1998). Note that the USA – and other countries – have no similar law.

4. A disclaimer against any legal responsibility for how any content on your site is used or interpreted by users.

5. If used, a notice explaining your site's use of cookies. This might include brief details of what a cookie is, which types are being used on the site, why they are used, and why the user should know about them.

Naturally, all of the above must be developed by legally qualified personnel – which, for most organizations, means outsourcing the work.

Other, more generic, online legal issues worth considering include:

- Unless you have an agreement to the contrary, the website designer will have copyright in that website – in other words, they hold the copyright, not you. Check the contract, if you have one.

- Using trademarks of other companies in the meta tags of your website is legally problematic.

- If you sell goods online then the 'offer' should be designed in such a way as to present an *invitation to treat*. This means the supplier makes a request for a potential customer to make an offer to the supplier. This gives the seller the freedom to reject the offer if they so wish. For example, you can reject orders for products that have been incorrectly priced because someone typed a decimal point in the wrong place.

- Any site selling goods online must bring the buyer's attention to the 'Terms and Conditions' of that sale. The best way to do this is to have the site designed in such a way that the buyer must either (1) open the 'Terms and Conditions' page in order to buy the goods, or (2) tick a box confirming that they have read them before the transactional page is opened.

- As with any form of advertising, your website must not say anything that is misleading or that may be misinterpreted.

- If an organization sponsors any element of digital marketing, then that sponsorship must be made clear. For example, if a personality is paid to extol the virtues of a product in a tweet, that association must be made obvious in the tweet.

- The EU's Consumer Protection (Distance Selling) Regulations 2000 lay down certain regulations in order to protect consumers. Key to this is that consumers purchasing at a distance – including online – can cancel an order within seven working days without having to give a reason.

- Ensure that customers are aware of any tax issues related to the product; for example, is it included in the price or is the customer responsible for paying any tax due when goods are delivered outside the home country of the seller?

Though not pertinent to many – if not most – B2C traders, the issue of child protection is a serious consideration. Whilst most legislation is with regard to the sexual abuse of children – and so not a concern for any legitimate business – in the USA there is also the Children's Online Privacy Protection Act (COPPA), which mandates that websites must obtain parental consent before collecting, using or disclosing personal information from children under the age of thirteen. Though no such law exists in the EU, complying with COPPA would be good practice, particularly if you trade in the USA and your product or service might appeal to minors.

DECISION TIME

As previously stated, this section seeks only to raise awareness of issues upon which the online marketer should seek specialist help. Essentially, therefore – as with all aspects of offline trading – the law is not a subject to be (1) taken lightly, (2) ignored or (3) guessed at. It is my experience that online these three are far from uncommon, with 'hoping nothing goes wrong' being the dubious strategy – and cost being the reason behind the poor practice.

A further decision that is strategic (rather than many of the above, which are operational) is: to which country's legal system will the organization be held responsible? Normally this will be the home country of the company – and the website's terms and conditions will make this clear. However, there are complications. For example, in Section 3.6 we consider the global website, in which case the local site for each country may be accountable to local laws. Another contentious issue is the country in which a site's server is located. Many website publishers – often in the adult entertainment industry or engaged in selling counterfeit products – flaunt global laws by hosting their sites on servers in countries or regions where online law enforcement is not as stringent as in others. For the legitimate organization this is a poor idea, as they will be perceived as being dubious even if their trading is perfectly legal and above board.

The main decision in this section, therefore, is *when* – not *if* – will legal help be sought?

YOU DECIDE

Advise Martha and her team at the Phelps Online Department Store (case study 13) on what legal issues will be particularly relevant to that organization with regard to its online trading.

Alternatively, conduct the same exercise for your organization or that of your employer.

CHAPTER EXERCISE

Giving justifications for all your decisions, advise Quincy Adams Wagstaff and his staff at Huxley University (case study 10) on all aspects of digital marketing covered in this chapter.

Alternatively, conduct the same exercise for your own organization or that of your employer.

CHAPTER QUESTIONS

Follow the link from the chapter's web page to a series of multiple-choice exam-type questions that will test your knowledge and understanding of the various elements of this chapter.

REFERENCES

Blackmore, J. (2011) Quoted on gerrymcgovern.com.

Boag, P. (2013) Is your organisation web-compatible? Available at www.econsultancy. com/uk/blog/62781-is-your-organisation-web-compatible.

Butler, P. and Peppard, J. (1998) Consumer purchasing on the Internet: process and prospects. *European Management Journal*. Volume 16, number 5, pp. 600–610.

comScore (2013) 2013 mobile future in focus. Available on comScore.com.

Forrester Consulting (2012) Driving SMB revenue in a tough economy. Available on actonsoftware.com.

Gay, R., Charlesworth, A. and Esen, R. (2007). *Online Marketing: A Customer-Led Approach*. Oxford University Press.

Hotchkiss, G. (2010) The integration of online behaviour. Available on searchengineland. com.

Hughes, T. (2007) Regaining a seat at the table: marketing management and the e-service opportunity. *Journal of Services Marketing*. Volume 21, number 4, pp. 270–280.

IDC (2013) Always connected. Available at https://fb-public.box.com/s/3iq5x6uwnqtq 7ki4q8wk.

Kenshoo (2013) UK online retail Christmas shopping report. Available on kenshoo.com.

McGovern, G. (2002) Information architecture versus graphic design. Available at www.clickz.com/design/site_design/article.php/945631.

McGovern G. (2011) Help people do things, don't keep them on web pages. Available at www.gerrymcgovern.com/nt/2011/nt-2011-09-19-Help-people.html.

Nielsen (2012) State of the media: the social media report. Available on nielsen.com.

Papacharissi, Z. and Rubin, A.M. (2000) Predictors of Internet use. *Journal of Broadcasting and Electronic Media*. Volume 44, number 2, pp. 175–197.

Peterson, R.A., Balasubramanian, S. and Bronnenberg, B.J. (1997) Exploring the implications of the Internet for consumer marketing. *Journal of the Academy of Marketing Sciences*. Volume 24, number 4, pp. 329–346.

Pew Research Center's Internet and American Life Project (2005) Digital divisions. Available on pewinternet.org.

Pew Research Center's Internet and American Life Project (2009) The mobile difference. Available on pewinternet.org

Pew Research Center's Internet and American Life Project (2012) Digital differences. Available on pewinternet.org.

Rappa, D. (1998) Managing the digital enterprise. Available on digitalenterprise.org.

Sandvine (2013) Global Internet phenomena report. Available at www.sandvine.com/news/global_broadband_trends.asp.

Schmidt, E. and Cohen, J. (2013) *The New Digital Age*. John Murray.

Stokes, T., Cooperstein, D.M. and Hayes, A. (2013) *How to Build Your Brand with Branded Content*. Forrester Research.

TNS, TRU and Marketing Evolution (2007) *Never Ending Friending: A Journey into Social Networking*. Fox Interactive Media.

Zinkhan, G.M. (2005) The marketplace, emerging technology and marketing theory. *Marketing Theory*. Volume 5, pp. 105–115.

Chapter **2**

Getting started online

Chapter at a glance

2.1 Introduction
2.2 Domain names
2.3 Website hosting
2.4 Who 'owns' the web presence?
2.5 Website analytics and e-metrics
2.6 The Internet as a tool for market research

2.1 INTRODUCTION

Where the Internet is concerned, there is a strange phenomenon that is pretty much unique in a business environment – and it is this. In all other aspects of business – be it commercial or not-for-profit – any expenditure is assessed on its potential benefit to the organization, what the return on investment (ROI) is likely to be and what might be the negative impact of not committing to that spending. On the subject of digital marketing, however, that reasoning seems to leave by the nearest window. Things are getting better, but we are far from being anywhere close to perfect. For example – in my personal experience – I have come across businesses that have paid thousands of pounds on a sign for the building's reception area (which will be seen by only a few customers), but have the website (that is available 24/7/365 throughout the world) developed by the owner's daughter's boyfriend for £50 cash. Similarly, the purchase or lease of a van would involve careful consideration of how many miles it would be expected to travel, its payload, maintenance downtime and a whole host of other issues before any decision on a specific vehicle from a particular supplier was made. Yet the company's web presence is barely discussed before its development is given the OK.

> So why is business commonsense so absent in so many aspects of digital marketing?

So why is business commonsense so absent in so many aspects of digital marketing? My opinion is that the key issues are a balance between managers (a) being uneasy about computer technology, and (b) not realizing the importance of the role that *digital* plays in contemporary business. In this chapter – as its title suggests – you will be introduced to the key elements in getting started in the online environment. If it is not the case already, by the end of it you will know that the Internet is not scary and that it *is* important in contemporary marketing. You will also know that it is not the exclusive domain of the folks from the IT department.

GO ONLINE

If you want to see what the web looked like in times gone by, follow the link from the chapter's web page to the excellent Wayback Machine.

2.2 DOMAIN NAMES

First impressions can be crucial. In an online environment, the organization's domain name may well be the first point of contact between it and a potential customer. First impressions are all about perception, and a 'good' domain name can influence how a potential customer might perceive the organization – that is: poor domain name equals poor company, good domain name equals good company to do business with. Although this notion is far from absolute – and may even be nonsense – given the price of a domain name, it costs little to pander to a customer's perception.

PRACTICAL INSIGHT

A domain name is not just for a website

Although technically they are not domain names, the digital marketer should apply all of the lessons in this chapter to the choice of 'domain name' for all of the organization's presences on the web – in particular, social media. Brands should always look to register their own name on the various channels, for example:

facebook.com/nike and twitter.com/nikefootball (@nikefootball);

facebook.com/Amazon and twitter.com/amazon (@amazon);

facebook.com/cocacola and twitter.com/cocacola (@cocacola).

Given that social media presences can be set up and discarded more easily than websites, it is also common – and potentially good – practice to use *quirky* names, such as promotional tag lines, as Facebook pages or Twitter handles.

Choosing an effective domain name – often referred to as the organization's address on the Internet – is a crucial decision for any organization. It is primarily a marketing decision and not one to be taken by other staff who do not appreciate the value of a domain name in marketing terms.

To have a web presence, an organization must have a domain name, and if they must have a domain name, then they should give some thought to not just having a *good* domain name, but the *right* domain name. Before the online marketer can select the *right* domain name, they must first understand a little about the subject.

What is a domain name?

Every presence on the Internet is identified by a series of numbers (142.56.89.43, for example) – called the Internet Protocol, or IP, address. To make these IP addresses easier to remember, the early proponents of the Internet decided to allocate a *word* (or series of characters) to each IP number. As no two sets of IP numbers are the same, no two domain names can be the same either.

Domain names are, and always have been, allocated on a first-come, first-served basis. The majority of generic, one-word domain names were registered in the early to mid-1990s – and as registration was free at the time, many were registered by IT students (who were amongst the first to use the Internet on a regular basis). It is the generic .com domains that many consider to be the *best*. It is also difficult to trademark a generic word. By definition, that means that generic .coms are the most valuable domain names.

The domain name system is run by the Internet Corporation for Assigned Names and Numbers (ICANN), which is responsible for a range of technical aspects of the Internet, including the Domain Name System (DNS), which allows for the registration of domain names within a number of registries known as 'top-level domains' (TLDs). TLDs fall into two broad categories:

- Generic Top-Level Domains (gTLDs), such as .com; and
- Country Code Top-Level Domains (ccTLDs), such as .uk for the United Kingdom.

Each country has its own *naming* authority that runs the domain name system for that country – referred to as *sponsoring organizations*. To register a name for that country you must apply to that authority for 'permission' to use that name. Effectively, those who register the name are the *owners* of that name and as such are the only ones who can use it. There are organizations that act as intermediaries between the customer and the naming agencies. It is with these *registration agents* (or registrars) that the vast majority of people or entities register their domain name.

Domain name construction

When a name is registered it takes the suffix of the registered naming authority. There are a number of suffixes to choose from (more of this later) but to illustrate how domain names are constructed this example will use the best-known suffix – .com (dot com). The domain used as an illustration is yagahit.com.

As the suffix is considered to be the *primary*, or *top level*, domain, combining the 'name' with the suffix creates a *second* level domain:

e.g. yagahit.com

When indicating their use as the URL (Uniform Resource Locator) of a worldwide website, it has become accepted protocol to use the prefix 'www' on the primary domain name:

e.g. www.yagahit.com

As the dot com suffix now has two distinct *words* before it, this is now a *third* level domain name.

Any subsequent *words* placed in front of the primary name, but separated by a full stop, make the URL a fourth/fifth level domain name. Theoretically, there is no limit to the number of *words* that can be placed in front of the domain. In practice, however, three or four is really the limit:

e.g. www.sunderland.yagahit.com

When used as a ccTLD, the domain name takes on an extra level to indicate its country of origin. Figure 2.1 shows the make-up of a domain on the .uk ccTLD.

There is a very unambiguous limit to the characters that can be used in a domain name. They are: all the letters of the Latin alphabet (A to Z), plus any number (0 to 9), and a dash/hyphen (-). Note that these rules apply to domain names that use the English language – others, known as Internationalized Domain Names, are available in different languages. A domain name must begin and end with a letter or a number, no spaces or other characters are allowed. Any amount of dashes can be used, but must not be placed together. Domain names must be at least three and less than sixty-three characters in length (excluding suffixes). Although two letter domains do exist, they are only allocated to organizations that can prove that they are universally recognized by a two character name. Communications giant O2 for example, uses O2.co.uk and Hewlett Packard, HP.com – realistically, however, unless an organization is in the same league as these examples, they can forget two character domains.

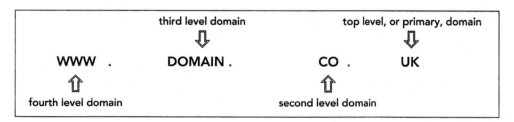

Figure 2.1 How a domain name is constructed

Just having fun dot com

Given their low price, domain names are ripe for funsters to amuse themselves. For example, the imaginatively named 'the longest list of the longest stuff at the longest domain name at long last' website – can be found (of course) on www.thelongestlistofthelongeststuffatthelongestdomainnameatlonglast.com.

Finally – and this is important for marketing reasons – domain names are NOT case sensitive. From a technical standpoint, it is possible to set up a website's host server so that it recognizes upper and lower case characters in a domain name (so making a domain case sensitive) – however, this is (virtually) never practised, it being the standard operating procedure to set them up as being non-case sensitive.

Suffixes

The most common domain name suffix is .com (dot com). This is the suffix for the USA and is considered to be the *global* name as it has no country identification (such as .uk for the UK). In reality, it has no country identification because it was the first suffix made available (there is a rarely used .us domain that is normally linked to state abbreviations, for example .fl.us for Florida).

There are over 250 countries with a country-specific domain, for example: .de for Germany .jp for Japan .fr for France and .gr for Greece – even the Vatican City State has its own .va suffix. Two global regions also have their own suffixes, but although .eu – for Europe – and .asia have become well established, plans for other regions have been dropped.

GO ONLINE

For a full list of the suffixes available from around the globe and tips on the legal aspects of domain names, follow the links on the chapter's web page.

Whilst some countries impose restrictions on who can register their names, more than eighty countries are *unrestricted*, meaning anyone anywhere can register any names. Some of these unrestricted names have been heavily promoted, but they are still considered as *novelties* in the majority of business fields – they include .tv (Tuvalu) and .cc (Cocos Islands). Indeed, such is the use of the .cc for *dubious* websites that in 2011 Google removed from its index all websites using that suffix.

As well as country-specific suffixes that use Latin characters, there is also a growing number of Internationalized Domain Names (IDNs) – also referred to as Multi-Lingual Domain Names – which use characters outside A to Z, 0 to 9 and the hyphen. At the time of writing, around 39 additional character sets are available, supporting over 350 languages including Arabic, Hebrew, Korean, Russian and Greek. Applications of IDNs for the marketer are limited, however. The most obvious issue is that if the domain uses non-Latin characters, only the keyboards of users in countries where those characters are used can type the domain name into a browser.

Perhaps the biggest shake-up in domain name suffixes came in 2013, when ICANN introduced a model that allowed organizations to 'buy' permission to use their own suffix. The idea is that, for example, Nike has the brand name as its suffix – has sites of the likes of football.nike and tennis.nike. Or perhaps a company – or the Greater London Authority – could register .London, and 'sell-on' domain names such as hotels. London and dining.London. As with the .com domain name gold rush of the early 1990s, generic words are also up for sale as suffixes. Applications for generic words have included Johnson & Johnson with .baby and L'Oreal with .beauty, .hair, .makeup, .salon and .skin. Time will tell whether the cost of these suffixes will benefit those who intend to use them, but you can be sure that at an initial fee of $185,000, plus an annual fee of $25,000, you won't be seeing my website with a .charlesworth suffix any time soon.

RESEARCH SNAPSHOT

Domain names add to email credibility

Having your own domain name means that you can use it for your email address. Research by Microsoft UK, published in 2008, found that almost half of respondents said that they would rather not use a company that had a personal email account – for example hotmail or gmail – rather than a company email address. I would suggest that in the years since that research use of the Internet has become so common that users are even more aware of the implications of personal emails in a business context.

Choosing the right suffix is dependent on the use to which the website is to be put, and the essential questions to be addressed are what is the nature of the organization and where does it trade – or hope to trade? If the organization is a business then the main choice is between the local suffix and .com. Using .co.uk as an example: if the business trades only in the UK then .co.uk is the suffix to choose – if the business trades globally, then .com is better. Of course, this is rather simplistic and other options exist in the grey areas that sit between the black and white – a hotel, for example, might seek to attract customers from around the globe but using the country code of its home country will identify where it is located geographically. For example, nicehotel.com could be located anywhere in the world, but nicehotel.co.uk is in the UK.

Creating the right domain name

Although there are guides for creating domain names for specific purposes, each having different criteria for the selection process, there are some issues that are generic to all purposes. They are:

- Length – in general, when picking a name, less is more.
- How easy is it to recall the name?
- How will it be communicated (e.g. verbally or in print)?

Other general considerations include:

- Is the domain name a representation of the organization and/or business?
- What is it to be used for (e.g. website, email address, company name)?

RESEARCH SNAPSHOT

Coffee is more important than a domain name, apparently

Research has revealed that the UK's small businesses are rushing their choice of web address, with 41 per cent taking less than an hour to make the decision – around the same length of time they took to source their coffee making machine. This was despite most of them recognizing that their domain name could have a lasting effect on their business, with one-third of businesses believing that their revenue would improve as a direct result of having a better web address, and a quarter admitting they had 'concerns' about the effectiveness of their domain name. More than 60 per cent of respondents did not seek a second opinion, and only 10 per cent of businesses considered the long-term effect of their domain name on their business image. Little surprise then, that so many British businesses believe that their choice of domain name could have been better.

Source: www.fasthosts.co.uk

For those new to domain names, it is worth reiterating that all (useful) generic words have long since been registered, so for a toy company wanting to register www.toys.co.uk or www.toys.com (both owned by Toys"R"Us) it is too late. So, assuming that a suitable generic word that represents the product or service being marketed is not an option, how does an organization choose a suitable domain name? Options include:

- Take the company name and add a suitable suffix. If I were a consultant, alancharlesworth.eu would be an example of this – although businesses often use the possessive 's' in the name, for example charlesworth's, which might be problematic for the domain name.

- Although the company might be known by the owner's name, surnames are rarely still available to register – a simple solution is to add the product or service offered to the company name. A business known as Alan's Ltd that makes toys might use alanstoys.co.uk.

- Along the same lines – add the location to either the company name or the product – alansofyork.co.uk or yorktoys.co.uk, for example.

- Register the name by which the company is commonly known – such nicknames are common where the organization's official name is particularly cumbersome or formal.

- Use the abbreviation of the organization's initials – Alan's Toys of York Ltd using aty.co.uk or atoy.co.uk, for example. This option is severely limited as most three- and four-character domain names have been registered.

- Abbreviate some or all of the words in the company name – an engineering company from Philadelphia, for example, could easily shorten that to phillyengineering.com.

It is worth noting that in the USA the use of the dash (-) in domain names is shunned, 'all one word' being the norm. However, this is not so much the case in Europe, with there being three significant examples of when it should be considered. First is where your 'first choice' domain name has been registered – simply split any words with a dash. Second, where the dash makes the domain name 'read' better (perhaps because the term would be grammatically correct if a dash were used). And third, there will be occasions when two words run together to create an unfortunate term. For example, a company that provided an expert consultancy service called Experts Exchange registered those two words as its domain name – unfortunately, the subsequent term read ExpertSexchange.com.

PRACTICAL INSIGHT

Capital practice

Earlier in this section it was mentioned that domain names are not case sensitive. This can be very important aesthetically when the name is presented in print. The following are all the names suggested as examples in the previous section – but all are presented using upper-case characters where pertinent. Not only do they look better, they sometimes make more sense grammatically:

alancharlesworth.eu	AlanCharlesworth.eu
alanstoys.co.uk	AlansToys.co.uk
alansofyork.co.uk	AlansOfYork.co.uk
yorktoys.co.uk	YorkToys.co.uk
phillyengineering.com	PhillyEngineering.com

Note that the suffix is always presented in lower case.

Registering a domain name

This process is relatively easy – and conducted online. There are two main choices:

1. Register it yourself using any one of the hundreds of online domain name 'registrars'.
2. If professional services have been employed to develop a web presence that organization will normally register the domain name as part of the package – though they should not choose it without discussion with the customer (you).

Whichever is chosen, there is one vital issue to note. Part of the registration process includes a section that requires details of the registrants – effectively who is the *owner*. It is not unknown for unscrupulous operators – both registrars and service providers – to list themselves in this section and not their clients, so make sure you or your organization is listed as the owner.

MINI CASE

Renew it or lose it

Although you may 'own' the registration of a domain name – you must renew the registration periodically; if you don't, you will lose the name and it will go back on the open market. Over the years there have been a number of embarrassing examples of major organizations and brands – Microsoft and Amazon have both been guilty in the past – forgetting to renew, but they were able to recover their domain names as there were trademark issues.

Buying a 'pre-owned' domain name

Transfer of ownership of domain names is not only possible, it is a business model for some companies and individuals. Over the years many names have been registered simply because their buyers felt that one day someone, somewhere would want that name – and so they would be prepared to pay for it. It is also the case that an individual or business (particularly a small one) might have a website, or be trading on a name, that is coveted by another organization. In such cases the owner might be willing to put up with the inconvenience of establishing their website on a new domain if the compensation is worthwhile. For the buying company the purchase price of the name might be considerable – but still only a small percentage of the overall marketing budget. Note that Chapter 6 considers the search engine optimization advantages of purchasing an existing name and/or site.

DECISION TIME

Choosing the *right* domain name requires two decisions:

1. Which suffix to use.

2. The composition of the actual name.

However, because so many names are already registered, domain name selection is often a case of second, third, fourth (or worse) choice. A common compromise is the name of choice with a substitute suffix or the first-choice suffix with a concession being made with the name.

1. Suffix selection revolves around the organization's target market and its location. Considerations include:

- Where is the market? Global markets are often best served by a .com.

- How does the organization wish to be perceived? Again, a .com might best serve objectives in this case.

- Even in a global market, if a product or service is identified with a specific country (perhaps its unique selling proposition is that it originates from a distinct region), then that country's suffix is better.

- If the business trades in Europe – rather than globally – then .eu is a serious possibility.

2. Name composition is often dependent on the name of the offline company, its brand names or those of its products or services. As shown in the earlier examples, it is often easy to simply employ the organization's name – or a variation of it – as its domain name. It is always recommended to have a recognizable connection between the offline and online names – particularly if the offline brand has been built over many years. To go online with a new 'name' is to start from scratch with regard to credibility and customer recognition – unless, of course, the online product is separate from the offline entity. Particular care should be taken with the use of SMS text-style abbreviations, for example, the use of the character '4' to replace 'for', or a single 'u' instead of 'you'. Whilst this works well for the mobile phone company Phones4U (they have built their brand around the notion), if an established, 'traditional' offline business were to use such abbreviations it could easily lose credibility in its market segment. Obviously, if the target market is made up of teenagers, then the text language might work.

For the new, pure-play online company, the situation differs in that the domain name is the trading name of the company – effectively, its brand. Whilst this has the advantage of having a blank canvas for name choice, it is hampered by the fact that so many names – particularly generic ones – have already been registered. It is the lack of availability of names that is behind the phenomenon of companies with fabricated words as their name. An example is the travel website Opodo. The major advantage of choosing this name was that no domain name with any suffix had been registered for the word.

GO ONLINE

Choosing a domain name

For more information and advice on registering the *right* domain name, follow the link from the chapter's web page.

And for some examples of poor use of domain names, follow the link to Good URL, Bad URL.

YOU DECIDE

Advise Milo Minderbinder and his management team at 22 Catches Fish Products (case study 7) on the particular problems they might have when choosing a domain name for the company's website as well as the wider issues related to the registration of names that might be relevant to that organization.

Alternatively, conduct the same exercise for your organization or that of your employer – is your 'ideal' name the one that is being used?

2.3 WEBSITE HOSTING

Websites are hosted on a computer that is permanently online, and so available for access from any other computer around the world. Such computers are known as web servers – or more commonly, simply *servers*. Outside of the major online e-commerce sites, few organizations operate their own servers, leaving their website hosting to companies that have the rental of web space as part of a business model. Such organizations (commonly referred to as Internet Service Providers – ISPs, or Application Service Providers – ASPs) operate server farms – banks of servers that can spread the workload of demand on hundreds or thousands of individual websites. ASPs will also normally offer a dedicated server facility, where only one site is hosted on a single server. Single-page websites can be hosted for only a few pounds per year (possibly as part of a domain name registration deal), though naturally, dedicated servers cost far more.

When choosing a website host, server-related issues to consider are: (1) speed of download; (2) downtime; (3) security; and (4) IP integrity. Let's consider them in more detail:

1. Speed. Like all computers, not only is technical capacity relevant (both hard- and software), but the greater the demand, the slower the operating speed. Therefore, a small-capacity server which hosts numerous websites, each of which attracts thousands of visitors at the same time, will deliver web pages slower than a large-capacity server that hosts only one moderately busy website.

2. Downtime. This is the term used to describe a website being offline. Whilst zero downtime is the target, it is also somewhat utopian. All manner of problems from

simple human error through fire or flood to malicious attack might render a server inoperable.

3. Security. How easy would it be for a hacker to access the server and so damage or delete your website or download any information stored on it? For those sites that conduct financial transactions online, the use of a *secure* server is essential.

4. IP Integrity. It is the case that at any given time there will be more websites than there are people who wish to view them, therefore many websites will be sitting on their server with no one wanting to download them. Hosting companies know this, and so only allocate an IP address when a site is requested — a practice known as dynamic IP addressing. A significant problem that can arise is that if the server is used to host websites that infringe search engine (or email) protocols, then innocent sites that share the nefarious site's dynamic IP address might be punished, along with the offending site.

A further consideration is that of having a website hosted on multiple servers spread around the globe. The advantage of this is that if you trade (for example) in Europe, the USA and Asia, then if your server is located in just one of those then requests from the other two must travel a long way. Having a server in each of the regions will increase download speeds in each location. It is also commonly assumed that there is an advantage in search engine optimization to this practice where geographic search is favoured.

DECISION TIME

As with all business applications, quality of service is related to cost, therefore the requirements of the site should be balanced against cost when choosing a server. For the likes of Amazon to have their website to go offline is a buisness disaster; even reduced download speeds will cost them sales (see the following mini case). Therefore, such companies own and maintain their own servers – and many of them.

MINI CASE

The cost of downtime?

Even the biggest and best are not immune from technical glitches. Microsoft (in December 2009), Facebook (September 2010 – reports say that this one was cured by turning the whole system off and turning it back on again – the same as we all do to solve PC problems!), Foursquare (October 2010) and, on the eve of the Olympics in July 2012, Twitter.

However, sometimes a website being unavailable is totally avoidable. For example, November 2011 saw the launch of a new range of Versace products available only at retailer H&M (H&M × Versace). As hordes of shoppers descended on H&M stores around the world and Donatella Versace arrived at the H&M London Regent Street store, thousands of customers logged on to HM.com to snap up a designer outfit. Or rather . . . they didn't – because the website crashed. So, despite all the money that was spent on the launch, nobody thought to beef up the servers to cope with the demand? I doubt that anybody forgot to book security staff for Donatella or make sure the shops were fully staffed that morning. So why was the website's availability not a key aspect of the strategic planning for the launch?

Conversely, a small offline business might get only a couple of visitors a day (or even per week), so slower speeds or two hours' downtime once a year is not a significant issue. Similarly, the chances of a malicious hacker accessing the site of a small offline trader is not only small, but they would be unlikely to inflict significant damage. However, if an e-commerce site were to have its database of customer details stolen, this could – ultimately – result in the failure of that business. For the pure-online trader who depends on organic search engine results for their business, being blacklisted by Google because of a shared IP address is disastrous, whilst for the offline business whose website is accessed only by customers who have been referred to it in offline promotions a high search engine listing is not so important.

YOU DECIDE

Advise the directors of Clough & Taylor Engineering (case study 2) on the most suitable hosting solution for them – include a brief justification for your decision.

Alternatively, conduct the same exercise for your organization or that of your employer.

2.4 WHO 'OWNS' THE WEB PRESENCE?

Although it has improved over the years, a situation still exists in digital marketing – and, in particular, website development – that causes problems in effective strategic and operational online marketing. That is: who, within the organization, 'owns' the organization's web presence? This does not mean who does the work on it, but who has responsibility for ensuring that work takes place and who has control over the presentation and content? Who has the final say on its development? In *Online Marketing* (Gay *et al.*, 2007), I suggest that, although the finance department has an obvious interest too, website ownership is often a 'them versus us' debate between IT, design and marketing. I go on to point out that in the most successful and groundbreaking websites this is not an issue – with the best skills from IT, design and marketing combining to work as a single unit. Sadly, this is not always the case, particularly in smaller businesses.

Any readers who feel my stance on who 'owns' the web presence is somewhat radical should take a look at this from expert practitioner and writer Gerry McGovern. Before quoting from his excellent article, 'Strategy and online' (2013), I'll offer a comment that kind of introduces the passage: 'one thing I hear again and again is that senior management doesn't get the Internet'. In 'Strategy and online' McGovern says:

From an organizational standpoint the online revolution has happened very quickly and many senior managers are really struggling to understand it strategically. Some senior managers don't even consider online as being part of the strategic puzzle. They think it an 'IT issue' or something like that; something that can be delegated. Online has become much too important to delegate. I've been working as a web professional since 1994 and one thing that has always surprised me is how little time senior management spends thinking about and engaging with online. In 2012, we surveyed over 1,000 web professionals and their number one challenge was not competitors but their own senior management's lack of engagement and understanding.

The origin of the problem dates back to the early days of the commercial web when businesses that were looking to go online turned to the IT department – they being the 'computer people'. It is, however, hubris on the part of marketers if they didn't accept some responsibility for this state of affairs, with too many not being computer-savvy (or even being computer-phobic) and so were either (1) not in a position to stop IT taking ownership of the website, or (2) glad to let them get on with it. But if, in the early days of the web, too many marketers shied away from the Internet as they too considered it to be all about computers, they were mistaken. Of course, it is not – no more than advertising on TV is all about television technology. Furthermore, although that situation has improved, it has still not been eradicated completely. As Kelly Mooney (co-author of *The Open Brand: When Push Comes to Pull in a Web-Made World*) stated in an interview with MarketingProfs.com in 2009: 'Quite frankly, most marketers haven't learned to love technology and to see it as an enabler in solving their problems. Rethinking the role of the Internet in business as a strategic enabler is critical to the future success of any brand.'

A further problem exists that is, perhaps, the result of all of these issues, and it is that too many decision-makers perceive that the best digital marketing is that which uses only *sexy* technology. As we will see in the course of this book, that is not necessarily the case. As David Meerman Scott (2007) says in his influential book *The New Rules of Marketing and PR*, 'I've seen many examples where site owners become so concerned about technology and design that they totally forget that great content is the most important aspect of any website.' Only time will tell if the new generation of marketers – perhaps those reading this book – who have grown up with computers and digital technology will more readily accept their use in their chosen profession.

RESEARCH SNAPSHOT

Marketing versus IT

In 2013, when the Chief Marketing Officer Council asked its members to describe their relationship with their Chief Information Officer (CIO) or Information Technology (IT), the results suggested that all was not well between the marketing and CIO/IT department.

Source: CMO Council, 2013

It is also the case that in large organizations, as well as any central marketing function, each of their marketing channels had an interest in digital applications (Hughes, 2007) – advertising, sales and PR, for example. Yet none was – or is – willing to take overall responsibility for the new medium (although the latter has been quick to 'claim' social media as theirs). The result of this was that websites were developed from the perspective of technicians or designers, with many sites being little more than a forum for them to exhibit their design and technical skills with little regard for the website's visitors – or, as the marketers called them, *customers* (that is, those who pay the bills). Meeting online marketing objectives invariably required less glamour and more usability, something few appreciated until the dot-com *boom* ended with a resounding *bust* as the twenty-first century dawned.

DECISION TIME

The answer to the question 'who owns the web presence?' will normally be determined by the size of the organization and its online objectives. For the SME which has little dependency on the web for its marketing, whoever has responsibility for sales and marketing is the obvious choice. However, this is often the owner, a co-owner or a director – for whom the website is an unwanted addition to their job role. In these scenarios the work is often outsourced, with the danger that the outsourced provider becomes the de facto manager – if not owner – of the web presence. The potential problem being that if that provider is IT or design centric, the organization's web presence may not meet any marketing objectives that might have been allocated to it. Larger organizations tend to have marketing departments, in which case that department should take ownership of the web presence – though it is this scenario that sees IT and design wishing to have control. As we will see in Section 3.2 when we consider management of the web presence, outsourcing of some or all aspects of the web presence is common practice (as is the case with many elements of digital marketing), in which case the *owner*'s role is more akin to project management. For the pure play online business, the web presence *is* the business, and so its ownership is that of the owner or directors. However, whilst they should be responsible for decisions at a strategic level, there should still be an operational manager who has responsibility for the web presence. Indeed, it is in this scenario where a 'them versus us' debate can come to the fore – with each group of specialists feeling that their role is the most important, so they should lead the decision-making by having ownership.

YOU DECIDE

Advise Quincy Adams Wagstaff and his executive at Huxley University (case study 10) on the most suitable web development solution for them. What internal issues might arise?

Alternatively, conduct the same exercise for your organization or that of your employer.

2.5 WEBSITE ANALYTICS AND E-METRICS

Marketing is the aspect of business in which it is hardest to determine if a return on any investment (ROI) has been made from any costs incurred. Brand advertising, for example, *may* or *may not* influence *some* buyers at an undetermined point *some time* in the future. The nature of online marketing has, however, gone some way towards addressing this marketing Achilles' heel, with digital analytics not only telling us *what* happened, but helping us to determine *why* it happened, and so make predictions for the future. This is because any visitor to a website, or recipient of any email, leaves a digital footprint from which marketers can glean data.

> " The nature of online marketing has, however, gone some way towards addressing this marketing Achilles' heel "

Sadly, not everything in the e-metrics garden is rosy. The digital footprint, for example, can give details of the (potential) customer's activity on the website, but as there is rarely any correlation between online activity and offline sales it is difficult to measure the impact of online activities on the organization's overall performance. Not only is the ability to collect data an issue, so too is the will of organizations to conduct any online analysis and the importance they might place on it. Furthermore, e-metrics does not escape the digital malaise described in the previous section in that ownership might be shared by multiple stakeholders with it being rare for any individual or department to be responsible for assessing online performance. As a result, analysis of existing digital performance is rarely used at a strategic level.

E-metrics is a perfect example of how IT and marketing staff must work together in order to be effective. Without the marketer's input, IT do not know which data are worth collecting and which are useless – even if the information is easy to collect. Conversely, without IT's help, the marketer has no way of implementing the technology to gather the data that they can then turn into valuable marketing intelligence.

As with other elements of the online presence covered earlier in this chapter, there is the question of whether to conduct e-metrics in-house or outsourcing the job. The answer lies in the objectives determined for the website. For the offline business which has a lead-generation website that might attract a dozen visitors a month, one of the many DIY tools offered by web hosting companies will be quite sufficient. At the other end of the spectrum, for the pure-online operation, analysis of its web operations is an essential element of its business – and one that requires significant expertise.

Key issues in online analytics include:

- What metrics are needed to help make both strategic and operational decisions?
- How should that data be collated?
- How should that data be collected – technically?
- How should the data be stored and mined?
- How is the data to be converted into information and then analysed so as to produce intelligence that is beneficial to the organization?

Although all of these issues should be addressed in equal measure, in practice that is rarely the case either strategically or operationally. A further problem – which is frequently the reason for e-metrics to be rejected as a practice – is the scarcity of qualified analysts. Outsourcing to a specialist company is, obviously, an option, but one that is rarely taken up if the organization has no real belief in the value of digital analytics in the first place.

GO ONLINE

With new technologies being constantly developed and practices evolving, the terms used in website analytics are dynamic – even the phrases *website analytics* and *e-metrics* can mean different things to different people. There are also problems with some of the terms themselves, with different phrases used to describe the same thing. For a full list of definitions of terms used in e-metrics – and a comment on what a 'web page' is in e-metric terms – follow the link on the chapter's web page.

What to measure?

Digital communications offer the marketer something never before available – the ability to gather statistics on every aspect of their marketing that is related to the online environment. In the early days – and still today to a limited extent – the ability to gather an almost infinite amount of data was seen as an opportunity not to be ignored. As a result – and this was more often than not driven by technology providers – vast mountains of data were collected. This was then stored until it went out of date (sometimes a matter of days) and then destroyed before any analysis was conducted on it. Best practice is to gather only data that (a) can be analysed, and (b), as a result of that analysis, provides information on which decisions can be made. Although resources may impact on the decision, the primary issue is to determine the purpose of any analytical efforts – with the objectives of the online presence underpinning that decision.

PRACTICAL INSIGHT

Hits are a miss

Used in reference to the Internet, a *hit* means a request from a web browser for a single file from a web server. Therefore, a browser displaying a web page made up of three graphic images and a paragraph of text would generate five hits at the server – one for the HTML page itself, one for the file of text and one for each of the three graphics. In the early days of the web (and occasionally still today) hits were *the* way of expressing how popular a website was. In contemporary e-commerce, however, a hit is a next-to-useless term of reference. Saying a website has a thousand hits a day, for example, is an almost pointless statement. It could mean ten visitors went to a website that has a hundred files, one visitor downloaded a thousand files, or anything in between. The chances are, however, that the first of these is most accurate. The use of 'hits' (in a press release, for example) to indicate the success of a website would suggest that the organization is (a) using hits as a metric in order to inflate numbers as the visitor count is relatively low, or (b) out of touch with contemporary practice.

However, life in the Digital Marketing environment can be confusing to the newcomer – and an example of this is that each download of a video is commonly referred to as a hit (e.g. 'It had 5000 *hits* on YouTube'). This is, of course, correct, as the video clip is only one file being downloaded.

(Note that the first paragraph of this is taken from my book *Key Concepts in e-Commerce*, 2007.)

As discussed in Section 1.8, online marketing objectives can include such things as income generation, brand development and customer service. However, just as each of these strategic objectives can be subdivided, so too can the purposes of the e-metrics that might be used to assess their success or failure. In addition to assessing *strategic* issues, e-metrics can be used to assess individual tactics that are employed to achieve those strategic aims. For example, a website's strategic objective might be to sell *x* thousand pounds worth of goods per annum – a metric that is easily measured. However, individual sales can be broken down by customers, value, items per customer or myriad other components. Often referred to as key performance indicators (KPIs), some of the most commonly collected online metrics include the following:

1. Brand development
    - Visitor numbers – more visitors means more people being exposed to the brand.
    - Number of visits by individuals – returning visitors might suggest brand loyalty.
    - How deep into the site visitors go – more pages accessed implies an interest in the brand's offerings.
    - How long visitors stay on the site – the longer they stay, the greater the affiliation to the brand.

2. Provision of after-sales services

   - Visits to, and time on, FAQ page – too many and too long might suggest problems with the product and/or instructions, whilst every visit might represent offline cost savings (e.g. at call centres).
   - How long a visitor stays on the site – a lengthy stay might suggest that the sought information is not easily available.
   - Downloads of pages that have been developed to provide specific information (e.g. pdf-formatted assembly instructions).

3. Lead generation

   - Conversion rate – percentage of visitors to website versus sales achieved, or percentage of visitors to website who go on to contact the firm versus sales.
   - Promotions acted on – discount coupons downloaded, for example (which can then be identified when used to make a purchase).
   - How many, and which, pages are downloaded – more pages featuring product details might suggest greater interest.
   - How long a visitor stays on the site – a lengthy stay might suggest that the information presented is of interest to the visitor.

4. Online sales

   - Sales volume – is the site generating income?
   - Sales trends – time of day/week/month/year, geographic, etc.
   - Average order size – bigger order values suggest customer satisfaction.
   - Average items per sale – fewer customers buying greater numbers is normally better (for logistical reasons).
   - Conversion rates – sales (volume, items) per site visits. Millions of visitors but few sales is not a statistic to boast about – something is wrong with the site or its marketing.
   - Click stream – the way a visitor navigates their way around the site might give clues to cross-selling opportunities.
   - Point of exit – ideally, this should be the page that confirms a sale; anything else suggests improvements can be made.
   - Repeat visitors – returning to buy after looking around, or simply comparing prices?

5. Maximize visitor numbers (to increase ad income)

   - Visitor numbers – falling, rising or constant?
   - How deep into the site visitors go – more pages accessed implies an interest in the content.
   - How long visitors stay on the site – longer stays suggest interest in the content.
   - Point of exit – home page or page of arrival means the content is of no interest.
   - Repeat visitors – any site with dynamic content would depend on these.
   - Subscription numbers – a subscriber expressing commitment to the site and/or its content.

As social media sites becomes more influential, there are also metrics that are specific to that aspect of online marketing (see Chapter 9). For example, you might wish to track:

- How many new users joined your online community over specific periods.
- The number of positive – and negative – listings for your brand, product or organization on review sites.
- How many people have subscribed to your blog's feed.

MINI CASE

Task Performance Indicators

Practitioner and author Gerry McGovern has developed what he calls Task Performance Indicators (TPIs), suggesting the website visitors' tasks – the reasons they have accessed the site – have three key metrics:

1. Success rate – if customers can't complete the tasks that they came to the site to complete, the website has failed. Naturally, to assess any success the website publisher must understand the tasks. Obviously, a negative success rate is a *failure* rate.
2. Disaster rate – a disaster is where the visitor thinks they have completed the task, but have in fact got the wrong answer. McGovern points to out-of-date content as being the main culprit for such *disasters*.
3. Completion time – if the first two are 'the basics', then this is best practice – McGovern suggests that saving people's time online is paramount. If McDonald's is fast food, the web is fast tasks.

Source: McGovern, 2010

Website analytics can also provide information that is useful across the range of objectives. One such example is data which reveal where a visitor was immediately before they arrived on your site. Again, that data helps the marketer assess prior activities and plan for future tactics that might achieve the objects of the online strategy. Essentially, there are three ways to get to a website:

1. By entering the domain name or URL into a browser – clicking on a 'favourites' list or 'bookmark' has the same outcome. A high percentage of visitors using this method would suggest that your site is established in the minds of the users (good), but it would also indicate a lack of new visitors (bad).
2. By clicking on a hyperlink on another website. A high proportion of this method would suggest that your site is held in high regard in the online community – enough for them to be proactive in including a link on their page (good), but perhaps your site is not listed high on search engine results pages (bad).
3. By following a link from an identified search engine listing. Having most of your visitors arrive by this method – and in some markets the proportion is over 80 per cent – means you have got your search engine optimization right (good), your search engine advertising is working well (good, but more expensive) or perhaps that all of your customers are new (which can be bad for many businesses).

PRACTICAL INSIGHT

Keyword tips from your e-metrics

A further vital piece of information gleaned from the e-metrics on search engine referrals is that the keywords or phrase used in the user's search are shown (the importance of keywords is covered in Chapters 6 and 7). This analytic can help in the selection of keywords, or confirm whether your optimization and advertising efforts are appropriate.

It is also the case that some of the metrics described previously might be misinterpretations of website performance rather than indications of user behaviour. For example, a short stay on the site might be interpreted as a visitor landing on the site and leaving immediately because the products on offer are of no interest to them – whereas the user might have been put off by the download speed, layout or presentation and decided not to stay long enough to view the products. Similarly, many visitors and few sales might be interpreted as a pricing problem, yet the answer is that the checkout facility on the site is poorly designed.

Yet again, there is an emphasis on strategic planning – without knowing what the objectives for the website are, what you are trying to achieve and how you are trying to achieve it, even the most comprehensive e-metrics are of little value.

DECISION TIME

Although the operators of major e-commerce sites appreciate the benefits of web activity analysis, this view is less common in other organizations – particularly offline businesses and SMEs. As with previous elements of this chapter, the decision is one of in-house or outsource – and again, the answer lies in the objectives of the web presence. For the pure-online operation particularly, employing an expert who can analyse e-metrics – or engaging an outside company to do the same – is essential. A further consideration is the way the data are collected and made available. Before e-metrics software was widely available, analysts had to read through pages of a website's log files – the results of the requests made to the site's server – to glean data. It is rare for this manual method to be used. Figure 2.2 is an example of a simple web page log file. This section shows only that data detail a single visitor's visit to a couple of pages. You can imagine the complexity of such files for, say, Amazon. Figure 2.3 is a breakdown of what each element tells you about the file.

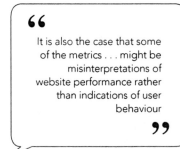

> " It is also the case that some of the metrics . . . might be misinterpretations of website performance rather than indications of user behaviour "

```
#Date: 2008-06-01 00:54:19
#Fields: date time cs-method cs-uri-stem cs-uri-query cs-username c-ip cs-version cs(User-Agent) cs(Referer) sc-status sc-bytes
2008-06-01 00:54:19 GET /partners/home.cfm - - 67.195.52.118 HTTP/1.0 Mozilla/5.0+(compatible;+Yahoo!+Slurp;+http://help.yahoo.com/help/us/ysearch/slurp) - 2(
2008-06-01 00:55:06 GET / - - 12.169.2.152 HTTP/1.1 Mozilla/4.0+(compatible;+MSIE+6.0;+Windows+NT+5.1;1813) - 200 17426
2008-06-01 00:55:10 GET /includes/stasisvalidation.js - - 12.169.2.152 HTTP/1.1 Mozilla/4.0+(compatible;+MSIE+6.0;+Windows+NT+5.1;1813) - 200 6294
2008-06-01 01:01:52 GET /help.cfm - - 74.6.22.121 HTTP/1.0 Mozilla/5.0+(compatible;+Yahoo!+Slurp;+http://help.yahoo.com/help/us/ysearch/slurp) - 200 17517
2008-06-01 01:06:23 GET / - - 220.181.32.22 HTTP/1.1 Baiduspider+(+http://www.baidu.com/search/spider.htm) - 200 167
2008-06-01 01:08:52 GET /includes/stasisvalidation.js - - 80.87.80.54 HTTP/1.1 Mozilla/5.0+(Windows;+U;+Windows+NT+5.1;+en-US;+rv:1.8.1.14)+Gecko/20080404+Fi(
2008-06-01 01:08:57 GET /partners/partner.cfm id=95 - 80.87.80.54 HTTP/1.1 Mozilla/5.0+(Windows;+U;+Windows+NT+5.1;+en-US;+rv:1.8.1.14)+Gecko/20080404+Firefo(
2008-06-01 01:08:57 GET /css/main.css - - 80.87.80.54 HTTP/1.1 Mozilla/5.0+(Windows;+U;+Windows+NT+5.1;+en-US;+rv:1.8.1.14)+Gecko/20080404+Firefox/2.0.0.14 h(
2008-06-01 01:09:02 GET /css/print.css - - 80.87.80.54 HTTP/1.1 Mozilla/5.0+(Windows;+U;+Windows+NT+5.1;+en-US;+rv:1.8.1.14)+Gecko/20080404+Firefox/2.0.0.14 (
2008-06-01 01:09:04 GET /images/banner/banner2.jpg - - 80.87.80.54 HTTP/1.1 Mozilla/5.0+(Windows;+U;+Windows+NT+5.1;+en-US;+rv:1.8.1.14)+Gecko/20080404+Fire(
2008-06-01 01:09:05 GET /images/waiaalogo.gif - - 80.87.80.54 HTTP/1.1 Mozilla/5.0+(Windows;+U;+Windows+NT+5.1;+en-US;+rv:1.8.1.14)+Gecko/20080404+Firefox/2(
2008-06-01 01:09:05 GET /images/w3cxhtml1.gif - - 80.87.80.54 HTTP/1.1 Mozilla/5.0+(Windows;+U;+Windows+NT+5.1;+en-US;+rv:1.8.1.14)+Gecko/20080404+Firefox/2.(
2008-06-01 01:09:05 GET /images/w3ccsslogo.gif - - 80.87.80.54 HTTP/1.1 Mozilla/5.0+(Windows;+U;+Windows+NT+5.1;+en-US;+rv:1.8.1.14)+Gecko/20080404+Firefox/2(
2008-06-01 01:09:06 GET /images/wave.gif - - 80.87.80.54 HTTP/1.1 Mozilla/5.0+(Windows;+U;+Windows+NT+5.1;+en-US;+rv:1.8.1.14)+Gecko/20080404+Firefox/2.0.0.1(
2008-06-01 01:09:07 GET /images/stasisbg.gif - - 80.87.80.54 HTTP/1.1 Mozilla/5.0+(Windows;+U;+Windows+NT+5.1;+en-US;+rv:1.8.1.14)+Gecko/20080404+Firefox/2.0(
2008-06-01 01:09:07 GET /images/Partners/aidimalogo.gif - - 80.87.80.54 HTTP/1.1 Mozilla/5.0+(Windows;+U;+Windows+NT+5.1;+en-US;+rv:1.8.1.14)+Gecko/20080404+(
2008-06-01 01:09:08 GET /images/sidebar/guestbook.gif - - 80.87.80.54 HTTP/1.1 Mozilla/5.0+(Windows;+U;+Windows+NT+5.1;+en-US;+rv:1.8.1.14)+Gecko/20080404+Fi(
2008-06-01 01:09:08 GET /images/lynxlogo.gif - - 80.87.80.54 HTTP/1.1 Mozilla/5.0+(Windows;+U;+Windows+NT+5.1;+en-US;+rv:1.8.1.14)+Gecko/20080404+Firefox/2.0(
2008-06-01 01:09:10 GET /images/sidebar/seemseed2.gif - - 80.87.80.54 HTTP/1.1 Mozilla/5.0+(Windows;+U;+Windows+NT+5.1;+en-US;+rv:1.8.1.14)+Gecko/20080404+Fi(
2008-06-01 01:09:10 GET /images/sidebar/1st-fp6-logo.gif - - 80.87.80.54 HTTP/1.1 Mozilla/5.0+(Windows;+U;+Windows+NT+5.1;+en-US;+rv:1.8.1.14)+Gecko/20080404-(
2008-06-01 01:09:10 GET /images/sidebar/FP6-oval.gif - - 80.87.80.54 HTTP/1.1 Mozilla/5.0+(Windows;+U;+Windows+NT+5.1;+en-US;+rv:1.8.1.14)+Gecko/20080404+Fi(
2008-06-01 01:09:11 GET /images/skipnavbg.png - - 80.87.80.54 HTTP/1.1 Mozilla/5.0+(Windows;+U;+Windows+NT+5.1;+en-US;+rv:1.8.1.14)+Gecko/20080404+Firefox/2.(
2008-06-01 01:09:11 GET /images/navbar/figure.jpg - - 80.87.80.54 HTTP/1.1 Mozilla/5.0+(Windows;+U;+Windows+NT+5.1;+en-US;+rv:1.8.1.14)+Gecko/20080404+Fir(
2008-06-01 01:09:11 GET /images/chinaflag.gif - - 80.87.80.54 HTTP/1.1 Mozilla/5.0+(Windows;+U;+Windows+NT+5.1;+en-US;+rv:1.8.1.14)+Gecko/20080404+Firefox/2(
2008-06-01 01:09:11 GET /images/menu-bg-off2.gif - - 80.87.80.54 HTTP/1.1 Mozilla/5.0+(Windows;+U;+Windows+NT+5.1;+en-US;+rv:1.8.1.14)+Gecko/20080404+Firefox(
2008-06-01 01:09:11 GET / - - 61.135.168.39 HTTP/1.1 Baiduspider+(+http://www.baidu.com/search/spider.htm) - 200 167
```

Figure 2.2 A small section of a log file

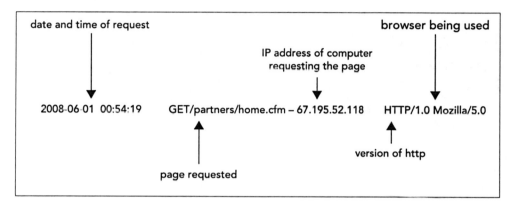

Figure 2.3 The interpretation of part of a line from the log file

Many website hosting companies provide inexpensive analytics that will often suffice – particularly for the offline trader who simply wants to check on visitor numbers, which pages are the most popular or on which pages visitors arrive. This information is made available – online – in simple charts that can be manipulated for specific time periods. Google is one organization which offers free website metrics to publishers – normally the only requirement being to simply need to add a piece of html to the site's source code. As you might expect, paying a fee will get you far more data and higher levels of analysis.

Figures 2.4–2.7 are screenshots of some of the metrics provided by Google for alancharlesworth.eu.

A further advantage of outsourcing the analytics is that the work can be done on a regular basis, with a periodic report delivered which highlights significant events or returns. Without this it is easy for the manager – who probably has a multitude of other things to do – to forget to examine the statistics regularly.

For those who want to take the other extreme and be 'hands-on' in tracking metrics, software is available that allows you to monitor site traffic in real time – as it happens.

	Page	Pageviews ↓	Unique Pageviews	Avg. Time on Page ?	Entrances ?	Bounce Rate ?	% Exit ?
		1,480 % of Total: 100.00% (1,480)	**1,165** % of Total: 100.00% (1,165)	**00:01:40** Site Avg: 00:01:40 (0.00%)	**700** % of Total: 100.00% (700)	**70.14%** Site Avg: 70.14% (0.00%)	**47.30%** Site Avg: 47.30% (0.00%)
1.	/index.html	218	175	00:01:46	149	65.10%	54.13%
2.	/alans-musings/online-retailing.html	134	123	00:02:02	123	92.68%	91.04%
3.	/internetmarketing/index.html	108	76	00:00:18	43	9.30%	10.19%
4.	/ACs-books/internet-marketing-a-practical-approach.html	55	43	00:01:50	22	54.55%	34.55%
5.	/internetmarketing/chapter1.html	51	41	00:03:17	18	50.00%	52.94%
6.	/good-and-bad-practice/index.html	48	37	00:00:52	24	79.17%	50.00%
7.	/cleethorpes-explanation.html	46	40	00:07:48	40	90.00%	86.96%
8.	/internetmarketing/chapter9.html	42	23	00:03:51	7	42.86%	30.95%
9.	/ACs-books/index.html	40	31	00:00:12	1	0.00%	7.50%
10.	/internetmarketing/assignment-tutorial-videos.html	36	30	00:08:07	27	59.26%	63.89%

Figure 2.4 Visit details of the most popular pages of the site. Compare this with a snapshot of the log file shown in Figure 2.2

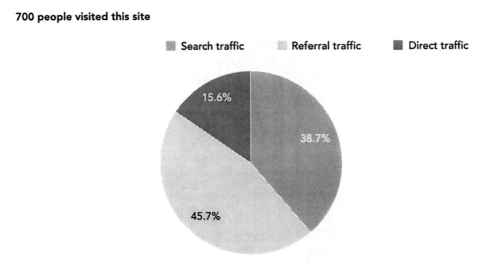

700 people visited this site

■ Search traffic   ■ Referral traffic   ■ Direct traffic

15.6%

38.7%

45.7%

Figure 2.5 How the 700 visitors to the site over a seven-day period came to be on the site

	Mobile Device Info		Visits ? ↓	Pages / Visit ?	Avg. Visit Duration ?	% New Visits ?	Bounce Rate ?
			86	**1.51**	**00:01:14**	**75.58%**	**82.56%**
			% of Total: 12.29% (700)	Site Avg: 2.11 (-28.56%)	Site Avg: 00:01:51 (-33.21%)	Site Avg: 65.86% (14.77%)	Site Avg: 70.14% (17.70%)
☐	1.	Apple iPad	46	1.72	00:02:03	73.91%	82.61%
☐	2.	Apple iPhone	15	1.27	00:00:28	86.67%	80.00%
☐	3.	(not set)	5	1.00	00:00:00	100.00%	100.00%
☐	4.	Samsung GT-N7100 Galaxy Note II	4	2.25	00:00:48	0.00%	50.00%
☐	5.	Samsung GT-N7000 Galaxy Note	3	1.00	00:00:00	33.33%	100.00%
☐	6.	Apple iPod	1	1.00	00:00:00	100.00%	100.00%
☐	7.	HTC 9292 EVO 4G	1	1.00	00:00:00	100.00%	100.00%
☐	8.	HTC A8183 Desire	1	1.00	00:00:00	100.00%	100.00%
☐	9.	HTC S710E Incredible S	1	1.00	00:00:00	100.00%	100.00%
☐	10.	LG P705 Optimus L7	1	1.00	00:00:00	100.00%	100.00%

Show rows: 10 ▼   Go to: 1   1 - 10 of 18   ‹ ›

Figure 2.6 Which mobile devices were most popular for accessing the site over a seven-day period

1 ▓▓▓▓▓▓▓ 17,958

Figure 2.7 Where in the world visitors were located when they visited the site
The darker shading indicates the most popular home countries of visitors. The darkest is, as you might expect, the UK, with nearly 18,000 visitors over the period of the analysis. Additional data informs me that I have had virtual visitors from 165 countries/territories. For me, this is simply interesting information – but in a commercial scenario I could be looking where to concentrate, strengthen or withdraw my marketing efforts based on where my 'customers' were located geographically.

Real-time analysis is particularly useful for social media sites, this means you can pick up on emerging trends and so take action to stay ahead of the crowd. Of course, it also means someone watching the analytics every minute of every day – and so you would have to be sure the organization was going to benefit from the commitment of such resources.

Essentially the decision is governed by:

1. What are the objectives of the site?
2. How can those objectives be best assessed, given:
    *   the data available;
    *   how it is collected and presented; and
    *   the expertise available to complete the analysis.

However, all of the above is a pointless exercise if the ability – and will – to act on any information gleaned is not high on the organization's agenda.

YOU DECIDE

Advise Phil and his team at the Cleethorpes Visitors Association (case study 4) on which web analytics should be collected to help meet their online marketing objectives.

Alternatively, conduct the same exercise for your organization or that of your employer.

2.6 THE INTERNET AS A TOOL FOR MARKET RESEARCH

Although this section on market research is included in this (early) chapter, marketers will be aware that research is actually an ongoing process – more commonly referred to as market *intelligence*. However, given that research into the market should take place early in any strategic or operational planning, it makes sense to include it at this stage of the book. It is also worth noting that online provides only part of the organization's market research – so, although it is covered as a distinct element here, it should be seen as part of the overall research process. I should also add that this is not a section on market research *per se*; I am not going to address such issues as sample selection, for example – that belongs in another book.

As with its offline cousin, data can be gathered online in both primary and secondary formats. Primary online research is either where a study is conducted on the organization's website or the Internet is used as a medium for gathering data on the organization, the brand or its products. Secondary online research is where existing websites are used as sources of information that the organization can use to its advantage. Let's now consider how primary and secondary information can be gathered using the Internet – as with any research, I'll start with the collection of secondary data.

Secondary research

Although it has always been available in libraries and similar public facilities, detailed market data is now commonly available online from specialist researchers like Mintel (www.mintel.co.uk) and Keynote (www.keynote.co.uk). Such organizations frequently offer valuable information as summaries that act as 'tasters' to full reports – which will be available to purchase online. Similarly, trade associations and organizations such as local Chambers of Commerce frequently publish industry and market data that is freely available on their websites. The UK government's Office for National Statistics (www.statistics.gov.uk), for example, has useful data on potential consumers, and the Department for Business, Enterprise and Regulatory Reform – BERR (www.berr.gov.uk, formerly the Department for Trade and Industry) – has a wealth of information on all aspects of commerce. For ongoing environmental and industry-specific information, news aggregators, blogs and press releases are available by either visiting websites or signing up for email newsletters or notifications via social media.

As with offline practice, competitors in your market or industry can also provide a wealth of information for the researcher. By definition, there can be only one market leader – the rest are followers. There is no shame, therefore, in taking the ideas of others and copying or adapting them for your own organization. When considering what information can be gathered from the websites of others in your marketplace, the marketing mix provides an excellent guide, for example:

- Product research – offerings of competitors, positioning, new products in the market, customer perceptions, new markets for existing products and opportunities to adapt products for existing markets.

- Pricing research – pricing policies of competitors, customer perceptions versus quality and demand elasticity.

- Promotional research – studies of competitors' advertising and any promotional activities associated with them, the reaction or response of customers to competitors' ads and promotions, media reaction to types of promotions, the development of new technologies used in the delivery of online ads.

- Distribution research – attitudes and needs of customers and alternative methods of distribution.

PRACTICAL INSIGHT

Digital support for competitor research

1. Google trends – compare interest in any topic by entering up to five topics and see how often they've been searched on Google over time and the geographic location from which people have searched for them most. This is a great way to compare your website, category, brand or product lines with your competitors'.

2. Search engines – check the ranking of competitors for the main keywords in the industry or market (I consider the importance of keywords in Section 6.3), or search for a competitor's future intentions. For example, search for competitors':

   - name plus terms like 'plans' or 'strategy' (you may even find something on their own websites which is not supposed to be open to the public);
   - products plus terms such as 'rumour' (trade publications may comment on gossip); and
   - key employees (a story of one moving to a country where your competitor manufactures a specific product range).

3. Pay per click ads – similar to search keywords, these can suggest competitors' online competencies or aggression in the marketplace.
4. LinkedIn or similar – follow companies and key employees for trends in recruitment and talent searches.
5. Slideshare or similar – a PowerPoint presentation revealing plans might find its way there in error.
6. Twitter search – tweets can suggest competitors' key influencers, employee opinions/morale, upcoming conferences.
7. Facebook or similar – follow competitors' fan pages for discussions amongst their customers and advocates – or look out for announcements that might betray future plans.

Additional research might include:

- Market studies – what is happening in the environment in which you trade or operate?
- Industry studies – consumers', competitors', distributors' and financial institutions' perceptions of how the sector is performing
- Corporate research – what are the major businesses in your industry with regard to – for example – corporate social responsibility?
- Social media sites – in particular user generated content where customers give their opinions of products and services.

Note that in Chapter 9 we look at the use of social media websites in marketing – which includes the use of such sites as sources of information, and in Section 9.7 consideration is given to online public and press relations, where the issue of corporate reputation management is covered in detail. This includes the methods of researching how your own organization is being discussed or treated on the various types of website.

Activity equals research

Search giant Google claims it can predict the opening weekend performance of a movie within 92 per cent accuracy. This is achieved by analysing search queries for the film and the volume of clickthroughs on SERP ads related to the movie clicks. Although this data is collected immediately before the opening weekend, Google also includes the movie's trailer-related searches up to four weeks prior to the release date.

Source: Google, 2013

Primary research

The first point of call for any Internet-based primary research must be the metrics of your own online activities. Having covered these in detail in the previous section there is little more to add other than to point out that although analytics are generally performance-related, the data that is gathered can be used in planning for the future as well as correcting the past. Other methods of collecting primary data using the Internet are – effectively – online applications of traditional offline techniques.

Note that the following is concerned with using the Internet in conducting research on behalf of the marketer – hosting questionnaires for other organizations and/or collecting data that can then be sold to third parties is a business model in its own right.

The most common form of research offline is the survey – where selected respondents are asked to answer questions or complete questionnaires. Naturally, there is an inherent flaw in conducting surveys online in that the only respondents are those who have access to the web – which is fine for online-related questions, but not so for other research. Whilst email can be used simply as a method of communication for questionnaires – as the post is offline – the interactive nature of the Internet can increase response rates.

On-page surveys do not have to be full-blown questionnaires, however. A small box in a prominent position on a busy web page, for example, could provide a wealth of data about customer behaviour with a simple question like 'how did you get to this site?' with a 'check-box' response for: 'search engine', 'link from other site', 'saw web address in ad', 'knew web address' or 'in my favourites/bookmarks'. It's very simple, but it gives human – rather than e-metrics-sourced, technical – data. Even more simplistic is a simple yes/no response to a direct question that is related to a product or service offered on the site – 'have you ever purchased a holiday online?', for example – or, as in Figure 2.8, a direct question at the foot of a FAQ page.

Long questionnaires are too complex to include on a web page, but they can be accessed from a link – perhaps a banner or a pop-up promoting the survey. To use websites other than your own it is necessary to engage agents who develop then host or distribute

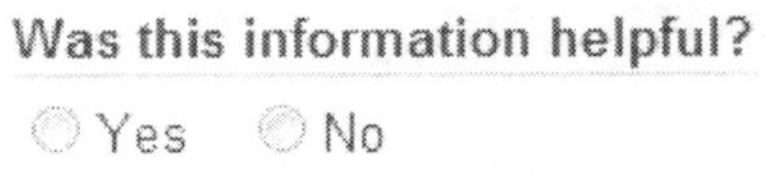

Was this information helpful?

◯ Yes   ◯ No

Figure 2.8 A simple yes/no response form

questionnaires. It is also worth noting that the results of research – if not confidential – can be released into the public domain, making surveys achieve the double objectives of data gathering and PR – and subsequent search engine optimization as a spin-off.

As well as using the Internet to host and distribute questionnaires, it is also possible to host online focus groups. Although this technique has flaws, the cost of assembling a group of individuals in a chat-room scenario is significantly cheaper than bringing them together physically. It is also the case that participants can be drawn from a much wider geographic area – even different continents – for just as low a cost, so expanding the scope for research.

Building on the notion that secondary research can be gathered through observation of consumer activity (for example, the use of keywords, covered in the previous section on secondary research) is the concept of *ethnography* – an overt or covert participation in the everyday lives of people over an extended period of time (Hammersley and Atkinson, 1997). Dubbed as *netnography* (Internet-ethnography) in an early study by Kozinets (1997), the online version of this social science is practised by joining online social media sites and entering into community discussion. Whether or not the researcher should disclose their [true] identity and purpose is an ethical question that is frequently debated by netnographers, but whichever path is chosen, valuable data on consumer behaviour and attitudes can be gleaned. As with any marketing-oriented involvement on social media sites, however, care must be taken not to be perceived as advertising products or brands – even when a bias has been declared. This may lead to the exercise being (a) rejected by community members, (b) flawed through 'unnatural' responses or (c) effectively becoming an online focus group.

Note that how online marketers can use social media sites as part of their marketing efforts is covered in Chapter 9. Methods include observing user behaviour in what might be described as *basic* netnography; this could be considered as an element of intelligence-gathering.

DECISION TIME

Although marketers might refer to research and intelligence with regard to data collected, for many – especially small businesses – the information is no more than that knowledge gained as part of their everyday commercial operations. Tracking a competitor's activities has always been something that is expected – almost naturally. In pre-digital days this meant that you signed up for competitors' mailshots (to your home – not business – address, of course) in order to track their promotions, and rang up for fictitious 'quotes'. Now, instead of having to physically visit the stores of competitors (in a previous career,

I spent many hours noting prices in competitors' shops), the prices are on their websites – or you might be able to use a comparison shopping engine (see Section 4.6) to do the job for you. You can even set up numerous 'hotmail-type' email accounts and register for competitors' email campaigns.

PRACTICAL INSIGHT

What – and tell my competitors?

In the mid- to late 1990s I spent time both 'preaching' the advantages of the Internet as a business tool and representing a company that designed websites. After 'it's a fad and it won't catch on', the biggest excuse I came across from small business owners for not having a website was that they thought it would make it too easy for competitors to find out details of their products and organization.

For the uninitiated, please note: I am not talking about any kind of 'industrial spying' here – that is illegal. Simply gathering information that is in the public domain is very much an expected aspect of doing business. Now, simply by spending a few hours a week surfing the web (it can even be at home, after 'office' hours – an important issue for small business owners and managers who spend all day actually running their business), you can:

- keep up to date on what is happening in your industry and/or market;
- track competitors' activities by visiting their websites;
- read what customers have to say about you or your competitors on 'review sites';
- find new markets – by, for example, visiting the websites of organizations that might use your products or already use those of your competitors; and
- develop new product offerings – the owner of a small hotel, for example, could visit the websites of national or global chains and 'adopt' their ideas for their own accommodation.

More specific data-gathering efforts – primary or secondary – will depend on the objectives of that research, what information is required from the data and how it will be used. Essentially, the same criteria for offline market research should be applied to online research initiatives – and data should certainly not be gathered simply because technology makes it easy to do so (see website analytics in the previous section). Any subsequent research will then be expected to give a return on investments made.

MINI CASE

Do it yourself – with a little help

As a marketer, you might know the questions you want to ask – but are not aware of how to use digital technology in order to ask them. Although some companies will handle the whole package for you, others offer the opportunity to develop it yourself. SurveyMonkey (www.surveymonkey.com) facilitates the creation of your own surveys that can be (a) hosted on your website or blog, or (b) distributed by email.

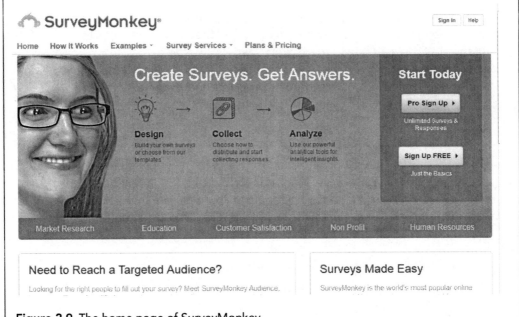

Figure 2.9 The home page of SurveyMonkey

YOU DECIDE

Advise members of the consortium that owns The Gilded Truffle Hotel (case study 3) on what kind of data could be gathered using online market research, how it might be collected and what use could be made of it.

Alternatively, conduct the same exercise for your organization or that of your employer.

CHAPTER EXERCISE

Giving justifications for all your decisions, advise Two Cities Manufacturing Ltd (case study 11) on all aspects of digital marketing covered in this chapter.

Alternatively, conduct the same exercise for your own organization or that of your employer.

CHAPTER QUESTIONS

Follow the link from the chapter's web page to a series of multiple-choice exam-type questions that will test your knowledge and understanding of the various elements of this chapter.

REFERENCES

CMO Council (2013) Big data's biggest role, aligning the CMO and CIO: greater partnership drives enterprise-wide customer centricity report. Available at www.cmocouncil.org/download-center.php?id=259.

Gay, R., Charlesworth, A. and Esen, R. (2007) *Online Marketing: A Customer-Led Approach*. Oxford University Press.

Google (2013) Quantifying movie magic with Google Search. Available on gstatic.com.

Hammersley, M. and Atkinson, P. (1997) *Ethnography: Principles in Practice* (2nd edn). Routledge.

Hughes, T. (2007) Regaining a seat at the table: marketing management and the e-service opportunity. *Journal of Services Marketing*. Volume 21, number 4, pp. 270–289.

Kozinets, R. (1997) I want to believe: a netnography of the x-philes' subculture of consumption. *Advances in Consumer Research*. Volume 24, pp. 470–475.

McGovern, G. (2010) *The Stranger's Long Neck*. A. & C. Black.

McGovern, G. (2013) Strategy and online. Available at www.customercarewords.com/strategy-and-online.html.

Scott, D.M. (2007) *The New Rules of Marketing and PR*. Wiley.

Chapter **3**

Developing the online presence

Simplicity is the ultimate sophistication.

Leonardo da Vinci

Chapter at a glance

3.1   Introduction
3.2   Web presence management and development
3.3   The basics
3.4   Online credibility
3.5   Content development
3.6   The global web presence

3.1 INTRODUCTION

In the first edition of this book, this chapter referred to the development of the web*site*. However, I feel it is now necessary to refer to the web *presence* – that is, the development of any aspect of the web that represents the product, brand or organization. For many organizations, a single website no longer represents its online presence – we should think of it more as a portfolio of digital assets. Although it is still the case that for most organizations this will be their website, content that is not hosted on the organization's servers – social media sites such as Facebook, Twitter, YouTube and blogs, or sales outlets such as eBay are obvious examples – should also be given the same level of consideration as the 'corporate' website. As Gord Hotchkiss (2010) states, websites are under the organization's control, but others are either completely or partially out of their control. He goes on to say that although the website is still at the core, there is a ripple effect spreading out, usually with lessening degrees of control.

> all online marketing – be it strategic or operational – revolves around the web presence

Whilst there are other essential elements to digital marketing, it is an inescapable fact that all online marketing – be it strategic or operational – revolves around the web presence. The importance of the website is acknowledged by the fact that three chapters of this book are devoted to the subject. Readers should note, however, that whilst other aspects of e-marketing depend on the website, it too relies on elements of marketing that go beyond what the customer sees on their computer screen.

PRACTICAL INSIGHT

Time to turn the page?

When the web first appeared an obvious metaphor for what we saw on the screen in front of us was web 'page'. Although many web 'pages' are still the static objects of the mid-1990s, we are now used to accessing sites which produce content on the fly (i.e. in real time) in response to the user's, publisher's or advertisers' needs. However, although there are examples of alternatives from academia (e.g. Yale University's professor of computer science, David Gelernter, suggests the web is a 'lifestream' – a heterogeneous, content-searchable, real-time messaging stream) and marketing (e.g. Coca-Cola describes its 'Journey' site – cocacolacompany.com – as a 'rich, socially enabled digital platform'), I think it will be a long time before we refer to the image on our viewing screen as anything but a *page*.

Going back to the early days of the web, Nielsen (2000) argued that 'users have more choice than ever. Why should they waste their time on anything that is confusing, slow or that doesn't satisfy their needs?' Reflecting on early websites, Levine *et al.* suggested in *The Cluetrain Manifesto* (1999) that 'many large companies offer flashy bread-and-circus entertainments on the Web. These offerings have all the classic earmarks of the mass market come-on: lowest-common-denominator programming developed to package and deliver market segments to mass merchandisers. This is not what most people want.' Although many – perhaps most – organizations have since seen the error of their ways, there are still far too many websites that are designed for the organization, not the customer.

As proof – if proof is needed – that this issue is still pertinent to the new generation of web users, consider this from *The Times Higher Education*. Hannah Fearn (2010) asked a panel of sixth-formers for their opinions of university websites. One replied, 'most university websites don't show you information you want to know, they just show you the information that they want you to know. That's quite stupid really.' The same comment could be applied to too many websites.

Huang and Christopher (2003) suggest that web designers must understand the key stages and influences in the purchase decision if they are to design an effective e-commerce application – something I alluded to in Chapter 1.

Many references cited in this – and the next two – chapters come from publications around the turn of the century. There is a reason for this. The late nineties saw the development of the Internet for commercial use and during that time there was experimentation amongst those seeking benefits from the new medium. It was also the period when graphic designers and programmers wielded an unhealthy influence over website development, with a concentration on technology itself rather than its effective use. The failure of so many so-called 'dot-com' companies at the end of the nineties helped focus attention on what actually works online from a business perspective. Practitioners began to publish the results of empirical experiences and academics began to publish theoretical research. That few writers, practitioners or academics have subsequently produced little that either significantly adds to or contradicts the basic concepts and models from this period owes more to the quality of those early publications than the lack of research and/or publications since. Effectively, the principles of good website design in 2000 are still valid for effective website design in 2014 – and they are likely to remain so for some time to come. There is also a certain irony that the main change to Internet access in the last couple of years – the use of mobile devices (something that was only a dream in 2000) – has seen contemporary designers hark back to the basic tenets learned by their predecessors nearly twenty years ago. Note that this issue is addressed elsewhere in the chapter.

Concentrating on presentation, usability and navigation, this chapter considers best practice in the development of the organization's web presence so that customers needs are met and organizational objectives achieved. Note that this chapter – in keeping with the philosophy of the book – considers the marketing elements of web design and not the technical (IT) issues. This 'non-technical' approach is not meant to ignore or devalue the input from programmers – this is particularly the case for *back-end* design (the visible page is the site's *front-end*). Google, for example, has a very simplistic page design and presentation that efficiently and effectively help users achieve their aim (generate a search). It is behind the scenes in the back-end design – the search algorithm – where Google's engineers and programmers earn their pay.

PRACTICAL INSIGHT

The technical basics

From a technical perspective, there are many ways of developing a website. The most basic is using hypertext mark-up language (HTML). This is a programming 'code' that makes the content of a document appear on a computer screen. For example, to make a word appear in bold you place <b> (start bold) in front of it, and </b> (end bold) after it. Other types of coding are more complex, from Cascading Style Sheets (CSS), which fix the presentation of pages within a site, through those referred to in this book as 'Flash'-type, to pages produced 'on the fly' by complex algorithms and software applications. As with other technologies that they can use such as TV and radio marketers do not need to know how the technology actually works – only how to use it effectively. If you want to check the code of a web page in Internet Explorer (IE), right click on your mouse and then click 'view source' – or on Firefox/Netscape, right click, then click 'view page source' – and you will see the source code used.

The main issues of a web presence – like marketing itself – do not exist in isolation, with each aspect having influence or effect on the others. Online credibility, for example, might be influenced by the presentation of the site and the quality of its content – all of which depends on the way the site is managed. However, to aid the learning process, I have presented all of the key aspects in separate sections.

If the objective of this chapter is to address the issue of developing an effective web presence, we must first consider what constitutes a *good* website.

A review of the academic research reveals a preponderance of similar criteria for assessing the quality of website design (note that I have deliberately repeated the references from the first edition of this book, this is because research subsequent to these have added nothing new). For example, note the commonality of the terms used by the following when presenting their key aspects of quality website design: ease of use, aesthetic design, processing speed, security (Yoo and Donthu, 2001); business function, corporate credibility, content readability, attractiveness, structure, navigation (Kim *et al.*, 2003); accessibility, communication, credibility, understanding, appearance, availability (Cox and Dale, 2001); usability, usefulness, adequacy of information, accessibility, interaction (Yang *et al.*, 2004); usability, information quality, service interaction (Barnes and Vidgen, 2002); core service, supporting services, user interface (Van Riel *et al.*, 2001); quality of information, service, security, playfulness, design (Liu and Arnett, 2000).

GO ONLINE

When you're inside the bottle, you can't read the label

Although this philosophy can be applied to all marketing, it is particularly relevant to website development. Essentially, it means that if you are too close to the design of a website (inside the bottle), you do not see the site (the label) in the same way that the site's visitors might. For more on my views follow the link from the chapter's web page.

Note that these all of these terms have an element of intangibility about them, and that the qualities could well be perceptions of users – perceptions that might be different from those of the site's developers. It is also the case that the underpinning of these criteria is mainly strategic: that is, they do not tell the developer how to *practically* apply these things to a website (e.g. what is 'ease of use' and how do you achieve it?). Worthy of further comment is that in this – and subsequent – research, little mention is made of any weighting for the criteria. If, for example, in Kim *et al.*'s criteria listed above, the home page of the website was not attractive to the target audience, or the navigation was poor, the users would leave the site before the other four criteria could even be addressed. Similarly, if students feel that the answer to an assignment question can be found within the text of a website they will ignore criteria of readability, attractiveness, structure and battle their way through poor navigation in order to track down that assessment solution.

Readers should note that this is the first of three chapters that cover website development. In this chapter we look at the basics that are applicable to all sites. In the two subsequent chapters elements of website design that are specific to B2C and B2B are addressed.

PRACTICAL INSIGHT

WWW – what, who and why

The website address begins with www, so when developing a website think 'www':

- **W**hat are the site's objectives?
- **W**ho are the visitors going to be?
- **W**hy are they visiting the site – what need is being met?

I am still amazed by how many sites are designed without these questions being asked – never mind answered – before the development begins.

3.2 WEB PRESENCE MANAGEMENT AND DEVELOPMENT

Management

Although in Section 2.4 we addressed the issue of who 'owns' the organization's web presence, in this chapter we consider not only the management of the web presence, but who is responsible for its development. Although these could be separate elements of the chapter, I feel they are so intrinsically linked that to consider them separately would be an error.

As with all business-related applications of the term, website *management* can mean different things depending on the size and character of what needs to be managed. Whether the web presence is a couple of pages acting as a lead generator for an SME offline business or a pure-play retail site with thousands of pages, an element of management is required if it is to effectively meet the organization's objectives for that site. As discussed in Section 2.4, there is the issue of who owns the web presence – essentially who has responsibility for it – and that there is often a 'turf war' between IT and marketing. The solution comes from offline practice. If a website is considered to be a publication, then it is best managed as such – like a newspaper, for example. Gerry McGovern (2002) describes the core objective of publishing as getting the right content to the right person at the right time at the right cost – that there is more than a hint of the marketing mix there suggests who should have control of the web presence.

The key role in publishing is the editor – or *managing* editor. As editor, it is their job to commission, source, select, proofread or reject content – and then decree the way in which that content is presented. As managing editor they also take on the wider responsibility for production and publication, so giving them responsibility for any technical aspects of the site. Naturally, the best editors (managers) do not dictate, but take advice and input from their staff – but a strategic outlook is essential. As a marketer, I am biased in my proposition that the web presence is part of the organization's strategic marketing communications mix and so say that the managing editor should have a marketing background. Though exceptions exist, in my experience, it is rare for the other two professions that might provide a proficient managing editor – IT and media – to have had the necessary strategic marketing education and/or experience.

As well as ensuring that strategic online goals are met (in conjunction with offline objectives) the editor also has responsibility for operational website management. As previously mentioned, there is the content – textual and otherwise – to be developed. This can be an in-house operation, outsourced or (as is most likely) a combination of the two, with subject experts being brought in to supplement employed talent when necessary. For the offline-trading SME this process is performed only once – when the site is first launched – with minor updates as and when required. For the pure-play online retailer or publisher who generates income through selling advertising, however, this is an ongoing process that is not confined to a standard nine-to-five, weekday-only operation. If the site is open to customers 24/7, then the site's management must be also.

PRACTICAL INSIGHT

Content management software

To describe such software as content management tools can be misleading to some. Content management software actually helps you *administer* the content, not *write* it. Think of a blog, for example, where the process of accessing the websites is made easier (than having to write HTML code and FTP the content online) with the writer using WYSIWYG software much the same as typing a Word document. However, that is the limit of any *management* that it offers. It does not think up subjects and put those thoughts into words in such a way that the content meets the objectives of the site.

As well as producing the website's content, there is the maintenance of the existing content to manage. Although the issue should be addressed during the original site design, it is essential that extensive consideration is given to the site's structure with regard to directories and file names. As a site expands over time, it might become necessary to add to, or modify, its navigational structure. Links to your website (from other sites) might be around for years to come, so rearranging your site can cause major irritation to potential customers. It is also the case that as search engines will have indexed your original URLs, changing them might well result in your search engine optimization (SEO) value dropping.

RESEARCH SNAPSHOT

Harder to continue than to start

Although the inventor of the web, Tim Berners-Lee (now *Sir*), was talking about educational materials online, I feel his comments on content are valid across all online content. He said that keeping web material up to date takes a lot more time and effort than that required to create it in the first place. I would add that keeping content up to date includes removing anything that is outdated or no longer relevant to the site's visitors. Corporate and public authority sites are usually most guilty of this fault.

Also part of the manager's role – though in conjunction with the organization's PR department – is contingency planning to ensure that unforeseen circumstances are dealt with efficiently and effectively. Server downtime or errors with the content of the site are two obvious disasters that may need to be *recovered from* with the minimum of fuss, damage or embarrassment.

Other issues constantly requiring *management* might include:

- Out-of-date material that has been either superseded or simply run its course. Though an effort should be made to avoid such problems in the editing stage, it is not always possible to present textual content in a 'timeless' fashion, it being sometimes impossible to avoid the present tense. The problem for managers is that if content refers to something that is currently happening (perhaps a new product being developed) – at some time in the future it will be completed, but unless your website is updated, it will still say it is *being* developed. Similarly, there is nothing worse than reading about a 'future event' that actually took place some time ago!

- Archiving of material that might be accessed by users in the future. This will also include its addition to any on-site search engine databases or navigational links. However, just because a website has an infinite capacity for retaining content (unlike a printed document, for example), managers should not keep old content for the sake of doing so – worthless content should be culled. Furthermore, the decision should be guided not by what the organization thinks should be retained, but by what the visitor is likely to access.

- Links away from your site need to be checked regularly (software is available to do it for you) to make sure the target pages are still there – if they are not, the user will blame you for the faulty link.

Naturally, on a website that sells goods there will always be product descriptions and prices to maintain – but sometimes a concentration on sales pages can lead to other pages or sections being neglected.

PRACTICAL INSIGHT

Practitioner Patrick Tam (2010) reflects the frustration felt by many digital marketers when he says: 'Digital marketing is about communications, not technology. Too often too many people get too caught up in the technical mumbo jumbo.' The title of the article from which this quote comes is also indicative: 'I'm a digital marketing pro, I don't work in IT'.

Development

The issue of technical and design versus marketing which was introduced when considering both the ownership and management once again has an impact on the development of any web presence – though, obviously, decisions made in the ownership and management stages will influence that development.

The skills required to develop an effective website are diverse. In the first edition of this book I suggested a list of skills required for website development – such a 'dream team' now includes: programmers, graphic

> " a 'dream team' now includes: programmers, graphic designers, usability experts, content writers, copy writers, search engine optimization specialists, sales staff, merchandisers and marketers "

designers, usability experts, content writers, copy writers, search engine optimization specialists, sales staff, merchandisers and marketers. And this doesn't include specialists in the likes of on-site security, checkout facilities, imaging, video – indeed, the list goes on and on.

My inclusion of offline sales staff – who should be at least consulted during the development of any commercial web presence – is questioned by some. However, in both online B2B and B2C marketing sales staff can have a real impact, for three key reasons:

1. Experienced staff have been there, seen it and done it. They know the product, the industry, the market and the customers. To ignore their input would be negligent. Beware, however – the website is a different medium from the face-to-face contact sales staff are used to, so allowing them to develop the content themselves is not a good idea.

2. Involving 'sales' in the site's development will help integrate the two elements of the organization's marketing. Too often sales personnel see the website as a competitor for customers rather than an ally in the task.

3. The majority of B2B websites concentrate on lead generation (see Section 5.4), and so when the potential customer contacts the firm – by whatever means – it is to the sales team that their enquiry should be directed. If they have had a hand in the development of the site then the sales staff will be better prepared to respond effectively to that initial communication.

A further consideration is that the ethos and philosophy of the organization will play its part in the management and development of its web presence. Gerry McGovern has done a lot of work with web development teams, and I feel his views on this subject are too good to reduce too much. Writing on his Giraffe Forum (McGovern, 2008), he makes the point that: 'It is impossible to create a website with excellent service if there is not a culture of service within the web team that manages the website . . . many web teams are unfortunately filled with people who have little interest in serving. In fact, many web teams don't even accept that their primary job is to serve customers.' He goes on to suggest that some web design teams:

● Think that their job is to manage technology. They spend their time thinking about technology.

● Think about traditional communications. They want to communicate at, rather than to, customers, and they expect customers to listen.

● Are excited by things like branding and graphic design. They often change a website because they're bored with the old one. They sometimes create website designs more for their peers to admire than for customers to use.

● Tend to be isolated from customers, and, because of this isolation, a culture of service rarely exists. In some organizations, web teams are not even allowed to talk to customers!

Although McGovern is being specific about websites that aim to help customers 'self-serve' themselves to products or information, all users arrive at a website with an objective in mind – McGovern's ethos will help them meet their needs and wants. I would conclude this section by pointing out that although it is not an absolute, staff who care about customers are more likely to have a marketing or sales background than an IT or design background.

PRACTICAL INSIGHT

The worst possible way to design a website

In the introduction to Chapter 2 of his excellent book *The Stranger's Long Neck*, before going on to detail how a website *should be* developed, Gerry McGovern says:

The worst possible way to design a website is to have five smart people in a room drinking lattes and posting Post-it note ideas. The longer you leave them in the room, the worse the design will become. It's a proven fact.

The second-worst way is to have 10 customers in a room drinking lattes and giving their opinion on what they want from a website.

Later in the book McGovern makes the comment that:

The web is not some back-end IT activity, it's a customer-facing, task-focused one. It's not about writing code and servicing machines, but about observing people so that you can serve them better or, more importantly, allow them to serve themselves.

Web teams need to be out front, not back-office.

If you have any role to play in the development of an organization's web presence, reading McGovern's book is not an option – it is essential.

Source: McGovern, 2010

In the first edition of this book I mentioned the phenomenon of the amateur website developer. Although their influence has waned over the years, it is still the case that some organizations – particularly SMEs – still have their website developed by someone who does not earn a full-time living from the occupation.

The *amateur* made an appearance in the early days of web design for a number of reasons, though most significantly because they were – and they still are – cheap. Normally associated with SMEs, the original amateurs were the IT students who, as part of their computing course, had learned the fundamentals of HTML and website design. Those computing programmes and courses, however, include little or no marketing or sales content. Subsequently, the advent of WYSWYG software meant that anyone who could use Microsoft

Word could produce a website – but not one worthy of the organization it represented. Long (2002) made a good analogy, pointing out that owning a camcorder does not mean you can write, produce and edit your own TV commercials. However, the amateur's low cost and the facts that the emerging web industry was not yet geared to provide *professional* web-design services and (sadly) that few organizations had yet come to appreciate the full value of the Internet as a medium of communication meant that the amateur web-designer business was booming. Although the amateur developer still exists, those who seek to meet organizational objectives from an Internet presence appreciate that a successful website requires the input of a variety of skilled professionals. And while it is true that a few amateurs have produced successful websites, it is a very small number – of amateurs *or* professionals – who can boast proficiency in all of the skills necessary to develop a truly effective website.

DECISION TIME

The well-used phrases 'you get what you pay for' and 'if you pay peanuts, you get monkeys' are pertinent in this scenario. Much depends on the marketing objectives for the web presence. For the successful offline business that has traded locally for many years through word-of-mouth referrals, a fairly basic web page – containing little more than the company name, contact details and what they are good at – developed by an amateur *might* be sufficient.

A more recent development related to the amateur consideration for organizations is the rise of the do-it-yourself (DIY) website. DIYers are guided through the process of making their own websites by a hosting company which offers templates, image libraries and industry-relevant content. These website-service provision sites are marketed at SME owners as a cheap alternative to professional website development, and as it is the business owner and/or employee who builds the site, I categorize them as *amateur* websites. Can they work? The answer is a guarded yes – in the right circumstances. The obvious key is the website's objective and its role in the marketing of the organization, but it also depends on the skill set of the person building the site. You might expect, for example, that someone who wants a basic website for their flower arrangement service might have a good eye for the aesthetic appearance of a website. Or an experienced salesperson might make a reasonable attempt at writing sales copy for their new venture. However, the templates are limited, and I must refer you back to my 'dream team' of skills requirements for the most effective sites, before recommending such facilities unreservedly.

> ### MINI CASE
>
> Below are four examples from the author's websites which use templates provided by the sites' hosts. Notice how 1 and 4 are virtually the same, that 3 has a grey 'blank' area on its right and that 2 includes an advert for the hosts at the bottom of the page. Although these 'cookie-cutter' sites *can* serve a purpose, none gives the visitor the sense that the site was designed for a specific purpose.

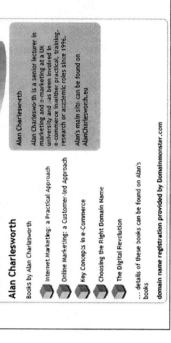

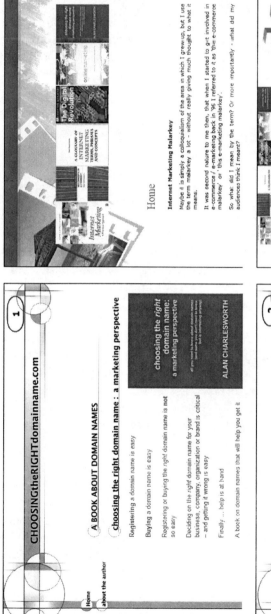

Figure 3.1 Four pages from the author's websites which use templates provided by the sites' hosts

The higher the stakes of what is expected from a site – its objectives – then the higher the gamble of not paying for a professional job. Conversely, any expenditure must give a return on investment – paying tens of thousands of pounds to a big-city web design company for a website that generates little income, does nothing to develop the brand and/or provides no effective customer support is not a sound business investment.

However, the prime consideration must be given to the visitor to the proposed site and what they expect. Schlosser *et al.* (2006) suggest that 'investment' in site design can enhance trust – and so increase purchase intentions. Whilst it should be appreciated that the 'monkey–peanuts' argument is valid, and that Schlosser *et al.* have a point, (a) highest cost does not necessarily equal highest quality, and (b) can a website visitor really tell how much 'investment' has been made in order to make a judgement?

PRACTICAL INSIGHT

Luxury hotels – luxury website?

As I mentioned in the Preface, I made the decision that throughout the book I wouldn't mention the costs of any of the services or products I talk about. However, I will break that rule for this story. When the Four Seasons Hotels and Resorts' new website was revealed in 2012 many eyebrows were raised at the reported (and staggering) $18m price tag – I hasten to add that most websites cost a lot less than eighteen million dollars. Furthermore – once we reviewed the new site I wasn't the only commentator to question just where the money was spent.

For those organizations with a significant online presence, the issue of site management is likely to be addressed at the beginning of the development stage – with the manager probably leading the development from initiation to going live online. Note that it is common for the development of a website to be incorrectly referred to as a *project* – this is wrong because projects have a completion date. Too many organizations have outdated websites because they were developed as a project, and when that project ended no one took – or was given – responsibility for maintaining (managing) the site's content.

Essentially, the decision is *who* will have responsibility for the site in an ongoing role. Strategically, the content itself should be determined by the site's objectives, but operationally – tactically, if you will – someone must have responsibility for the running of the site. Obviously, for big sites, that job is full time and requires someone with the experience to handle the varied duties it involves. But even for the SME with a minimal site made up of only a few pages it is still essential that *someone* within the organization takes responsibility for its management.

As with most elements of running a contemporary organization, the manager must decide whether tasks are undertaken in-house or whether they are outsourced. Website development is no exception. Given the list of skills described above, it seems doubtful if all, or even any, of the necessary talent can be found within the organization – though it is worth noting that *unskilled* staff who are either co-opted to, or volunteer for, the task rarely produce effective websites.

Realistically, few organizations will have the 'dream team' experience in-house. Even the likes of Tesco who will have their own 'online' department will use external suppliers for specialist functions of the website (the checkout facility, perhaps). Indeed, there are many software companies who have built businesses around supplying specialist elements of e-commerce sites – everything from keeping product images up to date, through 'customer experience management', to linking customers' online orders to the company's logistical support. As with all other aspects of digital marketing, the answer lies in the organization's dependency on the web. I have developed (and maintain) everything on my own website (alancharlesworth.eu) myself, and I have very basic 'design' and 'technical' skills. However, I do have considerable online marketing skills and my business or livelihood does not depend on this site; it is a support service for the book. A similar argument can sometimes be made for many offline organizations, particularly SMEs – and it is to them that the amateur's low price looks appealing. Such organizations should always remember the axiom *you are your website*. At the other end of the spectrum are organizations like Amazon that depend on the web for 100 per cent of their income, and so employ all the skills necessary to compete effectively in their market.

YOU DECIDE

Compare the different website management requirements for the Rockridge Museum (case study 1) and The Gilded Truffle Hotel (case study 3).

Alternatively, conduct the same exercise using one of these companies and your organization or that of your employer.

3.3 THE BASICS

An often-used comment on website development is that designers design for themselves instead of designing for the user, which invariably means using technology for technology's sake – something Loizides (2003) describes as 'one of the worst offences [online] marketers can make'. Although for the best examples of successful websites this is not true – sadly it is still the case for many sites. Dadzie *et al.* (2005) advocate that website features can be categorized into website design features and customer service functions. Although this might be considered a sensible way of separating the *design* and *marketing* elements of the site, it may also suggest to some that design and customer service are divorced – which is not the case. A common example of technology for its own sake is the use of 'splash' home pages. Online marketing practitioner and trainer Dr. R.F. Wilson (2003) defines 'splash' pages as 'home pages with dancing logos powered by Macromedia Flash technology designed to annoy and turn away visitors before they reach the real home page'. His opinion is shared by many – myself included – but not necessarily by all designers.

For designers, web pages such as those on my website (alancharlesworth.eu) carry no kudos – indeed, they might brand mine as being 'bad' because it is so basic. My argument is that the site is designed for its target readership – and if you were to visit that site it would be for easy-to-find information, not entertainment. Sadly, that 'splash' pages do nothing to meet the needs of visitors is too often not a concern of those who design them.

MINI CASE

Plain beats flashy

In 2013 it was a website that swept aside offline designs from some of the world's best creative architects, such as the iconic London Olympics Cauldron, in a top design award. In itself that was something of a shock. That the website in question could only be described as 'plain' – and was the website of the UK government – created even more of a reaction. Commenting on the result on his website, web content expert Gerry McGovern said:

Design is not just how it looks. Design must also be concerned with how it works. For things to work on the Web they must be findable. That requires a focus on search and navigation. When these are found the customer must be able to do something with them; complete a task.

I can add nothing to that other than to endorse every word – and applaud the award's judges.

Source: gerrymcgovern.com

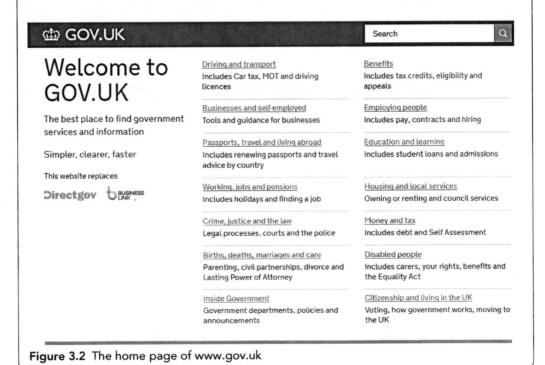

Figure 3.2 The home page of www.gov.uk

In Chapter 7 I have included a quote from advertiser Alvin Hampel, who makes the point that if an ad is clever and entertaining but sells no products, it has failed as an advert – the same can be said of websites. Writing in a white paper on website design, practitioner Rick Tobin (2008) sums up this subject well. He suggests that the web page is (or should be) designed for a key audience – the content written for them in a voice they want to listen to; the navigation intuitive to them specifically; and the benefit messaging built around their needs. He goes on to say that more often than not this is an accepted best practice in other media but is frequently ignored in website design because:

- web designers build for ego and flash, not users;
- web designers test sites based on a coolness factor and not on how a user actually interacts; and
- design theories are based on a push media perspective, where a glossy graphic grabs attention and brand association – very few focus on a pull medium, where the user is in the driver's seat and has explicit intentions.

Although the situation has improved since 2008, it is still the case that in far too many examples Tobin's observations are still valid.

GO ONLINE

The use of Flash-type technologies in website design is a hotly debated subject. See the chapter's web page for a link to the web page that first fuelled much of the debate – 'Flash: 99% Bad' by Jacob Nielsen.

In this section we will consider the basic elements of presenting information on a website. These are presented as guidelines, not rules. Obviously, the objectives of the site might dictate how the guidelines are interpreted – but they are ignored at the publisher's peril. It is also worth noting that this book is about marketing on the Internet – and so this chapter refers only to sites that perform a commercial or public service and from which a return on investment is required. If you want to create an 'all-about-my-favourite-rock-band' website, then ignoring the guidelines will not impinge on any objectives – commercial or otherwise. In fact, the chances are that only your family and friends will ever visit it, and so the design is of little consequence.

In addressing the basics of website development we are going to start by looking at two fundamental issues: presentation and usability. As with many aspects of digital marketing, opinion is divided on what is meant by various terms and concepts, and this section is no exception. In this case I will be combining website *navigation* with *usability* – others might consider them separate subjects.

GO ONLINE

Ads on your home page

Some business owners mistakenly believe that featuring ads on their websites will provide a good source of income. Although this is valid for organizations that seek to gain income from publishing web content, it is just the opposite for the business web presence. As I have said to a number of 'guilty' business owners and managers, 'would you have ads for your competitors on the side of your vans?' The answer is obviously 'no' – so I then ask, 'why do the same on your website?'

Presentation

As with so many things in life, 'keep it simple' is an excellent maxim to follow when developing a web presence. Usability expert Steve Krugg attempts to get the message across in the title of his book on the subject: *Don't Make Me Think* (2000). His point being that using the site should be instinctive – leaving users to concentrate on the objectives of their visit.

GO ONLINE

Just *plain* good

Some websites have a very 'basic' appearance – but this is not necessarily a bad thing. Follow the link from the chapter's web page for examples of 'clean' websites where the publishers/owners practise what they preach on the subject. You should note that all are considered to be experts on the subject of website usability.

Presented in no particular order, the following are some of the key issues in presenting a website to its visitors:

- Download time. In the early days of the web, research suggested that around eight seconds was as long as most people were willing to wait for a page to download. The widespread availability of broadband then reduced this waiting time – research conducted by Forrester Consulting in 2009 found that 40 per cent of shoppers will wait no more than three seconds for a page to download before abandoning a retail or travel site. It would seem that web users are an impatient lot. Web designers who ignore download speed – technology-heavy sites download slowly, simple ones quickly – do so at their peril. Or should I say at the peril of failing to meet the site's objectives. There is even a double-whammy from Google with regard to slow downloading sites. Not only might your site turn people away, but they might not even get there in the first place. Google has confirmed that it incorporates website speed into its algorithm for website rankings in its search results (there is a lot more about how search engines work in Chapter 6). Furthermore, not only has the increased use of mobile devices to access the web – many of which have slower connection speeds – returned the topic to prominence, but research from the Pew Research Center's Internet and American Life Project in 2012 revealed that four in ten American adults do not have a high-speed broadband connection at home. Cutting-edge technology certainly has a place – but is it on your website?

PRACTICAL INSIGHT

Same page, different name – vital importance

The first page of a website can be referred to as the *home* page or *front* page. Programmers usually call it the *index* page as that is the designation of the file that represents it. In marketing terms, however, it is the most valuable 'real estate' that you own on the web. Its content and presentation will determine whether or not a surfer might become a customer. If you doubt this, consider: would you go into a shop to buy shoes if nothing on the outside of the shop suggest that it sells footwear? Or would you enter a restaurant if the entrance was dirty? Here are a few tips.

1. The front page should:
   - download quickly
   - be short and to the point
   - offer a value proposition – a reason for visitors to stay
   - be professional
   - *inspire* visitors to go deeper into the site
   - *direct* visitors deeper into the site
   - appeal to the target audience
   - include contact details.
2. The front page should *not* have:
   - Flash/splash-type technology (e.g. it has a 'skip intro')
   - self-serving statements
   - a company description
   - advertising banners
   - any 'award' logos
   - the designer/developer's name or logo
   - a 'home' button
   - external links.

A footnote to this is that it is now common to arrive on a website as the result of an online search, in which case the user is more likely to arrive on any other page of the site other than the home page. Therefore – if *any* page could be the home page, shouldn't *every* page meet the criteria listed above?

- Make things easy on the eye – both aesthetically and with regard to making things undemanding to read. Avoid garish colours, flashing or moving images, music or any other 'novelty' that does nothing to help your site meet its objectives. Newspapers are white with black text – the lesson to take is (a) it makes the print easier to read, and (b) people expect it. Black on white might be a little 'basic' – but a dark text on a light background is a must. In some circumstances you may get away with white text on a dark background, but be aware – this will print as white on white. In other words: a blank sheet! Once again, the emergence of mobile devices to access the web has served to emphasize this aspect of design. As screens get smaller, the text gets harder to read if it is not dark on light. Need evidence? Apple Inc is generally perceived as being at the forefront of technological development – but which colours do they use for writing text messages on their iPhones? Yes, black on white. By the way – the Apple website is another example of aesthetically 'simple' design – with the text being mainly black on white.

RESEARCH SNAPSHOT

It *will* happen to you

Although it might be a long way off for most readers of this book (though, sadly, not its author) we all suffer loss of vision, dexterity and memory as we get older – and we need all three when using the Internet. According to research from the Nielsen Norman Group (2013), seniors – defined as being aged sixty-five and older – are 43 per cent slower at using websites than users aged between twenty-one and fifty-five.

As well as the obvious things like small font sizes, seniors are uncomfortable trying new things and twice as likely to give up on a task when they are online. Despite websites being better designed and seniors becoming more skilled at using the web, in an aging society which has an ever-increasing percentage of older people going online, it is a foolish web designer who ignores the needs of a demographic that has the disposable income to pay his or her wages.

- Font size. Also associated with making text easy to read is the size of the characters. This is another aspect where basic HTML scores – it being easily adjusted in size on the user's browser, whereas some Flash-type design has fixed text size. The same is true when text is integral to an image. The issue is particularly sensitive if (a) the target audience is older – and so (statistically) more likely to have failing eyesight, or (b) your website is likely to be viewed on a smartphone. I could add a (c) here – older people who use mobile devices to access the web. Younger readers might scoff at this comment – but consider this. In a B2B environment, the person you are hoping to do business with probably uses a mobile device and is almost certainly older than you.

PRACTICAL INSIGHT

Learn from history

Hundreds of years of print have shown that readability of textual content is optimal at 1.5 to 2.5 alphabets per line – normally around 65 characters. Few publications deviate from this rule, no matter how large or small the text is. Generally speaking, the easier to read the book is hoped to be, the fewer words there will be on a line – a 'holiday' novel that will be read on the beach, for example. Ironically, academic textbooks are some of the most guilty of breaking this rule – including this one – though not by much. The average line is around 75 characters long.

- Uniformity. Maintain a corporate image with offline publications, livery and so on – and every page in a site should follow the same layout and structure.

- Get the important content on the screen. The old newspaper axiom of 'above the fold' translates well to a web page – with 'below the fold' being any content that requires downward scrolling to see it, and 'above the fold' being what is on the screen when the page opens. People will scroll down a page if they feel it has something they need or will find useful, but they shouldn't have to scroll down to find the name of the organization whose front page they are looking at or the value proposition that should influence the user to stay on that page. Google recognizes 'above the fold' as providing a good user experience, stating in their Webmaster Central blog (googlewebmastercentral.blogspot.co.uk) that sites that have important content below other content (adverts, for example) would be penalized in the search engine's ranking.

- Page width. This is a contentious issue – with designers usually wanting to fill the screen, but good usability practice is against it for most applications. The key issue is that the developer does not know, and cannot control, the size of screen that the user will view the page on. To maintain control over the page's presentation, it is common practice to set the page width as one that can be seen by the majority of – if not all – users. The time when controlling width becomes a necessity is where the content is predominantly text – text that stretches all the way across a computer screen is difficult, if not impossible, to read (try it, see the link on the chapter's web page). It is far easier to hold the reader's attention if shorter lines are used. Again the lesson comes from the print media where newspaper content is presented in columns. Text is also best presented in short paragraphs with bold introductions or titles so that the attention of visitors 'scanning' the content is drawn to key subjects.

PRACTICAL INSIGHT

React or respond?

It has become more common for users to access the web using smartphones or tablets – and, as I write this in the Spring of 2014, there are tablets almost as small as smartphones, and smartphones almost the same size as tablets. Who knows what you will be using by the time you read this? Website developers are, therefore, facing up to the problem of how best to provide web content that is as readable on a tiny screen read on a train as it is on a PC on the user's desk.

One option is to use basic website design which the user can adjust for the screen on which they are viewing it. However, this involves some consideration of the different screen sizes and – it might be argued – results in a website which is 'okay' for all screens but perfect for none. This book's website would be such an example.

Another choice is to develop one site for larger screens (e.g. PCs and laptops), another for mobile devices – and perhaps another for 'mid-size' devices (e.g. tablets and notebooks). While this might be an ideal solution, it is very expensive and requires the organization to direct visitors to different URLs for each site.

Other alternatives exist which are based on the World Wide Web Consortium's (www.w3.org/) concept of *One Web*, which they define as: 'making, as far as is reasonable, the same information and services available to users irrespective of the device they are using'.

However, this does not mean that exactly the same information is available in exactly the same representation across all devices. The context of mobile use, device capability variations, bandwidth issues and mobile network capabilities all affect the representation. Furthermore, some services and information are more suitable for, and targeted at, particular user contexts.

Most commmonly referred to as 'responsive web design', this is a way of designing websites so that they have a fluid layout, but the coding adapts the content to the screen on which it is being viewed so that it displays appropriately. The key advantage of this is that the organization needs to develop and maintain only one website for all of its customers. The main disadvantage – as alluded to above – is that the mobile user's experience will be limited when compared to viewing a bespoke, mobile-only site. This is relevant because, as was addressed in Section 1.7, people use mobile devices in a different way to the way they use PCs or laptops. For example, booking a cinema ticket for a specific movie at a specific time at a specific location while on the move is a very different experience to reviewing movies to decide which movie to watch and where and when is the most convenient to you.

Another alternative for some organizations – particularly those which seek inter-action with the digital customer – retailers, for example – is to replace the website with an app (application software).

As with every aspect of the subjects covered in this book, however, the answer lies with what the customer expects and what the objectives of the organization's digital marketing are – a combination will provide the route to the answers to the questions raised above.

Because this subject is sure to change significantly over the lifetime of this book, I'll keep this section updated on the chapter's web page.

- Printed pages – also on the subject of page width, some pages will be printed by users (instructions, for example) – if this is the case, the page should be set accordingly. In standard format, printers will print a maximum width of 750 pixels – and often the default setting is 600. Setting the page width above this will result in the ends of each line being chopped from the printout. If you expect the user to print out the page – confirmation of an order or flight booking are examples – offer them the option of a 'print this' page which is designed to fit an A4 sheet of paper.

- Respect the conventions of the web. Links within text, for example, should be in a different colour, and usually underlined. In plain HTML developed sites this happens automatically – it is not the case in Flash-type design. Visited links should also change colour – in a long list it is easy to forget where you have already been and where you have not. Similarly, underlining words is frowned upon as they are misinterpreted as being link words. Online, words in all upper case are deemed the same as shouting – and rude. Furthermore, using all capitals actually reduces readability by around 10 per cent. Note that the issue of link colours can be overruled by the user's browser settings, but you should still design for the majority.

GO ONLINE

For more on how text looks on the web, follow the link to my web page on online text presentation.

- Avoid non-standard characters that not all browsers can read. The superscript ™ for example, does not appear as such on some browsers.

- Home page link. So that a visitor is never completely lost on your site, or because they may have arrived deep in the site from a search engine, there should be a link to the home page on every other page on the site – although it is surprising how many home pages include a link to themselves.

- Ensure the design features of the site are appropriate to its objectives. You would expect the presentation of a website for a funeral director to be different to that of an amusement park. An extreme example perhaps, but what sort of website might your target audience expect to find?

PRACTICAL INSIGHT

Knowledge of all fonts?

The most easily read font on a website is one from the Arial/Helvetica family. Times New Roman, the most commonly used font in printed media, should be avoided.

The reason is in the presentation of the fonts. Arial and its cohorts are *sans serif* fonts – they have no 'tail' at the end of each line in the letter. Times New Roman is a serif font – it has the additional tails. In print, characters are 'solid' and so the tails make the words easier for the human eye to identify – and so read. Online, however, all characters are presented in pixels – effectively thousands of dots on the screen that when put together represent letters, numbers and so on. Because of this pixelation it is better if each character is distinct from the next – and the tails in serif fonts tend to 'blend' each character into its neighbours, so making it more difficult to read on a computer screen.

Incidentally, this issue also makes words in italics difficult to read online – so they should be avoided.

Follow the links on the chapter's web page to see my examples of how different fonts look online.

- It may be true that a picture paints a thousand words – but online there are caveats. Be aware of using large images on a website (and never on the front page) as they can take a long time to download. If your product sells on what it looks like, then pictures are essential – but make sure consideration is given to the file size of any image (for download times). Also, the quality of any pictures is important – they should be professionally produced. Having pictures on a website simply because 'they look nice' is not good practice. The custom of having a picture take prominence on a web page is a legacy from the print media and advertising. Often referred to as 'the hero shot', having a big picture of a film star next to a story about a film in which they are starring might work in magazines, and images of gorgeous women on perfume ads might work offline, but online such illustrations simply take up valuable on-screen space.

PRACTICAL INSIGHT

The right pictures sell clothes

For an elite few so-called *e-comm models* an income of up to £20,000 a week is a possibility – but only if the clothes they are pictured in sell online. This means that the 'supermodel' look is out and 'girl-next-door' is in – if the potential buyer cannot see herself in the outfit then she does not buy. Getting the right model in the right outfit is also essential, with one online insider claiming that if a dress does not work on one girl, they'll shoot it on another, and she can boost sales by 800 per cent. Older buyers – those over thirty – however, are more likely to buy off a 'headless' model as they do not relate to the girl to buy what she is wearing.

Source: *Sunday Times Magazine*, 3 March 2013

- Grammar and spelling. Sadly, this final point should go without saying, but unfortunately it is a common problem on pages ranging from blogs to corporate sites. Ensure any textual content is grammatically correct and has no spelling errors. How credible is a business if it cannot even take the effort to have its website content checked for errors?

Usability

> usability is all about how easy it is for a visitor to achieve their objectives for visiting the site

Website usability is all about how easy it is for a visitor to achieve their objectives for visiting the site. If the objective is to find the address of a local store – is there a prominent link on the front page that says, 'store locations'? If it is to purchase a silk tie as a present – is there clear categorization: e.g. menswear > ties > silk? Any block on the visitor's smooth flow through the site is a reason for them to leave – and any click on the back button represents a lost sale. Naturally, the opposite is also true – an easy-to-use site is more likely to result in the site's objectives being met. Although the term *usability* is the 'scientific' term to describe this concept, it has been common practice to employ the term *user experience* – often abbreviated to UX – which I think better describes the objective of the exercise.

RESEARCH SNAPSHOT

According to research from the Nielsen Norman Group (McCloskey *et al.*, 2013), those of us who assume that teens are techno-wizards who surf the web with abandon are wrong. Nor do they like sites laden with glitzy, blinking graphics. The research also found teens perform worse than adults when using websites for three reasons: (i) insufficient reading skills, (ii) less sophisticated research strategies, and (iii) dramatically lower levels of patience – so, if you are trying to improve a site's usability for teens, you must consider all three of these factors. Earlier research from the same organization (Nielsen Norman Group, 2010) also found that teenagers disliked waiting for Flash pages to download – reaching for the back button being the most common reaction. And this is from a generation who will grow up considering the Internet to be a utility. In the same way that recent generations grew up expecting household electricity at the flick of a switch, today's children will grow up expecting websites at the click of a mouse – or the touch of a finger on a screen.

In Gay *et al.* (2007) I make the point that in website design, familiarity breeds *acceptance* and so endorse the commonly used – and so easily acceptable – 'header–columns–footer' model. Because the design is so frequently used – not least by some of the most visited sites on the web – when people arrive on a page with this design characteristic they are immediately at ease with the presentation.

MINI CASE

Don't confuse your site's visitors

My own website and that of the first edition of this book uses a standard 'header–columns–footer' layout. Some designers have tried to move away from this as they consider it unadventurous, however it will only take you a few minutes of visiting the most popular websites on the Internet to appreciate that it might be boring – but it works. As I mentioned earlier in this section, the similarity to newspapers is no accident.

Figure 3.3 The page construction of the home page of alancharlesworth.eu, which uses three columns, and the home page of this book's first edition, which uses two

Navigation

Website navigation refers to how visitors find their way – *navigate* – around your website. If you have only a couple of pages this shouldn't be an issue, but if the site has more than three pages this is vital. It is also the case that in an era when search rules the web, many visitors will arrive not on your front page – but deep in the site. Navigation systems should take this into account so that potential customers do not simply bounce straight off your site because (a) they are not aware of other content, or (b) can't find their way to it.

As Gerry McGovern (2009b) says, 'Good web navigation is unsubtle. It is clear, precise, familiar, consistent, boring, unemotional. Good navigation is ugly and functional.' For the designer who has spent several years at university being taught how to express themselves in their designs, ugly and functional is alien and they are tempted to eschew conventions – but as McGovern goes on to point out, phone directories are still best presented in A to Z, no matter how conventional that is. This topic is taken up by another practitioner–expert, David Bowen (2009), who says that: 'Consistency and convention are not "sexy" or innovative concepts but they are the bedrock of smooth journeys online just as driving on a particular side of the road is offline – it would undoubtedly be exciting if the side changed without warning in different parts of town . . . but it's not something you would want to have to think about.'

McGovern (2009a) also makes the point that when people are on the web, they are instinctive, impatient, impulsive and in a hurry. They click on the first link that looks in any way right – the reason why designers should not change obvious navigational aids to be 'sexy'. The offline example he uses is that even the most state-of-the-art new aircraft will still use the term 'exit' over the doors. Don't mess with established navigation conventions, he says, be as familiar and consistent as possible. Perhaps designers should take note of Leonardo da Vinci, who said, 'Simplicity is the ultimate sophistication.' Readers might be more familiar with that quote from the original brochure for the Apple II.

PRACTICAL INSIGHT

There are right visitors, and there are wrong visitors

Over the years numerous commentators, authors and practitioners have made the point that there are several distinct categories for people who arrive at a commercial website – and they should all be considered in the design of the site. Nearly all agree that the list is something like this:

1. They're there by mistake – they followed a link, mistyped a URL, misinterpreted the domain name – or one of a dozen other reasons. No part of your web development efforts should be aimed at them.
2. They don't really know what they are looking for, but they think you might have it – think of the window-shopper who wanders in off the street. A front page which says whose site it is and what they offer – plus a clear navigation bar, should tell this visitor whether they belong there or not.
3. They have some inkling of what they want and believe that you sell it – perhaps because they have been on the site before. As with the previous group, clear navigation should help them out – though as they know what they are after, more comprehensive listings might be necessary – or an in-site search facility.
4. They know what they want and they know that you sell it. For these visitors 'one-click' type navigation is necessary so that they can get to their purchase as quickly as possible.

Of course, grey areas will exist in this list – and developers should never forget that a visitor who is #4 for one product might well be a #2 or #3 for others.

Although you may know your way around your own site, you should not assume others find it as easy. Pages, sections, categories, products – whatever your site is made up of – should be signposted clearly. There should be an unambiguous contents list. If every page has a 'return to home/index page' link, then the visitor is only ever one click away from base – where they can start again. If your website is massive – provide an in-site search facility. Seen by many as essential to navigation around major sites, internal search facilities can be problematic – suffering from what I call 'red sweater syndrome'. The problem lies in who is responsible for the development of any search facility – and it is too often left to IT staff. By the very nature of computer programming – it is binary – coding is developed in a yes/no way. The algorithm is asked for a 'red sweater'; if there is no 'red sweater', the search return is 'none found'. And this is where marketing must work with IT in developing the facility. Here's the reason why.

Different people recognize the same products by different names and descriptions – a red sweater and a maroon pullover, for example – so marketing input is required to ensure provision is made for matching searchers with products that meet their needs; e.g. a search for 'red sweater' will trigger the response that 'maroon pullover' is actually the same thing. To avoid the 'no return' page – which is bound to send the potential customer elsewhere – marketers should help make sure that:

- If there are no matching products, a *marketing* message is offered (e.g. 'you might want to try . . .' or 'no shirts in this colour are available, but you might want to consider this range [link] that has other colours that might work with your outfit'.
- As indicated with the red sweater, where synonyms are used, the search terms that visitors might use should be predicted. This also includes popular terminology (e.g. a car enthusiast might search on 'alloys', not 'alloy wheels').
- Common misspellings (in the products and descriptions) can be predicted – similarly, different international terms should be catered for.
- Too many results are as bad as none. The visitor has used the search to save them time in navigating the whole site. Therefore, it's no good presenting them with a list that is longer than the site's navigation bar. Multiple results should be categorized, or if necessary an 'advanced search' option should be offered to help users narrow down their alternatives.

Other problems can stem from the nature of the content being sought. For example, most in-site search facilities cannot 'read' pdf files – so the sought-for content might be part of the website, but the search engine tells the searcher that it is not. Technical staff can address all of these elements when building the in-site search engine's parameters – but they should not be expected to determine those parameters themselves. I have previously emphasized the importance of input from sales staff in website development. This is a good example of where their experience is essential – it is they who know what customers ask for.

PRACTICAL INSIGHT

If readers think that I'm exaggerating on the issue of users searching for the same product using different search terms – as in sweater/jumper/pullover – consider this. In a keynote presentation at SES San Jose in September 2009, Nick Fox, Google's Business Product Management Director for AdWords, stated that people had searched for *cashmere sweaters* seventy-three different ways during the previous year.

Although good navigation is important for *branding* and *service* websites, for revenue-generating sites *important* becomes *absolutely essential*. As the site's objective is more tangible – make a sale, for example – the web designer can look to influence the way a visitor navigates their way around the site. One way of doing this is to use an online adaptation of the sales funnel. (Note that the sales funnel is a development from the buying cycle and AIDA concepts – both of which are covered in more detail in Section 1.6.) In the traditional version, potential customers might be exposed to an advert (the top, or widest, part of the funnel). People interested in the product might respond to the ad by ringing up to request a brochure (they enter the funnel). After reading the brochure, the prospective customer then contacts the firm to arrange a demonstration of the product, and so on until a purchase is made (they fall out of the funnel at its narrowest point). At each step the customer can either (a) go deeper into the funnel, or (b) step out by rejecting the firm's offer. Sales (and marketing) teams can then study users' progression through the funnel – and address any issues that cause them to step out at the various stages. It is also the case that customers can be 'rejected' at any stage if sales staff identify them as 'not-serious' purchasers.

Online, web designers might consider the website to be the 'funnel'. Potential customers might arrive at the front page (the mouth of the funnel) from a search engine. What they see on that page will determine whether or not they click deeper into the site (funnel). At each stage the prospective customer might withdraw (click away). The final stage – the narrow end of the funnel – is where the customer clicks on the link that fulfils their need and meets the site's objectives, be that 'buy now', 'download now' or 'find your nearest store'.

RESEARCH SNAPSHOT

Leaving is easy

If a website is difficult to use, people leave. If the home page fails to state clearly what a company offers and what users can do on the site, people leave. If users get lost on a website, they leave. If a website's information is hard to read or doesn't answer users' key questions, they leave.

Source: Usability guru, Jacob Nielsen, 2003

The funnel model is applied in a concept (championed by Bryan and Jeffrey Eisenberg) called 'persuasive – or persuas*ion* – architecture', where the navigational design of the site leads a prospects to the objective of the site by having them follow a series of commands. For example, a product description page might sell its attributes and end with the comment 'to find out what colours are available, click here', 'to select a size, click here' – and so on. However, the model also depends on the hyperlinks to each be a 'call to action' that motivates the user to move to the next stage. A persuasive call to action can be the difference between a visitor continuing down the funnel or leaving the site. For example, consider how the inclusion of a benefit and an imperative – or *active* – verb helps make the second of these hyperlinks more persuasive:

1. Bob discovered a work opportunity that changed his life. <u>**Read More**</u>
2. Bob discovered a work opportunity that changed his life. <u>**See how Bob doubled his earnings in less than a year**</u>

As with its offline version, the online sales funnel can be used as an analytical tool. If, for example, most prospects leave the site from the 'price' page then this suggests that either (a) there is a problem with the content of that page, or (b) there is a problem with the product's price. To find out which of these is the main problem, testing is the answer.

GO ONLINE

Whilst there is no definitive 'right' way for website design, numerous 'design guides' exist – follow the links on the chapter's web page to see some of the best.

Testing

Although testing should be considered as a basic element to website development it is too often the case that it is seen as an add-on, a luxury or worse still – not the necessity it is in reality. Before any site is made live to the public it should go through two stages of testing – *technical* and *human*. It should also be noted that this testing is related to the end user and how they are able to access and use the site. Aesthetically beautiful websites that win design awards or feature high in search engine results pages are not necessarily user friendly. As with all marketing, the only truly important opinions are those of the end users – the customers.

Technical issues that can be tested and addressed during development include:

*   Performance on the various browsers which customers might use, including not only the most popular (Internet Explorer, Chrome and Netscape/Firefox) but also Safari, Web-TV and any other system made available through Internet service providers.
*   Download speeds on a variety of broadband and dial-up facilities – with high- and low-specification PCs and laptops also being brought into the equation.
*   How pages present on various sizes of computer screen – including mobile devices if the target audience is known to use them.

It is also worth noting that testing should not end when the site goes live. Whilst ongoing improvements can be made to all of the elements listed above, other aspects of the site can be constantly tested for better results. For example, the text used in calls to action as part of the sales funnel can be tested for increasing clickthrough rates. For major online retailers like Amazon, such testing is constant for virtually every aspect of the web presence, including (but not limited to) background colour, headlines, copy, graphical images, banner ads, PPC ads, button colours – indeed, anything where there is the potential to improve the response and measure the improvements – being subject to testing in order to achieve maximum sales.

Human – or *usability* – testing is task oriented and should not be performed by anyone who has been involved in the project as they will have an insight into what is expected and how they should act. Nor should questionnaires or focus groups be used as people rarely say how they *actually* act online – few people like to admit they struggled with a task that they think others will perceive as easy. Although advanced testing using such techniques as eye-tracking (where the user's eye line is tracked as it moves around a web page) are available, much can be learned by taking a member of the Internet-using general public, and simply putting them in front of the site's home page and asking them to perform a series of commands. If the website has a specific target market, then people who fit the right demographic profile should be used for the testing. The respondents should be observed (and un-prompted – keep the design team out of the room) as they, for example, find the organization's postal address, a complaints phone number, the cost of shipping a product to America, a white paper download, how many colours a shirt is available in or make a purchase. Essentially, ask them to perform tasks that ordinary users will expect to complete (easily) in order to meet their objectives for visiting the site. Simple observation will tell the developers whether or not the site is usable.

PRACTICAL INSIGHT

'White van' versus 'eye candy' websites

Also known in the US as *panel van* websites, these are commercial sites of limited content and functionality, but which meet the objectives of the business they represent. The term comes from the ubiquitous vans that are a staple of businesses around the world that need to transport goods from A to B with the least fuss and best return on investment. Like their namesake websites, white vans are not a glamorous aspect of business, but they get the job done – hence the analogy. The opposite of such a site would be an *eye candy* website that looks good but does not meet any business objectives.

Note that these descriptions draw on content from my book *Key Concepts in e-Commerce*.

DECISION TIME

This section follows on directly from the previous chapters where the website's objectives and who takes responsibility for its development are addressed. In my experience, however, it is not always the case that these two fundamental issues have been addressed before work starts – or is even completed – on the site.

From the strategic objectives will come the answers to such issues as:

- What technology is most appropriate for the target market?
- What devices will the target market use to access the site?
- What style of presentation best suits the organization, brand and customers?
- How will the site be used – quick information-gathering or deeper research?
- Are there existing offline brand aesthetics that should be mirrored online – corporate colours, logo fonts, etc.?
- Should the site meet with accepted online conventions – or will the target market expect something more unusual?
- Will pictures add to the users' experience of the site – or detract from it?
- What method of navigation best facilitates the user meeting their on-site needs – and the objectives of the site?
- Is an in-site search facility needed, or will good navigation suffice?
- What testing is necessary to ensure both user experience and site objectives are optimized?

The answers to these issues will give the designers a direction to take in the way the site is developed to best suit target users.

YOU DECIDE

Advise Quincy Adams Wagstaff and his staff at Huxley University (case study 10) on what aspects of the basic website design are specifically relevant to the university's web presence.

Alternatively, conduct the same exercise for your organization or that of your employer.

3.4 ONLINE CREDIBILITY

This section is predominantly concerned with either online-only organizations or offline businesses that do not have a recognized offline brand name. In other words, those organizations whose website visitors do not know anything about the organization's reputation before arriving on the site. Obviously, if a brand is well known offline, online credibility is not an issue – Tesco online is the same Tesco as the company with hundreds of offline stores, for example.

In the *real* world, customers can use all of their senses in making a judgement on a brand or organization. They can *look* at the building they are in – how it is decorated; how well maintained; how clean. They can *listen* to what staff say – and note their tone of voice for sincerity or humour. They can *touch* the product; feel the characteristics; assess the quality. They can *smell* the product – or if relevant, the place in which it is processed or sold. They can *taste* the product – or ingredients. They can also use their *sixth* sense – the one that gives them an *insight* into the organization – its ethos and culture, for example.

Online they are limited to the square foot or so of computer screen on which the words and images that make up your web presence appears. On the Internet relationships and transactions are more impersonal and anonymous, making the building of *online* trust an essential component for organizations to succeed in the digital environment.

A term I have used for some time in an effort to emphasize to organizations that cost cutting on website development will come back to haunt them in the future is *online, you are your website*. Essentially, this notion reflects the fact that in the intangible world that is the Internet the only thing on which the (potential) customer can judge your organization is what they see on their computer screen. Of course, 'bad website equals bad organization' is a perception – but then so too is much of marketing. If *online, you are your website* ever carried any validity, it is with regard to online credibility. Long before the commercial Internet, Mowen (1987) made the point that the consumer evaluates a retailer and its products/ services before deciding on whether or not to develop a relationship with them. Not only is this equally true in the online marketplace, but it can be applied to B2B trading as well as retailing.

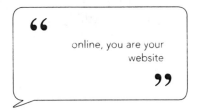

" online, you are your website "

I should add at this point that – as I have said previously – for *website* you might want substitute *web presence*. A poorly developed Facebook page will reflect badly on the organization, not Facebook.

MINI CASE

Fast-talking advice

When asked about the secret to success, Groucho Marx replied: 'The secret of life is honesty and fair dealing. If you can fake that, you've got it made.'

Whilst you should always look to present your organization in as good a light as possible, beware of overstepping the mark. Such is the nature of the digital world that you will be found out.

So how do we build trust and credibility into a website? Founder of Stanford University's Persuasive Technology Laboratory, B.J. Fogg (1999), suggested credibility is a combination of trustworthiness – unbiased, truthful, good and honest – experienced, intelligent, powerful and knowledgeable. However, P. Poirier (2003) attempted to be more objective by suggesting that visitors to a website form impressions about your company based on the totality of the experience they have whilst on your site. He goes on to make recommendations as to what makes up that *experience* – including ease of navigation, clarity of writing, quality of customer service and professional visual presentation of material. You will note that all of these issues appear elsewhere in this chapter as being examples of effective website design.

A number of writers offer more tangible solutions, though many are based around the aforementioned Stanford University's Persuasive Technology Lab's research into web credibility – whose guidelines include:

- Making it easy to verify the accuracy of the information on your site.
- Showing that there's a real organization behind your site.
- Highlighting the expertise in the organization.
- Showing that honest and trustworthy people stand behind your site.
- Making it easy to contact the organization.

However, the limitations of the computer screen can also be an advantage – particularly to the smaller business. Online, all organizations are measured in the pixels of a computer screen – and so a well-crafted site can be a great equalizer in a competitive marketplace. Providing they can meet the needs of their customers, the small business that is tucked away on a trading estate in an unfashionable northern town can be a *credible* online competitor of that mega-corp based in London's Docklands.

PRACTICAL INSIGHT

Look outward, not inward

When Jonathan Kranz, the author of *Writing Copy for Dummies*, was asked (in an interview in 2007), 'what is the most common mistake that you've seen companies make in crafting its collateral?', he replied:

Narcissism. We think we can distinguish our business from the competition by talking about ourselves: our company, our mission, our philosophy, our products. Yet the more we talk about ourselves, ironically, the more we sound like everyone else . . . and we lose potential customers as a result.

Source: marketingprofs.com

DECISION TIME

For the pure online organization, the website is everything – and so it should receive all the attention that the sole source of income demands. However, for any twenty-first-century marketer it is likely that the Internet will play an important role in any marketing strategy – and so how the web presence represents the organization is an essential consideration. The site must present a credible organization so that trust with customers can be developed – as Gefen and Straub (2004) point out, the higher the degree of consumer's trust, the higher the degree of purchase intentions of consumers.

Just as every business – and marketing mix – is different, so too is every website. However, there are a number of issues that should be addressed in order to suggest credibility to the customer. These might include such things as:

- Incorporate contact details, including full mailing address.
- Provide details of staff to make the organization real.
- Have an FAQ section that answers all potential customer questions.
- Include details of complaints procedures.
- Explain in full the organization's email and data protection policies.
- Use customer endorsements.

However, these are generic topics, and each publisher should also look for specific issues that are relevant to that site's visitors. For example, a guaranteed delivery by a certain day might suggest credibility through reliability. Also – as is a constant theme throughout this book – multiple aspects of Internet marketing impact on each other, such as ranking high in a search engine results page raising the credibility of that company within its field. Note however, that whilst we have considered trust as a distinct aspect of website design, effectively all the other elements of this chapter are components of online credibility. Furthermore, any of those issues listed above may not be relevant to any given organization or website. Indeed, the inclusion of some of them might actually be detrimental to the objectives or usability of the website. For example, for someone who trades from home, including their address online might not be a good idea for security reasons. Similarly, an FAQ section on a small website should be redundant as all of the questions a customer might have should be addressed within the limited content.

YOU DECIDE

Advise Robert Terwilliger (case study 9) on specific issues of credibility with regard to the website for the Modeller's Stand that would be important to potential customers, and suggest how they might be addressed.

Alternatively, conduct the same exercise for your organization or that of your employer.

3.5 CONTENT DEVELOPMENT

As we established in Section 1.6, it is the in the consumers' search for information that the web has the greatest impact on marketing – as content expert Gerry McGovern (2009c) says, 'customers don't arrive at your website to know less. They want to know more.' McGovern's assertion – based on his vast experience – can be supported by research from Jansen *et al.* (2008), who found that around 80 per cent of search-engine searches are informational in nature (the remainder are evenly split between searches that are navigational and those that are transactional). However, this should not come as a great surprise, as customers' thirst for information to aid their purchase decision has long since been recognized as a key element in the buying process –

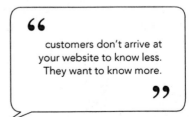

> " customers don't arrive at your website to know less. They want to know more. "

Glazer (1991) makes the point that a major component of exchange is the exchange of information.

If it is a search for information that is the primary motive for visiting a website, then that information must be not only of a high quality – but presented in a way that is acceptable

> **"**
> textual content is often the last thing considered in website development
> **"**

to the visitor. It is necessary, therefore, that further examination of this aspect of website development is included here. Although content developers have long argued the value of their contribution to the success of a website, their arguments have been equally long ignored by too many developers. Indeed, it is the experience of many – including myself – that the textual content is often the last thing considered in website development. It is not unusual for a site to be months in development and the content written in the last few days before it goes live – with it often being simply lifted from existing offline publications. Not only that, but the task is delegated to anyone who might be available at the time. So it is that arguably the most important element of the website – that will be available to customers 365 days a year, seven days a week, twenty-four hours a day – is written by the office junior or intern.

GO ONLINE

Quid quoddam pondus rudera

For evidence that textual content is the last consideration in the development of some websites, follow the link from the chapter's web page.

Author and practitioner David Meerman Scott (2007) acknowledges that website design is important, but suggests that it dominates the focus of too many organizations' online thinking, to the detriment of good content development – in his opinion, this happens because it is *easier* to do so. Supporters of quality content development point to traditional media, where professional input has always been a prerequisite of any content that is put into the public domain and attributed to an organization – and yet that ethos is largely ignored where websites are concerned.

PRACTICAL INSIGHT

Content is king!

On a commercial website, visitors arrive looking for information that will meet the needs that have driven them to the website in the first place. That information is the *content* of the website. While much of the sought-after information will be in textual format, do not forget that appropriate images, graphics, audio and video content can add to the readers' stimulus.

Good content will overcome basic design – but excessive design will not disguise poor content.

And who decides whether the content is good or bad? It is the website visitor – if it is relevant to their needs, then the content is good. As with all marketing, however, the trick is to know what the potential customers' needs are. A woman seeking reviews of bodice-ripper novels for her holiday reading expects to be directed to something published by Mills & Boon – and for advice on sunscreen lotion, a pharmacy site. Both will provide the would-be holidaymaker with relevant information – but each will be written and presented in the appropriate tone if they are to be effective.

So perhaps this insight should have been called 'the *right* content is king!'

One thing that sometimes confuses students is the difference between *content* and *copy*. Indeed, the common misuse of the two words would suggest the confusion spreads to practitioners and writers also. It is important to appreciate that while the two may blend into each other, in marketing terms there is a fundamental difference between content and copy. Essentially, content has the objective of being informative. Copy, on the other hand, is persuasive in its nature – hence the common term, *sales* copy. It is copy that will encourage a visitor to become a customer. The textual content presented in an advert will have been developed by a copywriter. Online, this aspect of the web content is often referred to as the *call to action* – 'click here for more information' is a basic example. The online blurring of where one stops and the other starts is commonly found in product descriptions. If a product is described only by its attributes or capabilities ('it is 50cm long and will last two hours on one charge'), then that is content. However, if it is described by how it best meets a customer's needs ('smaller than its competitors at a mere 50cm and practical in hundreds of outdoor applications because of its astonishing two-hour charge'), it is copy. That many website developers are confused by the terms only emphasizes their lack of awareness of the importance of both.

Having determined the importance of a website's content, let's now consider the development of that content by looking at the two distinct elements: (1) textual, and (2) images and other features.

The development of textual content

A common mistake in many aspects of marketing is that organizations are organization-centric rather than customer-centric. This manifests itself in website content development in that too many organizations determine the content by asking 'what do we want to say?' rather than 'what does the market want to read?'

> too many organizations determine the content by asking 'what do we want to say?' rather than 'what does the market want to read?'

In content development there are four key issues that need to be addressed. In chronological order, they are: (1) The solution to what need is being sought when the target market chooses to visit your website, (2) What information does the target market expect to be told to help meet that need, (3) How does the target market expect that information to be presented, (4) How is this information best developed? Let's consider these in more detail.

1. The solution to what need is being sought when the target market chooses to visit your website. This is a natural progression from the objectives for the website. As discussed in Section 1.8, key objectives for a web presence are essential prior to any development taking place – and this is a clear example of how a website cannot possibly be successfully developed without those objectives being clear.

2. What information does the target market expect to be told to meet that need? Obviously, specific information will vary from organization to organization, product to product, brand to brand and site to site – and, most importantly, customer to customer. However, the developer must be clear what constitutes information in the perception of the website visitor. This would be another example of the value of a 'dream team' being responsible for the website. An IT or design specialist working alone could not develop this aspect of the web presence. In this case, not only should an accomplished writer be involved, but there could be input from both marketing and sales staff.

3. How does the target market expect that information to be presented? An overriding consideration in this regard is that the information is easily read, understood and interpreted by the target audience. As stated earlier in this chapter, dark characters on a light background are easiest to read – but this does not address the *style* in which it is presented. First of all, it needs to be appropriate. If you sell goods to pensioners, for example, your target audience will expect a certain tone in the text, perhaps formal and reserved, certainly respectful – though not straying into being condescending. A further consideration is the *character* of the site. Martineau (1958) proposed that a retail store has its own personality – this is also true of a website, or more accurately, it reflects the personality (or culture) of the brand, product or organization. Although its aesthetic presentation will also have an influence, it is the presentation of the textual content that will best determine that personality.

Similarly, the *language* used in the text needs to be appropriate – and I do not simply mean English, Spanish, Chinese and so on (see later for more on this particular subject). What I am referring to is that in the same way that 'yo dude, wassup?' won't work on a website selling long-stay holidays to retired people, neither will 'good morning, ladies and gentlemen' suit a site selling skateboard accessories to teenagers. Another consideration is the use of jargon associated with the product. For many B2C markets, the jargon and the *style* may be closely related – not least in the teenage market or anything that is sport, hobby or interest related. Essentially, you use jargon if the target reader will understand it – indeed, in some circumstances, to explain terminology might be perceived as insulting to the experienced reader. However, a caveat is that in some markets the *buyer* may not be the *consumer*. Parents, for example, looking to purchase a present for their teenage offspring may not understand the terminology used – and so will not make a purchase. In a B2B environment, jargon becomes even more important as it can be part of the description of the product or its application – I look at this in more detail in Section 5.3, where I consider the impact of the decision-making unit.

MINI CASE

The Gobbledygook Manifesto

Author of *The New Rules of Marketing* and all-round expert on web content David Meerman Scott was so fed up with self-serving nonsensical comments in PR releases and on websites that he established the Gobbledygook Manifesto to help rid the world of 'corporate' phrases like *scalable, groundbreaking, cutting-edge, situational fluency* and *paradigm shift*. (What do these terms mean when an organization uses them to describe itself?) In his book, Scott highlights that in their marketing, Disney talk about 'quality entertainment content', and points out that is simply 'movies and TV shows' to you and me. I liked this phrase from a software company's website: 'We're dedicated to developing applications that empower users to be more productive.' It sounds to me like they might make bigger shovels. This phrase is an example of a *value proposition* (VP) – a common practice offline that is often presented as a tag (or strap) line in ads and promotions for the organization, product or brand (Nike's 'Just Do It' is a classic example). Online, the VP can be a repetition of an offline version or – better – can be specific to the online offering which might highlight the advantage(s) of the web-based offering. Used effectively, a tagline – or *online* value proposition – at the top of a web page should tell the user that they are on the right page to meet their objectives as soon as the page starts to download.

To read the Gobbledygook Manifesto follow the link on the chapter's web page.

Source: Scott, 2007

Another key issue that is pertinent here – and another that is too often forgotten by website developers – is this: where is the customer on their buying cycle? As was discussed in Section 1.6, the buying cycle is a model that describes the buyer's behaviour from problem recognition to purchase. The problem for content developers is that if you design the site to meet the needs of someone who is at the 'information search' stage, then that content will do little to satisfy someone who has reached their 'purchase decision' stage – and, of course, vice versa. Unless you are certain that site visitors are always at a certain stage, the content must try to meet both groups' needs – and so is a compromise to all stages in the buying cycle.

A final consideration that is an accumulation of all the factors covered in this section is how the presentation of information impacts on the relationship that will (hopefully) develop between customer and organization. In an attempt to assess the relationships between users and websites, Maulana and Eckhardt (2007) asked respondents to imagine websites they visited regularly as people – with three primary relationship types: just friends, good acquaintances and soul mates. Of course, back in 2007 social media as we now know it was in its infancy – and it was impossible to *like*, or *friend*, an organization as customers can now do on the sites such as Facebook. However – and as we will see when studying social media marketing in depth in Chapter 9 – *liking* an organization, brand or product on Facebook is usually as a result of a relationship originally formed offline. With the exception of pure-play online businesses (of which there are actually very few when compared to the number of offline entities), few sites operate in isolation in developing a relationship with users. For example, my affinity to Nottingham Forest is with the football club, not any website that features the club. In behavioural terms, this is an issue of what need I am meeting when I visit a site – let's say to find out the latest news about a player's injuries – and how well the site meets that need. However, how that information is presented to me might help develop a relationship.

When discussing online behaviour in the first chapter I commented on how the development of a relationship with a website can vary depending on what need the website meets. To continue the example of my relationship with websites that contain news about my favourite football team, it could be that a number of sites meet that need – but I might develop a relationship with a particular site depending on the style of the writer(s) of that site. For example, the 'official' site is more formal – presenting the news as fact, whilst other sites use a more informal style – with the addition of personal opinion. Essentially, it is that personal opinion or attitude – the *personality* of the site – which will help develop my relationship – but put off others. In marketing we call this segmentation.

MINI CASE

The virtual voice of the terraces

An example of how a writer's personality can attract repeat visitors to a website that – essentially – carries the same content as a number of other sites is the nffcblog.com – an unofficial site covering the activities of Nottingham Forest Football Club. On the page pictured below – lauding a long-awaited success – the club's site matches this one for its celebratory mood, but the nottinghamforest. co.uk page was more formal in its presentation. Can you imagine an officially sanctioned report where the writer announces that he is 'off to the pub'? The writer catches the mood of the fans – for they too were all going to the pub to celebrate, as was I.

Figure 3.4 A page from nffcblog.com

The story and the screenshot image were those used in the first edition of this book. I also made the case in the first edition that 'passion can sell' when it comes to writing content.

It is rare, but sometimes amateur content can score over that which is professionally written. The primary reason for this is that the writer's enthusiasm for their subject comes through in the text. Naturally, proofreading to correct any major errors in spelling or grammar should be conducted – but poor syntax can sometimes add to the charm of the content. The drawback to this approach is that the site is dependent on the writer to continue as the voice of the site. In the case used as an example above, it is impossible to produce a newer screenshot as the author has decided to discontinue his blog. This is now more of an issue in social media marketing than it is in website development because it is with social media that customers are now more likely to interact – and so form a relationship.

How is this information best developed?

In this section it is impossible to divorce the issue of *how* (is the content best developed) from *who* is responsible for its development. Therefore, although we address the issue of website management in detail in Section 3.2, before we continue to consider the *actual* content, let's consider who writes it. As mentioned earlier, it often falls to junior members of staff to produce the textual content – and, with the greatest respect to office juniors around the world (who may one day become *great* content writers), they are the wrong people to whom you should give this crucial task. In the same way that without the necessary education and training not everyone can write a book, or a newspaper article, or advertising copy – why should they be able to write website copy? At the least a professional should be paid to *edit* the text. At the *very* least, someone who knows what they are doing should check the spelling and grammar. I find personal assistants and secretaries good for this task – indeed, if you *must* insist on 'DIY' content writing, such employees (who are used to writing things *properly*) will do a better job than most. Of course, this is an option of last resort – as an expert in the practice, Bob Bly (2003) says, you should write your own copy *only* if you: (1) are an excellent copywriter, (2) enjoy writing copy, and (3) have the time to write copy. In other words, he is saying to the vast majority of people: don't do it.

In order to get the style of the content right, the copywriter must get a feel for the product, service, organization or brand about which they are writing. Copywriting expert John Carlton (www.john-carlton.com) calls this process 'sales detective work'. *Clues* would come from such things as previous ads, brochures, reports, press releases, technical manuals and product specifications. As well as also interviewing staff from senior management through to shop-floor workers, online social media sites can provide an insight into how the organization, brand or product is perceived by the general public – that is, its customers. Perhaps most importantly – if it is possible – Carlton recommends that speaking directly to existing customers will help in presenting the content in their 'language'. I have to wonder how many organizations go to these lengths when developing online content. My own experience is that organizations dismiss this as unwarranted expense – and yet those same organizations will spend hundreds of thousands of pounds (or whatever) on a single promotion that will be seen by comparatively few people. At the lower end of the scale, firms are willing to pay for the technical aspects of the website, but not for the textual content. This is, of course, illogical – for an insight into the reasons for it I refer you to my comments in Section 2.4 with regard to who – in the organization – 'owns' the website.

> 66
> to get the style of the content right, the copywriter must have a feel for the product, service, organization or brand about which they are writing
> 99

GO ONLINE

For some excellent illustrations of how to inject some of the organization's culture into a website, follow the link on the chapter's web page for some examples of innovative '404' messages.

A common mistake made in website development – because it requires no further effort or cost – is to simply reproduce content that was written for other media. Even in the digital era's early days this was identified as a flawed practice. In 1997, Jacob Nielsen made the point that a movie is not made by filming a play – although the story and characters are the same, the two media require different presentation skills. Content written for offline publication has been developed to be read in a different context than it is on a website. On the web, any tangible aspects of the publication – you physically hold a book or newspaper, for example – do not exist. Where printed content is linear (the last word on page two leads to the first word on page three, for example), web content not only exists on a *bottomless* page, but it has links to multiple other pages – allowing users to read them in any order. Similarly, this page (that you are reading now) exists as part of a book – would this page be useful without the content and context of the rest of the book? Web pages, on the other hand, must be able to exist in their own right, meaning that the content must provide the context and purpose of every page so that a user arriving deep in a site from a search engine, for example, will comprehend what the page is about.

PRACTICAL INSIGHT

Don't sell a product – solve a problem

Although this phrase could be a motto for not just website content but all marketing messages, online it serves another purpose in that it is applicable to good on-site navigation. Links to content deeper in the web should be clear on how the visitor will benefit from clicking on the link – and eventually buying the product. For example, a company that specializes in lawn products might have the following as the links on its home page navigation bar:

- I need a greener lawn
- I need to get rid of moss
- I need to get rid of weeds

Or maybe:

- My kids are ruining my lawn
- My dog is ruining my lawn

Notice how all of these examples are written in the first person (I, my), which (a) makes the issue personal, and (b) gets away from 'we' and 'us' – the language of an organization that is talking about itself.

A further consideration in the 'don't take it from other literature' argument is the way in which we read the textual content of web pages. Simply put, we find it harder to read text on a computer screen than we do printed on paper, so we rarely read whole pages of textual content. Instead, we scan the text, picking out keywords, sentences and paragraphs of interest and skipping over other text that has no appeal to us. Obviously, therefore, the web writer must pander to this practice by writing content that uses descriptive headers (and sub-headers), short paragraphs, bullet points and content that gets to the point quickly. Finally, on the subject of writing specifically for the online context, web pages have hyperlinks that can be used to direct readers to associated or supportive information – and they certainly won't be present in any offline publication.

The question of whether the textual content of websites should be short (to retain attention) or long (to cover the subject in detail) is one that has experts in the field arguing. The answer, of course, comes in what the customer expects – but that is too simplistic. Consider the customer's position on the buying cycle issue discussed in the previous section, for example. In real life the competent salesperson knows within a minute or so if the customer is new to the product or is a repeat buyer – and so can adjust the length (as well as content) of their sales presentation accordingly. Online, we cannot make that decision about the customer and so have to gamble on long or short – or present a compromise that may or may not suit all customers. That content developers are left between a rock and a hard place with regard to the short versus long debate is confirmed by research into health information websites by Huntington *et al.* (2007). They found that although users found shorter content easy to read, they thought the information presented was too short to meet their needs. As with a number of aspects of web development covered in this chapter, publishers must accept that they can please some of the people all of the time and all of the people some of time, but not all of the people all of the time. This same adage can be carried into the consideration of the *actual* content.

In his influential book *The Long Tail*, Chris Anderson (2006) suggests examples of criteria people might use for their evaluation of content – whether it is high or low quality.

High quality	Low quality
Addresses my interests	Not for me
Well made	Badly made
Fresh	Stale
Substantive	Superficial
Compelling	Boring

As Anderson rightly points out, beauty is in the eye of the beholder – the assessment being not one of the tangible quality of the content (i.e. well researched and written, grammatically correct, to the point, etc.) but how *appropriate* it is to them (for some years, I have actively used the term 'beauty is in the eye of the customer'). For example, a website on the subject of horse riding would – for me – definitely be 'not for me' and 'boring'. A teenager who has recently taken up horse riding would obviously think the opposite for these two criteria, but they might also – being a newcomer to the subject – be happy enough with 'stale' and 'superficial' content. Similarly, if the content addressed her interest, would poor spelling and grammar ('badly made') be an issue?

However, someone who has been riding horses for many years would have yet another opinion of the same website content, potentially finding it ticks all of the boxes in the 'high quality' column while at the same time determining it was 'not for me' because she has seen it all before.

PRACTICAL INSIGHT

Testimonials work – if you treat them right

Sean D'Souza, ace content writer and founder of PsychoTactics (www.psychotactics. com), endorses testimonials but warns against 'the-company-was-wonderful-I-would-recommend-them-to-anyone' type tributes. He advises you to use the following structure:

1. Paint a detailed picture of the customer giving the testimonial.
2. Explain the situation before the customer made the purchase. Make sure to put in the reluctance factor.
3. Explain the result of having made the decision and how the customer has benefited.

Practised correctly, this method helps the potential customer visualize how they might benefit from the product or service on offer.

The *actual* content of the website will depend on the objectives of the site – but there are some elements that are essential to most (if not all) sites if they are to be successful. Although no list can be absolute – and inevitably, grey areas will exist – Figure 3.5 is a rough guide to what users might find (a) essential, or (b) useful or interesting. It is the latter which differentiates the online presence of the organization. Note that in a competitive environment, all competitors' websites are likely to contain the 'essential' elements. It is the 'useful or interesting' content that adds value and so differentiates the organization in the marketplace.

PRACTICAL INSIGHT

Stand out – or run with the crowd?

In markets where many companies offer what is essentially the same product you need to differentiate yourself – including online. So are you one of the crowd? Try these:

1. Take your website content – in particular the 'about us' section. Now substitute the name of your biggest competitor. If the content still makes sense, you are in with the crowd.

2. Take the content of your competitor's site and substitute your organization's name. If the resulting text is not accurate when your name is substituted then your competitors have made an effort to differentiate their online offering.

Note that earlier in the chapter I mentioned the use of hosting companies that provide templates for DIY websites – how do you think sites using such facilities would fare in this test?

You will note that I describe this as a *rough* guide – in all aspects of marketing there is rarely, if ever, a single right answer. The value-added list is a list of things that *might* be included on a website; it is not an absolute directory for every website.

Essential	*Value added*
• The organization's name. • What the organization does – its business or, if non-commercial, its objectives. • Where the organization is located (address). • Full contact details. Note that all of these should be on the site's front page. On an extensive site that is likely to have visitors arrive deep in the site from search engines, the first two should be on *every* page. • If the website facilitates online transactions or collects visitor data then legal notices are also a must (see Section 1.9).	• How the organization/brand/product/service will meet the needs of the reader. • Extensive product/service descriptions, including static or – where appropriate – moving images. • Articles about topical issues in your market or industry sector – these can be written in-house or commissioned. • An insight to the organization – over and above the standard 'about us'. Pen-pics of staff, perhaps. • Reviews of products – car accessory retailers commenting on the performance characteristics of cleaners and polishes, for example. • Endorsements or testimonials from satisfied customers. • A frequently asked questions (FAQ) section – this has the added advantage of reducing repetitive requests from the public. • A directory of useful books and websites – a brief review of each adds a personal touch. • A glossary of terms used in your industry – particularly if your business attracts customers who are new to the marketplace.

An addendum to the above could be a 'do not include' list, which would include:

• Self-serving statements – 'we are . . .', 'we do . . .' 'our . . .'. Customers want to know how the company can help meet their needs, not how wonderful the organization thinks it is.
• Errors in grammar and spelling.

Figure 3.5 Website content

The development of images and other features

After text, the next most common type of content is pictures. As mentioned in Section 3.2, pictures are often included on a web page for purely aesthetic purposes – they look nice. However, the organization's website is its online real estate (with the front page being prime property) and so taking up space with a picture that does nothing to meet the online needs of the target market is a waste of that valuable resource – with the aforementioned 'hero shot' being the worst offender.

PRACTICAL INSIGHT

When an image isn't a picture

For the newcomer to website design the term 'image' can be confusing. This comes about because – in terms of hypertext code – pictures are listed as images. This is fine if we are talking about, for example, the online reproduction of a photograph. Using any of the software commonly available, however, it is possible to create images that are not *pictures* – an obvious example would be a chart or graph. However, the main confusion comes about because text can be produced as an *image* – so if a website designer refers to an image, they do not necessarily mean a picture. Follow the link on the chapter's web page for a sample page of 'images'.

That said, of course, there will be sites where pictures are an essential element of helping to meet the customers' needs. An obvious example is the product picture, though this is by no means universal; hardly necessary were the pictures of drawing pins that I once saw on a stationery retailer's site! Similarly, pictures of the interior of a hotel room or the view from the room's balcony will always say more than textual descriptions. If a picture is an advantage, then care should be taken to show the product at its best. Multiple product images are relatively easy to offer as the pictures can be presented on the product pages as small images – dubbed 'thumbnails' – that enlarge when clicked on. Multiple pictures of a product should add to the buyer's understanding of, and attraction to, the product. In offline car sales, for example, the salesperson will walk the customer around the car and then invite them to sit in it – a series of photos should do the same job. For some items – clothes come to mind – pictures from various angles will help to give the (potential) customer a better idea of how the product looks. Indeed, some retailers have taken this a stage further by allowing users to 'build' a virtual model (an avatar) that matches their measurements – and then add clothes to the model to give an even better idea of how they will look on the buyer. More basic than the virtual model, but more advanced than the static picture, is the 360-degree picture – which allows the user to move around either a fixed 3D object (an ornament, perhaps) or a space (a hotel room, for example). Using a 'panoramic' facility available on many digital cameras can really make the viewer think they are there – ideal for tourist destinations or services.

As with text, there is the temptation to 'do it yourself' when it comes to images of products. This is particularly the case now that digital cameras seemingly make the process so easy. However – as with the textual content – professional input is best sought, particularly as the photos will be best captured with digital online reproduction in mind.

Another aspect of the web presence where pictures can work is in developing the supplier–customer relationship. Perhaps more relevant in B2B environments than B2C, a picture of the member of staff who deals with your required product might add a little *personality* to the web page, and perhaps encourages the customer to contact your organization rather than a competitor who has a similar product at a similar price.

GO ONLINE

Infographics

As their name suggests, infographics are a method of presenting information or data in pictorial form. They are more popular on websites than in printed media as a web page is endless, so the infographic can be scrolled down. For some examples of how infographics can be used, follow the link from the chapter's web page.

Of course, you can go one better and have *moving* pictures. Driven by the increased availability of broadband, that sites such as YouTube make it easy to embed videos on websites and that search engines return videos in response to searches, means that many sites now include videos as integral elements of their content. Like all content, however, it should be used only if it helps meet the objectives of the site, and so the user must perceive it as being useful – or they will never click on the 'play' button. For example, some products lend themselves to the 'instructional' video – such as those that have been used at in-store point-of-sale for many years, and so give added value to the website visitor.

RESEARCH SNAPSHOT

Why do videos work?

Behavioural psychologist Dr Susan Weinschenk – dubbed 'the Brain Lady' – suggests four very human reasons why we are drawn to video:

1. The fusiform facial area makes us pay attention to faces.
2. Voice conveys rich information.

3. Emotions are contagious.
4. Movement grabs attention.

Dr Weinschenk (literally) talks the talk to support her theory by presenting this concept in an online video. To watch it, follow the link from the chapter's web page.

There are a number of other ways in which video can be used on a commercial website, other than as content as part of a YouTube-type business model. These might include any of the following:

- An introduction to the organization – available as a link from the home page, such a video can give personality or character to the organization.
- Testimonials – as with the introduction, having a 'real' person talk about how your product solved their problem gives a more human interpretation than the printed word.
- Product demonstration – how the product can be used – an armchair with multiple adjustments for back and legs, for example.
- Service demonstration – a commentated visual 'walk-round' of a hotel, perhaps.
- Instructional – fitting, assembly or maintenance instructions can be complex when presented on paper, and easily lost. The online video is not only always available, but customers can see how something is done at the same time as hearing the instructions.
- More interesting for some applications might be a 'day in the life'-type story, where an employee is followed as part of a recruitment strategy. Theatres could record snippets of plays and cut them into comments from actors or backstage workers. Similarly, a church could video sermons and intersperse them with commentary from officials and flock.

While quality will always be an issue – as with images – modern technology has made the playing field a little more level for small businesses when it comes to developing videos to be shown online. Pre-digital video creation was expensive, and normally handled by media agencies. Now, however, compelling videos are within reach of all businesses – not just those with media budgets big enough to afford a professional film crew.

RESEARCH SNAPSHOT

The top image-related issues as far as online shoppers are concerned are: quality of the image (80%), alternative views of the selected item (64%), being able to see products in different colours (61%) and professionally produced videos (57%), although video is very important to half of the shoppers.

Source: e-tailing group and Invodo, 2013

Note that no matter which of the above you use, all videos should be:

- As short as is feasible to get the message across – any more than a few minutes and you should condense the message.
- Of *professional* quality – poor video quality will be perceived as representing an organization that has little emphasis on quality. Although the 'amateur' shaky, hand-held production can have a certain appeal, effective examples are extremely limited. Readers might be surprised to realize just how many of those 'amateur' videos are in fact very professionally produced to look that way.
- Of benefit to the user – grandiose rhetoric from the CEO or MD extolling the virtues of the organization or any aspect of it are for the presenter, not the customer.
- Keyword tagged according to their content – more and more search engines are presenting videos in response to searches.

Spoken content is a further option that has become more viable due to the popularity of both MP3 players and MP3-player facilities on smartphones. This means that verbal content from a website can be easily downloaded and replayed at a time that is more convenient to the listener. Dubbed the podcast as the iPod brand dominates the MP3 arena, such digital recordings can also be used in more creative ways than simply being a spoken version of a written article. A spoken explanation of assembly instructions for flat-pack furniture, for example. Or what about a spoken recipe? In this case, the listener/cook can easily pause or replay sections where necessary.

PRACTICAL INSIGHT

Idle symbols?

I have long cautioned against the use of icons in place of text. This is not simply a personal opinion. Back in 1985, after finding that pretty but unlabelled icons confused customers, the Apple Computer Human Interface Group is said to have adopted the motto *a word is worth a thousand pictures*. After that, a descriptive word or phrase was added beneath all Macintosh icons.

For bricks-and-mortar traders, interactive maps – such as those from Google – can make finding the store easier than just directions or a *static* map. Similarly, a hotel can use such maps to emphasize how good a location it is in. The caveat remains, however, interactive maps should be used to satisfy the needs of the customer, not 'jazz up' a website whose textual content is poor.

Other interactive website content includes:

- Widgets – pieces of scripting code that facilitate the delivery of live content from a third-party site without the website owner constantly having to update their

Figure 3.6 Examples of commonly used widgets

site. Applications include such things as calendars, clocks, weather forecasts and calculators.

• Although many organizations have moved them away from their websites to social media platforms, online forums allow customers to ask questions about products and services. Although viewed with suspicion by some users – they are often perceived as not being independent of the organization hosting the forum – some companies have successfully used forums as an effective form of after-sales service that is provided by the consumers themselves, so reducing costs in that department.

DECISION TIME

As website development practitioner and writer Gerry McGovern (2007) says, 'there are three things a great website must be: useful, useful and useful'. Note that McGovern doesn't use terms such as 'entertaining' or 'a showcase for the designer's skills' or 'at the cutting edge of Internet technology'. If these things help meet the needs of the target market, fine. But for the majority of visitors that need is information – presented in a way they find easy to access and understand.

The content of a website is wholly dependent on the objectives the organization has for that site. Essentially – the four key decisions to be made are:

1. The solution to what need is being sought when the target market chooses to visit your website. Why are people coming to your site? Remember, the web is a pull medium – they have chosen to go to your site – what is it they are going there for?

2. What information does the target market expect to be told to help meet that need? Visitors are on your site to solve a problem – what is it that they think will help them?

3. How does the target market expect that information to be presented? What language – over and above that of nationality – will the visitor want the information in? Put simply, how will they best understand and accept what you have to say?

4. How is this information best developed? Should the content be purely text – or can pictures help meet the customers' needs? Or are video clips or podcasts a better solution? And finally – who is responsible for its development?

YOU DECIDE

Advise Lindsey Naegle (case study 12) on what type of website content will best satisfy the needs of those people who visit the site seeking the service she has to offer.

Alternatively, conduct the same exercise for your organization or that of your employer.

3.6 THE GLOBAL WEB PRESENCE

When businesses are considering moving into new countries, the primary strategic decision is whether to standardize or localize. This means the organization must decide on whether the marketing mix it uses domestically will be successful globally, or will the mix need to be adapted to suit various local markets? For the online marketer there is a similar decision to be made with regard to the web presence for each country, except that rather than there being two options there is a third option that falls between them. The *standardize* approach is to have one website of a domestic organization that caters for a global audience – normally in English, though verbatim translation of some or all pages into other languages may be included. The *localize* approach is to develop different websites for each country in which the firm aims to trade. Using the domain names of the local countries (and being hosted in those countries), the content and presentation of these sites is adapted to address local culture and issues – though there may be some translation from the domestic site.

The approach that falls between the two is the most popular option for those firms that are – or want to become – worldwide brands. Common amongst American brands, this is where the global organization develops *local* websites for each country in which it has a physical presence, but in this case each web presence would have a standardized brand image and the usage of common logos in uniform colours and layouts – but with content that is localized where applicable.

PRACTICAL INSIGHT

Personalize your site to where your customers are

IP geolocation – the use of a computer's Internet Protocol address to determine where in the world that computer is – can be used to change the content of your site to suit each particular visitor. For example:

- Product localization – promotions on a clothing retailer's site could differ depending on whether the user was in a hot or cold climate.
- Show prices in the local currency.
- Offer localization – an airline could feature discount flights from the user's nearest airport.
- Inform customers where their nearest offline store is and if the product they are looking at is in stock there.
- Deliver an optimized site depending on the device being used (e.g. PC or smartphone).
- Adjust delivery cost according to location.
- Modify checkout facility to suit location (e.g. state/province/county).

Considerations for any global website development include:

- Which version of 'English' is to be used – UK or US? In truth, it matters little whether 'colour' is spelled with or without a 'u' – so long as there is consistency on all sites (this is of course, problematic for the US company's UK website.)
- If any of the content is translated, consideration should be given to meta-data for search engine optimization – Google, for example, searches in over 100 languages or dialects.
- The relative length of languages. Multilingual web designers know that German can take up around 30 per cent more space than English, while Chinese characters are considerably more compact. This is a particular issue when designing mobile-optimized sites, where space is at a premium.
- Have translations checked by a native speaker of the translated-to language, as literal translations rarely work – with wording or phrases being changed to suit local nuances. 'Going the extra mile for customers', for example, might suggest to some that the organization's staff do more walking than most.
- Develop a clear web design template that can be easily used for all country sites, taking into consideration all issues that might arise in the various countries being targeted. For example, a site using leading-edge technology might be fine in the US, where broadband is prevalent, but users in other countries might be dependent on slower methods of downloading the site.

PRACTICAL INSIGHT

Size matters

If the site's content is likely to be printed – consider where the user is. In the USA the printer default setting will be for 'letter' size, whereas the rest of the world favours A4.

- If all country-specific sites are available from the 'home' site, consider the links. The link to the German site, for example, should say 'Deutsch', not 'German'. Flags are an option, but beware of using the UK's Union Flag for English-language sites – not all English speakers are from the UK.

- Ensure country-specific cultures and practices are taken into account. Not all countries follow the UK and US practice of a person's last name being their family name, for example – which may be an issue for online form-filling.

- Beware of countries where many languages are spoken or cultures are represented – Malaysia would be an example of such a country.

- Studies also suggest that the way in which audiences look at a website is influenced by their cultural background. Research by the Korean Advanced Institute of Science and Technology (Dong and Lee, 2008) found that Chinese and Korean users tend to register more 'areas of interest' in a short time period, and are less likely to use a sequential reading pattern, than American viewers.

- Be aware of units of measurement – metric or imperial units, for example – if in doubt, offer both. Dates can be problematic – 4/5/15, for example, could refer to days in the first week of April or May depending where in the world you are. Similarly, a conversion facility should be included on the page if prices are listed only in the 'home' currency.

- Colours also need to be considered – red meaning stop, or danger, for example, is not universal. Investors studying Chinese stock market reports might be surprised to find red is used to symbolize 'up' and green 'down' – the opposite of the Western norm.

- Numbers can be tricky – in English the number thirteen has negative connotations and so is rarely used but in Mandarin the same applies to the number four.

- The culture of the market. Arab culture, for example, not only eschews credit card payment in favour of cash, but they favour face-to-face communication. Furthermore, the context of the communication process is more important than the content (Yasin and Yavas, 2007). Thus, oral communication is more highly valued than written – not a good omen for email marketing.

DECISION TIME

The first consideration for the 'global' web presence is whether or not there will be sufficient customers to merit the expenditure. For the pure-online UK company, for example, that does 90 per cent of its business in this country, it is not really worthwhile optimizing its site for the dozen or more countries from which it might take orders – the assumption would be that overseas website visitors would be able to read English (or even *be* English). Similarly, the Greek refrigeration engineering company that carries out work only in the Athens' city boundaries needs one site – in Greek. However, if that firm wants to extend its trade services into Albania or any of the former Yugoslavian republics, then sites in the local languages will be necessary.

If a global presence is required, the key decision is whether to standardize or localize. Can a straightforward reproduction of the domestic site with the content translated into various languages meet the needs of a worldwide public? Or would each market expect to find a website that is localized to their region? And if that is the case, how do you ensure it still presents a global brand presence despite the localization?

Having decided on the type of website globalization you are going to use, a further decision is on whether each country's site will be developed locally or centrally. Although having each country be responsible for its website offers the advantages of local knowledge, there can be problems. Subsidiaries of a multinational company in each country may differ in organizational size and human resources and so be unable to meet the standards required by the parent company. It is for this reason that many global organizations prefer to move 'local' developers to a single location – normally the firm's 'home' country – so that uniformity and quality control are more easily maintained.

YOU DECIDE

Advise the board of Matthew Humberstone Foundation Hospital (case study 6) on whether or not they should localize their global presence, and if so, how?

Alternatively, conduct the same exercise for your organization or that of your employer.

CHAPTER EXERCISE

Giving justifications for all your decisions, advise Philip Ball and his staff at the Cleethorpes Visitors Association (case study 4) on all aspects of digital marketing covered in the chapter. This includes taking a look at the 'dummy' website that can be found by following the link from the chapter's web page.

Alternatively, conduct the same exercise for your own organization or that of your employer.

CHAPTER QUESTIONS

Follow the link from the chapter's web page to a series of multiple-choice, exam-type questions that will test your knowledge and understanding of the various elements of the chapter.

REFERENCES

Anderson, C. (2006) *The Long Tail*. Hyperion Books.

Barnes, S.J. and Vidgen, R.T. (2002) An integrative approach to the assessment of e-commerce quality. *Journal of Electronic Commerce Research*. Volume 3, number 3, pp. 114–127.

Bly, B. (2003) Should you write your own copy? *Bob Bly's Direct Response Newsletter*, September.

Bowen, D. (2009) Forensic pathways: sowing confusion. Available at www.bowencraggs.com/best-practice/tips/942.

Cox, J. and Dale, B.G. (2001) Service quality and e-commerce: an exploratory analysis. *Managing Service Quality*. Volume 11, number 2, pp. 121–131.

Dadzie, K.Q., Chelariu, C. and Winston, E. (2005) Customer service in the Internet enabled logistics supply chain: website design antecedents and loyalty effects. *Journal of Business Logistics*. Volume 26, number 1, pp. 53–78.

Dong, Y. and Lee, K.P. (2008). A cross-cultural comparative study of users' perceptions of a webpage: with a focus on the cognitive styles of Chinese, Koreans and Americans. *International Journal of Design*. Volume 2, number 2, pp. 19–30.

e-tailing group and Invodo (2013) How consumers shop with video. Available at www.e-tailing.com/content/wp-content/uploads/2013/03/EtailingGroup_Whitepaper_3.pdf.

Fearn, Hannah (2010) Deciphering the code. *Times Higher Education*. Available at www.timeshighereducation.co.uk/story.asp?storycode=413004.

Fogg, B.J. (1999) What variables affect website credibility. Presentation at the CSLI IAP Conference, November.

Gay, R., Charlesworth, A. and Esen, R. (2007). *Online Marketing: A Customer-Led Approach*. Oxford University Press.

Gefen, D. and Straub, D.W. (2004) E-commerce: the role of familiarity and trust. *International Journal of Management Service*. Volume 28, pp. 725–737.

Glazer, R. (1991) Marketing in an information-intensive environment: strategic implications of knowledge as an asset. *Journal of Marketing*. Volume 55, pp. 1–19.

Hotchkiss, G. (2010) Google defines 'you' on the fly. Available at www.mediapost.com/publications/article/138900.

Huang, A.S. and Christopher, D. (2003) Planning an effective Internet retail store, *Marketing Intelligence and Planning*. Volume 21, number 4, pp. 230–238.

Huntington, P., Nicholas, D., Jamali, H.R. and Russell, C. (2007) Health information for the consumer: NHS vs the BBC. *Aslib Proceedings*, New Information.

Jansen, B.J., Booth, D.L. and Spink, A. (2008) Determining the informational, navigational, and transactional intent of web queries. *Information Processing and Management*. Volume 44, number 3, pp. 1251–1266.

Kim, J., Suh, E. and Hwang, H. (2003) A model for evaluating the effectiveness of CRM using the balanced scorecard. *Journal of Interactive Marketing*. Volume 17, number 2, pp. 5–19.

Krugg, S. (2000) *Don't Make Me Think*. New Riders.

Levine, R., Locke, C., Searls, D. and Weinberger, D. (1999) *The Cluetrain Manifesto: The End of Business as Usual*. Basic Books.

Liu, C. and Arnett, K. (2000) Exploring the factors associated with website success in the context of electronic commerce. *Information and Management*. Volume 38, number 1, pp. 23–33.

Loizides, L. (2003) Lesson in the art of Flash. INT Media Group. Available at www.clickz.com/mkt/capital/print.php/2240791.

Long, B.S. (2002) How to avoid common web mistakes. *Public Relations Tactics* (online journal). Volume 9, number 11.

Martineau, P. (1958) The personality of the retail store. *Harvard Business Review*. Volume 36, pp. 47–55.

Maulana, A.E. and Eckhardt, G.M. (2007) Just friends, good acquaintances or soul mates? An exploration of website connectedness. *Qualitative Market Research: An International Journal*. Volume 10, number 3, pp. 227–242.

McCloskey, M. *et al.* (2013) *Teenagers (Ages 13–17) on the Web* (2nd edn). Nielsen Norman Group.

McGovern, G. (2002) Demystifying content management. Available on clickz.com.

McGovern, G. (2007) *New Thinking*. Newsletter, July.

McGovern, G. (2008) Web professional: are you ready to serve? Available at giraffeforum.com/wordpress/2008/01/27/web-professional-are-you-ready-to-serve/.

McGovern, G. (2009a) The drawbacks of talk aloud usability testing. Available at giraffeforum.com/wordpress/2010/12/05/the-drawbacks-of-talk-aloud-usability-testing.

McGovern, G. (2009b) How to create clear web navigation menus. Available at giraffeforum.com/wordpress/2009/11/15/how-to-create-clear-web-navigation-menus/.

McGovern, G. (2009c) What the web is really for. Available at giraffeforum.com/wordpress/2009/01/25/what-the-web-is-really-good-for/.

McGovern, G. (2010) *The Stranger's Long Neck*. A. & C. Black.

Mowen, J.C. (1987) *Consumer Behaviour*. Macmillan.

Nielsen, J. (2000) *Designing Web Usability*. New Riders.

Nielsen, J. (2003) Usability 101: introduction to usability. Available at www.useit.com/alertbox/20030825.HTML.

Nielsen Norman Group (2010) Usability of websites for children: design guidelines for targeting users aged 3–12 years. Available on nngroup.com.

Nielsen Norman Group (2013) Senior citizens (ages 65 and older) on the web. Available at www.nngroup.com/articles/usability-for-senior-citizens.

Pew Research Center's Internet and American Life Project (2012) Digital differences. Available on pewinternet.org.

Poirier, P. (2003) Can your site stop your telephone from ringing? Available on marketingprofs.com.

Schlosser, A.E., White, T.B. and Lloyd, S.M. (2006) Converting website visitors into buyers: how website investment increases consumer trusting beliefs and online purchase intention. *Journal of Marketing*. Volume 70, number 2, pp. 133–148.

Scott, D.M. (2007) *The New Rules of Marketing and PR*. Wiley.

Tam, P. (2010) I'm a digital marketing pro, I don't work in IT. Available at www.clickz.asia/916/im-a-digital-marketing-pro-i-dont-work-in-it.

Tobin, R (2008) Barriers on a website. Available on enquiroresearch.com.

Van Riel, A.C.R., Liljander, V. and Jurriens, P. (2001) Exploring consumer evaluations of e-services: a portal site. *International Journal of Service Management*. Volume 12, number 4, pp. 359–377.

Wilson, R.F. (2003) 12 website design decisions your business or organisation will need to make correctly. *Web Marketing Today*, 9 July. Available on wilsonweb.com.

Yang, Z., Cai, S., Zhou, Z. and Zhou, N. (2004) Development and validation of an instrument to measure user perceived service quality of information presenting web portals. *Information and Management*. Volume 42, number 4, pp. 575–589.

Yasin, M.M. and Yavas, U. (2007) An analysis of e-business practices in the Arab culture. *Cross-Cultural Management: An International Journal*. Volume 14, number 1, pp. 68–73.

Yoo, B. and Donthu, N. (2001) Developing a scale to measure the perceived service quality of Internet shopping sites (sitequal). *Quarterly Journal of Electronic Commerce*. Volume 2, number 1, pp. 31–47.

Chapter **4**

The B2C online presence

> *I am the world's worst salesman – therefore, I must make it easy for people to buy.*
> *Frank W. Woolworth*

Chapter at a glance

4.1 Introduction
4.2 Multi-channel retailing
4.3 The retail website
4.4 Checkout process
4.5 Fulfilment
4.6 e-marketplaces and comparison shopping sites
4.7 Third-party retail websites

4.1 INTRODUCTION

This chapter concentrates on selling goods to the end consumer via a website – essentially, retailing. It is, however, impossible to divorce the subject of this chapter from that of others throughout the book – the most obvious being the previous chapter that looks at website development. It is also the case that some aspects of this chapter are also relevant in the next, where sales might be made online but in a B2B context.

RESEARCH SNAPSHOT

Online shopping: a steep rise – then stability

In 1999 fewer than 15 per cent of web users shopped online – but in 2000 this had rocketed up to 85 per cent. However, the first thirteen years of the new century have seen no significant increase in that figure, with some statistics even suggesting it has dropped slightly. Note, however, that in some countries the figures differ. In South Korea, for example, 99 per cent of web users have shopped online – but the figure plummets to 38 per cent in China. However, those people who do shop online are spending far more money in the digital environment.

Sources: Forrester Research (forrester.com); the Nielsen Company (nielsen.com); eConsultancy (econsultancy.com); US Commerce Department (commerce.gov)

Online retailers can be divided into two main categories:

- Pure-play – where the organization trades online only. In this case, the online sale is the be all and end all of the site's objectives. The site's design and content must reflect this.
- Multi-channel (so-called 'bricks and clicks') – where the firm sells goods both offline (bricks) and online (clicks). Although online sales are important in this instance – the website also acts as a sales lead generator for the bricks element of the business. So popular has multi-channel retailing become in recent years that the concept is now more popularly recognized by the buyer-centric description of 'click-and-collect', which is covered in the next section.

A third group is offline retailers who have a web presence but do not *sell* online. In essence, such traders are using their web presence for brand development, lead generation or customer service (see Section 1.8), and so the web content is developed accordingly – in this chapter I concentrate on those sites that facilitate online B2C transactions.

Before considering the role of the Internet in any retail strategy, let's consider its impact so far. Throughout this book I have attempted to present facts and figures that are both relevant and accurate. However, when considering what percentage of retail sales are made online, the data is complex or biased, resulting in it being confusing – or both of these. The complexity comes from different bodies' interpretations of what 'retail' is within their research. For example, some include services such as the online purchase of insurance or booking of holidays or flights, whilst others include only tangible products. This has an obvious impact in that just one family trip booked online would be the equivalent of dozens, if not hundreds, of low-cost items purchased online (it is worth noting that Germany-based travel giant TUI reported that 40 per cent of its UK customers booked online for summer 2013, with the Nordic countries having an even higher figure of 67 per cent). Also, do downloads of music and games count as online retail sales – and what about Internet gambling? Other statistics, such as those from the UK's Office for National Statistics (ONS), include 'online' with other 'non-store' retail figures – but this does not include any services. The problem itself is compounded by researchers not always publishing their own definition of what they have counted as 'retail'.

Bias comes in the form of research published by organizations that are in some way involved in – or would gain from – online retailing, and so may have a natural inclination to be positive about any numbers involved. It is also worth mentioning that even in countries where the Internet plays a significant role, usage is not 100 per cent – indeed, in the USA that figure has stalled at just over 70 per cent of the population. Combine this with those web users who do not shop online and there may well be around a third of the population who will never shop online. Although it is likely that this 30 per cent represent the poorer segment of society and so their retail

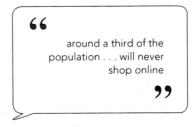

" around a third of the population . . . will never shop online "

spending will be low for many classifications of product – their mere existence will prevent online sales achieving a majority of overall retail sales.

Although online sales have increased exponentially since the birth of the web – and no matter how much pro-web evangelists might extol its virtues – online sales still represent only a relatively small percentage of all retail sales – so whilst online B2C sales will represent a significant sum of business for a relatively few retailers, it will always be a minority of overall retail sales. Indeed, this could well be used to support the argument that the Internet's main benefit in B2C trading is as a marketing platform used to influence offline consumer purchases, rather than an additional channel of distribution.

GO ONLINE

Online sales stats update

Follow the link on the chapter's web page to read the author's tracking of this subject.

In the mid-1990s, the low cost of entry into (theoretically) global markets saw a wave of new online retailers. At that time most of the major offline – 'bricks-and-mortar' – retailers shied away from the web, many thinking it was simply a fad and others concerned that they could not operate both physically and electronically without one cannibalizing the other (Gay *et al.*, 2007). Those that did go online did so with a half-hearted effort that was neither e-tail nor e-marketing strategy. Although the situation is changing fast, it is still the case that a significant number of retailers either do not sell online at all, or offer only a limited range. This is not to say that offline retailers do not use the web – they do, but as part of their strategic marketing effort – branding and after-sales service being the most common online objectives.

Whatever their online objectives, the offline retailers have now entered the online environment with a vengeance – and so present competition to those entrepreneurial dot-com retailers who were first to sell to consumers online. Despite this, there is still a tendency for retailers to treat online as the poor relation. However, they neglect the standard of their web presence at their peril – the contemporary shopper sees the website as part of the retailer's brand and may reconsider shopping at an organization's physical outlets if they have a poor online experience.

PRACTICAL INSIGHT

Customer, consumer – or both?

Fundamental to marketing – and equally essential online – is the customer/consumer issue. Basically, the customer pays for the product and the consumer . . . well, consumes it. This can, of course, be the same person who buys a chocolate bar and then eats it. However, they might have bought the chocolate as a gift for their daughter – in which case the child is the consumer. In marketing this is important as the marketing message might be targeted at the consumer or customer – babies' nappies are an obvious example.

Online, the customer/consumer targeting issue is important in that it determines the nature of the content of the website – and its presentation.

If established offline retailers were slow to react to the digital age, there was one group who were swift to recognize the opportunity presented by the Internet. I have classified this group as 'micro retailers', although as some sell in specialist markets, they could just as easily be called 'niche operators'. Such retailers may or may not have a physical retail presence, but are smaller businesses than both the pure-play and multi-channel companies described above. It is worthwhile considering the role that the Internet has played in the development of micro sellers and niche markets in the B2C environment. It has always been the case that a segment of small retailers has operated in specialist markets that are too small (or specialized) for mainstream retailers to contemplate. Although they might attract customers who are willing to travel long distances, such buyers are few, with the majority of customers coming from the locale of the shop. By definition, this means that turnover is low – but still sufficient for small businesses to make a reasonable living. This return on limited turnover stems from two basic business principles: (1) low costs – such shops are rarely in premium-rent malls or high streets, and (2) high selling prices – anyone who is willing to search hard for a particular product will not expect to purchase it at discount prices.

The niche outlet is normally proprietor-run, and the owner is likely to be an expert in the product being sold – often because the product area relates to their profession or long-standing hobby. Fishing tackle, equestrian supplies, model-making kits, tapestry materials or musical instruments would be typical examples of such – though also common are outlets dedicated to specialist elements of popular markets. An example of this might be the bathroom fittings supplier who stocks more unusual products than can be found in national-chain DIY superstores.

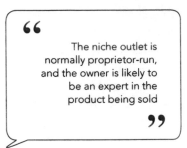

> " The niche outlet is normally proprietor-run, and the owner is likely to be an expert in the product being sold "

GO ONLINE

The largely untapped online shopping market in China is a great temptation for Western retailers and brands – but how easy is it to set up shop in China? Follow the link on the chapter's web page for an excellent article on the subject. Note that it was written at the end of 2012 and research with my own Chinese students suggests it is accurate – but the main reason I have included it here is for you to judge how accurate the points raised are now.

For existing *bricks-and-mortar* niche operators, the introduction of the Internet provided an obvious additional outlet for their products, but in the early days of the commercial web most saw it as an *add-on* to the offline store rather than being an essential element of an integrated retailing strategy. It did not take too long, however, for the more forward-thinking traders to realize that niche products featured highly in search queries on related subjects and so online sales could easily eclipse those made in the physical shop. The next logical stage was for people who were experts in a topic to open online-only (pure-play) outlets. For many of these individuals, selling goods related to their particular interest was a long-held dream, but the cost – and financial risks – of opening a physical store meant that it had remained a dream. However, websites could be set up for very little, minimal stock holding is required for the e-shop and – equally importantly – you do not need to be on the retail premises for all the hours the shop is open. This last point is the reason for it to be common for many small, niche e-shops to be run part time, with the owner being either (1) in full-time employment (so guaranteeing income), or (2) a parent who fits in the online business with childcare responsibilities. So common is this model in the USA that the terms 'mom and pop operation' and 'stay-at-home moms' are both closely linked with part-time online trading. The concept is not limited to the US, however. In 2013 the insurer Direct Line for Business presented research that suggested that around eight million people in the UK run online retail businesses from homes – either buying or making their own goods for sale online.

A further issue that played a vital role in the spread of the online niche retailer was the advances in software that made the provision of online sales facilities both easy and relatively inexpensive. However, e-commerce has developed in such a way that you do not even have to develop your own website. A number of Internet brand names offer shop facilities within their web presence – charging either a fixed or a commission-based fee. Such sites not only offer the niche seller a platform for online sales and guaranteed virtual footfall, but also lend their brand value, promotional activities and – importantly – search engine rankings to the small business. A further attraction is that the host brand will facilitate online payment (on eBay, it is through PayPal), meaning that sellers need not set up their own credit-card account. The use of such third-party websites is covered in more detail later in this chapter.

MINI CASE

The long tail of online business

Closely associated with the Internet – not least because it was promoted virally online – Chris Anderson's Long Tail model (Anderson, 2006) is based around the concept of niche marketing. Anderson, using the music industry as an example, suggests that whilst the main retailers (off- and online) concentrate on selling only the top twenty selling CDs at low prices, there is a long tail of less popular CDs which cannot match sales figures of the top sellers, but can still sell in numbers that are sufficient to generate profits for niche sellers. The Internet connection is that the web not only helps niche sellers reach potential customers, but social media-type recommendations ('if you enjoy this, you might like this . . .') can make buyers aware of artists they have not previously considered – or even heard of.

Although focused on the Long Tail model, Anderson's book provides an excellent background to the development of B2C e-commerce. For my review of the book, follow the link on the chapter's web page.

4.2 MULTI-CHANNEL RETAILING

Although the issue was introduced in Section 1.6, where we looked at online buying behaviour, it is worth highlighting the options open to the contemporary shopper. Only fifteen years ago, for many products, the consumer was limited to visiting a single retail outlet, considering the options available there, and making a purchase. Now, however, not only can shoppers use the web to research products and suppliers, they have a choice of purchasing off- or online as well as having the product delivered or collecting it from a local store. The latter has become known as 'click-and-collect' – and the concept is now the cornerstone of multi-channel retailing – which, in turn, has become *the* business strategy for many retail brands.

Defining multi-channel retailing, one of the leading publications on the subject says: 'the cross-channel ideal envisages the customer being able to walk through the store door after a few hours of surfing the web to purchase or pick up the perfect product, with the expectation that the local store should be aware of their order and able to fully support them' (*Internet Retailing*, 2008). Although research in the early days of this concept suggested that shoppers use the method to save shipping expenses or because it is convenient, for *some* buyers this is now *the* way of shopping. In other words, click-and-collect *is* shopping, and any retailer who is not participating takes the chance of not being viewed by some customers as a *proper* retailer. Could it be that by the time the third edition of this book is published I might have to explain to a new generation of shoppers that buying online and collecting offline has not always been the norm?

> " click-and-collect is shopping "

RESEARCH SNAPSHOT

Click-and-collect

Research from Graham Charlton of econsultancy (2013) found that 40 per cent of shoppers used 'reserve and collect' over Christmas 2012. An obvious advantage to multi-outlet retailers over pure-play and smaller competitors, even this high take-up is less than the same organization's previous research which suggested that taking the year as a whole, the figure is closer to 60 per cent.

That shoppers do not use such a facility for all purchases is reflected in figures from multi-channel retailer Argos, who revealed that sales via their online 'check & reserve' service represented just 29 per cent of total sales in early 2012.

By contrast, auto parts and cycle retailer Halfords say that fully 86 per cent of all its online sales are for in-store collection.

Sources: econsultancy.com; argos.co.uk; halfords.com

Although it was towards the end of the century's first decade that click-and-collect grew in popularity, its potential had been recognized by some retailers over ten years earlier. However, these were mainly large department stores that catered for a local market for whom visiting the physical store was not a problem. What these shops discovered was something that has become the foundation for many traditional retail brands' acceptance and promotion of click-and-collect – and that is when customers visit the shop to collect their ordered goods they are very likely to make other purchases while they are there. In other words, the sale of one – or some – items online is actually a form of associated or up-selling. Or is it simply an inducement for the customer to visit the shop in the same way as posters in the window or ads in a newspaper? Only time will tell.

PRACTICAL INSIGHT

To app or not to app

A problem facing the contemporary e-tailer is whether to develop a smart phone app, a 'mobile' website or simply have a website that is equally usable no matter what device is used to access it. Apps are certainly trendy – but they restrict the number of customers you can appeal to in that the app must be downloaded to individual devices. Mobile websites are developed specifically to not only download on the smaller screens, but have small touch screen usability built in. Websites that are equally usable on all types of device are by necessity rather simple in their design, and so cannot include some of the *tricks* so loved by designers – but do offer a single cost (in development and maintenance) rather than having additional costs for each application. At the time of writing the jury is out on what is best – with experts and practitioners equally split. However, as is always the case, it will be the customer needs that will make the final call.

DECISION TIME

The decision on multi-channel retailing needs to be considered from two points of view – the offline retailer going online and the online retailer developing a 'bricks-and-mortar' presence. Let's consider the latter first.

> we now have the situation where major online-only retailers are having to consider the possibility of opening physical stores

In many cases – particularly for the niche retailer – the online presence is actually a development of an offline business, with the online fulfilment being handled from the bricks-and-mortar store – something that can add to the credibility of the e-commerce website. For others, the online business is only profitable because there are not the costs (both fixed and variable) associated with running a physical outlet, with many eBay-type retailers running their operation as a part-time venture. Furthermore, the goods are normally dispatched outside of the immediate area, so having a single outlet would not increase sales to a wider demographic – and multiple stores is simply not a consideration. However, if the business is full time, and premises are rented with stock held, it does make sense to open to the public. In a complete reversal of the early days of the web, we now have the situation where major online-only retailers are having to consider the possibility of opening physical stores to meet the wants of customers who expect to be able to collect goods they have purchased online.

More significant is the first issue raised – that of bricks-and-mortar stores moving online. For many retailers the potential of channel conflict was the reason for their being slow to join the online revolution. This was a situation I always found puzzling – and yet many senior executives thought an online presence would take sales away from their physical stores. In my opinion, a sale was a sale, no matter where it was made. It is rather ironic, therefore, that some of those same laggards are now the leaders of the click-and-collect approach.

PRACTICAL INSIGHT

Online while in-store

Some retailers bring multi-channel facilities directly into shops by allowing consumers to place online orders on point-of-sale terminals or web-enabled mobile devices for employees to use. Others have sections of the premises dedicated to space for Internet-enabled kiosks where customers access the shop's website, which may well feature more products than are available in the physical store.

Marks and Spencer have taken this concept a stage further at their store in Cheshire Oaks, where they have introduced high-definition TV screens to showcase products, staff equipped with iPads, virtual counters – such as the virtual make-up counter – widespread use of QR codes and free wi-fi throughout the store. Furthermore, their Amsterdam concept store included what M&S introduced as the world's first *virtual rail*, which was composed of three stacked forty-six-inch screens and three physical rails, each holding fifty items of clothing.

Selling intangible service lends itself even more to the virtual showroom. The year 2013 saw TUI Travel launch its next generation of high street shops. In the new-look shops brochures are replaced by self-service laptops and interactive tables and maps. Free in-store wi-fi, either in shared areas or private booths, facilitates customers using their own devices.

However, as with all marketing problems, the answer lies with the retailer's customers. If they *expect* a web presence on which goods can be purchased or ordered, then that retailer should have an e-commerce website that supports their offline sales and marketing efforts. Schoenbachler and Gordon (2002) suggest that there are three issues to consider when identifying customers' expectations with regard to their channel choice: demographics, past experience and convenience. Whilst these will vary from seller to seller, the concept has its roots in *traditional* segmentation models. Briefly considering each of Schoenbachler and Gordon's points in turn:

● Demographics – this might apply to geographic issues (where are your customers; are there local shops?) but be more specific to Internet users' demographics. If your product is aimed at affluent thirty-year-olds who are cash-rich but time-poor then online has to be an option. A target segment of low-income families, on the other hand, is not likely to have access to the Internet, or even a credit card, and so would never use a website to purchase goods.

- Past experience – do your competitors have online sales? If they do, then people in your market will expect an online option – to not have one is to send customers to your competition.

- Convenience – as with the cash-rich but time-poor segment, do your customers value the convenience of online purchases? Insurance and banking services would come under this heading. Also of significance is that not only do customers like to be able to pick up merchandise at a store after ordering online but they see it as a significant advantage (of the online shop) if they are able to return online purchases to a physical outlet.

YOU DECIDE

Advise Frank and his staff at Hill Street Motorist Shop (case study 8) on extending their limited online offering and how it can be further integrated into their overall sales strategy.

A second option is to identify a well-known high street retailer that does *not* sell online and consider why it has taken that decision.

Alternatively, if your organization or that of your employer is a retailer, consider the implications of integrated off- and online retailing.

4.3 THE RETAIL WEBSITE

GO ONLINE

Outsourced specialists

Although some students might find some of the subjects in this book complex, in reality I am only introducing the *basics* of those subjects. If you doubt this, go to the chapter's web page and take a look at the list of the kind of Internet retailer services that can be outsourced and see just how specialized some aspects of online marketing can be. In reality, for students who are seeking a career in digital marketing, a lot of the jobs are with the companies who offer these services.

In this section we will look at elements of website design that apply specifically to websites on which consumers can make purchases. However, to concentrate only on the online purchase element is to undervalue the site as a retail outlet. As mentioned in the introduction to this chapter, there are two types of retail website: pure-play and bricks and clicks. Although both offer online purchase facilities, the latter must also consider the customer who might be on the site as *part* of their buying process, with a decision to buy being made either off- or online and the actual purchase made in the other medium. Similarly, few customers will make a purchase on their first visit to a site. This being the case, the website must cater not only to the potential online purchaser but those who have not yet made up their mind. Recognizing that all visitors to the B2C website can be valuable, Moe and Fader (2001) identified four types of online shopping visit that the customer might make:

1. Directed-purchase visits. The consumer is ready to make a purchase.
2. Search and deliberation visits. The consumer is researching not only the product, its price and availability, but also the terms, conditions and credibility of the site – although they do intend to make a purchase eventually.
3. Knowledge-building visits. The consumer is engaged in exploratory browsing that *may* lead to a purchase at some time in the future.
4. Hedonic-browsing visits. The consumer is doing electronic window-shopping – that is, shopping for pleasure or recreation.

Offline, it is easy for the experienced salesperson to identify these groups. Online, the website must cater for them all – for even the latter is a recipient of a branding message that may eventually influence a purchase.

PRACTICAL INSIGHT

Shoppers' personality traits

Aubrey Beck of e-commerce company SteelHouse lists ten online shopping personality traits:

1. The distracted shopper
2. The premium shopper
3. The determined shopper
4. The active shopper
5. The free shipping hunter
6. The thrifty shopper
7. The loyal shopper
8. The methodical shopper
9. The impatient shopper
10. The wish list shopper.

For descriptions and advice on how to market to them, follow the link from the chapter's web page.

We have seen this notion of different *types* of website visitor in previous chapters – notably in Sections 1.6 and 3.3 – where we considered the issue of buyer behaviour and where potential customers are in the buying cycle. A concept popular in offline retailing is that of the early-stage buyers and late-stage buyers. In this model, the salesperson takes a different approach to customers depending where they are in their buying decision-making process. Early-stage buyers are looking for information that will help them make a purchase decision, while late-stagers have already done their research and are ready to buy. Getting it wrong in-store costs you sales – the same is true online. As with Moe and Fader's four types of visitor, in the offline environment identifying the different kinds of shopper is relatively easy for the experienced salesperson. Online, however, it is not possible to immediately identify which category each visitor is in, so the site must pander to both. This is particularly true if the goods have a long buying cycle – with the website having to cater for visitors who are at all the stages in the cycle. This could be discreet or obvious. For example, links on the front or product page might say something like 'weighing up the options?' and 'ready to buy?' Subsequent pages for each link would have appropriate content – details of finance schemes or delivery schedules in the latter, for example.

It is also important to take note of *why* people shop online. According to a 2013 report by econsultancy.com (which was based on research from MIT, Facebook, Google and Target (Le Grice, 2013)), the seven most popular reasons for people buying online rather than in a physical store are:

1. Value – 75% said prices were more competitive.
2. Open – 63% highlighted the ability to shop at any time of the day.
3. Delivery – free delivery scored high at 59%.
4. Speed – the element of 'next day' came in at 55%.
5. Ease – 48% noted online shopping is simply easier.
6. Range – stock availability at a glance won the hearts of 46%.
7. Choice – 40% cited the ability to buy new or otherwise unavailable items.

However, other research from Statisticbrain.com (2012), which quotes the US Commerce Department, Forrester Research, Internet Retailer and comscore.com, produced rather different results:

- Time saving – 73%.
- More variety – 67%.
- Easy to compare prices – 59%.
- No crowd – 55%.
- Lower prices – 49%.
- Spend less on fuel – 40%.
- Less tax – 30%.

Although essentially very similar, the last two points are worth comment. Could, for example, increasing fuel prices signal the end of the bricks-and-mortar store? Furthermore, in America states have their own sales taxes, which differ from state to state – so if you live in an 'expensive' state you can buy goods from an online retailer based in a 'cheaper' state.

An obvious advantage that virtual retailers have over their offline counterparts is that there is no display-product cost. Part of the success of Amazon, for example, is that the online store need only list a description and cover image of a book to display it for sale. Therefore, millions of books can be listed with no stock-unit cost – no physical store could ever afford to stock and display the extensive range offered by the online sellers. Note that there will be a cost of page development and website hosting, but this would be nothing like the cost of buying even one copy of each book offered for sale – although online stores do keep stock of top-selling items – with just-in-time deliveries tied to a comprehensive stock-control system making sure stock levels do not reach zero. Or as is the case with Amazon, deliveries are made direct from associates.

> An obvious advantage that virtual retailers have over their offline counterparts is that there is no display-product cost online.

PRACTICAL INSIGHT

In much the same way that businesses seek new markets outside of their home country, so it is that more and more online stores are looking to cross-border retailing as a way of increasing sales and profits. We have addressed the issues of having websites developed for specific countries or regions (see Section 3.6) – cross-border retailing is more to do with selling products from a 'home' website to customers in other countries. Some of the issues are obvious, such as language and currency, but these can be overcome without too much difficulty. Similarly, the issue of some electrical products not being suitable for all countries is fairly well known. However, others are less apparent. Import and/or export taxes, for example. And what about goods being returned or goods' warranties being applicable in all countries? Or which laws are applicable in the event of a dispute? In such instances it might just be a case of *seller* beware.

This issue of stock cost extends beyond simply displaying a book on a shelf – there is also the matter of merchandising to increase sales volume. For example, a bricks-and-mortar bookstore must decide on whether a book is displayed by author, genre or subject. To display a book in more than one category means increasing stock holding by that multiple – for the chain retailer this number is then multiplied by the number of stores. Online, however, books can be 'listed' in multiple categories at no extra cost. The same concept can be applied to other product categories – men's polo shirts, for example, could be listed (displayed) in 'casual wear', 'summer shirts', 'sportswear' and 'gift suggestions' as well as by manufacturer or brand. This ability to multi-list goods means that stock can be arranged by consumer need, so providing an efficient navigational structure for the website from a consumer perspective (Taylor and England, 2006).

DECISION TIME

In essence, the issues raised in this section mirror many of those included in the previous chapter on website development. However, it is worthwhile emphasizing some elements in the online shopping scenario. Key issues will vary depending on the product being sold, but the following should be common to most sites:

- Navigation. Obviously important to any website, good navigation is absolutely essential for the retail website where customers will soon click away to a competitor if they cannot easily find what they are looking for.

- Product pages. Textual and visual description is crucial – and the visual element of the B2C website is an opportunity for designers to show the full range of their skills and programmers the added value that technology *can* bring. Textual descriptions should follow all the criteria covered in Section 3.5 – and, as ever, it is the needs of the customer that should be paramount. For example, giving an extensive technical description of the inner workings of a laptop is not what the average customer is looking for – they simply want to know what that technology does for them, for example, will it play DVDs and have the power for online gaming?

  In some instances a simple one-dimensional image of a product is sufficient to display its qualities – a book cover is a book cover, no matter what angle you view it from, for example. However, common software now makes possible applications that allow the customer to move around the image as if it were in three dimensions. Cars, for example, can be moved so that the customer can view it from 360 degrees, or a hotel bedroom can be rotated so all of its attributes can be viewed. The widespread use of broadband also makes video clips of products feasible for many markets. This could be instructional (using a mobile phone), a demonstration (how to use a power tool safely) or aesthetic (a video tour of a cruise ship).

- Cross- and up-selling. Also known as associated selling, this technique is well established in offline retail – and technology can be used to transfer it online. The model for cross-selling is for the salesperson to offer related or associated products to increase sales. Done properly, the practice is perceived by the buyer as being part of good service – drill bits with a drill, or matching tie with a shirt, for example. Up-selling is where the salesperson offers an upgraded or higher-specification product to increase sales value. As with cross-selling, this can be seen as being part of good service. For example, a customer might select a laptop off the shelf, but when the salesperson asks pertinent questions they discover that the buyer needs a higher specification machine to handle the uses for which they are buying the computer, and so advises one with a higher spec. Online, carefully prepared software programs can take the place of the attentive salesperson, with an automated notice of the need for an accessory or advice on an associated product appearing when a purchase is made. Whilst technology can be applied to automate these facilities, human input from an experienced salesperson (to identify the associated products) is essential.

- Frequently asked questions. These pages can be extremely useful for both customers and the selling organization (they reduce the necessity to employ staff to respond to telephone or email enquiries). As with all aspects of the website content, the FAQ section should be developed by sales and marketing staff who will be aware of (a) the kind of questions that might arise, (b) what the answers are, and (c) how the answers should be presented. The page could be

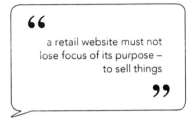

divided into sections, for example questions on products, shipping, payment methods and so on. It can also be dynamic, moving the most frequently asked questions to the top of the list in response to customers' enquiries.

- Calls to action. Part of the site's sales copy (see Section 3.5) and the site's sales funnel (see Section 3.3), a retail website must not lose focus of its purpose – to sell things. To this end, the visitor must be constantly prompted to make a purchase. The most common call to action is an 'add to shopping basket' message (within text or as a button). Simply having such a message at the bottom of a product page is not enough – the customer might not read down that far.

- Wish list. It could be that the website visitor might not be ready to purchase on a particular visit to a website, in which case a 'wish list' facility can be offered. Originally designed to be a list of products that you would like to own that is available for others (friends, family) to access if they wish to buy you a gift, it is now commonly used by people who like to remind themselves of products they have come across on a site and might purchase sometime in the future.

- In-site search facility. Already covered in detail in Section 3.3, for the retail site that lists a wide range of products this is considered by many to be essential. However, some observers – including me – question the value of a search facility on *all* B2C websites. Our argument is that a good navigation system will allow visitors to easily find what they are looking for in a couple of clicks or so. In addition, while they are on their way to the sought product they may come across

something else that takes their interest. Like me, most supporters of this notion come from a traditional retail background – where it is accepted practice to put the most commonly purchased goods at the *back* of the store so that customers must walk past – and be tempted by – numerous other products on their way to the goods and back to the checkout. Having visitors navigate their way to what they want is the online equivalent of this practice.

MINI CASE

Walking the walk on in-site search

I have deliberately chosen not to include a search facility on my digital marketing website (www.alancharlesworth.eu) – and cost or technical ability is not the reason – they are available free from a number of sources, including Google. My reasoning is this.

Students – the site's target audience – tend to be too focused in their search for information that will help with an assignment and so ignore the wider perspective of the subject area they are researching. If my site had a search box on the front page, the student might type in (for example) 'Facebook'. This would return perhaps one or two pages. However, if the student follows the path from the front page: 'interesting articles', then 'social media marketing' – in only two clicks they are on a web page that lists, with my comments, links to articles on the subject. As they scan down the page they will come across the articles on 'Facebook' – plus numerous others that might be useful for their assignment – which they would never have seen if they could have just searched for 'Facebook'.

Research suggests that customers who favour in-site search engines and those who do not use them are evenly split. Perhaps one solution lies in the number of products being sold. Research on actual websites by Roger Willcocks suggests that if a site sells around a thousand or fewer items, then the average usage of on-site search is less than 6 per cent. However, when that small percentage of visitors did use a search facility, they were nearly twice as likely to make a purchase. Suggesting perhaps that they knew exactly what they wanted to buy and went straight to it – in other words, they were at the end of the sales funnel discussed in Section 1.6.

Source: Roger Willcocks of e-commerce specialist company Screenpages (www.screenpages.com), as reported on econsultancy.com in March 2013

- Contact information. This is essential for a number of reasons, not least the issue of online credibility (as covered in Section 3.4). From a sales perspective, however, a customer may wish to speak to someone to seek advice on the product they are interested in. In this case the shop can offer a contact phone number (freephone or ringback are best), a direct email address (with enquiries answered as soon as possible) or maybe a 'chat' facility where a sales assistant conducts a conversation with the customer.

- Price details. Although you may consider this to be a basic of retailing, it is surprising how many sites don't go into enough detail. For a UK site that sells tangible products only in the UK, a single selling price is enough – as is the case in a bricks-and-mortar shop. However, if overseas customers are targeted, considerations such as tax should be included. A short note informing an overseas customer on how they may be able to reclaim VAT might be the difference between a purchase and a lost sale. Another problem is making clear *exactly* what the price covers. Hotels, for example, should make it clear that the displayed price is per person, per room, per night or per stay. It should also be made clear if any local taxes are included, or yet to be added. This is problematic for US services where local taxes vary from region to region. Any potential customer who decides on a hotel at a certain price is bound to feel cheated if that price rises after the initial 'quote'. Even if the additional cost is relatively small, the buyer is likely to take their custom elsewhere.

- For all customers – local and international – there is also the issue of shipping costs that should be easily available to the shopper. The issue is covered in detail in section 5 of this chapter.

PRACTICAL INSIGHT

Incentives work online too

Retailers running promotions to encourage purchasing is as old as retailing itself – and the Internet offers new opportunities for incentives, both online and using email. As well as the tried and tested methods such as discounts and free shipping, the e-marketer can be more inventive. For example:

- Wish lists give a strong indication that the customer is serious about a potential purchase. Why not have a promotion giving customers the opportunity to buy everything in their wish list at a special rate?

- Software can remember things much better than humans – so why not use technology to automatically send out personal incentives on people's birthdays (if you have the data), or on each anniversary of their first purchase or registering with your site?

- Product reviews – they are very popular with customers, increase your review numbers by offering incentives to write them – a percentage refund if you review a purchase, for example.

- Gift vouchers are fairly common – but what about reminding customers in January and February about redeeming those they might have received at Christmas?

- Another promotion that is popular offline is the 'refer-a-friend' concept. Online, only a click of the mouse and entry of an email address are required. Incentives for both the referral and any resulting purchase can be offered.

- Printer-friendly pages. Particularly in the early stages of the buying process and with complex products, customers may visit numerous sites in their research. In order to collect information the shopper may wish to print out information to either (1) compare product attributes, or (2) show to and discuss with a partner. If the products you sell may fall into these categories then the information should be on easily printable pages or optional pdf files.

- A product comparison facility. Many retail sites will offer similar products from different manufacturers, and so customers may need to decide on which meets their needs best or which is the best value for money. To do this, sites can use technology to allow customers to select product information pages and see them side-by-side on the same page. As the information on each product is presented in the same format, comparison becomes a far more straightforward task.

The importance of all of these aspects of online selling can be summed up by a comment from Amazon founder Jeff Bezos, who said: 'the best customer service is if the customer doesn't need to call you, doesn't need to talk to you. It just works.' This is in line with my 'three objectives' principle. Amazon concentrate on selling things (income generation), and as a result of the quality of how they commit to that the *service* element of my objectives is not required.

GO ONLINE

Customer experience the Amazon way

Follow the link from the chapter's website to read ten customer-experience sound-bites from Jeff Bezos.

Note that I consider online checkout facilities to be such an important element of the B2C website that I devote the whole of the next section to them. Similarly, shipping is covered in Section 4.5, which covers all aspects of fulfilment. Worth a reminder is the option of using third-party turnkey solutions offered by a number of Internet brand names (see Section 4.7). Not only do the likes of eBay offer such facilities, but most hosting companies offer 'easy-fit' templates for e-shops – including checkout facilities. However, it should be noted that these companies provide only the technology – the textual and marketing content will still need to be added by the organization that is making use of that technology.

YOU DECIDE

Advise the Rockridge Museum's management (case study 1) with regard to their online B2C trading.

Alternatively, conduct the same exercise for your organization or that of your employer.

4.4 THE CHECKOUT PROCESS

All the effort, cost and resources applied to the online shop's design are wasted if the *browser* cannot convert to being a *buyer* because they have problems with the site's checkout procedure, hence, there is no more important element of the online shop than the checkout facility.

Many people – mistakenly – think the checkout procedure starts at the moment the customer clicks on the 'buy now' link. Although this may be the case with the purchase of a single product, it is not so when the customer is buying more than one item. In reality, the process starts when a customer adds the first product to their basket.

PRACTICAL INSIGHT

You say tomatoes, I say potatoes

Quite why some terms become more popular than others is something of a mystery – a point I make in the introduction to my book *Key Concepts in e-Commerce*. Although there is an argument that the subject of this section is influenced by offline use in the USA and Europe – as far as the online shopper is concerned 'cart' and 'basket' (plus either of these prefixed with 'shopping') both mean the same thing. For many, 'checkout' has the same meaning – though *online* it is normally used as the verb describing what you want to do rather than a noun describing where you do it. So universally accepted are the terms that many sites simply show an image of a trolley or basket – with shoppers will know exactly what is indicated by the icon.

Important considerations for any checkout facility include:

- It must be easy to use. Although the entire site should have good usability, it is *essential* in the checkout process. While surfing around the website the customer can stumble and make mistakes and still stay on the site. When they get to the checkout, however, their personal data and their credit-card details are at risk – and they are not prepared to take any chances with them.

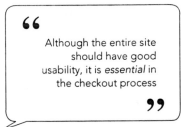

> " Although the entire site should have good usability, it is *essential* in the checkout process "

- Make it constantly available. Too many sites allow you into the checkout process, but not out again. Right up to the final click of the 'buy' button, it should be easy for users to return to the main site to shop for more products. Having a link, or better still a running total, constantly visible on every viewing page keeps the basket constantly in the shopper's focus.

- Following from the previous point – make it easy to change the basket at any time. Not only should actual products be easily changeable (i.e. added or deleted) but details such as size or colour should be effortless to adjust.

- Abandoned carts. Like the trolley full of shopping that is left at the offline checkout, any online basket that is filled, but not purchased is a concern for the retailer. With some shopping facilities it is necessary for the potential customer to initiate a checkout procedure in order to see the final cost. However, for most products, if a visitor has spent time on the site, researched and reviewed products, added them to the basket but then not completed the purchase, then the online retailer must investigate what has gone wrong – and seek to correct it. Several scenarios – and solutions – are possible. Most serious is where the shopper has abandoned the filled cart because they cannot, or do not know how to, use the checkout facility. In this case, the fault lies with the website's development. Obviously, this should be tested before the site is launched, but frequent cart abandonment should ring alarm bells for the site's manager. The site's log files will identify exactly where the user leaves the process, which will help identify problematic aspects. The problems may range from a technical error that means the checkout simply doesn't work through to a badly worded instruction that results in users not being able to follow the procedure correctly.

  Beyond the control of the website, however, is that it could be that the customer has simply changed their mind about the purchase, has not got their credit-card with them, needs to double check the required size or measurements for the product, or perhaps they don't have the time to complete the purchase (it is common for users to 'shop' on their lunch break using their employer's Internet facility). For these scenarios – and they do not know what the reason is – the online marketer must be proactive in finding out which one applies and recovering the customer.

PRACTICAL INSIGHT

Re-marketing

The confusion between re-marketing and re-targeting (which is covered in Chapter 7) is not helped by the fact that re-marketing is not even an obvious choice of term for the practice it represents. Re-marketing concerns the issue of customers putting products into their virtual shopping basket, going to the checkout – but not actually going through with the purchase. Given that 43 per cent of UK consumers have abandoned an online shopping basket in the last twelve months (Whisbi, 2013), simply ignoring them and giving them a virtual wave goodbye, stores have realized that it is worth trying to get them back through re-marketing. If they have reached that stage, it is likely that the store has the email address of the customer (they have either completed the checkout form or are a registered customer) and so the shop then sends an email – or more than one until a result is achieved – to the shopper which comments on the abandoned basket. Methods vary from a 'did we do something wrong?' question, through reminding the customer of an offer they would have qualified for in that sale, to offering some kind of incentive to complete the purchase.

PRACTICAL INSIGHT

Trade globally, think locally

Sometimes checkouts fail for simple reasons that are obvious when pointed out – and yet again emphasize the importance of a marketing input to the site's design – in this case, the development of the shopping cart's fields. A common error I come across repeatedly is where US sites will not accept a form with no 'zip code' on it. That addresses outside the USA have no zip code seems to have escaped them (for an example, follow the link on the chapter's web page).

- Accept multiple methods of payment. Although many – if not most – people are now willing to give credit-card details online there will always be some who would rather pay cash on delivery. Many shoppers are also used to using a payment facility such as PayPal for all of their online purchases – and may go elsewhere if that facility is not available on the site. Alternatively, provide a freephone number so that customers can give their credit-card details over the telephone if they prefer to do so.

- As is covered in the next section, fulfilment is an essential element of online retailing – and during the checkout process the customer should be offered a range of delivery options.

- Finally, there is the question of security. A checkout should always be hosted on a secure server. Not only will customers be unwilling to use unsecure sites, but the lack of such will have a major impact on the site's credibility (see Section 3.4). So important is this issue that all genuine sellers use secure servers – it is very unusal to find a reputable seller using an unsecure page.

As pointed out earlier in the chapter, 'retail' includes more than just shops. In particular, travel-associated vendors need to have both efficient and effective checkout facilities – except in these examples the term 'checkout' is replaced by 'booking'. In itself, this can be problematic. On a shop site, each product's price is listed next to the description. For services such as flights or hotels, however, the prices are rarely fixed – therefore the customer must enter certain criteria before an exact price can be given. Let's take a hotel room as an example. It is common practice that to get a quote the customer, having selected the type of room they want and how many guests there are, must enter the dates they wish to stay and then are obliged to click on a link that is too often labelled 'make a reservation' or 'book now'. In fact the link does not make a reservation, it is merely the next step in the process, but unwary users may shy away from clicking because they want only a quote – not to make a firm booking.

Insurance is another example of this situation, with the customer having to submit personal details before a quote is given. However the insurance sellers always make it clear that this is a quote – rather than a sale – with customers having to indicate specifically when they wish to convert the quote into a purchase. The insurance industry is particularly efficient in this regard as they will inform the potential customer that the quote is valid for a set period – with follow-up emails used to pursue the sale up to the end of that period.

DECISION TIME

Worth noting at this point is that in *marketing* terms – in much the same way that a 'customer' might not hand over any cash for a service – an online 'checkout' need not include a financial payment. For example, if the web page has an objective of signing up users for a free newsletter, the form they have to complete for the service is, effectively, the checkout. Similarly, the form that I complete in order to register my interest in a new service offered by my local council should be designed with the same criteria as a checkout on an online retail site.

Although a reasonably effective website can be developed with limited technical expertise, a checkout facility is a specialist area that needs either expert in-house skills or – as is common – it is outsourced. The latter is popular as not only are specialist skills required, so too is a secure server. Most small companies will pay for secure hosting – business website hosting companies offer a full checkout facility on their servers. A further option is to use a third party for both checkout and payment handling. As is mentioned in Section 4.7, using a shopping site such as eBay is a sensible option for small online retailers.

PRACTICAL INSIGHT

S is for secure

To identify when you are on a secure site, take a look at the URL in the browser window. A secure site will start with 'https://'. If the site is using the secure check facility of a hosting company, the URL will switch from that of the website (e.g. www.retailwebsite.com) to that of the secure server (e.g. www.secureservercompany.com). Although you have moved to the secure server when you clicked on 'buy now', it is the norm that the page will carry the same livery as the company site – all part of the secure hosting service.

Another option for traders – though in a limited number of industries – is to use agents to accept customer payments. One example of this is hotels. It is the travel and tourism industry that has seen most sites that – as a business model – operate as intermediaries for numerous hotels, airlines and car hire companies. These companies then seek high listings on both organic and paid listings for keywords related to locations in which they have clients. For individual hotels, partnering with one or more online booking agencies alleviates the problem of maintaining an online booking form. Obviously, a fee will be involved, but such sites will normally feature highly on search engine listings and so generate business that the hotel might otherwise miss. So widespread are the online booking agents that many hotel chains use them in addition to their own online booking systems.

4.5 FULFILMENT

As with its offline equivalent – commonly referred to as 'logistics' – fulfilment is often the neglected element of online B2C trading. Nevertheless, despite its less than glamorous image, making sure the customer receives the product they have ordered is just as important as any other aspect of online retailing. As customers become more at ease with shopping online, their expectations are that the purchase is a seamless process from recognizing a need to having the product in their hand – with failure at any point reflecting badly on the seller.

> "fulfilment is often the neglected element of online B2C trading"

In this section we will consider the four key building blocks of online fulfilment: stock control, shipping costs, outbound logistics and returns. Although each is an element of the business (i.e. a cost) and so in itself an integral aspect of any strategic decision, in this section we will focus on the important operational aspects and how they are presented to the customer on the website.

Stock control

One of the great advantages of selling online is that customers do not expect to carry the goods out of the shop with them, so you do not have to hold them physically in stock. Therefore, if a supplier has short lead times – next-day delivery is common – the e-tailer can source the ordered product from a supplier (or the manufacturer) and still offer delivery to their customer within a reasonable period.

For the company that actually carries stock, the same issues of stock control that impact offline apply online. However, with regard to out-of-stock (OoS) products there are a number of issues are unique to the online sales environment. These include:

- In an offline store the salesperson can direct customers to substitute products or the customer – having made the effort to visit the store – will look for alternatives. Online, however, in one click of their mouse or prod of the screen, consumers can easily switch to another website which has the goods in stock.

- Online, it is easy to withdraw a product from sale or post a temporary 'out of stock' notice – preferably with an indication of when it will be available again.
- If the OoS is temporary (e.g. a day or two), the customer need never know if shipping/delivery time is outside that period.

Shipping costs

In a B2C environment it is common practice for the customer to pay for both actual shipping (transport) costs and 'handling' or 'packaging' (in the UK, the term 'post and packaging' is an accepted term to describe the cost). These two costs should be considered in isolation:

- Packaging. This element also has two aspects: the cost of labour and that of materials. Firstly, all products must be placed in a package that is appropriate – for example, packing for fragile items. All packaging – even the ubiquitous 'Jiffy bag' – costs money. Similarly, the operation of physically placing the goods into the packaging can be labour intensive – and so, expensive. Obviously, for a high-volume retailer automation is an option, but that would involve significant capital expenditure (for any machinery) that is beyond the resources of a smaller business. Any costs incurred must be recovered in either (1) the shipping cost charged to each customer, or (2) the product's basic selling price.

MINI CASE

Quick fingers and small boxes

Several years ago – before music downloads became popular – I became involved in the marketing of an online-only business selling CDs. This was a 'cottage industry' in the truest sense of the term – with the entire operation being run from a picturesque village in the North Yorkshire Dales. As our marketing and SEO improved, so did the sales. But therein lay the biggest problems we had. Having solved the issue of reasonably priced, high-quality boxes in a variety of sizes (two-CD cases are bigger than those for single units), we were then faced with the time it was taking to select a CD from the boxes in which they arrived (we purchased CDs only in response to orders and had them delivered in bulk), place it in the appropriate box and print and affix the address label. With practice, our best worker got this down to a couple of minutes, but the average was more like three. I never bettered five minutes per order. Simple arithmetic tells the story. We increased sales to around 500 orders per day. So 500 times three minutes equals 1500 minutes. Yes, we needed twenty-five person-hours per day to dispatch the customers' CDs. Effectively, three full-time members of staff. Despite healthy sales, the owner sold the business shortly afterwards – the cost of fulfilment meant that making a profit in a competitive market was simply not possible.

- Transport. The cost of transport can be fixed quite easily by weighing every item in advance to calculate how much to charge the customer (note, don't forget to weigh the products with any packaging – boxes can be quite heavy). If you sell only a few products, weighing each will take only a few minutes – even with a wide range of products on offer it is not too onerous a job, and it will be a one-off task. By adding a fixed sum to cost to cover packaging, either shipping charges can be listed in a chart (weight × location) or software used to tabulate the same numbers based on customers selecting (1) product, (2) where they are, and (3) shipping option (first class, etc.). Although this sum can be shown as a total at the end of the checkout process, best practice would be to include it as a running total in the shopping basket. This is particularly the case if you offer free shipping when an order reaches a set total – seeing that they are close to the 'free' figure will often prompt shoppers to buy extra items. A report from Forrester (Mulpuru *et al.*, 2012) revealed that 27 per cent of shoppers admitted to buying unplanned items to get free shipping.

GO ONLINE

How to offer free shipping without going broke

Follow the link on the chapter's web page to read an interesting article on the business decisions behind offering free shipping for online buyers.

A further consideration of packaging is whether the shop offers special wrapping services – a product that has been purchased as a gift, for example. Although this service does add value to the overall product offering – and it can be offered at an additional fee – it does add to costs in terms of both time and packaging (the gift wrapping).

PRACTICAL INSIGHT

Shipping: a cost or nice little earner?

Not uncommon is the practice of lowering the selling price of a product to near its cost – and then increasing the 'shipping' charges in order to generate a profit. Most customers see this juggling of numbers for what it is, and object to the notion of being cheated. Recognizing this, eBay has introduced an element to its feedback section that prompts the customer to comment on how reasonable they consider the postage charges to be. Those sellers who consistently overcharge are brought to book by the online auction site – or simply lose customers.

Outbound logistics

After the ordered product has been sourced and packaged, delivery to the customer must be arranged. The costs are not a significant issue for the seller because they will have been paid by the customer – either specifically, or intrinsic to the buying price. Neither is a dispatch problem, as most carriers will collect. The most significant problems arise at the other end of the delivery chain – where, and how, the customer actually takes possession of the goods. Although research from IMRG (2012) suggests that around 92 per cent of deliveries are made without problems, that means 8 per cent do have significant problems, and a further 4 per cent are not delivered on time – which means that twelve orders out of every hundred result in a disappointed customer. Furthermore, the IMRG UK Valuing Home Delivery Review (2012) considered the cost (to sellers) of the six most common reasons for delivery failure. They are, with the calculated loss per annum for each:

1. Failed first delivery – re-delivery required/arranged: £55,368,358
2. Failed first delivery – collection by customer: £0
3. Late delivery: £60,693,444
4. Order lost – replacement sent: £73,834,056
5. Order lost – loss of customer goodwill: £100,805,834
6. Order undelivered and returned to sender: £34,772,947.

> " although customers considered delivery service a vital component of customer service, online retailers were not matching expectations "

For some items there is no problem. A boxed DVD, for example, will go through the average householder's letterbox. However, if the goods are bigger, or a signature is required for the delivery, there must be someone at home to accept that delivery – or an alternative must be offered by that seller. Sadly, this final stage of the sales process is too often not given the same level of attention as other aspects that lead up to it. For example, research by Micros (2013) found that 32 per cent of online retailers did not offer next-day delivery, and only 19 per cent could deliver on a nominated date – the latter despite the fact that carriers typically offer such a service (although at a higher cost). Similarly, carriers also provide tracking facilities and accept specific delivery instructions from addressees – but these are offered to online buyers by less than a quarter of the retailers sampled in the Micros research. That research by IMRG UK (2012) found that nominated day delivery was identified by customers as being one of the most significant issues that would improve their perception of online delivery makes such omissions particularly questionable. Furthermore if such options are made available by the seller, the buyer must be made aware of them (see Section 4.4 above, where the checkout procedure is discussed) – research from Page-Thomas et al. (2006) found that, although customers considered delivery service a vital component of customer service, online retailers are not matching expectations concerning the information they provided about the delivery of ordered goods. It would seem that this situation has improved little in the years since that report was published.

MINI CASE

Delivering on delivery

I had ordered a water pump for my 'classic' Toyota MR2 and I was waiting at home for it to arrive when I got this text:

Figure 4.1 A helpful delivery text

The full message advised me that I could text to have the parcel delivered to a neighbour or other options. 'Ian' duly arrived at 11.35.

Over the years a number of initiatives have been tried to address the issue of missed and deferred home deliveries. These include basic arrangements such as having the delivery driver phone the recipient an hour or so before their expected time of arrival or more accurately predicted delivery times using GPS tracking. Other more complex schemes have been the subject of numerous start-up business models – all recognizing that any system that might be widely accepted will generate healthy profits. The following have been, or are being, tried, but to date nothing has really caught the public's imagination:

- Re-delivery services – the customer directs goods to a depot from where they collect them.
- Pick-up – and return – points at convenience stores and filling station forecourts.
- Removable boxes secured to an electronically controlled anchor point outside the recipient's house.
- Collection points at self-storage depots.
- Locker banks at supermarkets, including a card-swipe facility on the boxes.

Perhaps the answer lies in the delivery being considered to be just part of the selling service. June 2013 saw online fashion and clothes retailer asos (www.asos.com) partner with its logistics provider to offer a new 'Follow my Parcel' service where customers can live-track their delivery online monitoring the progress of their delivery with a real-time countdown to the actual delivery giving them their actual fifteen minute delivery slot. I would expect that by the time we get the third edition of this book such a service will be the norm and having to take a full day off work to sit at home awaiting a delivery that may or may not turn up will be a practice consigned to TV's History Channel.

PRACTICAL INSIGHT

The future of retailing?

Christmas 2012 saw eBay testing a new mobile app called 'eBay Now' that allowed shoppers to order from local stores and have the shop deliver the item – by cycle courier – to wherever they were (work, café, pub, park bench, home) within an hour. It should be noted that unlike other parts of the world, in the USA many – if not most – major retailers sell via eBay, making such a service more feasible.

A final issue with respect to delivery is that of sending to an address that is not the one associated with the name on the credit-card used for the transaction. Many firms, fearing fraud, will refuse to do this. However, for many people, being at home all day to receive goods is problematic – if not impossible. For the gift-seller (a florist, for example) such a policy would be a recipe for bankruptcy. There are ways around this, but it generally involves having the bank make further checks on the validity of the credit card – which involves a higher cost for the seller. For the smaller company, it makes sense to sell through a third party where PayPal-type facilities tackle such issues for the retailer.

PRACTICAL INSIGHT

There's more money in picks and shovels than gold

Although hard facts do not exist to support the notion, a number of industry insiders point to the profits made by the major delivery companies and suggest that of all the industries that have profited from the rise of the Internet, it is those courier and parcel services that deliver the online-ordered products who have benefited most. This is based on a similar hypothesis about the great American gold rushes in the nineteenth century. The adage was that the businesses selling mining tools made far more money than the prospectors who bought them.

Returns

Also known as reverse logistics, the organization must give consideration to customers who want to return goods to the vendor. The quantity of potential returns will depend on both the product and the organization's policies with regard to returned goods. Obviously, the law dictates that faulty goods must be accepted back and full refunds given – for the online trader, paying for the postage for returns is also good practice. However, goods that the buyer simply does not like do not have to be accepted back – though premier retailers see it as good business to do so. Offline, this is not a major problem as the goods are (normally) returned to the same store where they can be inspected and returned to stock. It is also the case that refunded cash is frequently spent during the same visit to the shop. Other than staff time, therefore, there is no cost to the retailer. For the online retailer, however, there is considerable inconvenience and cost involved – though note that multi-channel retailers can promote that online purchases can be returned to a physical outlet). This situation is not, however, new. Catalogue retailers have faced similar problems for years and build the cost of returns into their selling prices as an overhead. Experience from this channel is that such is the cost of paying for, accepting and sorting some faulty returns, it is cheaper to simply send out a replacement item and tell the buyer to dispose of the damaged original themselves. It is, perhaps, the policy of ready acceptance of returns on the high street that has resulted in shoppers using a company's returns policy as a barometer of its customer service – it was a generous returns policy that helped Marks & Spencer develop its brand. So it is on the web, where the tangible issue of returned goods also crosses to the intangible topic of online credibility. In a consumer-returns survey published in December 2007, returns management specialists, Newgistics, found that nine out of ten respondents cited a convenient returns policy as being at least 'somewhat important' in encouraging them to shop at a website that is *new* to them. I think that if that were the case back in 2007 it is even more the case now.

Throughout this book I have tried to emphasize the point that effective digital marketing does not consist of a series of disconnected events but that the successful strategy must be holistic in nature, with each element complementing the others. With that in mind, I will finish this section with a couple of examples that many would think belong in the website design sections of this or the previous chapters. The first is an online facility that helps customers select the right shoe size. Called Shoefitr, the app was introduced by Running Warehouse (www.runningwarehouse.com) in 2010 – and it is reasonable to expect that it might increase sales because customers would have more confidence in ordering the right size shoe. The second example is that of a facility called Virtusize (virtusize.com) which although it had been used on other sites in Europe for a while, first came to my notice when asos rolled it out on their site. The very clever, but easy to use, tool allows customers to compare specific measurements of potential purchases with an item they already have by overlaying silhouettes of both garments. So, two smart facilities that might increase sales – but here is the kicker. Shoefitr reduced fit-related returns rates at Running Warehouse by 23 per cent and Virtusize already had a track record of reducing fit-related returns by up to 50 per cent before asos adopted it. So, you decide, where is the biggest ROI on these tools – increased sales or increased profits by reducing returns? I'm going with the latter.

CASE STUDY

Getting it right when the customer gets it wrong

I recently bought a belt from clothing retailer Orvis (orvis.co.uk). I had already had an excellent buying experience with this company (follow the link from the chapter's web page to read that story) and so had no qualms about using them again – this despite the fact that many of their products are shipped from their home base in the USA. Sadly, when the belt arrived I had picked the wrong size (could the on-site description have been better?). So I checked what was involved in returning the 'wrong' belt and getting one that was a size smaller. First option was to call in at one of their physical stores, but as the nearest is around eighty miles away that was not realistic. So I rang them up. Immediately a new belt was ordered – although, not unreasonably, I had to pay for it – and I was told to return the other belt using a return address label on the invoice. And here's the best bit: Orvis have a deal with an organization called Collect+ (collectplus.co.uk) which meant that I could drop the package at a local shop. The cost of the return postage was included in the refund for the original belt.

DECISION TIME

The nature of the product being sold will dictate much of the fulfilment criteria. Its size, value, perishability and how fragile it is, for example, will all impact on any fulfilment strategy. In deciding how to address an organization's fulfilment agenda it is worthwhile considering the four key elements introduced in the previous section:

- Stock control – although a central element of marketing, stock availability is normally handled by a designated person or team, often integral to the procurement department. It is an aspect of online retailing that is strategic to the organization.

- Shipping costs – cover expenditure, profit centre, promotional tool – or all three? Closely associated with product pricing, again this is a strategic decision rather than an operational task left to the online team.

- Outbound logistics – for the serious (rather than the occasional) online vendor, the choice of delivery service is essential in ensuring customer satisfaction, but it is also a cost centre that must be carefully selected and monitored. Long-term contracts or strategic partnerships with carriers are normally the best options. If any kind of 'drop-off' facility is offered, this too is a strategic decision.

- Returns – any commitment of resources in this area will depend on (1) the product (e.g. is it susceptible to easy damage or failure, or is it in any way size-related and so liable not to suit the buyer?), and (2) the company's policy towards returns (e.g. does any kudos gained by a liberal returns policy offset potential costs?).

Having considered all of these issues, and decided how they will be addressed both strategically and operationally, it is then important to describe them clearly on the website – both as instructions about what will happen when a customer makes a purchase and as an important development of the site's credibility – and so too, its brand.

YOU DECIDE

Advise the management team at Hill Street Motorist Shop (case study 8) about fulfilment-related issues that are specific to them.

Alternatively, conduct the same exercise for your organization or that of your employer.

4.6 E-MARKETPLACES AND COMPARISON SHOPPING SITES

Although definitions differ in various sources, in this book I will consider e-marketplaces and comparison shopping sites as being so similar that they can be addressed in this single section.

The advent of the web as a source of shopping information not only proved to be a boon for shoppers and – if they use it properly – marketers, but it also presented a business model that exploits shoppers' desire for easy access to that information. This comes in the form of shopping comparison sites (or, as they are more accurately called, comparison shopping engines – CSEs) and e-marketplaces.

Comparison shopping engines

A CSE is a website that, as a business model, elicits fees from the sellers of products that are listed in the comparison pages produced as a result of a potential customer's search.

Although CSEs have an element of search to them, they should not be treated as the same as organic search engines (see Chapter 6) but more like search engine advertising (see Section 7.5). This is because the CSE will only present your product's details to the searcher if you have not only agreed to be included in that search, but are willing to pay for any clickthroughs made from the search listing. CSEs are, essentially, searchable directories of products – but when the user clicks on a listed product they are taken directly to a web page where that product is offered for sale. For popular products, multiple listings appear in the CSE, with the user being able to compare each vendor's offering before clicking through on the one that appeals most – usually, though not always, the cheapest. Although sites such as Kelkoo (kelkoo.co.uk) include product details, they search mainly on price – and so are referred to as being price comparison sites (though note that many of these sites allow you to view products in order of their 'popularity' – though what determines that popularity is not always clear). Although common in the financial services industry where the user is required to submit personal details and so be presented with a personalized product that meets their needs, many other sites simply list the relative attributes of a variety of products – from cars to kettles. As with so many aspects of the Internet, it is the travel industry that has been the primary exponent of the concept – with sites like Expedia (expedia.com) and Travelocity (travelocity.com) being able to search their databases to present flight and hotel options for wherever the traveller wishes to go.

However, the convenience of free, on-demand product comparison comes at price – that being the lack of total impartiality of the options offered to users. Despite the fact that most CSEs explain their links with sponsors, it is often only in the small print – and how they generate income and how their commercial relationships affect their content is not always obvious to users. Similarly, when considering – for example – car insurance, whilst a number of brands might offer their own insurance policies, there is a limited number of policy underwriters. In a similar vein of questioning the independence of some CSEs, the problem might be one of conflict rather than allegiance. It is common practice, for example, to omit results from key suppliers in a market because they choose not to pay the fees charged by the comparison site.

As is the case in so much of online marketing, CSEs have added to their content to take them beyond offering comparisons of similar products. Not only are shipping and any other additional costs for each listed seller included in the comparison, but many now offer customer reviews (see Section 9.2) – essentially they are trying to present themselves as a kind of online shopping community site or one-stop portal for buyers of particular products or services. Add to the content network ads (see Section 7.6) or even affiliate links (Section 7.7) and it can be difficult for consumers (and some marketers) to differentiate such sites from e-marketplaces.

E-marketplaces

Although the term was originally used as a generic description for any kind of marketplace that exists online, e-marketplaces were originally normally associated with B2B trading in specific markets – hence I cover them in Section 5.5. However, it is now becoming common practice to refer to websites such as Overstock.com, Yahoo! Shopping and Buy.com as e-marketplaces (albeit sometimes with the prefix 'B2C'). That Amazon's facility is actually called 'Amazon Marketplace' reinforces this point. The name game continued when 2013 saw eBay re-launch its re-branded its Shopping.com site as the 'eBay Commerce Network'. Although it was described by many commentators at its launch as a CSE, the site more resembles what we have come to expect from an e-marketplace, with the *network* including more than 8,000 merchants around the world. This being the case – what is eBay? Operating an online marketplace can be a very lucrative business model, and I would expect that during the lifetime of this book we will see some other digital brands enter the market. Google, for example, have dabbled with the concept in recent years and one would expect that the search engine giant has the resources and know-how to tempt sellers onto any e-marketplace they might wish to develop. Similarly, after a number of experiments that might be described as *dipping their toe* in the market, is it only a matter of time before Facebook launches a full-blown *social* marketplace?

So how does an e-marketplace differ from a CSE? Perhaps the title of each give us a good place to start. The CSE is a search facility – perhaps for the customer who knows, or has a very good idea of, what they want to buy. Insurance for a a specific car or a holiday in a specific place and on specific dates. The e-marketplace, on the other hand, is more like a market, where the shopper has an idea of what they want to buy (e.g. a new dress) but would like to browse around a shop – or dip into a directory – by searching on less specific criteria with the result being a list of 'suggestions' rather than specific products. Naturally, there will be overlaps between the two – but this is a reasonable differentiation. That said, the issue is complicated still further by the fact that you could look for a product on, say, Yahoo! Shopping, and find that when you click on the 'view details' link for a product, you find yourself on eBay or Amazon.

> ## GO ONLINE
>
> Follow developments in e-marketplaces and the role played by social media on the chapter's web page.

DECISION TIME

As with all aspects of Internet marketing, using CSEs or e-marketplaces is not for every retailer, with advantages and disadvantages to the service offered. These include the following:

- The comparison results are price-based. If you offer a premium price for a premium service, then you may fare badly in the CSE results. Remember, CSE users are in the segment of the market that is shopping on price. If this is not your demographic then the use of comparison sites is questionable – although some sites do offer sub-categories based on quality versus price. Hotel sites, for example, offer price comparisons for different star ratings.

- Not all of your products have to be listed. Selected products can be used to raise the seller's profile – the equivalent of the long-established offline loss-leader principle.
- The major CSEs and e-marketplaces rank highly with search engines. If you are struggling with both SEO and search engine advertising, perhaps the CSE can put your product on the search engine results pages.
- There is a cost to the retailer of selling through a price comparison website. Whilst this can be built into selling prices and marketing budgets, paying a commission to sell your product cheaper than your competitors might be a risky long-term strategy.
- The CSE might not have many visitors, or its visitors might not be shopping for your products – though, in a pay-per-click arrangement, no traffic equals no cost (other than that involved in setting up the listing).

Although the CSEs and e-marketplaces all provide a guide on submitting to their engines, before adding products to their listings you should be prepared to provide details of all of the following attributes for each:

- The product's full name
- A clear description of the product
- The product's manufacturer and assigned part number
- The category in which you wish it to be listed
- How you want the product to be classified
- Your selling price – and retail price if you are discounting it
- The URL of the product's page
- The URL of any image to be presented on the CSE or e-marketplace
- Stock availability
- Shipping costs.

YOU DECIDE

Advise the owners how suitable the use of CSEs or e-marketplaces might be for The Gilded Truffle Hotel (case study 3). Explain both the positive and negative aspects of the practice for the hotel.

Alternatively, conduct the same exercise for your organization or that of your employer.

4.7 THIRD-PARTY RETAIL WEBSITES

In the previous section I asked the question 'what is eBay?' In an attempt to differentiate between comparison shopping sites, e-marketplaces and third-party websites, I am going to call it the latter.

Although the original concept was for the general public to sell off – by auction – unwanted items in a kind of online boot-sale, eBay is now more commonly used by small and micro retailers as a method of selling to a market that prior to the Internet was simply not possible. Furthermore, many shun the auction model, simply listing goods at a fixed price. Although some of these businesses do operate in niche markets (see earlier in this chapter), many do buy and sell mainstream products. They make much of the eBay site a facilitator of B2C retail transactions rather than the C2C auction site that it was originally. However, the reason I refer to eBay – in this context – as a third-party website is that the organization offers sellers not just 'advertising space' but also the facility to develop their own eBay store on the company's domain and – importantly – the use of eBay's checkout facility. Indeed, if it were not for the fact that many travel-based CSEs and Amazon also offer their businesses the use of their own checkout, this facility *could* be used as another differentiator between CSEs/e-marketplaces and third-party shopping websites.

Building your eBay store requires little in the way of technical knowledge – simply choose a name, pick a template and write a description for your shop and you are away. A customized logo and a colour scheme will help personalize your online presence. Up to 300 categories can be created for your store, so there are few products you cannot consider for this virtual shopping mall. Obviously, fees must be paid – eBay charges store owners a monthly subscription fee, a listing fee and a final value fee for items that sell. In addition, postage and packaging costs must be considered when deciding on a profitable selling price – but given that these will be the only marketing costs to be added to the products' cost price, healthy profits can still be made. Adopting the traditional retailing practice of 'loss leaders', common practice is to list 'bargain' products in auctions to attract browsers, and then direct them to your online store where all of your products are listed.

Despite eBay's easy-to-use shop-development tools, the online niche retailer should still exercise those elements of good practice covered in this and other chapters – writing textual content in such a way as to best promote products being an obvious example. Indeed, if I wanted to give examples of poor website development a short tour around eBay shops would produce numerous instances. Common errors include poor use of colour and size in fonts, low-quality photographs, inadequate product descriptions and very little sales copy or calls to action.

As a footnote, I have decided to use eBay as the prime example here as I expect that the majority of readers will be familiar with the company that is most recognized in this field. However, it is not the only site to offer such facilities to the niche retailer – and I would certainly be remiss if I didn't mention Tabao (www.taobao.com), which is widely regarded as the 'Chinese eBay'.

DECISION TIME

The use of third-party websites to host online shops can offer significant advantages for some organizations, particularly small or micro businesses. Many of the issues raised in Chapter 2 (website hosting, for example) are negated by partnering your business with a branded website in much the same way as *concessions* have worked in traditional retailing for scores of years. The use of the third party's checkout facility can also be a deciding factor for the smaller seller.

However, such a route to market can have disadvantages, particularly if the organization has ambitions to expand beyond being a small player in a particular market. This is because the business is inextricably linked with the host organization and so all those benefits gained from the partnership can be an impediment in developing an online brand of its own – not least because the third-party retailer can be perceived by customers as being just that – a business that is too small to trade in its own right.

The use of such sites is not limited to SMEs, however. Though not as popular in other parts of the world, in America a number of high street brands use eBay (or similar) auctions to sell off goods that might be end-of-range, unpopular sizes or colours, or simply over-stocks.

YOU DECIDE

Advise Robert Terwilliger on the advantages and drawbacks of using a third-party website to sell the Modeller's Stand (case study 9).

Alternatively, conduct the same exercise for your organization or that of your employer.

CHAPTER EXERCISE

Giving justifications for all your decisions, advise Martha and her team at Phelps Online Department Store (case study 13) on all aspects of online retailing covered in this chapter.

Alternatively, conduct the same exercise for your own organization or that of your employer.

CHAPTER QUESTIONS

Follow the link on the chapter's web page to a series of multiple-choice, exam-type questions that will test your knowledge and understanding of the various elements of the chapter.

REFERENCES

Anderson, C. (2006) *The Long Tail*. Hyperion Books.

Charlton, G. (2013) Christmas 2012 online shopping survey report. Available at http://econsultancy.com/uk/reports/christmas-2012-online-shopping-survey-report.

Forrester Research (2008) US c-commerce forecast: 2008 to 2012. Available on forrester.com.

Gay, R., Charlesworth, A. and Esen, R. (2007) *Online Marketing: A Customer-Led Approach.* Oxford University Press.

IMRG (2012) IMRG UK valuing home delivery review 2012. Interactive Media in Research Group. Available on imrg.org.

Internet Retailing (2008) Out of touch retailers throw away high street sales. *Internet Retailing.* Issue 5, September.

JupiterResearch/Ipsos (2006) Insight retail consumer survey. Available on omniture.com.

Kamarulzamam, Y. (2007) Adoption of travel e-shopping in the UK. *International Journal of Retail and Distribution Management.* Volume 35, number 9, pp. 703–719.

Le Grice, C. (2013) Seven things customers demand online. Available at econsultancy.com/uk/blog/61972-seven-things-customers-demand-online.

Micros UK (2013) The 2013 online retail delivery report. Available at www.micros-ecommerce.com/research/

Moe, W.W. and Fader, P.S. (2001) Which visits lead to purchases? Dynamic conversion behavior at e-commerce sites. *Sloan Management Review.* Volume 42, number 2, pp. 8–9.

Morgan Stanley (2006) The state of the Internet, part 3. Available on morganstanley.com.

Mulpuru, S., Roberge, D., Sehgal, V. and Freeman Evans, P. (2012) US online holiday retail forecast, 2012. Forrester Research. Available on forrester.com.

Newgistics (2007) Holiday shopping and returns. Available on newgistics.com.

Opinion Research Corporation (2008) Ouch point survey. Available on opinionresearch.com.

Page-Thomas, K., Moss, G., Chelly, D. and Yabin, S. (2006) The provision of delivery information online: a missed opportunity. *International Journal of Retail and Distribution Management.* Volume 34, number 4/5, pp. 258–277.

Schoenbachler, D. and Gordon, G. (2002) Multi-channel shopping: understanding what drives consumer choice. *Journal of Consumer Marketing.* Volume 19, number 1, pp. 42–53.

Shop.org (2008) *The state of retailing 2008 marketing report.* Available on shop.org.

StatisticBrain.com (2012) e-Commerce/Online sales statistics. Available at www.statisticbrain.com/total-online-sales/.

Szymanski, D.M. and Hise, R.T (2000) e-Satisfaction: an initial examination. *Journal of Retailing.* Volume 76, number 3, pp. 309–322.

Taylor, M.J. and England, D. (2006) Internet marketing: website navigational design issues. *Marketing Intelligence and Planning.* Volume 24, number 1, pp. 77–85.

Whisbi (2013) Web-based buying habits of UK consumers. Available on whisbi.com.

Chapter 5

The B2B online presence

Business only has two functions – marketing and innovation.

Peter F. Drucker

Chapter at a glance

5.1 Introduction
5.2 B2B buying practices
5.3 The B2B website
5.4 Lead generation
5.5 E-marketplaces
5.6 Online auctions and tendering

5.1 INTRODUCTION

Where the last chapter – on the B2C web presence – built on the previous chapter on website development, this chapter is developed from both. Obviously, the basic tenets of website design (Chapter 3) apply to B2B sites just as much as a checkout facility on a B2B site should comply with the same guidelines as those covered in Section 4.4 on B2C. This chapter, then, concentrates on those issues that relate specifically to the B2B online presence – that it is relatively short should not give readers the perception that the subject is any less important than those covered in the previous chapters; it is simply that many of the key issues have already been addressed.

Also worth noting is that in a B2B environment, online marketing should be seen as part of the wider entity that is e-business. This issue is addressed in detail in Section 1.4 – the impact of the Internet on business – and referring to that section will be beneficial to your understanding of this chapter. Similarly, this book concentrates on the use of the Internet in marketing – and not the use of the Internet in business in its entirety. For example, it is now common practice to use the web as part of recruitment, project management and logistical operations, and although elements of good practice in web design will be incorporated on sites in those fields (e.g. navigation and usability), they are not marketing specific, and so are not covered in this book.

A final point of note is that I have differentiated only B2C and B2B in separate chapters. Essentially, this chapter – despite its title – actually considers *all* non-B2C online marketing, that is, marketing to organizations or entities rather than individuals as is the case with B2C. Therefore, where reference is made to a B2B market or environment, this could just as easily apply to selling to a government department or university as it could another profit-driven business. In this context, perhaps the term B2O – business to *organization* – should be in common use.

Two issues are significant in B2B marketing: (1) the method of both the decision-making process and the actual purchase differs from B2C, and (2) the range of products varies dramatically. The first of these is addressed in detail in both Section 1.4 (actual purchase) and the next section of this chapter (buying practices). The diversity of products purchased by an organization means that the marketer must be prepared to adapt their online selling to suit different product lines. However, in a similar manner to consumer markets, firms make use of the Internet in their purchasing as a source of information and, sometimes, as a transaction channel. This second point means that it is sometimes necessary to have a website that is – essentially – a retail site, with goods selected, ordered, paid for (using a credit card) and fulfilled in exactly the same way as on a B2C web presence. In Chapter 1, I gave the example of relatively low-value stationery being an illustration of this. In instances such as these, the website developer is advised to treat the site as a retail site – following all best practice used in that environment. It is perhaps this similarity between B2C and B2B sites with a 'shopping' facility that has resulted in all such sites being dubbed 'e-commerce' sites.

For other products – in total value terms, the majority – the website is not the medium on which the actual purchase is made. As we will see in subsequent sections of this chapter, the organization's online presence can play a significant role in the commercial buying process but rarely is it the end of the process, more often, being a medium for marketing communication.

5.2 B2B BUYING PRACTICES

Throughout this book it has been my intention to avoid covering *offline* marketing theory and models – there are plenty of books that do that – this book being about *digital* marketing. However, there are a number of offline issues must be addressed in order to practise online marketing and – as with buyer behaviour (Section 1.6) – how organizations go about their business purchases is an essential consideration for the B2B digital marketer.

GO ONLINE

'The role of search in B2B buying decisions' is a high-quality, must-read paper which considers how the web is used by buyers in B2B environments. It is a couple of years old, but that makes it no less relevant . . . and I would suggest that the web is used even more in procurement now than it was at the time of this research. To read the paper, follow the link from the chapter's web page.

Key to this issue is *who* makes the buying decision, and in this regard Webster and Wind's 1972 paper on the subject is still relevant. They suggested that the buying decision can depend on input from *some* or *all* of: initiators, users, influencers, deciders, approvers, buyers and gatekeepers. Dubbed the decision-making unit (DMU), these have remained the same in the online environment – with each of them being able to use the web to help them in their own aspect of the decision-making process. More recently, in a survey on B2B trading, search engine marketing firm Enquiro (2007) suggested that there are three elements to the contemporary Internet-using B2B buying unit:

1. The economic buyer – who releases funds and holds power of veto
2. The user buyer – who judges the impact of the purchase on the job
3. The technical buyer – who considers not only the technicalities of the product, but aspects such as logistics and shipping costs.

The same report also proposed that B2B purchases follow a chronological order of: awareness, research/consideration, negotiation and purchase – a sequence similar to the recognized B2C buying process. The difference being the inclusion of 'negotiation' – though it might be argued that the retail customer's ability to seek out lower prices online (for example, see comparison search engines, Section 4.6) is a B2C equivalent of 'negotiation'.

As previously mentioned, it would be rare for a purchase order to be raised based purely on information gleaned from a website. More likely is that the Internet will be used to gather information that will then be used to narrow down a field of potential suppliers, who will then be contacted on a personal basis. This reflects the way that B2B purchasing has been conducted for hundreds of years – with the web replacing (or supplementing) catalogues, brochures, trade shows and, to a lesser degree, advertising. This means that the B2B website has the key objective of lead generation – making the presentation of information an essential element. It is also the case that in a branding context, the site can help develop the relationship that is essential in B2B commerce. Supporting the argument that in a B2B context there is little opportunity for direct sales, but opportunities for lead generation and relationship building exist, Gummerson (1994) – one of the originators of the concept of relationship marketing – predicted that the Internet would only be exploited effectively as a marketing tool when practitioners moved beyond its ability to support transactions and recognized that information delivered online provides a foundation for developing relationships with customers. Needless to say, the quality of the web presence can end a relationship before it has a chance to begin – this is particularly relevant where an initial order (once negotiated) will result in repeat orders over a long period of time.

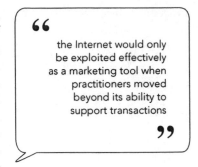

> the Internet would only be exploited effectively as a marketing tool when practitioners moved beyond its ability to support transactions

DECISION TIME

The key decisions to be made with respect to B2B buying practices revolve around being aware of:

- How your potential customers go about their buying decisions, and
- Who – within the buying organization – has responsibility for seeking information on the product that will meet its needs.

Both of these issues can be addressed by reviewing the B2B buying process – or *cycle* – that might follow a sequence something like that shown in Figure 5.1.

It cannot be emphasized enough how much this process can vary depending on the almost infinite number of products that might be purchased in the B2B environment. In describing consumer transactions it is relatively easy for a marketing tutor to use examples such as cars, mobile phones or soft drinks when teaching marketing practice. In a B2B scenario, however, students tend to be unaware of just how many B2B products are manufactured – and so marketed. These products range from the one-inch-long metal bracket that holds up the classroom whiteboard to the tons of concrete used in building a motorway flyover – and, yes, people earn a living marketing both of these products! It is also worth mentioning that the smartphone purchased by the end user is made up of thousands of components – each one of which has been purchased as a B2B product. Now think of all of the components of, say, a jet aircraft.

Having assessed the potential buying process used by the target market – or industry – the digital marketer can draw some conclusions as to (1) who is likely to make up the DMU, and (2) what information they might seek online – and how they will expect it to be presented.

A further consideration is that the web has now been with us long enough for the first Internet generation to have grown up and started work. This means that younger B2B buyers are – perhaps – not only more likely to shop online than their older counterparts, but they will expect the same standard of user experience they are used

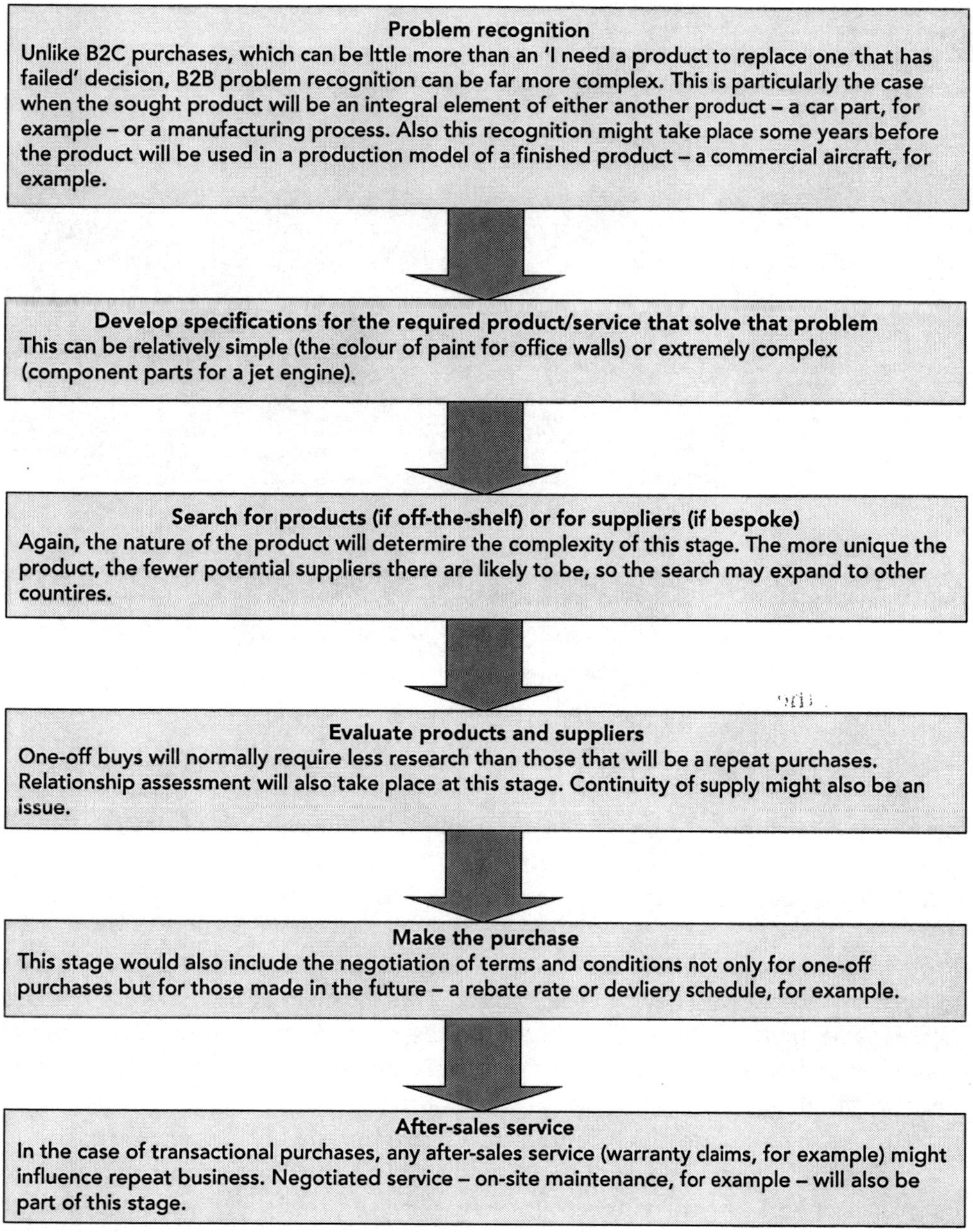

Problem recognition
Unlike B2C purchases, which can be lttle more than an 'I need a product to replace one that has failed' decision, B2B problem recognition can be far more complex. This is particularly the case when the sought product will be an integral element of either another product – a car part, for example – or a manufacturing process. Also this recognition might take place some years before the product will be used in a production model of a finished product – a commercial aircraft, for example.

Develop specifications for the required product/service that solve that problem
This can be relatively simple (the colour of paint for office walls) or extremely complex (component parts for a jet engine).

Search for products (if off-the-shelf) or for suppliers (if bespoke)
Again, the nature of the product will determire the complexity of this stage. The more unique the product, the fewer potential suppliers there are likely to be, so the search may expand to other countires.

Evaluate products and suppliers
One-off buys will normally require less research than those that will be a repeat purchases. Relationship assessment will also take place at this stage. Continuity of supply might also be an issue.

Make the purchase
This stage would also include the negotiation of terms and conditions not only for one-off purchases but for those made in the future – a rebate rate or devliery schedule, for example.

After-sales service
In the case of transactional purchases, any after-sales service (warranty claims, for example) might influence repeat business. Negotiated service – on-site maintenance, for example – will also be part of this stage.

Figure 5.1 An example of a B2B buying process

to on retail and social media sites. Research by the Acquity Group (2013) found that when making company purchases online there were significant differences between the generations, with 90 per cent of buyers aged 18–35 doing so, 68 per cent of buyers aged 36–45, 45 per cent of buyers aged 46–60 and only 29 per cent of buyers aged 60+.

As the youngest generation gets older, the percentage of online B2B purchasing can only get bigger. A caveat to this research, however, would be to suggest that the more junior a buyer is, the less responsibility for *strategic* purchasing they are likely to have.

YOU DECIDE

Advise Syd Carton and Charlie Darnay at Two Cities Manufacturing Ltd (case study 11) on what type of buying process might be common in their industry (or markets) and consider how that might impact on their web presence. Remember, you are looking at them as vendors, not buyers.

Alternatively, conduct the same exercise for your organization or that of your employer.

5.3 THE B2B WEBSITE

In Chapter 3, the importance of website content development was stressed, and the point is emphasized in B2B marketing because the site is likely to be visited by people – all of whom will have a different agenda in deciding whether or not they will buy from you. As we have seen in the previous section, the problem stems from the way businesses go about making their purchases.

In the previous section we considered a sample B2B buying cycle. In order to build a web presence that meets the needs of B2B buyers, it is worthwhile giving that cycle further consideration by looking at each element in more detail.

1. Problem recognition – likely to be an in-house decision, though buyers do use the web to keep up to date with news in their sector. This means that online press releases for new developments or products should be distributed to those sites that might be visited by industry workers – with the organization's own website including content on new products, new applications or any other advances that are important in the industry or marketplace. Such content might prompt the B2B buyer to recognize that they have a problem. The use of social media can be effective at this stage, with blogs or social network sites playing a role. Note, however, that these are more likely to be industry-specific rather than the more general Facebook-type sites.

2. Develop specifications for the required product/service that solve the problem – another issue that is probably completed within the organization, though as in the previous stage, staff may use the web to stay in touch with developments in their industry that may influence any specification decisions. The company website should address any issues that might be specific – although it should be inherent in any product description.

3. Search for products (if off-the-shelf) or for suppliers (if bespoke) – not only are there search engine optimization issues to consider, but the information that the buyers seek must be made easily available on the site – and in a format that they will find most useful.

4. Evaluate products and suppliers – offline, this would normally involve contacting the potential suppliers; online, this is not necessary. The phrase 'online – you are your website' (introduced in Section 3.3) is relevant here. Based on their perception of the organization from its website, a company may or may not make initial contact via email or telephone – a call that could lead to a multi-thousand-pound order or contract. Would you trust the manufacture of a vital, high-specification safety component for your product to a firm that couldn't be bothered to spell-check the text on its home page? Or returns '404' messages when you click on a product link on their site?

5. Make purchase – as stated earlier in the chapter, online purchase (i.e. with a credit card) is not the norm in a B2B transaction, except in the case of low-value products. However, the product might be suitable for online ordering – in which case a retail-style site might be appropriate. If the goods being sold lend themselves to regular repeat orders, then once the initial order has been negotiated (price, discounts, delivery, etc.) then an online provision should be made to accommodate those orders. This could be as simple as a designated email address or a more complex password-protected order form. It may even be an opportunity for a personalized web page, as described in Section 8.2.

6. After-sales service – as with other web presences, this can be a specific objective of the organization's online presence, be that website or a social media platform. In the B2B environment, this could go beyond a standard FAQ page to being part of any contractual agreement made with regard to the product – installation instructions or application updates, for example.

There are several caveats to add to this cycle that might impact on the digital marketer, including:

- The online information-gathering exercise might be given to a junior member of staff who is tasked with finding potential suppliers (via a search engine – another complication for keyword selection – see Section 6.3) who then simply prints out web pages that they think are relevant. The printed pages are then distributed amongst members of the DMU.

- A B2B buyer is often starting at square one with no knowledge of the market – therefore brand affinity does not play any part. On the other hand, if you have previously dipped a toe into that market, you might be drawn to a brand you have come across before.

- Inspecting, sampling and negotiation are integral aspects of B2B buying – although it might not be possible for them to be completed wholly online, they should be introduced on the website.

- In B2B purchases risk avoidance is a significant issue. Buying a shirt in a colour that doesn't suit you (in a B2C transaction) might be annoying. Ordering bespoke products that are not suitable for your application in a B2B environment could spell bankruptcy for the company or the buyer losing their job. Website copy should reflect this concern.

- Similarly, there is a lack of emotion in a B2B purchase. When buying for ourselves the axiom 'buy with the heart, justify with the brain' is often true. This is not the case in commercial procurement, where buying criteria must be adhered to.

DECISION TIME

In all marketing, the message and mode of transmission should correspond to customers' expectations, requirements and needs. Online, this is equally relevant. The additional problem, however, is that there can be a number of people involved in the buying decision – all of whom might be looking for something different on the vendor's website. For example, the *economic* buyer will concentrate on price, discounts, rebates and so on. The *user* buyer will care less for cost and instead will concentrate on whether or not the product will serve the purpose for which it is being purchased – with a natural inclination to desire the product that is actually *better* than they need – and will be looking for exact specifications and applications. The *technical* buyer may look beyond the unit price and application and pay greater attention to lead times, delivery schedules and shipping coats. Any web content that does not address all of these issues and panders to only one or two may find the 'neglected' group rejecting your offering and looking elsewhere.

How the relevant information is presented is another issue. Many products will be sold in niche markets where buyers will be experts in the industry. In this case, the content can be written in a language only they will understand. Indeed, a lack of jargon, acronyms and abbreviations may well give the impression that you are not a serious player in that industry. When preparing the content it is essential to consult closely with the firm's sales staff, who are familiar with the terms used in the industry.

In any DMU, the person who accesses the website might need to relay the information to the other decision-makers, and that may not be online – a board meeting, perhaps. Facilitating a printed format is an obvious requirement in this case – with pdf helping to ensure quality. However, as we covered in Section 3.5, video and audio can enhance textual content and can be effective in the conversion process. This is particularly true where video can be used to describe complex procedures, or an audio commentary from an expert in the product can bring to life the same content presented in one-dimensional fashion on a web page. This might be particularly relevant if members of the DMU are used to accessing the web on mobile devices. As with all issues related to content, sales staff who have a history of dealing with industry buyers will be able to provide invaluable information in this regard.

5.4 LEAD GENERATION

Such is the nature of B2B marketing and procurement that the key objective of the majority of B2B websites is lead generation. In essence, the website must present such a good impression of the organization and its products that potential buyers feel that both will meet their needs – and so they are *obliged* to contact the firm.

Having said that, any salesperson will tell you that moving the potential customer from *just looking* to being a genuine lead is far from easy. In real life, the salesperson can watch, listen and react to the prospect. Online, the website does not have such aids, and so the 'call to action' must be delivered in the right way. A common mistake of many B2B sites is to push the lead-generation aspect too early – that is, force the searcher to contact the organization too early in their buying process. Information should be made available to help decision-makers differentiate products and suppliers, so that when they do contact the vendor they are a more viable lead.

DECISION TIME

In my experience, far too many organizations have their websites designed so that the content does an excellent job in starting the customer down the sales funnel (see Sections 1.6 and 3.3), but then drops the ball when it comes to guiding them to the next step. This situation epitomizes the argument that websites must *never* be created only by folk with no sales and/or marketing

> websites must *never* be created only by folk with no sales and/or marketing experience

experience. The sales process is just that – a process – and experienced sales staff can do an excellent job in guiding potential customers through it. To ignore their experience when developing a web presence is a significant mistake. Furthermore, a lack of cohesion between online and sales often results in leads being captured by the website, only to be dropped by the offline sales team. To address this inexcusable state of affairs three issues should be resolved. They are:

1. What are the most appropriate calls to action? In Section 3.3 we looked at the concept of *persuasion* architecture, where the website content moves the visitor towards a desired action – in this case, to contact the organization. At the same time such navigation should also allow users to recognize if they are on the wrong site, that is, the seller cannot meet their needs – which is important as it cuts down the time wasted in responding to enquiries that will never generate sales. What *is* appropriate will depend on the product and the nature of the market in which it is being sold. For example, a product whose purchases are transactional (rather than relational) might suit a 'for a 10 per cent discount on your next order . . .' style of call to action. A lawyer offering to review an organization's health and safety policy, on the other hand, might be better advised to use a 'contact us before an injured employee does . . .' type of call. Websites for products where viewing samples of work would be an integral part of the buying process could give the contact details of the representative who covers the area in which the potential buyer is located.

2. What medium of communication is best? Again, custom and practice in the product's marketplace will dictate the answer. In some industries it is the phone number of the local agent or representative that is the normal method of responding to a promotion – so an online facility that allows the potential customer to find the telephone number of the person who covers their area would be preferable. In other industries the customer would expect to visit the supplier – to inspect quality-control practices perhaps. In this case a direct email address or phone number to the person (or team) who would play host to the visitor would be best. For the company that trades globally, phone numbers can be problematic because of time differences – in which case an email address would be favourable. If the organization has local representatives around the world, then it is their contact details that should be emphasized. The use of contact forms should be considered carefully. If the website has been developed to do its lead-generation job effectively, then the prospect will simply wish to initiate a dialogue – so the appropriate phone number or email address will be sufficient. To insist that the visitor (who has been successfully moved down the sales funnel by the web content) completes an online form is not good practice.

Any pertinent information can be easily gleaned in the initial conversation – yet a form requiring excessive fields to be completed (name, address, contact details, company size, etc.) might be enough to send the potential customer to a competitor who has a simple email address as a medium for the call to action. In some circumstances a prospect might wish to ask some pertinent questions, but not engage in direct email or phone contact – in which case an anonymous 'chat' facility might be an option.

3. Who handles the initial contact? In much the same way as fulfillment is the often-ignored element of online B2C sales, so allocating responsibility for incoming enquiries is frequently the Achilles' heel of lead generation. I have previously empha-sized the value of having sales staff involved in the development of a B2B website – not least because it is they who pick up the leads from the site. Other issues can include co-ordination of campaigns – for example, it is pointless having a PPC campaign running on the same week as the majority of the sales team are attending a trade show and so are not available to take sales-lead phone calls. For both email and phone contact details, wherever possible, a direct line should be established with the salesperson who will take responsibility for the customer. This might be geographic or product oriented – and is likely to have existed before the web was even invented. An effective design feature is to have key staff profiled on the website, so that if I am looking for 'mark 7 turbo yagahits' I can see on the web page that the salesperson responsible is Jane, read about her experience in the industry and contact her directly by phone or email. Practised effectively, the essential sales–customer relationship is developing before the two have even spoken. For companies who handle greater volumes of lead enquiries, employing the services of a specialist call centre – with its associated expense – is preferable to losing hard-earned online leads.

RESEARCH SNAPSHOT

Leads – what leads?

Research by the American Association of Inside Sales Professionals found that sales professionals were over optimistic about their performance in following up online sales leads. Findings included:

- 25 per cent of respondents said that they respond by phone to online leads within five minutes – in reality the figure was 5 per cent.
- Of the companies surveyed that had web contact forms, over 40 per cent failed to reply by either email or phone.
- When asked how many attempts their sales teams made to contact a lead, companies most often estimated 'more than five', but the most common number of attempts was zero.
- More than 90 per cent of the companies surveyed considered that their first response to online sales leads was by phone – whereas in reality, 67 per cent made their first contact by email.

- Only 20 per cent of companies thought that they took over a day to first respond by phone to online leads, when in actuality 31 per cent did.

Source: AA-ISP, 2013

YOU DECIDE

Following on from the last exercise, advise Sam and Chris at BethSoft (case study 5) on what is the best way to use their website to generate sales leads.

Alternatively, conduct the same exercise for your organization or that of your employer.

5.5 E-MARKETPLACES

Although marketplaces, where buyers and sellers come together, are the bedrock of trade – and marketing – it is the B2C version that most people will think of when they hear the term. However, the B2B market has had its own marketplaces for just as long as the consumer version has existed.

PRACTICAL INSIGHT

Networking moves online

In the offline environment, the B2B marketplace acts as more than a meeting place for buyers and sellers. It is somewhere to network with potential customers, to form alliances, and to seek the advice of acquaintances. The same is true online, with e-marketplaces providing similar services – resulting in them being called B2B communities or portals.

Often industry-specific, the B2B marketplaces are far less well known – which is to be expected as only those people with an interest in those industries will have cause to have heard of them. It is also the case that many offline B2B marketplaces are rather civilized – with competitors in both the supply and buying sides of the market working together to either best meet the needs of customers or get the best deals available from sellers. Neither is it unusual for competitors to form partnerships in order to best serve their customers. This spirit of co-operation has transferred to their online incarnation – the e-marketplace.

The online marketplace – 'a facility to link buyers and suppliers electronically to automate corporate procurement' (Porter, 2001) – as with the traditional one – has two interested parties: buyers and sellers. *Buyers* seek visible, knowledgeable sellers, better prices, a more efficient purchasing process and controlled spending. *Sellers* seek new markets and new customers. Also mirroring the offline entity, there is a third party – the marketplace provider. In rare circumstances, provision of the marketplace might come from one of the other two parties (a group of fruit farmers paying for premises in which they can all display their produce, for example), but normally the marketplace provider will do so as a business model. Profits are made from charging either buyers, or sellers or both to participate in the market.

There is a case to answer that the e-marketplace is an element of the procurement process – that is, it is a 'buy-side' element of business – and so does not belong in a marketing text. Whilst this is a reasonable argument, to be effective, marketers must be aware of the e-marketplace's function so that they can make best use of it in the promotion and distribution of their products – hence their inclusion in this text.

A target for venture capitalists at the end of the last century, many start-up B2B e-marketplaces suffered in the dot-bomb collapse along with other online ventures. However, whilst many of these had suspect business plans and overspent on promotion and technology, research into the reasons for their demise (Day *et al.*, 2003) suggests that the key issue was that it was impossible to replace long-standing relationships in the B2B supply chain with a website, therefore the e-marketplaces' greatest competition was existing ways of doing business. The intervening years, however, have seen a much more positive approach to the use of the Internet in the procurement and logistics fields – and so the use of e-marketplaces has become part of the way of doing business. Although some e-marketplaces are open to any and all members of an industry, many are restricted to membership of a restricted community – be they buyers or sellers.

DECISION TIME

Often cited as an example of how many organizations' adoption of the Internet as a business tool has been fragmented, it is not unusual for a firm's buying department to actively use one or more e-marketplaces in its procurement activities – and yet the marketing department ignores them in its sales efforts.

How effectively the online marketer is able to use e-marketplaces obviously depends on the extent the industry in which they operate is served by them. If there is good coverage – and there may be a dominant player – then committing to selling via an e-marketplace can release physical resources (members of a sales team, for example) to concentrate on areas of the business where online marketing is not suitable or accepted. As with all online marketing efforts, however, using an e-marketplace is not a 'fit and forget' solution. The site should be constantly monitored for activity, particularly if there is a 'community' element to it – social media sites now being popular as part of this role. It is not unusual for the first firm to respond to a 'chat-room' enquiry to be the one that gets an order. Similarly, frequent involvement in forums and the like will help build a profile of the organization and so help in any relationship marketing efforts.

Also worth noting is that e-marketplaces can be industry- or market-specific, and so the digital marketer might need to join several of them. For example, a table manufacturer might be a member of a 'tables' portal that attracts anyone who wants to buy tables, but they could also join e-marketplaces for suppliers to the hotel and catering industry, education and local government.

Whilst joining some online marketplaces can be as simple as entering your email address into a box, in order to join an e-marketplace that is linked to e-procurement facilities, the online marketer will need to complete an 'application form'. Whilst some of the content will be standard issues related to the organization in order to establish credibility, other sections are an opportunity to market the company and its products. For these sections it is essential that thought and preparation are given to the entry.

Data relating to your company might include:

- The registered name of your company and its full address
- Your company number (as registered at Companies House) and its VAT number
- The name of any parent company if your company is part of a group
- The name of your managing and any other directors – and their responsibilities
- The annual turnover of your company as in the last set of published accounts
- The number of employees in your company

Although these will add credibility to the firm – and several might be classed as essential for many buyers – it is the following points that require an element of 'sales copy':

- A description of the company – over and above the formal details listed above
- A description of the services and goods your company provides
- The URL of your website or social media presence to enable buyers to see more about your company
- If you are a supplier of goods, an indication of stock holding and product availability
- An indication of the types of organizations you currently supply, including a list of existing customers
- Details of any industry accreditation, such as ISO, Corgi, IIP, etc.

Finally, there is the section that *non-marketers* always ignore. Most forms will have a section for 'other information' – this is your best chance to make reading buyers contact you rather than any of your competitors. But remember, these will be professional buyers who will not be swayed by sales rhetoric.

YOU DECIDE

Spend some time online and see if you can find any B2B marketplaces that might be useful in the marketing of the Gilded Truffle Hotel (case study 3). Remember, you are selling, not buying – and, yes, the hotel has a significant B2B market.

Alternatively, conduct the same exercise for your organization or that of your employer.

5.6 ONLINE AUCTIONS AND TENDERING

Staples of B2B trading for decades, both auctions and tendering have gained a new lease of life in the Internet age. As with so many other aspects of marketing, the concepts remain the same online as they are offline – but the technology has vastly enhanced the services available to both buyers and sellers. Although closely related as methods of doing business, the two models differ in their practice – as you will see as we look at each in more detail.

Online auctions

Auctions are subdivided into two types – the *forward* and the *reverse* – the forward (or *ordinary*) being the original. In normal transactional trading, the seller places goods for sale at a fixed cost and invites (potential) customers to buy the goods at that price. In a forward auction, the quality, quantity, specifications and so on of the goods are made known and identified as 'lots'. At a given time and date interested parties make bids against each other, with the one making the highest bid being the winner of the lot – and so becoming the buyer of the goods. Also popular in B2C and C2C trading, auctions are normally seen as a way of selling goods you own but no longer have a use for – making them 'second hand' or 'used'. This is also the case in a B2B environment. Although it is a business model to buy new goods in bulk and then break them down into smaller units to be sold at auction, common auctions are for surplus or obsolete goods no longer needed by the organization – machinery that has been upgraded or furniture from refurbished offices, for example – the UK's Ministry of Defence even uses an online auction to sell surplus goods. Over-stocks of goods that have not sold as well as was expected are another popular auction item, with goods being sold in bulk lots to smaller retailers or – as is now common amongst a number of brand names – sold on the likes of eBay. Similarly, the assets of bankrupt companies are a familiar component of B2B auctions. Although there is a perception that auctions are for relatively low-value items only, this is not always the case. In the oil industry, for example, it is common practice to use auctions to dispose of drilling rigs and refinery facilities – all selling for millions of dollars.

Traditional auctions require the buyers to be present in a specific location at a certain time to make bids – or at least have a representative to bid on their behalf. Although these do still exist and are popular in some industries (antiques, for example), the seller can reach a much wider audience – and so achieve a higher price – by using the web to advertise the lots and allow bids to be made over a longer period of time. This means that the industrial buyer can constantly monitor auction websites – most are industry- or market-specific – and bid on products or services that are of interest. The online facilities mean that they can watch bidding in real time and so be aware of whether or not they are likely to win the bidding within their budget – something that is not always possible when the bidding takes place in a period of minutes some time after the goods were originally advertised.

With online reverse auctions – also known as *procurement* or *event* auctions – the role of the buyer and seller are reversed, with the buyer announcing what they wish to purchase and then inviting bids to satisfy those wants. Also, unlike the forward auction where the seller hopes to increase the selling price to its optimum, the reverse auction seeks to drive the selling price *down*. Although the buyer posts their requirements some time before (in order for the bidders to prepare their quotes), the event normally takes place over a short period, typically an hour or so. As the bidding is performed in real time via the Internet, the result is dynamic bidding – and so this helps achieve a downward price pressure not normally attainable with a traditional paper-based bidding process. This model can help organizations make significant savings – Procter and Gamble, for example, is said to have made savings in its supply costs of around 20 per cent by conducting reverse auctions (Hooley *et al.*, 2008). Whilst auctions are normally associated with tangible products, reverse auctions are also regularly used for services. A company might use one to secure cleaning services, for example.

MINI CASE

UK government shows the way in e-procurement

One area of B2B trading that has been proactive in the adoption of reverse auctions is government purchasing. Indeed, e-auctions are an integral element of the UK government's Procurement Strategy for central civil government. A natural extension to established tendering systems, bidders are evaluated for their ability to meet the requirement (of the product or service being bid on) before they are invited to take part in the auction. With these other issues being suitably resolved beforehand, the focus of the auction is on price.

Tendering

With its origins in fair and equitable trading – and the elimination of bribery and corruption – the concept of tendering has been common practice in the public sector for many years. The term itself is a form of legalese where an unconditional offer is made by one to another to enter into the contract of transaction of goods or services at a certain specified cost. A rudimentary description of what can be a complex process is this:

1. The buyer makes known their requirements. As with all aspects of B2B trading this can be as basic as the provision of pencils, to something as multifaceted as building a bridge or providing a computing infrastructure. Exact specifications are included so that interested parties can assess the potential costs in detail.

2. Potential bidders make known their interest and submit details of their organization, its resources and capabilities. These are then evaluated by the buyer to ensure that if the firm's bid is accepted it will be able to deliver on time and to the standard of quality stipulated in the requirements document.

3. If it meets the required standards, the company is accepted to submit a tender.

4. All interested parties submit a bid by a predetermined deadline. These bids are sealed – meaning that only the bidding organization knows its submission until all bids are opened after the deadline has passed.

5. The buyer reviews all of the bids. Although price will be the dominant factor characteristic of any decision, it is possible for a higher bid to incorporate better specifications – a shorter lead time or higher-quality materials, for example.

6. All entrants are informed of the successful bid, with the winner being awarded a contract for the work.

Before the Internet, this process was unwieldy, complicated and time consuming, particularly for small to medium-sized businesses – with big organizations often employing staff (or whole departments) whose sole job was to track, develop and submit tenders. However, online technology has alleviated much of this. For example, pre-Internet, a firm that submitted tenders to a local authority on a regular basis would have to complete all the documents on paper – much of the time repeating the same content over and over (company information, for example). Now that local authority will maintain an electronic database of suppliers that can be appended to any tender – so saving the business the task every time it submits a tender.

Another provision added to the online tendering systems of many public sector organizations is that of facilitating *joint* tenders. Whilst it was always possible for two, or more, small businesses to combine for one bid (joiners, electricians and builders for a housing renovation, for example), logistically this was problematic, particularly if the required skill-sets were not available locally. Online, however, individual firms can 'advertise' for partners or submit *partial* bids with the expectation that others will bid for other aspects of the contract.

DECISION TIME

I made the comment at the beginning of this chapter that much of the content is more relevant to the buyer than the seller (more e-procurement than e-marketing), and this section is a perfect example. Online auctions, along with other e-procurement tools, have changed purchasing and supply management processes. However, it is the foolish B2B marketer who ignores the impact of the Internet on the way in which their customers go about their buying process. Put simply, if customers expect the type of product you sell to be available in auctions, then you should be using auctions as part of your organization's overall marketing strategy.

PRACTICAL INSIGHT

An important aspect of B2B trading is the 'request for a quote' – more commonly known as the RFQ. As the term suggests, this is where the potential buyer contacts the vendor and asks them to quote a selling price for a specific product or service. On the website, this can be achieved by including an online RFQ form – but note that to be effective, the form should be at the end of a conversion funnel and not simply be an 'add-on' to the content.

Naturally, involvement in online auctions depends on the nature of the product, market and industry – and for some marketers auctions will simply not be an option or a consideration (though it will be worth monitoring them for their use in the future).

A further opportunity is the reverse auction, where the marketer is faced with a kind of reversal of roles. Although they are seeking to *sell* their product or service, they are – effectively – bidding to *buy* the permission to make that sale. As with all auctions it is easy to be caught up in the fervour of the event and bid beyond your means or intention – and so it is with the reverse auction. The marketer must make a firm decision on the lowest figure they can profitably provide the product for – and not allow themselves to bid below that amount.

Online tendering is a natural extension to its traditional predecessor, so the same rules apply. The web has brought two significant advantages, however: the whole process can be (1) easier – and so an acceptable option for even the smallest firm; and (2) there are more opportunities to put in joint bids with partners. The adoption of online tendering has also seen the development of a business model whereby companies – for a fee – will use software to track relevant tendering opportunities and help you submit a suitable proposal.

YOU DECIDE

Advise Syd Carton and Charlie Darnay at Two Cities Manufacturing Ltd (case study 11) on how they might use online auctions in the marketing of their products and/or services.

Alternatively, conduct the same exercise on your organization or that of your employer.

CHAPTER EXERCISE

Giving justifications for all your decisions, advise the directors at Clough & Taylor Engineering (case study 2) on all aspects of digital marketing covered in the chapter.

Alternatively, conduct the same exercise for your own organization or that of your employer.

CHAPTER QUESTIONS

Follow the link from the chapter's web page to a series of multiple-choice, exam-type questions that will test your knowledge and understanding of the various elements of the chapter.

REFERENCES

AA-ISP (2013) 2013 lead response audit. Available on insidesales.com.

Acquity Group. 2013 state of B2B procurement study. Available on acquitygroup.com.

Day, G.S., Fein, A.J. and Ruppersberger, G. (2003) Shakeouts in digital markets: lessons from B2B exchanges. *California Management Review*. Volume 45, number 2, pp. 131–150.

Enquiro Search Solutions (2007) The brand lift of search. Available at www.enquiro-research.com/brand-lift-of-search.aspx.

Gummerson, E. (1994) Making relationship marketing operational. *International Journal of Service Industry Management*. Volume 5, number 5, pp. 5–20.

Hooley, G. Piercy, N.F. and Nicoulaud, B. (2008) *Marketing Strategy and Competitive Positioning*. Prentice-Hall.

Porter, M.E. (2001) Strategy and the Internet. *Harvard Business Review*, March, pp. 154–162.

Webster, F.E. Jr and Wind, Y. (1972) A general model for understanding organizational buying behavior. *Journal of Marketing*. Volume 36, pp. 12–19.

Chapter **6**

Search engine optimization (SEO)

Man will not live without answers to his questions.

Hans Morgenthau

Chapter at a glance

6.1 Introduction
6.2 How search engines work
6.3 Keyword selection
6.4 On-site optimization
6.5 Off-site optimization
6.6 Strategic SEO

6.1 INTRODUCTION

In the first edition of this book I stated, 'some practitioners might argue that such is the power of the search engines that Internet marketing is, effectively, search engine marketing' and at that time (2009) it was a valid argument to make. However, two significant things have happened since that time to question that statement.

The first is internal to SEO – and that is the fact that it is no longer a secret art known only to a few experts. However, the basics of SEO have not really changed since it started in the mid-1990s and they are now common knowledge (Google has free guides online and books like this have helped with that) and relatively easy to practise. Indeed, contemporary content management systems (CMSs) now prompt users for effective SEO input. More important, however, is the external threat to *traditional* search from the meteoric expansion of the use of social media. As it has become the primary reason many web users go online, it is suggested that those users start their 'search' from there by asking friends for advice on, for example, good websites to buy certain products. Facebook's Graph Search (covered later in this chapter) is designed to take this several steps further and make social networking the hub of surfers' web activity.

So is search engine marketing (SEM) a dying practice – something that is no longer a necesity for the digital marketer? To make a judgement on that we need to dig below the hullabaloo that has surrounded the likes of Facebook and Twitter in the off- and online press that has diverted attention from the fact that social media is still used predominantly for *social* activities – and search engines for *commercial* activities such as buying things. Note, however, that things are changing and who knows how this introduction might differ by the time the third edition of the book comes around? Although we consider the now significant role social media plays in digital marketing in Chapter 9, to suggest that the importance of SEO has diminished would be an irrational oversight. Indeed, as the search engines evolve there may be an argument that their power is nowhere near its zenith. As Amit Singhal – the man in charge of search at Google – said in an interview with Mark Prigg of the *London Evening Standard* on 6 February 2012, 'Search engines are still at the information stage. Our objective is to make this a source of knowledge for our users' – suggesting, perhaps, that search engines will play an increasing role in our lives. Furthermore, the data that search engines are amassing is increasing at an exponential rate. As John Battelle suggests in his book *Search* (2005), Google is sitting on a goldmine of information that can help marketers better identify and reach their target markets. Battelle calls this collection of information the 'Database of Intentions', which he describes as 'the aggregate results of every search ever entered, every result ever tendered and every path taken as a result'.

It is the ubiquity of search engines and the way in which they encroach into all aspects of online marketing that prompted me to avoid a chapter that concentrated on search engine marketing (SEM). Although many might argue – with some validity – that marketing that employs search engines is a sub-discipline of digital marketing and so a subject in its own right, I disagree, preferring to divide the use of search engines in marketing into two distinct elements:

1. search engine optimization (SEO); and
2. the use of search engines as a medium for hosting ads – which is covered in the next chapter and is commonly referred to as *search engine advertising*.

That both rely on keywords and that organic results are listed on the same search engine results page (SERP) as paid ads is normally the basis of any argument to include them both under SEM is, I feel, too simplistic a notion. Although the same keywords are the fundamental reason that organic returns and paid returns appear on the same SERP – the way in which their presence is orchestrated is very different. In a nutshell – though as you will see in this and the next chapter, I am being simplistic when I say this – the marketer can pay to be top of the ad section, but it is the *search engine* that decides who is top of the organic listings. It is for this reason that I choose to cover the organic – or *natural* – search engine optimization in this chapter, and leave the paid advertising aspect for inclusion in the chapter covering online advertising.

Those new to search engine optimization often think the aim of the exercise is to somehow get the better of the search engines – when, in fact, the opposite is true. The search engines depend on websites for their business. They want to index websites that have content that matches the keywords of searchers, and so meets the needs of those searchers. They want to develop a relationship with your website. But, like any relationship, it has to be built – not imposed.

The search engine does not automatically trust the new website. It likes to check up on the validity of the content. It might even wait a few months before listing the site – just to make sure it is what it claims to be. It will check to see if any trusted sites link to the site. And that is why some websites sit at number one in the search engine results pages. Yes, they are optimized correctly – but they have the history. The search engine is confident that the site is what it says it is. The search engine trusts it. The searchers trust it. Your website won't gain that trust overnight – so be patient. SEO is all about the long haul – it's about developing a relationship.

> " SEO is all about the long haul – it's about developing a relationship "

PRACTICAL INSIGHT

SEO advice from the top

When asked, 'does search engine optimization work?' Matt Cutts, who has held a number of significant roles at Google, commented:

It does to some degree. Think of it this way: When you put a resume [CV] forward, you want it to be as clean as possible. If the resume is sloppy, you're not going to get interviewed for the job. SEO is sort of like tweaking your resume.

Source: Q&A session between *Wired News* and Matt Cutts, published on blog.wired.com in March 2008

What is SEO?

Before looking in some detail at the *what* and *why* of SEO, it is worth considering the issue from the point of view of the search engines – or at least, those who own and publish them. The operation of a search engine (SE) is a business model in which a service is provided that attracts users to a website – and any site that attracts significant numbers of visitors can sell advertising on that site. To be successful in attracting users, the SE must satisfy the needs of its users. To satisfy them best, the SE must respond to the users' searches with results that address the problem for which the searcher is seeking an answer. Therefore, if, for example, I am having problems with green fly on my roses, entering the phrase "green fly roses" should return pages that will tell me why it is happening and how I can prevent it.

PRACTICAL INSIGHT

It's not easy

In his bestselling book *Everything I Know about Marketing I Learned from Google* (2011), Aaron Goldman describes SEO as 'the practice of improving a brand or web site's visibility on Google and other search engines'. He goes on to say that 'it's not that complicated', but that 'doesn't mean it's easy to get to the top of Google'.

To present that information, the SE will look for pages that appear to address the issue raised by the query. They do that by seeking pages that include the words "green", "fly" and "roses" somewhere in the content or coding (more of this later). Naturally, there will be millions of pages that have the word "green" on them. The same goes for "fly" and "rose". There might even be a news item headlined 'Green Bay Packers fly to Rose Bowl', which includes all three words but has nothing to do with problems with insects in gardens (it alludes to an American gridiron football team travelling to a particular venue).

However, it is reasonable to assume that a *genuine* web page about problems with aphids and the like on roses will include the words "green", "fly" and "roses". Indeed, the title of the page might be "Growing Roses", and have a section called "dealing with pests", and that section will include advice specific to killing green fly. The SE, therefore, will pick such a page as the top result for the searcher. Following on will be every other web page that has the three searched-for words on it – ranked in order of what the SE decides is most relevant to least relevant (on the day this was written, the phrase "green fly roses" gave 2,200,000 returns on Google, 5,770,000 on Yahoo! and 5,590,000 on Bing, and they all led with gardening-based pages. They also addressed the issue that "green" and "fly" in this context are also presented as one word.) Of course, the SE has to *guess* in what context the searcher is using the sought words (gardening or gridiron football teams, in the example above), but then the whole issue is far more complex than my simplistic example above.

In essence, SEO is the practice of making a website attractive to a search engine by presenting its code and content in such a way that the search engine will assume that it will address a specific enquiry from a (human) searcher. In the gardening example above, I would be striving to make my web page about roses and greenfly appeal to searches on *keywords* (more on these later) on that subject. The issue becomes more important to me if I am trying to sell greenfly spray on my web page rather than simply presenting my 'hobby' page.

PRACTICAL INSIGHT

It's a key issue

Throughout this book when reference is made to what a user might type into a search box the term I use is *normally* 'keyword' or 'keywords' – hence the title of the section later in this chapter.

That some writers split the term into two words ('key word') is the least of the confusion caused by the lack of cohesion in descriptions in common use. It would seem that any combination of 'key', 'search', 'term', 'phrase' and 'word' is an option – for example 'key term', 'search term', 'key phrase', 'key term', 'search word' or 'search phrase'.

Whilst I can appreciate that a user might type a whole sentence in a search box and so 'keyword' is hardly an accurate description – for the sake of continuity I usually use only that – unless one of the other terms serves grammatical continuity better.

For many, this aspect of digital marketing is both mysterious and somewhat mystifying, not least because (1) it is dependent on some extremely complicated mathematical algorithms, (2) the term 'search engine optimization' is something of a misnomer – suggesting that it is the search engines that are being optimized, rather than the web pages, and (3) is it the same as search engine marketing (SEM)? Let's address these issues in turn:

1. Yes, the algorithms by which the search engines determine their listings are complex (more on them later), but the maths element is all 'behind the scenes', and the digital marketer need not hold a computer science or engineering degree to practise successful SEO.

2. Though widely known as search engine optimization, the phrase *optimizing* [your website] *for search engines* better describes the activity. Essentially, the e-marketer is looking to optimize a web page so that it best *attracts* the search engines.

3. The term search engine marketing is used to describe the wider impact that search engines have not only on *digital* marketing – but marketing as a whole. In that context, SEO is an element of SEM.

Let's consider this last issue in more detail. In this chapter we will look at how a web page can be optimized so that it appears high up in the search engines' *organic* listings. In the next chapter we consider the use of search engine results pages (SERPs) as a medium for carrying ads (also called paid placement). Both of these issues might be considered to be elements of SEM.

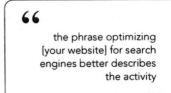

> the phrase optimizing [your website] for search engines better describes the activity

PRACTICAL INSIGHT

Searching for what you know is there

Although eBay is one of the best-known brands on the web, its name is also amongst the most searched-for keywords. Quite why a user would open up a search engine and type 'eBay' or 'Facebook' into the search box rather than simply typing 'eBay' or 'Facebook' into the browser – or clicking on the link in the browser's 'favourites' – is a mystery to some.

The answer (probably) lies in a practice known as *navigational search* (or *navigational query*). There are two main reasons for this: (1) in order to reach the required website, domain names must be typed into browsers *exactly* – and in some instances specific spellings of domain names can be tricky to remember – including which suffix is used, and (2) surfers are so used to using search engines that they automatically start with them. A third reason – that people are lazy – is probably covered within the second point.

For those who may doubt that navigational queries take place, follow the links from the chapter's webpage – and see how the most popular websites on the Internet are consistently the most searched-for terms.

6.2 HOW SEARCH ENGINES WORK

As you will discover in the section, search engines are something of a law unto themselves, caring little for the businesses in their listings (remember, their objective is to provide a service for the *searcher*, not those who want to be found). Therefore, any business – but particularly pure-online traders – should be wary of total dependence on search engines for their online traffic. A simple change in a search engine's algorithm or increased SEO activity from a competitor could see a prized top organic listing disappear overnight – reducing new customers to zero. Naturally, paid advertising might take up some of the slack, but it is doubtful that referral numbers will be maintained.

When considering how a search engine performs its expected duties, there are two issues to address: firstly, how it assesses websites for suitability in matching the search criteria (the algorithm), and secondly, how it presents the results of its assessment (the SERP). Before we consider these two in more detail, it is worth mentioning that the search engines use spiders (or bots) that spend their lives touring the web gathering up information on websites which the SEs store in their vast indexes. It is from these indexes that search results are gleaned.

If I could give here an absolute list of those elements of a website that score highly in the search engine algorithms – and so help propel a site to the top of the SERPs – this book

> **"** If I could give here an absolute list of those elements of a website that score highly in the search engine algorithms . . . this book would become an instant bestseller **"**

would become an instant bestseller, and I could retire to a luxury villa in a sunny location. The fact of the matter is that there is no 'magic bullet' solution to SEO. Those people who are outside the search engine companies can only really guess at exactly how they work – calculated guesses certainly, but still guesses. Despite the spurious claims made by some less scrupulous search engine consultants, there is no guarantee of achieving a place in the top ten results of a search. There are a number of reasons for this, not least that:

1. The specific factors in the algorithm used to calculate the rankings are unknown – Google is *said* to have around 200.

2. Other than that they are not equal, the weighting apportioned to each factor is unknown. Furthermore, it is changed regularly – so no one (outside the search engine companies) knows which elements of SEO gain most benefit and which have little value.

PRACTICAL INSIGHT

Now you see it, now you don't

Rankings for some keywords fluctuate constantly. Try searching for a phrase from a competitive market (car insurance, hotels or smartphones, for example) every fifteen minutes or so and you will notice that the top ten returns will rarely be the same.

Whilst the question of their weighting is important, it is the actual factors in the algorithm that take the concentration of the search engine optimizer – though naturally, if a specific factor is identified as having a significant weighting, it is common sense to make sure that factor is addressed correctly.

The relationship between the search engines and search engine optimizers is a strange one. On the one hand SEOs help website developers to ensure that their sites feature in the SERPs for keywords representing the content of the pages – which is exactly what the SEs want. That is, the searcher finds a page that will have the content they are looking for. Without some kind of optimization a web page – no matter how good the content is – might not be found by searchers. On the other hand, however, the search engines do not want their indexes 'influenced' by SEOs to the degree that the optimizer is dictating search results – particularly if 'black hat' spamming techniques are used to distort the search results. Indeed, recent years have seen the SEs penalizing sites that have been optimized by these illegitimate means.

PRACTICAL INSIGHT

Analysis of search results can provide a general guide, but it does not reveal the actual algorithms used by the search engines. For example, I have seen research which revealed that – in a survey – the search engine seemed to favour websites with a domain name that was thirteen characters in length. The likelihood is that, in that survey, a website with a thirteen-character domain featured highly in the search results, so skewing the data.

Note that the *length* of a site's domain name is definitely *not* part of the search engines' algorithms.

So what are the elements of the algorithms? For some facets there is a certain level of agreement between the industry experts. However, for many aspects of SEO there is a big grey area where confusion and controversy reign. For the purposes of this book we'll consider only what are deemed to be the most popular optimization elements, dividing the optimization into (1) the on-site placement of keywords, and (2) off-site issues that can improve the site's SE popularity.

GO ONLINE

A common thread in any SEO advice is that no one – not even the 'experts' – knows the search engine algorithms. This means that there is limited agreement between those experts – and some outright disagreement. For a perfect example of this, follow the link on the chapter's web page to 'Search Engine Factors V2'. Not only is there a comprehensive list of factors (I think I've got them all in the chapter), but there are ratings – and comments – on their importance from a gathering of the world's top SEO practitioners.

Personalization

In the first edition of this book I alluded to the fact that many practitioners and commentators thought that Google was personalizing users' search results depending on each searcher's search history. In other words, two people typing in the same search term at the same time will get different SERPs. Since that time personalization has become the norm for search engines. Personalized search considers the websites the user previously visited via search results to determine the results for future searches – so providing a more personalized experience. For example, if a user's normal response to a product search is to click on an eBay link then future product searches will have more eBay pages on the SERP. However, the service has received criticism as the results bias in favour of previous searches can mean that new information is limited. However, as the CEO of Google, Eric Schmidt, is often quoted as stating that the perfect search engine would deliver just one result – the right one – it seems likely that before the third edition of this book comes out we will have seen the search engines collecting (even) more user data and so providing us with our *own* search results. That the search engines already – effectively – do this for the delivery of ads means it is more a case not of *if*, but *when* this will happen.

The search engine results page (SERP)

The search engine results – or *returns* – page appears as a result of a request on a search engine. As it is the page that shows the results of a search, appearing on it is the objective of the search engine optimizer. The SERPs of the major search engines are presented in two columns. On the left will be the organic listings (the results of SEO) and on the right the sponsored listings (paid ads). Some search engines – significantly, including Google – also include ads above the organic list.

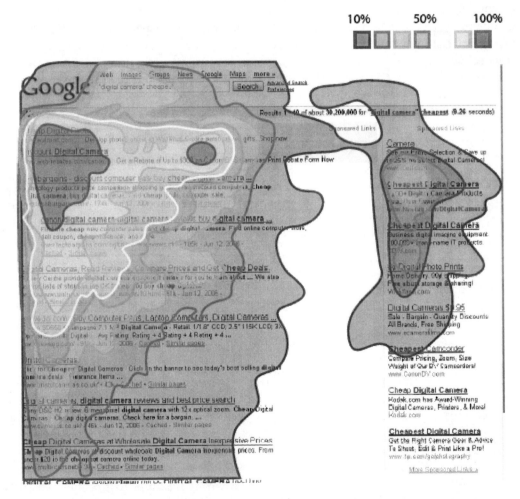

Figure 6.1 SERP heat map. This image shows how users look first at the top organic result on a SERP, with paid listings well down the scale. Still think it isn't important to be high in the natural listings?

It has been an evolution of the way in which we use the Internet (and in many ways a tribute to the abilities of contemporary search engines) that we rely on only the highest listings when we practise online searching – in how many searches do you go beyond the first page of listings? If featuring anywhere in an SE search result is the objective of the SEO, then appearing at the top of the first SERP is nirvana for digital marketers.

DECISION TIME

Before considering the decisions to be made with regard to SEO, it is worth noting that these issues are equally relevant to B2B traders as they are in the B2C environment. Chapter 5, which considered the B2B online presence, emphasized that organizations use the web to help with procurement – and search engines are used to find business products and services as well as B2C products. Indeed, commentators make the point that business buyers expect the same online experiences in their work environment as they have become used to in their personal online shopping.

The decision on involvement in SEO is determined by the organization's marketing objectives. These can be divided into three significant business categories: (1) the online pure-play, (2) the bricks and clicks, and (3) the offline only. As stated in the previous paragraph – these are equally valid in consumer and industrial markets. Issues for the three categories include:

1. The online pure-play business is dependent on the web for its income – therefore featuring high in the SERPs is essential.
2. For the bricks-and-clicks business it will depend on the ratio of their off- and online sales and how any online marketing efforts complement or replace offline sales – though it is normal for this type of organization to seek high search engine listings. However, offline marketing will always drive traffic to the website, so it is not as crucial as it is for the pure-play.
3. With the offline business, this issue is more difficult. Although it is more and more common for customers to use the web to find products or offline sellers, for some organizations the web will always be a minor source of customers. For these, obviously, high visibility in the SERPs is not a priority. Similarly, in some industries, businesses have operated offline for years – and their marketing is relationship- rather than transactional-oriented. For these, the web offers little by way of generating new business. In other areas, however, the web brings much to marketers. A further consideration to this is if the potential customer has been made aware of the existence of an organization – at a networking event, for example. Such is the nature of how SEs work that – providing the organization has a website with its name on it – simply typing the organization's name into the SE will bring up that organization's website on the SERP.

With regard to search engines there are three significant categories: (1) competitive markets – if you're not high in the SERPs, your competitors will be, (2) niche markets – where it is relatively easy to get to the top of the listings, and (3) companies that trade only locally, but whose customers use the web in the same way as they might a telephone directory to find local products or sellers. This has gained importance in recent years as *local* search has gained prominence.

Essentially, if you want your website to be found by potential customers, then appearing high in the listings on SERPs for keywords pertinent to your organization, product or brand is a given. Not to be high on the organic listings means that increased resources must be committed to other ways of driving traffic to your site – from offline efforts to online advertising – including paid advertising on the SERPs, which is covered in the next chapter.

YOU DECIDE

Take a look at all of the case study organizations and consider the importance for each of having high listings on SERPs for relevant keywords. List them in order of significance of SERP listings, with the organization for which high listings are essential at the top and the one for whom it isn't so important at the bottom.

Alternatively, consider the importance of high SERP listings for your organization or that of your employer.

6.3 KEYWORD SELECTION

As I explained in the introduction to this chapter, I have chosen to differentiate SEO from advertising on search engines. However, there is one area where they are inextricably linked – keywords.

This is because the structure of both organic and paid listings is governed by the keywords that are used by the searcher. Therefore, although this section is included in the chapter on search engine optimization, it is equally relevant in the sections on search engine and network advertising in the next chapter, as they are also developed around keyword matching. So why is deciding which keywords your website should be optimized for so important? Simply put, keywords are the core of all search engine marketing. If – as I described in the introduction to this chapter – the search engines are striving to match the searcher with websites that address their needs, it is the keywords that the searcher types into the search box that the search engine uses to make that match.

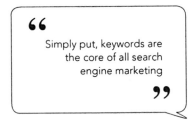

"
Simply put, keywords are the core of all search engine marketing
"

The issue for the online marketer is, therefore, to decide which terms the user will type into a search box when they want the product or information your website sells or provides. But, like many marketing problems, the question revolves around trying to get into the head of the potential customer to discern what they are thinking – not what you are thinking.

Some examples of mismatches are rather obvious – holidaymakers search for "cheap flights", but airline marketers sell flights that are *budget, bargain* or *best value*. Similarly, someone seeking medical advice after a relative has had a *heart attack* would search on those words – yet website content written by a doctor would talk about an *acute myocardial infarction*. Inward-looking keyword decisions also place too much emphasis on product names, jargon and brands. Even if your latest model, the '123–500 series rodent eliminator' is the best in the business – and already well known in pest-control industry circles – if I am new to the industry or I'm looking for the solution to a rat-infestation problem I'm going to type "rat killer" in my search box, not "123–500 series". This notion is reinforced by research from Jansen *et al.* (2008) which found that 80 per cent of searches are informational, 10 per cent navigational and 10 per cent transactional. The definitions for each – as identified in Andrei Broder's seminal paper 'A taxonomy of web search' (2002) – being:

- Informational – looking for a specific fact or topic
- Navigational – seeking to locate a specific website
- Transactional – searching for information related to buying a particular product or service.

For content developers this means that they should be looking to provide keyword-rich information that helps the searcher meet their needs. That may lead to an (eventual) sale or traffic that will achieve website objectives (e.g. advertising income).

Note that in research into search engine use, it is now common for the *keywords* to be categorized as:

- A *term*: a series of characters separated by white space or other separator – essentially, a word
- A *query*: a string of terms (words) submitted by a searcher – with *query length* denoting the number of terms (words) in the query.

PRACTICAL INSIGHT

Developing keyword lists for products, brands or organizations is problematic. One answer is to use the old sales and marketing trick of selling not the product but the benefits it can provide (in Section 3.5, I talked about selling green lawns, not grass seed).

Brad Geddes suggests that keywords can be chosen on the basis of:

- Explicit keywords, which directly describe the product – e.g. "plumber in Sunderland"

- Problems keywords, which describe the conditions the product solves – e.g. "flooded bathroom"
- Symptoms keywords, which describe the problem – e.g. "leaking pipe joint"
- Product names and part numbers, which are the actual product names and/or part numbers – e.g. "copper joint 234/567B".

Source: Geddes, 2010

Furthermore, the English language doesn't help the e-marketer, with some words being a heteronym – the same spelling, but different meanings. For example, 'bow' could be the front of a ship, a weapon used by Robin Hood, a hat decoration – or something you do when you meet the Queen or emperor. Similarly, 'lotus' can be a flower, a car or a yoga position. Furthermore, if you want to buy films featuring the secret agent with a licence to kill, typing 'Bond' into a search engine will not only give returns devoted to 007. Somewhere in the SERP will be DVDs from the James Bond franchise, but the chances are that the top return will be something to do with financial services. Plus there will also be entries for the UK organization for international development, which has the same name as the sought-after spy. There are also words for which foreigners use 'localized' versions instead of the names that natives use, for example the place names Munich/München and Majorca/Mallorca. Similarly, products are known by different names in different countries or regions. For example, that device you save digital files on is a *flash drive*, *USB drive* or *memory stick*, depending where in the world you are. In many of these cases the search engine will pick up on the duplicates – but it will be worth checking before you make keyword decisions.

Keyword problems do not end there, however. The level of competition in the market will also be a consideration. If your product is represented by popular keywords then your website is competing with every other website that has been optimized for the same terms. This is particularly true if you sell a product with a generic identification – such as 'smartphone', 'tablet' or 'car insurance'. One way out of this is to optimize for more unusual terms that address niche markets – the so-called *long tail* of keywords. However, for some companies this is not feasible – consider how many combinations of types of car and customer location in the UK a car insurer would have to optimize for to match all potential queries, for example.

Still considering grammatical issues, search engines will usually identify misspellings – offering auto-corrected alternatives – and treat singular and plural as the same search – but this is not always the case (try searching on "hotel Berlin" and "hotels Berlin" and check both returns). A similar situation arises with *stemming*. For example, a search using the word 'swim' in a phrase may produce different results than the same term, but with the word 'swimming'. In this example the chances are that the searcher was referring to 'movement in water', but the issue can be more complicated – the word 'swimmingly', for example, in a search term would have nothing to do with aquatic pursuits, but would refer to something going well.

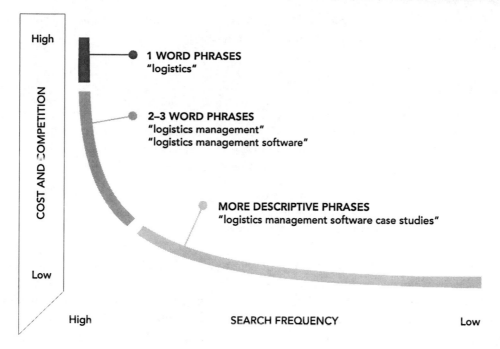

High

1 WORD PHRASES
"logistics"

2–3 WORD PHRASES
"logistics management"
"logistics management software"

MORE DESCRIPTIVE PHRASES
"logistics management software case studies"

COST AND COMPETITION

Low

High   SEARCH FREQUENCY   Low

Figure 6.2 The long tail of keywords. This 'infographic' demonstrates how search terms get longer as they move down the long tail of keywords

Source: © Elliance. All Rights Reserved

Localization

A subject that has evolved along with the development of the search engines is that of serving searchers with results that are locally relevant to them. This has come to the fore even more with the widespread adoption of mobile devices. No longer does the searcher sit in an office or house when seeking an outlet with a product in stock; they are on the high street, in a café – or even in one shop and looking for a cheaper price for a product in another store close by. Having a SERP tell me that there are 60,400,000 Greek restaurants listed (as Google did in the Spring of 2014) is pretty useless information if I want to eat out within a reasonable travelling distance from my home. My search is more likely to be 'Greek restaurant Sunderland', 'Greek restaurant Newcastle' or 'Greek restaurant north east England' – and so the restaurants in those areas should optimize their sites accordingly. Needless to say, having a restaurant in Sunderland topping the SERP of a searcher in California is equally useless – and the search engines know it.

Localization impacts on keyword selection in a number of ways, not least in that it can favour the smaller – local – business. The most obvious is in the address of the business, which – by definition – will include region, city or district that might be searched for by the customer. For the national (or even global) organization, having a web page *optimized* for every one of its outlets can be problematic – though not impossible for the can-do company. Another, less obvious, factor that can favour the local company is the use of *regional* phrases and terms. These are often difficult for the national company to adopt as they exist – and so are known – only in their own locale.

DECISION TIME

The best keywords must have both (1) strong relevance to your site – and so the product or service you are offering – and (2) high search volume – they should be the terms people *actually* look for. But how do you identify the right keywords? The following three options are available, and in most cases all should be practised:

1. Ask yourself. The chances are that you can think of a dozen or more keywords off the top of your head, but looking no further than these is a mistake. Your own ideas of what potential customers *might* use may differ wildly from what they will actually use.

2. Ask your customers. This can be offline or online and can be part of a formal campaign, or customers can be questioned in an ad hoc fashion as and when they have contact with the organization. Simply asking a regular customer (of an offline business) what keywords they would use to find your website can be quite an eye-opener.

3. Use technology. An extension of asking your customers, the first step is to look at the metrics of your website to see what keywords people who actually visited your site used to find it. This concept can be taken a stage further by visiting one of the many websites that provide keyword research tools. Such tools collect data on search engine queries that have been conducted over a period of time. You can see what terms are searched on – normally by market or industry – as well as getting advice on related terms including synonyms and popular misspellings. Although the most comprehensive keyword research tools must be purchased, both Google's AdWords Keyword Tool and Yahoo's Keyword Selection Tool provide keyword volume for free.

Another route to follow is to match your keywords with the *reason for a purchase* of anything that you sell. Perhaps most obvious is where the purchase is a gift – so the search term a distant uncle might use is 'Christmas present five-year-old girl'. Similarly, those looking for inspiration might use 'engagement gift ideas' or 'surprise present for my wife'. Along similar lines – and common practice in traditional advertising – is to provide a solution to a problem. In this scenario the searcher does not type in the name of a product (the solution), but the problem. For example, if the local wildlife is thwarting attempts to improve your lawn, you might use 'birds eating grass seed' as the search term.

YOU DECIDE

Advise Robert Terwilliger on what keywords might match up with what potential customers for the Modeller's Stand (case study 9) might type into a search engine. Bear in mind that most customers will not know of the existence of the product.

Alternatively, conduct the same exercise for your organization or that of your employer.

6.4 ON-SITE OPTIMIZATION

Search engine optimization is based on two distinct categories: those that are concerned with the website itself, and those that are outside the parameters of the site. In this and the following sections of this chapter we will look at these two elements in turn, starting with the on-site aspects.

Keyword placement

The SE algorithm will consider the placement of the keywords within the web page – and to fully appreciate these issues it is a good idea to put yourself in the place of the search engine. Its aim is to provide the searcher with results that will best satisfy their objectives for making that search. With this in mind, it is necessary to optimize your web pages to help the search engine achieve that objective.

The keywords can be placed in two aspects of the website: (1) that which is visible to the human visitor – its *content,* and (2) that which is part of the source code of the page and so is visible only to the search engines. Let's consider them both in turn.

The web page content

Also known as the body text – because it fits into the source code in the *body* command – this is the textual content of the website that the visitor will read. Some put forward the argument that this is the most important aspect of SEO, and there is some validity – and sense – in their line of reasoning which is this. If the search engine is looking to meet the needs of the searcher, then the keywords that they use should be an inherent, organic aspect of the site's textual content. For example, consider this chapter as if it were a web page. Obviously it is about search engine optimization – that is its title. Now consider the keywords you might type into a search box if you were seeking answers to the sort of questions and issues I address in this chapter. I will (almost) guarantee that those keywords appear within my text. Three obvious search terms would be: "search engine optimization", "SEO" and "keywords". Now have a quick look to see how many times those three phrases appear on the pages of this chapter. How could I possibly write about the subject area without using these terms? And that is the search engine's view as well – with the contrary also being true – a page that does not include those terms can't really be about SEO. Having said that, irrespective of the benefits of keyword inclusion, you do not want a web page with content that reads something like:

Search engine optimization, keywords, SEO are important to keyword, SEO and search engine optimization for web page's SEO, keywords and search engine optimization.

This too contains the keywords, but it makes no sense to the human reader – and the SE spider will realize that it is search engine *spam* (nonsensical content designed to appeal to the SE). How often the keywords should appear within the text is debatable, though there is evidence that the SEs take *frequency* into account. For this reason there is some sense in keeping textual content short – keywords appearing twice in fifty words is a better ratio than four times in 400 words. There would also appear to be an advantage if the keywords are the first words on the page, or at least in the first sentence or paragraph. Once again, however, I refer you to *organic* content – a web page (or book) about apples would be very strange if the word 'apple' wasn't in the first sentence or two.

PRACTICAL INSIGHT

Panda bites back and Hummingbird flies in

Responding to frustrated searchers who discovered that too many of the sites they clicked on from Google SERPs were little more than a list of ads or had no relevance to their search, February 2011 saw the search giant introduced a significant change to its algorithm – Panda. Google Panda saw many 'ad' sites disappear from the results pages whilst high-quality sites moved onto page one. At the time of writing, Panda's successor, Penguin, was still introducing updates to better satisfy the searching public. Google's commitment to high-quality content is thought to have been a significant driver in the popularity of *content marketing* – which we consider later in this chapter.

Not content with constant tinkering, September 2013 saw Google surprise the online marketing industry with a brand-new algorithm called 'Hummingbird'.

The source code

The argument for including keywords in a web page's source code is that this helps the SE spider identify the page's subject. In reality, with the exception of the page title – on which most agree – search engine optimizers disagree on the validity of this practice. However, given that each entry takes only a few minutes, the investment is not excessive – and as all of the entries should correspond with the actual content of each page it does encourage good content development.

The first batch of source code entries are the meta tags. These describe the contents of a web page, and can include 'status' information, the author's name or the name of the web design company, for example. In the early days of SEO, because the meta tags were there to describe the page, the SEs focused on them. However, they are easy to abuse and for this reason the search engines eventually reduced their reliance on them. The exception is the title tag – as it actually appears in the browser (at the very top of the browser window) it is a valid descriptor and so is abused only by the foolish. Other meta tags include the *description* and *keyword* tags. The latter is – it seems – universally ignored by the search engines. The former is also useless in SEO terms, but it is worth consideration as it can appear as the descriptive text for the web page on the SERP. Other places within the source code that may – or may not – be useful for SEO include:

- The *alt attribute* for an image. These are textual descriptions that appear as alternatives (hence *alt*) for images. Although the practice is dying out as broadband availability increases, some people surf with the image function turned off (pages download faster), so the textual description says what the 'missing' image is. More importantly, however, alt text tells the visually impaired what the image is – a legal requirement in the UK and much of the EU. Once again, the process is an exercise in *natural* SEO. If the image is a picture of a church in Humberston, the alt text should be 'Humberston church'. Not only does the visually impaired user know what it is, but the SE does also – so anyone searching on "Humberston church" will be presented with the page that features that picture. This is particularly true if the user has searched on the 'images' facility of the search engine. Sadly, many web designers treat both the disabled and SEs with some disdain and simply tag the image with the file name – for example 123.gif – or with nothing at all.

- The H1 tag. This is the source code instruction that is used on page or paragraph headers (hence 'H') which makes the text bigger and bold. Again, the *natural* aspect of SEO comes into play. If a website on Manchester United has a section on former players, there is likely to be a page for David Beckham. That page will – naturally – be headed with the player's name. Consequently, the words 'David Beckham' would be in an H1 tag at the top of the page. It is obvious, therefore, that a search engine looking to match a search on "David Beckham" would offer up that page as containing content that is about the footballer. Note that other H tags present the text smaller than H1 – although H2, H3, H4 and so on are not thought to carry the strength of H1 in optimization terms. The same principle applies to the 'bold' command – the notion being that if a word is bolded within a paragraph then it is important to the reader and the subject – so the SE gives it more credence than other words on the page.

- Hyperlink text. These will be relevant to the SEO of the page to which they deliver the user. Rather than making a link on, for example, 'click', or 'follow this link' – which mean nothing to a search engine – keywords should be used as the link text. Continuing the example of a Manchester United website, the 'former players' page would have a link on it to the 'David Beckham' page – if that link is on the words 'David Beckham', then that is telling the SE that the target page is, indeed, about that player.

- Part of the technical/design aspect of the website, but not in the source code, is another opportunity for keyword inclusion – the inclusion of keywords in the domain name and directory and file names used on the website. For example, consider the aforementioned David Beckham page. A logical URL for it would be: www.manutdwebsite.com/former-players/david-beckham.htm. This makes it clear to both humans and search engines what the content of that page is. Although some doubt is laid on the SEO value of these, giving web page files names that match their content seems to be the type of logical practice that SEs favour. My own website – alancharlesworth.eu – is not likely to be about David Beckham, for example. By the same token, however, having too many slashes (/) in the URL might serve only to dilute the value of the page.

Worth noting at this point is that websites originally featured text and images only. Now they include videos, pdfs, music, films and maps – which should all be optimized for the search engines. This is achieved by incorporating keywords in the titles and names of the various files. Other aspects of on-site SEO that fall outside of keyword placement include the following:

- Outgoing links to external sites. In the next section we will consider the value SEs place on incoming links, however, outgoing links also add to the validity of your site in SEO terms. This does not mean that a page of links to every site you can think of will be looked on with any favour. As with all of the other aspects covered so far, there is an element of how appropriate the link is – with SEs considering the quality and relevance of pages you link to. A link from my website to a site on dolls' houses, for example, will gain no credit from a search engine. However – as is frequently the case on my site – if I have a paragraph of text describing an aspect of SEO and it includes a link to an article on a search engine-related website that is rated highly by the SE, then that approval will rub off on my site.

- Advanced design technology. As with virtually every element of SEO, there is a divided opinion on how – or even *if* – the search engines spider websites developed in Flash or Ajax-type technologies. Without going too far down the road of how these technologies work, it is fair to say that any site navigation that is embedded in the likes of Flash is more difficult for the spiders to read than is basic HTML or cascading style sheets (CSS). Another application that SE spiders don't like is that technology which is used to produce pages 'on the fly'. These are pages that are generated only when a user requests them – the results of an on-site search, for example. This means that the pages do not exist *permanently* – so the SE cannot refer searchers to them. Put simply, you cannot index something that isn't there all the time. This is not to say that such technologies should not be used on websites, but if appearing high in SERPs is important to an organization, then using them repeatedly will hinder that objective.

- Search engines also try to assess the validity of the sites they are – effectively – recommending to their users, and so they look for elements of the content that suggest the site (or its publishers) are trustworthy. This might include such things as how comprehensive any contact details are – no phone number and only a PO box number as an address suggest the organization might have something to hide. Similarly, a comprehensive privacy policy would indicate that the organization takes its duty of care towards its customers seriously; a lack of one suggests the opposite. On a more technical note, any checkout facilities should be hosted on a secure server (denoted by having 'https' at the beginning of the page's URL) – a lack of secure trading does not reflect well on the trader.

It is worthwhile adding at this point that none of the issues raised in this section is an absolute. I have presented what is the most popular conception of the best way to develop on-site SEO at the time of writing. Indeed, by the time you read this, the 'rules' – the algorithms – may have changed. It is also the case that no two SEO professionals agree on *all* aspects of on-site optimization. And finally, it is quite possible to find a web page that appears at the top of a SERP for a specific search term and that page not feature the keywords anywhere in the content or code. Furthermore, there may be no evidence of any 'black hat' operations. Such are the mysteries of search engine optimization.

Having introduced the term 'black hat', it would be remiss not to give a brief explanation of the concept. Having said that, as it is a practice that all legitimate organizations should avoid, I will spend little time on the subject. Black hat search engine optimization is a description given to the profession of those who seek to gain high search engine listings by nefarious means. The term is based on the old cowboy axiom of good guys wearing white hats and the bad guys black. The idea is to use technology to present one set of content for a website to a search engine and another set for the human user – so-called 'cloaking' of the real content. Although some legitimate businesses use this illegitimate method of SEO (normally following ill-judged advice), the practice is most common for dubious business practices and adult websites. For example, the source code and content that the SE spider sees might say the website is about advice on buying property in Spain – but the site that downloads for the (human) user is an advert for (often spurious) overseas property investment. Search engines constantly look for the practice, and ban any sites that they identify as being guilty of it.

> " Black hat search engine optimization is a description given to the profession of those who seek to gain high search engine listings by nefarious means "

PRACTICAL INSIGHT

Poor rankings? Some negative aspects of on-site optimization

- The site's content is very similar to – or the same as – that on existing sites that have already been indexed. The SE assumes you have copied, rather than developed, the content and so downgrades your site.

- The content of your website is little more than a list of links to other sites – like those sites targeted by Google's Panda algorithm change.

- External links from your site go to sites judged by the SEs to be 'low quality'.

- Duplicate title and meta tags on pages. The purpose of the tags is to identify the content of each page – if every page has the same title and description the SE cannot give credit for them.

- Keywords used in meta tags and title do not match the content of the page (a kind of low-level black hat SEO).

- If a website requires a registration and/or a password to get in the SE cannot get past that page.

DECISION TIME

As we covered in Section 3.4, writing website content is no easy task – and one normally best left to experts in the art. However, there have been problems in content development where the author develops content that reads *properly* (i.e. correct grammar, syntax, etc.) and then along comes the SE optimizer and changes the text so that it contains more keywords. The result is that the content might satisfy the search engines – but not the visitors that the SEO is designed to attract. The best content writers already know about SEO, and will ask to be briefed on what important keywords should be included in the text (note that it is not their job to decide on the keywords – that is for the online marketer to do).

PRACTICAL INSIGHT

Submit to search engines? You might not need to bother

In the early days of search, website owners or publishers had to submit their websites to the various search engines in order that they might be indexed. Although the facility still exists on the major SEs, they all suggest that it is not necessary because their spiders will find your site anyway. Indeed, some observers suggest that the SEs penalize submitted sites – the logic being that if the sites aren't good enough to be found by the spiders (i.e. they have no links going into them), then they do not warrant being listed.

For the most part, keywords will fall *naturally* into a page's content. However, there will be exceptions. For example, I would like my website – alancharlesworth.eu – to be the number one return when anyone searches on my name. However, if you take a look at the home page, my name is not naturally part of the content. To address this, as well as including my name in the source code (the header image, for example), I have *artificially* added it to the textual content. For example, I have 'signed' the 'three purposes' message and added a copyright notice in my name. I don't think any are out of place, but strictly speaking, none is necessary for the non-SEO objectives of the page. Had I started the page something like 'Hi, my name is Alan Charlesworth . . .' it would – I think – have detracted from the validity of the site by making it too much like a sales pitch.

GO ONLINE

Choose your words carefully

The text that appears in the website link on the SERP is controllable – at least to a certain degree. Follow the link from the chapter's web page for my example of how it can be done.

YOU DECIDE

Write some textual content for the Modeller's Stand website (case study 9) that will appeal to the search engines for the keywords that the text contains. Use the keywords you selected in the previous section.

Alternatively, conduct the same exercise for your organization or that of your employer.

6.5 OFF-SITE OPTIMIZATION

Off-site search engine optimization can be divided into two to key elements: (1) the website's history, and (2) the links that go into it from other sites. Let's consider these in turn, starting with the one that SEOs have little control over – the site's history.

Website history

One of the more intangible aspects of SEO that is not obvious to researchers – and so it can be amongst the reasons why an apparently 'un-optimized' site ranks highly – is the site's history. As I alluded to in the introduction to this chapter, the SE looks to develop a relationship with each website, and the longer that relationship has existed the more trust the SE places in the site's content. Things the SE might consider include:

- How long the site has existed – its age. This is not so much that a ten-year-old site *must* be better, but that a new one has still to prove its validity. Note that the site's age is normally determined by the age of its domain name, that is, when it was registered.
- Within the overall maturity of the site, the age of each page is considered. This can be a two-way street, with older pages being perceived as authoritative while newer pages are seen as more contemporary.
- Frequently updated pages might be considered more valid in a dynamic environment. A page with the word 'news' in the title that has not been updated for three years, for example, carries little authority.
- The search engine's own metrics can be used in its judgement of the site. For example, a site that has – over a number of years – had a high clickthrough rate when it appears on a SERP would be rated higher. So too would a site that has a history of repeated searches for its domain name.

Inbound links

Although SEO staff can actively seek out inbound links, an effective and efficient integrated marketing strategy will *naturally* result in links going into the organization's site. For practitioners, this *natural* phenomenon is recognized as being SEO at its best as it goes closest to meeting the expectations of the search engines – that the website will best provide a solution or meet the needs of searchers. That such an approach is strategic – rather than tactical – also appeals to the search engines as the site's value is built over a long period of time, so endorsing its validity.

However, many – if not most – SEOs do not have the luxury of time, with publishers wanting high rankings not only immediately, but consistently. It is to this more tactical approach that the rest of this section is devoted – though it should be noted that any or all of the following might also be part of strategic SEO, which is covered in the next section of this chapter.

The philosophy behind the importance of inbound links is that the search engines use them as part of their search algorithm – in essence, a site with lots of links going into it *must* carry some legitimacy with those sites that include the links and so the site's SE validity rises also. The more links to the site, the more valuable it is assumed to be, and so the higher the rating. Like other elements of search engine ranking, however, the system is open to abuse, with black hat SEOs manufacturing links to increase a site's ranking.

> The more links to the site, the more valuable it is assumed to be, and so the higher the rating.

In an effort to take advantage of link popularity, less scrupulous search engine optimizers (the black hats) look to create links into their site by nefarious means – so-called link spamming. There are a number of ways to accomplish this, including:

- Create websites that exist only to include links to your site, or sites. Content for such sites is often *scraped* – stolen – from other sites. Given the low cost of registering a domain name and hosting a page or two on it, this is an inexpensive way of creating links.

- Visit websites that have facilities for visitors to leave comments (for example, chat rooms and blogs) and leave messages that include a link to your website. Although this can be done manually, it is more likely that a software program would be employed to complete the task.

- Pay for links. Whilst this can be borderline legitimate (Stanford University has sold links on its site), there are sites that are developed as a business model where profit is made by selling links – often called *link farms*. For a relatively small fee links are added to your pages. Considering the legitimate side of the argument, if on my website I – on my own initiative – endorse a website or company, is it unethical for that organization to pay me for adding a link to that site? Others argue, with some validity, that any ad carried on a third-party site serves the same purpose as a paid link.

- Partake in reciprocal linking. This is where you contact other site developers and trade links. Again, this can be legitimate – there are a number of websites to which I link from my site where their publishers have then considered that some content on my site would be of interest to their readers – and so add a return link. However, dubious reciprocal links are those that are the only content on a page that is hidden from the site's visitors – rather like a link farm.

Like other dubious SEO activities, the search engines look for and penalize link spamming. A crackdown which began in 2007 saw the search engines clamp down on the practice, with links from sites that have no obvious connection with the subject – or are paid for – being penalized in rankings. This was taken even further as part of Google's Panda algorithm update, introduced in early 2011.

GO ONLINE

Although the search engines are well aware of the situation and have implemented measures to address the problem, blog spamming is where messages left on blogs have the single purpose of gaining an incoming link to a site with the intention of increasing that site's search engine ranking. Each message will include the URL of the target site – so creating the link – but nothing relevant to the subject of the original blog. For an example of this, follow the link on the chapter's web page.

A further attempt by the search engines to address link spamming is to assess the quality (rather than just the quantity) of links going into a website. Hence – in theory – only sites considered authoritative (so-called *authority* sites) are used in assigning ranking value. A few links from quality sites will far outweigh hundreds of spam links. The appraisal of quality can include consideration of such issues as:

- The linking site's own standing in the search engine rankings.
- The suffix of the linking site's domain name. A .ac.uk site (.edu in the USA), for example, denotes a college or university and so is considered unlikely to include spam links, whereas a site with a 'novelty' suffix would carry less authority as these are rarely used by reputable organizations. To this end, July 2011 saw Google remove from its index all websites with a .cc suffix as so many spammy websites were hosted on that domain.
- The relevance of inbound links to both the linking and linked-to sites. To address this, the search engines will consider the text around the links to assess its relevance. As with all aspects of SEO, for genuine links this would be a *natural* aspect of the textual content of both sites.
- The frequency and timing of new inbound links to the site – a steady trickle over a long period of time is considered better than occasional surges.

Although link spamming is not considered acceptable by legitimate SEOs (or the search engines), leveraging the publishers of third-party sites to link to yours is perfectly acceptable. However, a grey area exists between what is acceptable and what is spam – with practitioners and commentators unable to agree on where black and white meet.

Although not directly an element of linking, a related issue is that of how the search engines use the social media standings of an organization. Facebook shares, likes and comments, Pinterest pins and Twitter tweets all add to the brand's, organization's or product's SEO rating – but most important for Google ratings will always be involvement with its own Google+ social media platform. Could that be the reason for the recent rapid increase in activity on Google+?

PRACTICAL INSIGHT

Poor rankings? Some negative aspects of off-site optimization

- Your website – or pages within it – has no links from other sites.

- Your website is either inaccessible to the SE spiders (it is 'down') or the server response time is slow – normally due to an unreliable hosting service. The SE is not going to recommend a site that is not available too often.

- Participation in link-trading schemes or buying/selling links. Having to buy links suggests that your content is not good enough to attract genuine links.

- Low visitor numbers to the site, in particular, clickthrough rates from SERPs. This is something of a vicious circle for the newcomer and a virtuous circle for the established site. Poor text showing on the SERP link may be a cause.

- Your IP address – or that of your hosting service provider – has been blacklisted by the seach engines.

DECISION TIME

The website's history is something that the optimizer has or has not. There is no opportunity to change or influence the way the search engines see the past of that site. However, there is a way around this – though generally, it is suitable only for pure-online businesses or at least those offline businesses that rely heavily on their web presence for branding or sales leads. This potential solution is to buy either a domain name or a name that has hosted a site for a long period of time. In the case of the domain name only, how long a domain has been registered – whether it is used to host a site or not – forms part of the SE algorithm. Hence, a name registered in 1994 will carry more status than one registered in 2008. Careful research on any of the hundreds of sites that offer domain names for sale, or simply checking on the owner of a not-live name or publisher of a website and making them an offer, may result in not only a name with history, but a website also. In the latter case – though it will cost more – it may even be the case that the website is already listed in the search engines for keywords that are relevant to your organization. Obviously, there is a cost involved with buying a name or site, but that cost should be considered as either a justifiable marketing expense – or even a prudent capital gain. See also Section 2.2 for more information on domain name registration and purchase.

Once it has been recognized that link spamming is neither a sound long-term strategy nor one that any legitimate organization should undertake, link development takes on a role that is akin to the offline practice of networking. That is, you need to get your organization, brand, product and reputation known in the online circles in which your customers move.

Before embarking on any link-building campaign, it is worth conducting an audit of what you have to offer, and how good you are at delivering it. This is for two reasons. Firstly, it is pointless 'promoting' anything that users will not be impressed with – they are not going to link to anything that does not in some way benefit them. However, more importantly, if you offer a good product at a reasonable price and deliver it with excellent service then satisfied customers will talk about you online – and that will inevitably lead to links to your site. Essentially, this is the *natural* growth of links that search engines are looking for and value so highly. As author and online marketing practitioner Seth Godin (2008) comments in *Meatball Sundae*, 'Business growth comes from . . . satisfying the people who can best leverage your idea.'

Linking strategies

In order to be proactive in building inbound links, there are a number of things the web marketer can do, including some or all of the following:

- Reciprocal links – although they are sometimes considered to be link spam, there are limited opportunities for genuine exchanges of links between associated or related sites. It is important to try to get links from web pages that are read by the audience you want. The best way to find suitable sites is to search on the same keywords that your site is optimized for – and then contact those non-competitive sites that top the listings. Because these sites are rated highly by the search engines, any links from them are considered to be authoritative.

- List a limited number of products with shopping comparison or auction sites. This does not have to be part of a distribution strategy, but simply part of the SEO strategy to create links.

- Submit to key industry, geographic and specialized directories – the advantage of this is twofold: (1) they direct traffic to the site, and (2) the link is recognized as quality by SEs. For more on directories, see the next section.

- Participate in social networks and online communities. When you add comments, replies or responses to forums or blogs, for example, there is normally the facility for your URL to be included, so creating a link.

There are a number of further tactics that can be used to attract links into a site – these are collectively known as 'link baiting'. Although the term itself has negative connotations, the practice is not spam-related. Link baiting is all about encouraging people to link to your site by producing quality content that attracts – *hooks* – those links. Baits might include:

- *News* hooks, normally in a specific environment, industry, etc.
- *Contrary* hooks, where the writer takes up a contrary stance to expert, or public opinion on a given subject.
- *Resource* hooks, where the website gains a reputation as the place to go for information.
- *Humour* hooks attract those looking to pass on to others some light relief (Charlesworth, 2007).

More specifically, there are a number of ways the baits can be laid – though these are two formats: (1) where the bait is cast to attract users to a specific web page's content; or, where the bait itself is the attraction, readers are then directed to the organization's website. Types of baiting include:

- Writing articles for inclusion in third-party newsletters or websites. This is common in the service industries, where the writer can develop a reputation as an expert in their field. Obviously, every article includes a link to the corporate website.
- Submitting articles to article directories. Such directories are used by publishers to source content for everything from newsletters to special reports.
- Publishing the results of research on your own site. The paper is then marketed as if it were a product in its own right, with online activity – for example email – driving visitors to the article.
- Submitting articles to social media sites. Such is the nature of sites like Digg.com that if an article appeals to readers it can be spread virally around the community site. Note, however, that this is likely to create a temporary 'spike' in both links and visits rather than long-term link development.
- Issuing online press releases for all newsworthy events or happenings related to the organization. (Online public relations is covered in detail in Section 9.6.)

It is important to note that with all of the methods described above it is essential that any text is exceptional in both its content and presentation. If the content is not relevant to the target readers (or publishers) and presented in the style that is expected by the target segment then the article will disappear into the mass of similar articles produced for the same purpose as yours. Worse still, poor quality content will be perceived by readers to be link spam – and so your site might suffer (rather than gain) from the practice. Note that this practice has a very close association to *content marketing*, which is covered in the next section.

One aspect of linking where the SEO can be proactive in furthering their cause is in the issue of the anchor text of any link coming in to the optimized site. Anchor text is the actual words that are hypertexted on the 'sender' site. The search engines give greater value to links where the anchor text matches the keyword used by searchers. For example, if a website publisher includes a link to my site, it might say: 'A site with many useful links to e-marketing articles is that of university lecturer Alan Charlesworth. **Click here** to go to his site.' In this example, *Click here* is the anchor text. However, if the link was my name – 'A site with many useful links to e-marketing articles is that of university lecturer **Alan Charlesworth**' – it would carry more credit with the SEs if anyone searches on my name. To achieve this, I could send a polite email to the publisher of the site thanking them for the link, but asking them if they could amend it. They might ignore me, but it's worth a try.

A final point to make is to remind Internet marketers that success in any search engine optimization strategy will be dependent on the competition that the website has in the online marketplace. Following the guides given in this and the previous chapter is relatively straightforward, and in a limited market will (probably) give satisfactory results. Take my own website as an example. If you search on "Alan Charlesworth" on any of the main search engines then you will find alancharlesworth.eu at, or near, the top of the SERP. My SEO success is helped by there not being too many people in the world with my name. There are even fewer with websites – and fewer still who see any benefit in having their website at the top of the search listings. Effectively, I'm successful because I'm not really competing with anyone else. If, on the other hand, my name was George Clooney or Brad Pitt my chances of getting to the top would be limited to say the least. Similarly, getting my 'hints and tips on search engine optimization' page to the top of the SERP for "search engine optimization" would be an almost full-time occupation. And so competitive is that market that I would be unlikely to succeed.

> **YOU DECIDE**
>
> Advise Lindsey Naegle on how she might develop links into her consulting website (case study 12).
>
> Alternatively, conduct the same exercise for your organization or that of your employer.

6.6 STRATEGIC SEO

Such is the nature and importance of featuring high in the SERPs, for some organizations SEO has moved on from being a matter of a number of operations and has become a significant element of the marketing strategy. Indeed, for the online-only company, it could be *the* marketing strategy. As a result, instead of SEO being carried out by a dedicated person or team, everyone involved in the online presence takes a role in the SEO of that web presence. This would include obvious departments such as public relations (PR) which would expect to be versed in the use of keywords in press releases, but also less obvious units, such as human resources (HR). In a large organization it is often the case that the HR department is the most regular publisher of information about the company on the Internet. Properly optimized, job descriptions and adverts on not only the organization's own site(s) but also on recruitment sites can bring both traffic and links into the main site.

Furthermore, the organization should look beyond the basic issue of getting pages at the top of a SERP and appreciate the wider role search engines can play in their business. As Gerry McGovern says on his influential forum (giraffeforum.com):

When a customer searches for "Dublin Rio Flight" they are advertising the fact that they want to fly to Rio from Dublin. The customer today is the advertiser. Search is a form of personal advertising. Customers are telling organizations what they want to buy and what they need to know before they buy. Most organizations are too busy shouting at customers about things the customer isn't interested in. Organizations need to listen a lot more.

It is not unusual for an international company with a global physical presence to have a web presence where the page numbers are in the thousands, hundreds of thousands or even millions. Effective optimization of such entities is referred to as *enterprise* SEO. Key issues faced by such organizations might include any or all of the following:

- multiple objectives
- keyword selection – and the mapping of content to them
- complex sites
- multiple countries – with subsequent localization and translation difficulties
- content development
- duplicate content
- inbound linking
- outbound linking
- localization for multiple outlets
- co-operation from all operational departments – some of which may be overseas
- stakeholder satisfaction
- particularly in B2B, long sales cycles
- recruitment of staff with, or the development of existing staff in, the necessary skills
- … and as with all aspects of business strategy; budgeting.

Content marketing

Although the tactic of creating content to attract potential customers is not new, the concept of *content* marketing has become increasingly popular in recent years – so much so that it is now recognized as a discipline in its own right. Defined by the Content Marketing Institute (contentmarketinginstitute.com) as 'a marketing technique of creating and distributing relevant and valuable content to attract, acquire, and engage a clearly defined and understood target audience – with the objective of driving profitable customer action', the practice has seen increased relevance due mainly to changes in search engine algorithms and the growth in social media which have placed an emphasis on the quality of online content. This focus on the importance of quality content is, in itself, a result of consumers blanking out traditional marketing messages – and focusing on information they find useful.

The objectives of content management can include increased web traffic, direct sales, customer retention, brand awareness, customer acquisition, lead generation or thought leadership, and it is equally valid in both B2B and B2C markets. Whilst content can simply be the 'non-sales' aspects of a website (e.g. describing how products can be used – which many people would consider to be good practice anyway), strategic content marketing would include the specific development of content to be published in such formats as social media (e.g. tweets, Facebook entries), blogs, articles, papers, case studies, research reports, guides, webinars, shared documents, podcasts, Q&A pages, videos, forums, infographics and PR. It is because all of this content – which is not necessarily hosted on the organization's website – can bring visitors and links into the site that it is sometimes referred to as *inbound marketing*. As is covered in this chapter with regard to website content, content for marketing purposes can also include non-textual items such as webinars, videos and podcasts. Throughout this book I have stressed the importance of having the right talent and management in place for effective online marketing, and this is never more valid than if the organization is considering strategic content marketing.

PRACTICAL INSIGHT

Search or social media?

Launched in March 2013, Facebook Graph Search is the social media giant's tool for searching its database of over one billion people, more than 240 billion photos and – apparently – over a trillion social connections. Unlike the search engines, which trawl the web, Facebook Graph Search is limited to Facebook – which raises the question of whether the facility belongs in this chapter or Chapter 9, on social media marketing. Given that it is about searching for , well, anything, I have decided to make it part of search – for the time being. Perhaps by the time the book's third edition comes out we'll have determined whether it is search or social media.

At the time of writing the content is restricted by each user's privacy settings and output is limited to pages, apps, groups, photos and places, with search results being personalized on the individual connections of the searcher.

Follow the links on the chapter's web page to monitor the development of something Facebook is pinning a lot of faith on as being 'the next big thing'.

Offline influences on search

Although the search engines provide the facility of online search, they are only part of the overall product search. Often, search engines are given the full credit for helping customers find a product – or information that will help them reach a buying decision. However, in many situations the search engine might well be the last step in the search, but it is not necessarily the first. Any contact with the product, whether that be physical (seeing a new model of car in the street), as a result of promotional activity (seeing an ad for the car on TV), in another media (a review of the car in a newspaper or magazine), online (a blogger commenting on the car) or simply word of mouth from a friend or colleague might prompt the user to go to a search engine to find out more about the car.

To consider how off- and online marketing can be integrated to good effect it is worth considering the concept of 'search plus'. Although people may use a search engine to seek further information on a product, brand or organization that they have come across in an offline environment, this concept relies on the marketer being proactive in either building search engine optimization or buying relevant keyword advertising for terms that are associated with offline marketing efforts for the period that they run. For example, a TV ad campaign might feature a memorable tag line – in which case the tag line would be purchased as a keyword so that when the phrase is entered into a search engine the top listing (organic, sponsored or both) is for the advertised product. Other search-plus applications include:

- Search-plus television – where ads and product placement can cause search spikes for relevant key phrases, for example "Keira Knightley dress" during the Oscars ceremony.
- Search-plus outdoor – both pedestrians and commuters often get only a fleeting glimpse of an outdoor ad, so they may search for details online when they reach their home or work.
- Search-plus word of mouth – in this instance, *word of mouth* refers to both the off- and online application (viral). Search advertising can be used to reinforce the positive, and respond to the negative, word-of-mouth message.
- Search-plus public relations – this can be proactive or reactive. Paid placement can be arranged in advance of a co-ordinated PR event, or pertinent keywords can be purchased to provide a reaction to bad news.
- Search-plus direct mail – where direct mailings – both off- and online – promote a product or service, keywords can be purchased so that if potential customers go online to seek further information on the promoted product the brand message is reinforced by appearing high on the SERP.

Note that this section is based on my description of 'search plus' in *Key Concepts in e-Commerce* (Charlesworth, 2007).

PRACTICAL INSIGHT

Directories

Where search engines rely on their spiders to crawl the web, directories have an element of human involvement in their development but they can play an important role in helping users find relevant websites. Indeed, in some circumstances they can complement, or even replace, the necessity to rank highly in the SERPs. For example, if you search on "London restaurants" on Google you will find the main listings are for directories of one kind or another.

Online directories are direct descendants of the *offline* directory – and in many cases the online version is produced by the same organizations that traditionally produced hard-copy versions. Industry or trade bodies, for example, listing their members as part of their online presence, a local Chamber of Commerce cataloguing all businesses in its area or a tourist information board might have a directory of accommodation listed by type and location.

Unlike search engines – which will find a site sooner or later – directories must be sought out by would-be listees. Ironically, the best way to find one is through the search engines – though to find them all does take some time and a little ingenuity in tracking them down. Indeed, that a directory appears near the top of a SERP is in itself proof of the value of being in that directory.

Being listed in some directories is free (local authority sites, for example), whilst others use the listings as a business model, and so charge either a one-off or an annual fee. An enhanced citation – as in telephone Yellow Pages directories – may be available for a higher charge. Whether potential returns will justify the costs must be decided on an individual case basis – with the hosting site presenting statistics to prove the visitor numbers to their site and their demographics. The higher the fee, the more visitor data you should expect.

An SEO off-shoot from being listed in directories is that each link from a directory can count towards the link popularity score of sites. This is particularly true if the directory is considered to be an 'authority' by the search engines.

DECISION TIME

Once again, the organization's off- and online objectives, the nature of its business and the market or industry in which it trades will determine its adoption or otherwise of strategic search engine optimization and the role it will play in the organization's overall marketing and business strategies (I hope business and marketing students will recognize that I just described the purpose of an environmental analysis prior to any strategy formulation).

For the global entity, finding any aspect of its operations – be that new products or corporate social responsibility – via an online search is such a common consumer expectation that effective SEO is a given. For such organizations investing in enterprise SEO is the obvious solution. However, such is the cost – and often lack of understanding of what is required – that SEO is often still seen as a sub-department of marketing or online and so does not get the resources required for successful implementation of the concept.

PRACTICAL INSIGHT

Optimizing for mobile

As users increasingly use mobile devices for search, the SEO has to take into account the differences between searches on PC and searches on mobile. Taking tourism and a visit to London as an example, PC searches will be made prior to a visit, with more generic searches such as "restaurants in London" or "where to eat in London". However, when actually walking around the city, that same tourist's search will be 'goal-oriented' and so they are more likely to use their smartphone to search for "restaurant near Trafalgar Square" – so if you have an eatery close to Nelson's Column, you should include those terms in your keywords.

Mobile searches are also likely to be time sensitive, so if you sell tickets for events, make sure your site is constantly updated so that 'today' is part of the relevant page's SEO.

At the other end of the essential search spectrum is the small local trader whose potential customers will either use search in the same way as the telephone's Yellow Pages were used a generation ago or they will use a mobile device to search for immediate fulfilment of a problem or desire. For them, 'enterprise' SEO will be less complex in that it is easier to encompass the *enterprise* in the practice. However – as with the global organization – failure to commit adequate resources will result in ineffective SEO. In the digital world in which businesses exist, they can be sure a competitor will appear in the SERP in their place.

YOU DECIDE

Advise the board of the Matthew Humberstone Foundation Hospital (case study 6) on aspects of enterprise SEO that are relevant to that organization.

Alternatively, conduct the same exercise for your organization or that of your employer.

CHAPTER EXERCISE

Giving justifications for all your decisions, advise Frank and his staff at Hill Street Motorist Shop (case study 8) on all of the aspects of search engine optimization covered in this chapter.

Alternatively, conduct the same exercise for your own organization or that of your employer.

CHAPTER QUESTIONS

Follow the link from the chapter's web page to a series of multiple-choice, exam-type questions that will test your knowledge and understanding of the various elements of the chapter.

REFERENCES

Battelle, J. (2005) *Search*. Nicholas Brealey.

Broder, A. (2002) A taxonomy of web search. *ACM Sigir Forum*. Volume 36, number 2, pp. 3–10.

Charlesworth, A. (2007) *Key Concepts in e-Commerce*. Palgrave-Macmillan.

Geddes, B. (2010) The four types of PPC keywords. Available at http://certified knowledge.org/blog/the-four-types-of-ppc-keywords/.

Godin, S. (2008) *Meatball Sundae*. Piatkus.

Goldman, A. (2011) *Everything I Know about Marketing I Learned from Google*. McGraw-Hill.

Jansen, B. J., Booth, D. L. and Spink, A. (2008) Determining the informational, navigational, and transactional intent of web queries. *Information Processing and Management*. Volume 44, number 3, pp. 1251–1266.

Chapter **7**

Online advertising

The business that considers itself immune to the necessity of advertising sooner or later finds itself immune to business.

Derby Brown

Chapter at a glance

7.1 Introduction
7.2 Objectives and management
7.3 Where to advertise online?
7.4 Online ad formats
7.5 Search engine advertising
7.6 Network advertising
7.7 Affiliate programmes
7.8 Landing pages

7.1 INTRODUCTION

Providing quality content that attracts readers and then selling advertising alongside that content has been a business model for publishers since printing came of age in the seventeenth century. So it is that, as a business model, website publishers and search engines sell advertising. However, whilst the marketer should not ignore the sell-side element of advertising, in this book I concentrate on the Internet as a medium for marketing and so the focus is on that aspect of online advertising. That is, how the Internet can be used to carry our ads, not how selling ad space can generate an income for online publishers.

Readers should also understand why search engine advertising is included in this chapter and not the previous one. I make the point in the introduction to Chapter 6 that I prefer to divide the use of search engines in marketing into two distinct elements. (1) search engine optimization (SEO), and (2) the use of search engines as a medium for carrying ads – which is what is covered in this chapter. There is, however, a connection between organic listings and paid ads – and that is keywords. Although the selection of keywords is covered in detail in Section 6.5, it is worth noting here that all of the criteria for selecting keywords for organic listings apply equally to their selection for paid ads.

GO ONLINE

Online advertising terms explained

To find out the language of online advertising, follow the link from the website to the UK's Internet Advertising Bureau's jargon buster.

Although advertising on the Internet started back in 1994, it was nearly fifteen years before global brands were switching their advertising budgets away from traditional media and going digital. Why it took online advertising so long to come of age is debatable, but reasons include:

- As with the Internet as a whole, there was (and still is?) a lack of understanding of – and interest in – the web by advertisers and advertising agencies.

- A reluctance to adjust to the new medium – before the web, good advertising people were well versed in the tools and techniques of reaching broad markets with lowest-common-denominator messages via interruption techniques (Scott, 2007). The Internet required new skills and methods – or that existing skills be adapted.

- No fixed pricing policies. The traditional media – TV, radio, print, billboards and so on – uses fixed 'rate cards' to assess costs. For example, a thirty-second ad shown during a TV programme watched by five million people at eight o'clock on a Friday evening will have a cost based on a matrix of fixed costs for those variables. The rate card system allows the marketer to calculate the budget for any advertising campaign. Online, however, no such rating system exists.

- Related to the rate card issue is that traditional media have recognized key 'broadcast times' – for TV it is after dinner until about 10 or 11 p.m., whilst radio has peaks during the morning and evening rush-hours (people listen in their cars). Online, however, each individual has their own 'prime time'.

- The web is fragmented. Advertising on traditional media is dominated by a limited number of players – on TV, for example, it is the commercial networks – and in print there is a narrow range of newspapers and magazines. Online, however, there are millions of websites, most of which have independent publishers. It is the development of the ad networks – predominantly Google's AdSense – that has opened up online advertising (ad networks are covered in Section 7.6).

However, as we will see throughout this chapter, these objections have been – or are being – overcome as the Internet has been adopted as a utility by the bulk of the population – that is, the people who respond to advertising messages.

As well as becoming an integral part of most people's lives, the Internet does bring three significant benefits to the advertiser that are limited in other media. They are targeting, analytics and interactivity – let's consider them in more detail.

1. Targeting. Not only are web pages subject specific, but as they must be *requested* by the visitor, there is an element of self-segmentation by all web users. For example, take a web page that has content about maintaining a good-looking and healthy lawn. It is a reasonable assumption that if someone arrives on that page they have done so because they have an interest in gardening and grass, and so have clicked on a link (from a SERP, perhaps – which means they have searched on a term related to lawns) or they have typed the URL directly into their browser. This means that if I am marketing a related product – grass seed, lawnmowers, fertilizer or garden tools – that web page is an excellent place to host my ad. By definition, because the visitor is on that page, they are almost certainly in my target market and a potential customer for my product.

> "
> Not only are web pages subject specific, but . . . they must be *requested* by the visitor
> "

2. Analytics. As department store mogul John Wanamaker famously said, 'I know half of my advertising is wasted, I just don't know which half.' The reason for this is that with traditional media there is little or no evidence that any advert has worked. Some metrics are available, but they are limited in their ability to assess actual results. For example, a TV ad might be shown during a programme that was viewed by ten million people – but how many actually saw the ad? And of those who did, how many took any notice of it – and in that group, how many had an interest in the product? This is particularly true of branding ads where no direct sales can be attributed to the ad campaign. Online, the very technology that runs the Internet can be used to assess the effectiveness – or otherwise – of any advertising. Whilst the issue of whether or not a visitor actually saw, or took any notice of a banner ad on a page is still in question, if the customer clicked on the banner that is a positive indication that the ad has succeeded in its immediate task. A further advantage of online advertising ROI

assessment (often called return on advertising spend – ROAS) is the primary way of costing online ads. That is that you pay only if the ad has appeared on a web page, or if the visitor has clicked on it – meaning that Wanamaker's 'missing half' doesn't exist. However, as we will see in the later section on network advertising, analytics have moved on at a pace, and clicks on ads are now only a part of the metrics available in assessing and implementing effective online advertising

3. Interactivity. A final attribute of the online ad that is absent in all other media is its potential for interactivity. Arguably, an offline ad that prompts the customer to 'ring this number' is interactive in that it prompts a response and so is the instigator of an interaction. Online, however, the ad is truly interactive because the user can click on it for direct action related to it – ultimately (or perhaps ideally) the customer could see an ad for a product and in a click or two, and within a few minutes, have purchased it without leaving their seat. And in the world of mobile connection to the Internet, that seat could be anywhere from on public transport to the beach. It is also the interactive capability of the Internet that has seen a rise in online promotions, including contests and coupons. Although, strictly speaking, these are not ads *per se*, many of them are presented in such a way that it is hard for users to recognize a significant difference (e.g. if an ad on a web page includes a coupon, is that an ad, a promotion – or both?).

PRACTICAL INSIGHT

Online segmentation of ad delivery is broken down into three core types of targeting – though the last can be used in unison with either of the first two and each has its own sub-categories:

1. Contextual – the ads served are relevant (in context) to the content of the web page.
2. Behavioural – ads are delivered in response to your prior actions on the web.
3. Geographical – the use of IP recognition to identify where in the world the surfer is, with location-relevant ads then being served.

7.2 OBJECTIVES AND MANAGEMENT

The objectives of any ad campaign – and there should always be specific aims – will largely determine the nature and type of ad used, how it is managed and what analytics should be used in tracking its results. Like its counterparts in traditional media, the objectives of online advertising can be divided into three key sub-groups:

1. Direct action – ads that seek to elicit a reaction from consumers. Although this is usually purchase-driven ('click here to take advantage of this limited offer'), or informs customers of a particular promotion ('50 per cent off in store this weekend'), the action is not necessarily a sale – it could be an opportunity to sign up for a newsletter, register a vote or make a donation to a charity, for example.

2. Lead generation – more common in B2B trading, the ad is designed to persuade the reader to contact the advertiser with a view to discussing a potential purchase.

3. Branding – ads that reinforce consumer perception of the brand, organization or product by frequent exposure.

PRACTICAL INSIGHT

What's being displayed?

According to the world's largest display advertising network, the Google Display Network, online *display advertising* broadly consists of banner ads, image ads and video ads. I'll be a little more unambiguous and say that if an ad is not text-only, it is a display ad. Note that earlier literature – including the first edition of this book – refers to display as *banner* advertising.

Although it is not an exact science, there is general consensus of opinion that display ads are best used for brand building while direct action ads are most effective in textual format. Certainly, text ads (see Section 7.4) are best placed to induce action – but for the many websites that carry ads, those ads will be from Google's network (see Section 7.6) and they are predominantly text only. This is (probably) because (1) those ads are derived from the ads on search engine results pages where text is considered best as it makes the ads 'blend' with the organic listings, (2) website publishers prefer the text ads as images may conflict with page design or content, and (3) images require more work. However, as display ads are now very much part of the networks' online advertising toolbox, they are a popular choice for brands that have the resources to develop them. Indeed, it takes only a cursory inspection of display-ad-filled sites to realize that they are dominated by major brands who are using the web as part of integrated marketing strategies.

A further consideration is the impact of the so-called 'last click'. This is where (as stated above) text ads are the most likely to induce action – the clickthrough – and so collect the plaudits for the conversion. However, that click can be at the end of a long buying process that might include image-based display ads that have helped build the brand – and so the credibility – of the purchased product or organization that is selling it. Note that a similar argument can be levied against search engine optimization, where the 'last click' is on a search engine results page, but the customer has been driven online by offline promotions.

The point was made earlier that Internet advertising has no 'rate card' for ad costs, instead there are three main ways of paying a publisher (or their agent) for carrying your ads. Before looking at these in a little more detail, it is worth noting that (1) in online advertising the terms are routinely referred to by their acronyms, and (2) where I have used *pay*, the word *cost* is also sometimes used – and so the two have become interchangeable. The three common methods of payment are:

1. CPM (cost per thousand impressions). Used almost exclusively for display ads, pay per impression advertising is not unique to the online environment. In case you are wondering, 'M' – the abbreviation of the Latin for a thousand (mille) – is used because ad impressions are sold in blocks of one thousand. The cost will depend on the sites that carry the ads, but might vary from around 50 cents to one dollar per thousand for non-prime sites to ten dollars or more for a 'brand-name' site – though, obviously, the more traffic a site has, the quicker your ad budget is spent. Note also that ad cost is almost exclusively calculated in US dollars, no matter where in the world you are. However, that the Internet Advertising Bureau's definition of what constitutes a successfully served ad is that 50 per cent of the ad must be seen for at least one second is hardly encouraging to the marketers paying for those impressions. Nevertheless, if an ad does become a *viewable impression,* then according to Google (in a press release in April 2013), a user is up to twenty-one times more likely to click on it than if it did not become *viewable.* Google also predicted at that time that viewable impressions would become the standard measure for online advertising in place of the 'served impression' metric used at that time.

2. Pay Per Click (PPC). The advertiser pays only on performance by paying for each click made on the ad. So, no clicks, no fee. The system is also known as CPC (cost per click) and less commonly, pay per action. The latter is where a visitor might complete an action from the ad – ticking a box to receive a newsletter, for example – and the publisher receives a (higher) fee only if the action is completed. This concept can be extended to paying a commission if the user actually makes a purchase after clicking on the ad. This model is difficult to track, however, and is more common in affiliate marketing (see Section 7.7). The cost of PPC varies wildly and is largely dependent on the keywords being 'purchased' (more of this in Section 7.6). Clickthroughs might range from a few cents to hundreds of dollars per click.

3. Pay Per Call. Popular in some industries, insurance, for example, this is where an online advert – or associated website – features a freephone number and software tracks any contacts made through that number and a fee is paid for each call. The fee charged for pay per call is higher than other pay-for-performance models, but the advantage to the advertiser is that callers are more likely to be high-quality leads and so the chances of achieving a sale are also much greater.

> Measuring the effectiveness of ads . . . has moved on significantly in recent years.

Measuring the effectiveness of ads – particularly banners – has moved on significantly in recent years. At the turn of the century, e-metrics would tell you only how many visitors had clicked on a banner. Now it is relatively easy to find out where they were (geographically) and what web page they were on when the ad was displayed. Not only that, but you can track the ad-derived visitor's path through your site all the way to (hopefully) a purchase. As with website metrics (you will use some of these to track ad results), ad analytics can be done in-house, be outsourced or be part of a service offered by an ad network.

DECISION TIME

If online advertising can help the organization meet its strategic marketing objectives, there are a number of operational decisions to be made with regard to how that advertising will be practised effectively. With the objectives of the ads (i.e. direct action, lead generation or branding) having been decided at a strategic level, it is the nature of the ads that will concern the e-marketing practitioner.

Current custom and practice for online advertising dictate that display ads should be used predominantly for branding and text ads for income generation. Operational decisions at this stage are: (1) how do we manage the ads, and (2) what metrics do we use to judge their effectiveness?

The management decision is – as it is offline – do we do it ourselves or do we pay someone to do it for us? In an offline environment it is common practice to outsource advertising to agencies that will work with the organization in developing the campaign and then manage the distribution. Their experience and expertise will ensure that the ads appear in the most appropriate media at the right time and at optimum cost. A key issue with regard to this is that to the outsider the offline advertising industry can appear as a 'closed shop', with personal contact – and established relationships – playing a significant role. It is normally the case, therefore, that even major brands will use an ad agency to handle their advertising. However, as online advertising both developed and proved its effectiveness, the feeling of some industry observers was that many established offline ad agencies missed the digital-marketing boat by failing to (1) recognize its impact, and (2) develop expertise in the field. This left a gap in the market for companies that understood the new digital environment and the technology used for advertising in it, and it is those firms that are now the brand leaders in the online ad-agency industry – with some of the pre-eminent names of the pre-Internet advertising world still playing catch-up.

PRACTICAL INSIGHT

Click fraud

Depending on which side of the table you sit, click fraud is either not really a problem or it is a reason for not using pay-per-click (PPC) advertising. The search engines say that the amount of click fraud is negligible. However, some advertisers – and independent investigators – reckon that up to 60 per cent of clicks could be fraudulent. So what is click fraud?

Basically, PPC works by having advertisers pay website publishers each time a user clicks on an ad. That no clicks equals no cost, and that each clickthrough is recorded, makes the model both cost effective and easily measured. Now, if I were a dishonest publisher or agent handling a site's PPC ads, and I knew that I received a payment for every click made on an ad on my website, I might be tempted to click on a few ads myself. Obviously, the search engines and ad networks are aware of this and are on the lookout for such activity. However, I could pay someone to click for me – perhaps someone in a part of the world where labour costs are low. Or perhaps not one person, but several. Or several hundred. Or several thousand. I can afford to do this so long as I pay less for each fraudulent click than I receive as income for each clickthrough – and for some keywords I might be receiving several dollars a click (some cancer-related legal keywords are reported to go for over fifty dollars a click). Of course, I could skip the overseas cheap labour and simply use a computer program to roam my sites and act like a human visitor clicking on ads.

Naturally, the ad networks strive hard to trace fraud – but as with most online fraud, the bad guys are always looking for ways to be one step ahead. Cynics suggest that the ad networks are not too keen to track frauds as they also benefit from them – they take a percentage of clickthrough fees – leaving the overcharged advertiser as the only victim.

With regard to the management, however, whether you use a specialist firm to handle the placement and control of ads or do it yourself, there are two avenues to follow – networks or individual publishers.

- Advertising networks. The role of the online advertising network is much the same as its offline relative – that is, to enable website publishers to sell more advertising space (commonly called ad inventory). Publishers can be represented by one network or they can use a number. They might use them for either all of their ad inventory or only seek their help to move any space that cannot be sold by their own sales staff. The basic model is that ad network operators have agreements with publishers so that contextual ads are delivered to participating sites. The ads are delivered on a PCM or PPC basis, with the advertisers paying the network and the network giving a portion of that revenue to the site that hosts the ad. The primary advantage of this model to the advertiser is that will their ads can be featured on a plethora of sites – although this might include many that will receive few, if any, visitors.

Networks vary greatly in their reach, pricing, metrics and contextual targeting ability. At one extreme are the networks that work as brokers on an arbitrage basis – treating ads and space as commodities that can be traded. Such networks generally offer only 'blind' buying – that is, the advertiser does not know on what sites their ads will appear and the seller does not know what sorts of ad will appear on their pages. Other agencies offer detailed demographics for audiences or organize their networks by topic, normally working closely with a relatively small number of publishers. The cost of advertising with the different types of agencies will be reflected in their ability to deliver targeted or more generic ad placement.

- Individual publishers. In this case the advertiser contacts the website publishers directly to negotiate price and placement of their ads. This can result in better returns from ads because publishers will usually have detailed demographics on their target audience and so facilitate better micro-targeting of audiences. On the downside, however, this task is extremely time consuming – perhaps prohibitively so for the small to medium business. An agency, on the other hand, should already have relationships with key publishers and so can handle multi-site ad management much more efficiently.

Selecting which metrics are most important to your campaign depends on its objectives. For example, if you are trying to maximize sales leads, then cost per lead is more important than impressions served. If you are brand building, impressions served is more important than cost per lead.

> 66
> Selecting which metrics are most important to your campaign depends on its objectives.
> 99

When considering the analytics to be used in determining the effectiveness of an ad campaign, the critical decision is – once again – whether to carry out the work in-house or outsource it to specialists. If the campaign management has been handed over to an agency then it is likely that they will include analysis of the results as part of the service they offer – and you pay for. Worth noting also is that if an outside agency is used for the management, it is important to involve them in the development of the objectives of the campaign's – or at least keep them informed. Without this participation they cannot possibly be expected to produce meaningful analytics.

If the analysis is to be conducted in-house there are software applications that can be used. Indeed, another advantage to using ad networks is that they will provide you with statistics – many of them in real time – on your ads' performance. As with websites (Section 2.5) and email marketing (Section 8.3), the actual analysis depends on the campaign's objectives. It is no use, for example, having a thousand users clickthrough on a sales-oriented ad if no one buys anything. However, there is a caveat to add with regard to measuring the overall success or failure of an ad campaign: it is entirely possible for all aspects of the ad to work perfectly – only for the experience of the customer after they have clicked on the ad to destroy that good work. The significant experience in question here is that of the *landing page* to which they are taken. So important are landing pages that I devote a full section to them at the end of this chapter. With regard to analytics, however, the advertiser should consider the whole process through which the respondent to the ad should pass in order to identify areas of failure – using a conversion funnel (see Section 1.6) is recommended. If a potential customer clicks on an ad, continues through a landing page to a product page but leaves without making a purchase then it is unlikely that the fault lies with the ad; rather, something further down the funnel.

7.3 WHERE TO ADVERTISE ONLINE?

A marketer's response to this question would be, 'those sites that members of the target market are likely to visit.' This is not the subject to be addressed in this section, however, moreover the question is what *types* of websites can be considered to carry your ads?

Obviously, online ad placement is limited to those pages whose publishers accept ads as part of their income generation model. Until the advent of the search engine operated networks (see Section 7.6), the majority of ads were limited to relatively few categories of sites. In 2003, for example, 51 per cent of online ads were hosted on the major portals such as Yahoo! and MSN (Nielsen/NetRatings, 2003). However, the ad networks have made it easy for even the smallest website publisher to include text ads on their pages, so opening up the scope for advertisers. The web has also changed since 2003, with social media sites – which were few in number at that time – now hosting ads.

With comments on their suitability, the following are all potential hosts for online advertisers' offerings:

- Social media sites. These can be heavily targeted, but there are question marks over 'banner fatigue' – that is, users ignoring ads on the pages. It is also the case that many social network members use them to 'escape' the barrage of ads that confront them in all other media. Simply reproducing that ad-saturated environment on social media sites may well turn users away from them.

PRACTICAL INSIGHT

Do advertisers 'like' social media?

Although – almost from its launch – Facebook has been popular with its users, those users have been reluctant to click on ads on the social media giant. Part of the issue is that when people go on the likes of Facebook they are in 'communication' mode rather than seeking to solve a problem – the mindset which makes them so receptive to SERP advertising. However, given that it is dependent on advertising income, Facebook has continually strived to make the ads on its pages more appealing to users. For example, its 'Customer Audiences' and 'Lookalike Audience' facilities (released in March 2013) both helped advertisers present their ads in front of better-targeted audiences.

To judge the data about users that Facebook can glean from its site, try looking at your Facebook page or that of a friend or even a stranger. Now build a potential product profile based on the entries and likes on that page. For example, a young woman who has announced she has booked a beach holiday might be interested in offers for bikinis and suntan lotion.

However, paid social media advertising is primarily used to support branding-related efforts, and this has created another concern for marketers that social media sites need to address – that of analytics of the ads. According to Nielsen (2013), to measure the effectiveness of their campaigns, advertisers 'would prefer to use the exact same metrics used in the offline medium, and additional metrics specific to the online. Very few media sellers, however, actually provide such metrics.'

- Search engine results pages. Contextually accurate in that the ad's keywords match those of the searcher, but some industries are extremely competitive.
- Portals. High traffic, but there is often limited targeting potential for the top-visited front page. Subsequent subject-specific sections can be better segmented, but attract fewer visitors.
- Community websites. Extremely good for targeting as, by definition, the page content is decided by the community members.
- Chat rooms, forums and message boards. Traffic might be low, but targeting can be accurate as the ads can be contextual to the subject being discussed.
- Blogs. Only a few blogs attract meaningful traffic – and readers are often more interested in the blog content than any ads. Targeting can be accurate, however, and advertisers may benefit from the 'halo effect' of having ads on the page of an expert in the subject area (e.g. a search marketing company ad being displayed on the blog of a recognized 'guru' in SEO).
- Virtual world sites. Opportunities for advertising on such sites abound, but a significant problem is that for advertising to be effective it must be targeted. To target customers you must be able to identify them – and in virtual worlds the inhabitants (avatars) are anonymous.
- Podcasts/video-clip pages. It is often the case that when a user clicks on a link to access an audio or video broadcast, it is hosted within its own 'page' – with any space (e.g. that surrounding the video window) being ideal for carrying display ads. This is particularly the case if the video takes a while to download – leaving the user as a captive audience for any ads that are running. Ads can also be embedded in the podcast or video – with the increased popularity of YouTube creating the opportunity for ads to be presented in front of a video clip. Users can click to skip the ad, but many simply let it run out of convenience.

PRACTICAL INSIGHT

Advertising on YouTube

The Google-owned video site makes a number of formats available to advertisers. They are:

In search

In the same way that search engines deliver keyword-related ads alongside search results, so does YouTube – with fees paid only if a user clicks on the video ad.

In slate

These ads only appear in videos that are more than thirty minutes in length (TV programmes, for example) and give viewers the option of watching one video ad from a selection before the programme starts or having a series of ad breaks through the programme. If the viewer chooses your ad to watch, this suggests they might have at least a passing interest in your product, brand or organization, which can be useful for branding or new product advertising. Advertisers only pay if someone selects their ad.

In display

These are promoted videos that appear down the right-hand side of the YouTube page, alongside the video a user is watching. They are relevant to the content of the video being watched. They should be attractive enough – or have a compelling message – for viewers to deem them worth watching when the video they have selected has finished. Note that these video ads can appear anywhere on Google's ad network that takes video.

In stream

These videos are the closest format to TV and appear as a pre-roll to popular videos (and not niche videos, as is possible with the other formats). Advertisers pay only if a user has watched the ad for thirty seconds (or the whole ad, whichever is shorter) – if users elect to 'skip after five seconds', the advertiser doesn't pay. It takes an engaging ad to stop the viewer clicking on the 'skip ad' button – but this can be an effective method for videos that the user has running in the background, for example, music videos where the user may be playing videos from their 'watch later' facility.

- Print pages. Often neglected, some pages lend themselves to being printed – which means the ad gets printed along with the rest of the content. For example, a money-off voucher for a hotel or restaurant that is on the path of a requested route-map.

- Newsletters. Although these are more 'email' than 'website', they are often in html and so could carry ads. As with other 'community'-oriented communication, the newsletter is likely to be very subject specific and so a good vehicle for targeted advertising – or perhaps better still, sponsorship, which might be more acceptable to readers even if they still perceive it as advertising.

- Emails (1). For the likes of Hotmail and Gmail, this is a business model in its own right – with users getting excellent web-based email facilities in return for their outgoing emails carrying ads. Although contextual matching can be effective, users of such services will vouch for the fact that any relationship between some ads and email content is ambiguous, to say the least.

- Emails (2). Having your own emails carry ads is an option for some organizations, though this must be practised with care. Having an ad on emails that go out in response to customer enquiries, for example, might work. However, adding an ad to every email that leaves the organization is questionable. How would a supplier, complaining customer, union spokesperson or government official – for example – feel if their business correspondence included an ad for your latest promotion?

- Question and answer (Q&A) websites. The name of these sites rather gives away their purpose, but the questions are both posed and – hopefully – answered by users. As the questions are on a multitude of subjects, every page is an excellent host for contextual ads.

- Any other website. A curious category perhaps, but as the major networks now make it a relatively simple task to include ad-script in the code of a web page, it is possible for your ads to turn up virtually anywhere that there is a contextual match-up between your ad's keywords and the content of the web page.

A further consideration for ad hosting is online gaming. Frequently disregarded because they are not websites *per se*, the use of ads within the games played online has a number of applications and advantages in reaching certain target markets – particularly as players have moved online (away from consoles) to play against competitors around the world. Methods of in-game advertising include:

- Static in-game – ads that are shown either within the game (on a billboard feature within the game, for example) or on a menu or leader board.

- Dynamic in-game – where displayed ads can be changed depending on location, day of the week and time of day.

- Inter-level ads – displayed during natural breaks in game play, such as between levels – hence the title.

- Game skinning – sponsorship of display units around the game and/or custom branding integration into the game.

- Product placement – as with its film and TV equivalent, branded products are featured within the game – a mobile phone or car used by a character, for example.

- Sponsorships – where the advertiser 'owns' the game or an aspect of it. This might be sponsorship of a tournament, level or session of game play.

- Post-game – ads that appear on screen following completion of the game.

- Pre-game – ads that appear on screen before a game commences, possibly while it is loading.

RESEARCH SNAPSHOT

Advertising on location-based gaming

Although the iconic Tetris game was available for playing on mobile phones in 1994 and Angry Birds arrived in 2009, it is the more recent, almost universal, adoption of smartphones that has seen a meteoric rise in both mobile gaming and location-based social networking. Combine the two, and you have location-based gaming which allows users to play out virtual scenarios in real-life settings – and presents advertisers with a unique opportunity to connect with a niche of their audience in both an online and physical world.

A footnote to this section is that although, as online marketers, we are concentrating on which sites can carry our ads, we should not forget our own publications for in-site ads. An obvious example is including ads for specific promotions or products on the front page of an online retailer's site. Less common, however, is consideration of other pages for carrying a promotional message. Suggestions would include the following – but there will be others depending on the objectives of the site:

- Searching page. If the site offers such a feature the process might take a few seconds – so instead of a blank page or a 'please wait' message, why not feature a search- or site-relevant message? For example, a hotel searcher might be informed that the site also offers travel insurance at a competitive rate.
- Search results page. As with the major search engines, an in-site SERP could include an ad for a product that is related to the search. A search for 'casual shirts', for example, could include an ad for a range of polo shirts that are on promotion.
- Purchase confirmation. When an order is made it is normal practice to show a page confirming the details – why not include a pertinent ad? Admittedly, this comes at the end of a purchase procedure, so instant action is unlikely, but a branding message can be easily embedded on the page.

A caveat is that to be effective these need to be carefully prepared and presented. Indeed, if they are badly executed they could actually put customers off – the opposite of the hoped-for response. Note that this model uses the same concept as described in Section 8.3 – email as a medium for marketing messages. A warning with regard to hosting ads on your own website is that unless it is part of your business model, you should never host ads for other companies – it will simply devalue your site and impact on your credibility.

DECISION TIME

Though segmentation and targeting are staples of marketing, it is worth remembering that wherever an ad is delivered the response rate will be determined by its relevance to the audience of the publication. So it is online. At its most basic, we are talking about women's cosmetics being advertised on a website that attracts women users and car tyres on a site whose visitors are most likely to be car owners – and so on.

An advantage of online advertising is that – like magazines – the content of a web page will determine its viewers, making contextual advertising relatively straightforward – though far from simple. As you will see in later sections of this chapter, both search engine and network marketing are generically contextual in nature. It is very much the case, therefore, that the digital marketer must have identified the target market for the product or service they are advertising before online placement is even considered. Once that decision is made then website demographics can be matched with those of the target segment – with those demographics largely dictating the categories of sites that will be most effective as vehicles for the organization's ads.

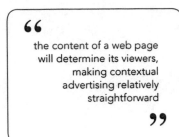

> the content of a web page will determine its viewers, making contextual advertising relatively straightforward

YOU DECIDE

Advise Howard Johnson on what categories of website might be most suitable for carrying ads for the Rockridge Museum (case study 1).

Alternatively, conduct the same exercise for your organization or that of your employer.

7.4 ONLINE AD FORMATS

The formats available to the e-marketer for online ads are determined by two issues: (1) the objectives of the ad, and (2) where they are to be displayed. The former is a decision that is made by the organization but the second – though there may be a preference – is determined by the publishers of the ad-carrying sites. For example, SERP ads on the big three search engines are text only – therefore, if you want to advertise there your ads will not include images (note that this was true at the time of writing and may well change in the not-too-distant future). Portals, on the other hand, will often insist on banner ads. Ad formats are, therefore, loosely divided into *text only* and those that include images – now commonly referred to as *display* ads.

Text-only ads

These can be divided into two categories: (1) within textual content, and (2) stand-alone.

Text-link ads

As the name suggests, this kind of ad is one that is 'embedded' within a line of textual content on the web page. The concept stems from the practice of making links out of references to a product within textual content – something that is effective when compared to other methods of on-page advertising. It is, however, problematic for publishers to insert such ads because they can impact on the actual content and distort the natural flow of the narrative. It is common, therefore, that in-text ads are used only on sites where the publisher is also the advertiser – with affiliates being the prime exponents of the craft (affiliate marketing is covered in Section 7.7). For example, a film-related website might include an article on Brad Pitt – with the name being a hyperlink to the movie star's auto-biography on Amazon. Whilst this might be considered a valid practice on some sites, it would be more dubious in, for example, a review of a film in which the actor starred.

It is also the case that the actual content might be *tainted* by the inclusion of an in-text ad. Take my own pages about the city of Athens as an example (see Figure 7.3, p. 254). Essentially, it is simply my thoughts about Athens that might be useful to someone looking to visit the city. I have included textual 'network' ads on the pages as a demonstration for students (and readers of this book). It is clear that any ad is just that – an advert independent of my content. However, if, on my page about hotels, I was to say, 'I think the **Hotel Alan** is the best hotel in Athens', with the name of that hotel being a hyperlink to a hotel-booking agency that would pay me for any clickthroughs, then my credibility becomes an issue. The consideration for the reader is: do I trust the author in his advice on the hotel, or is he simply recommending it to get a payment? If such a doubt enters the reader's thoughts, then they may not have confidence in any of the other content. On the other hand, if the recommendation is *genuine*, it will generate a higher CTR than other ads because the reader takes it as a sincere recommendation from the writer.

As we have seen in other aspects of this book, some of the terms and phrases related to digital marketing can be confusingly similar – or even interchangeable – and here we have another example. The basic – and original – concept of *text-link ads* is as I have described above. However, technology has presented us with an augmented version of the original – dubbed *in-text* advertising. This is where the hyperlinked words do not take the user to a new website, but open a small pop-up ad when scrolled over by a mouse – the reason for them also being known as *rollover* ads. Depending on your point of view, these are either an excellent source of income or an unwanted annoyance when reading website content. For publishers and content providers this is an additional form of income generation as they can 'sell' words or phrases that are *naturally* included within an article. For readers, the usability of the page is compromised by the intrusion of the ads, and content writers argue that their credibility is threatened as the ads can intrude on serious articles or content – as with my Brad Pitt example above, perhaps.

GO ONLINE

Follow the link from the chapter's web page for an example of poor in-text advertising.

Stand-alone text ads

These are *probably* the most common type of online ad (sources on the subject differ, and none seems absolute as ad definitions within surveys are mixed), if only because they are used by the search engines and network ad providers (see later sections of this chapter). Not only do these ads appear on nearly every SERP, but their easy availability to any website publisher has resulted in them being (almost) ubiquitous on any site that is not published as part of the online marketing strategy of a specific company, brand or product. Depending on the network used, the format of these ads will be fixed, though they will normally have a headline, body text and advertiser's name – with each having a character-related limitation.

Also included in this category is the advertorial. A kind of crossover to the in-text ad in that the actual ad is integral to the textual content, advertorials can be used to great effect to reach consumers who switch off to conventional ads. However, there is an issue of delineating where advertorials stop and content marketing (see Section 6.6) starts. This is important because the search engines penalize content that is too much like an advert – whilst rewarding legitimate content.

> ### Display ads

Previously known as banner ads, these were first used in October 1994 but faded in popularity as their cost-effectiveness was called into question. They have, however, made a comeback as technology has taken what were once little more than static advertising banners (hence the name) into dynamic and creative advertising spaces that use *rich media* to appeal to both advertisers and web users. Although use of the term 'banner' is decreasing, the traditional sizes of static banners are still used for display ads so that website designers can allocate suitable space within ad-hosting pages. See Figure 7.1 for examples of the most common sizes.

Despite the use of the term 'banner ad' being on the decline – perhaps because of the public's negative perception of it – the 'old-fashioned' static image with a marketing message and a link to the advertiser's website or landing page can still be effective in the right circumstances. However, as technology has advanced, so too has the imagination of ad developers, and it seems hardly a week goes by without web users being presented with ads in a new format. I wonder how many of these new styles will go on to have the longevity of the basic banner – and how many will follow the path of the universally annoying 'pop-ups'?

DECISION TIME

Having decided on the objectives of an online advertising campaign the digital marketer must decide on which sites (or types of sites) the ads will appear. Essentially, the decision on the management of the ads, and the sites on which they will be hosted, will largely determine the type of ad to be used – Google SERP ads, for example, are predominantly text only.

A constant thread to this book is that there are *some* aspects of online marketing that are best left to experts, and ad design fits into that category. That said, the development of ads to be used online is far more achievable for the 'do-it-yourself' marketer than ads in many other media. Indeed, as many display ads use the same scripting as websites, they

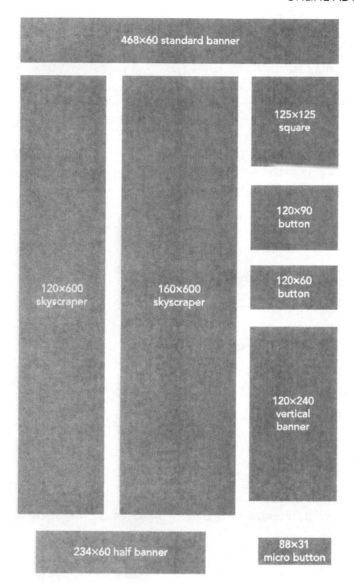

Figure 7.1 Common types of banner ads

can be developed by members of the web-design team. Similarly, if someone is employed to write web page copy, they too could be engaged in writing the ad copy. The following points are a guide to what ad developers should consider when working on them.

As with other elements of online advertising covered in this chapter, the objectives of the advertising campaign will determine the actual ad design. For example, an ad that seeks to generate income (e.g. stimulate sales) will need a strong call to action and perhaps a picture of the product. A branding ad, on the other hand, will require livery, name and logo to be prominent. Although the technology used will have an influence, the more significant issues will come under one of two headings: aesthetic (how it looks) and textual (what it says).

Aesthetic

Any ad should grab attention, generate interest, create desire and invoke action (AIDA, see Section 1.6) – and to do this it should, in some way, stand out from the page. One way to do this is with the visual appeal of the ad – its aesthetics. An important consideration is the size of the file, or files, that make up the ad. As a large-file ad will delay the downloading of the page and may cause visitors to leave the site, publishers are likely to impose file-size limitations. This is particularly relevant to banners that incorporate new-media applications.

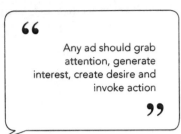

> " Any ad should grab attention, generate interest, create desire and invoke action "

PRACTICAL INSIGHT

Ads appeal to our basic instincts – apparently

Usability expert Jakob Nielsen suggests that there are three design elements that are most effective at attracting attention:

- plain text (i.e. no pictures)
- faces
- cleavage and other 'private' body parts.

J. Nielsen, 2007

Technically, an ad can be placed anywhere on a web page, though common practice has resulted in there being a number of 'standard' placements:

- the top of the page – above any other content
- to the extreme right or left of any page content
- in the middle of the page between sections of content
- at the bottom of the page – below other content.

Note that the 'header–columns–footer' web page design (see Section 3.2) lends itself to accommodating ads in any of these placements. Whilst few can agree on which is the best of these options, it is generally recognized that being 'above the fold' – that is, on the screen as the page opens, before any scrolling takes place – is the place to be.

Textual

Whatever the objective of the campaign, each ad must convey a message to the target audience. This can be a simple communication telling of a promotion – 'the XXXX sale starts on Friday', for example – or something more complex. However, it is rare that a message can be delivered in picture form only. Even Nike's series of branding ads featuring pictures of famous sports stars will carry the tag line 'Just Do It' (and the 'swoosh' logo) – without which the ad is simply a picture of a sportsperson.

Essentially, the textual content of the ad has two primary objectives:

1. Let the audience know what benefit they will gain from purchasing the product (or whatever the objective of the ad is).

2. Make clear the *call to action*. I considered this in some detail in Section 3.3 with regard to website copy, and the same principles apply to email marketing – but in the online ad it is essential that *something* entices the audience to take some kind of action, normally to click on a link that will start them down the sales funnel. As with websites and emails, the call to action should be specific and highlighted within the ad, for example featured on a red button.

A final consideration that has grown in importance in recent years is that of what device the user will see the ad delivered on. If the ad message is to reach the intended audience then they must be able to see and/or read it. For many years screen sizes were relatively large and operating systems were predominantly Windows based. However, smartphone and tablet screens are much smaller and deliver web pages differently than on PCs or laptops. For on-mobile advertisers there is also the problem of using Flash software in delivering ads. Apple devices do not run Flash technology, and with the iPhone and iPad having over 50 per cent of their respective markets this creates a problem for the ad makers. At the time of writing these issues have required savvy digital advertisers to have separate *mobile* ad campaigns – however, I think we will see the main network providers address these problems in the near future.

PRACTICAL INSIGHT

Advertising has a job to do

The following quote about ad development is attributed to acclaimed advertiser Alvin Hampel:

> If you remember the joke in my commercial while forgetting my product, the joke is on my client. If my presenter grabs you but you ignore what she's trying to sell you, I've blown it. If you are struck by my cleverness but remain unsold by my ideas, I've bombed as a copywriter . . . the very things that are remembered most may contribute least to making the sale.

I would add that the comment is equally valid with regard to website design.

Web users are canny folk, however, and well used to being advertised *at*. They are also wary of scam-type statements – 'you have won a prize, click here to claim it', for example. Such copy should be avoided by the reputable organization or they too will be perceived as scammers. Similarly, while witty headlines might raise a smile, they seldom help the ad meet its objectives. In his 1985 book *The Copywriter's Handbook*, Robert Bly suggests that headlines have four functions:

1. Get attention.
2. Select an audience.
3. Deliver a complete message.
4. Draw the reader into the body copy.

Bly (echoing Hampel's sentiments) adds that a copywriter's chief job is not to be creative or amusing – it is to sell. The history of offline advertising is littered with ad campaigns that won awards from the designer's peers, but failed to register the brand in the consciousness of the viewing public – making them failures in business terms. The digital marketer would be well advised to take heed – their ad is, first and foremost, published to achieve the campaign's objectives – not win awards. As with websites, do not allow design to overcome substance.

YOU DECIDE

Consider the different types of online ad formats and offer Philip Ball advice on which might be the most suitable for the Cleethorpes Visitors Association (case study 4).

Alternatively, conduct the same exercise for your organization or that of your employer.

7.5 SEARCH ENGINE ADVERTISING

It is important to appreciate that *advertising* on search engines is not the same as being featured in their *organic* results – that element of search engine marketing is covered in Chapter 6. In this section we look at the listings on SERPs that are *paid for* – hence it often being referred to as *paid search*.

MINI CASE

The origins of paid search

The concept is accredited to Bill Gross, who launched the first paid search engine, GoTo.com, in September 1998. At the time, search engines were inundated with spam – particularly from adult websites (it is generally recognized that pornography and gambling sites were always at the leading edge of any developments in search engine manipulation). Gross thought the only way to combat spam was to have businesses pay to have their sites listed. This would lead to users being more likely to use a spam-free engine and, more importantly for GoTo, far greater income from PPC (pay-per-click) advertising – which would replace the CPM (cost per thousand impressions) method more common at the time.

Gross realized that the inherent value of intentional traffic was far greater than that of undifferentiated traffic. He also realized that some keywords and phrases were more valuable than others, so ad prices were not fixed, they varied depending on demand. Although GoTo's arbitrage-based business model (it purchased links from other sites for a flat rate per click in a CPM deal, and then resold those clicks on a PPC rate on its own site) is still used, more common is the concept's development into the search engine and ad network application of paid placement. Note that this description draws on content from my book *Key Concepts in e-Commerce*.

Although most people (though not all, see the Research Snapshot 'Ad, what ad?') recognize paid search results as adverts, the search engines still seem to be evasive in identifying them as such. In the first edition of this book I said that on their SERPs, Google calls them 'sponsored links', Yahoo! opts for 'sponsor results' and MSN Live 'sponsored sites'. I went on to comment that marketing students should know there is a difference between 'advertising' and 'sponsorship' – and that the search engines seem to be using a loose interpretation of what *sponsorship* is. Only months after that book's publication the search engines proved me wrong by changing their description of paid ads to *ads*.

However, as I write this – in 2013 – the situation at Google, Yahoo! and Bing still seems to be in a state of flux. For example, the once standard practice of changing the background colour of ads from white to (usually) light blue or faded yellow is flexible. Furthermore, depending on the type of screen you are using, the blue and yellow backgrounds are that it is almost impossible to distinguish them from white. Moreover, when Google replaced its free *product search listings* with its paid-for *Google Shopping* facility the new listings were described as 'sponsored'.

RESEARCH SNAPSHOT

Ad, what ad?

Research from UK company Bunnyfoot (bunnyfoot.com) in 2013 suggests that many people are unaware of the difference between *paid* and *organic* search listings – with 40 per cent not knowing some listings were actually adverts. Furthermore, many of this group believed the ads were the most authoritative links. In searches for specific products (car insurance was used in the research) 81 per cent of users clicked on Google AdWords listings as opposed to organic search results.

Search engine advertising is based on the concept of matching the searchers' keywords with links to pages that will satisfy the objectives of those searchers. In search engine optimization, the chosen words are placed on the web pages (see Section 6.3). With search engine advertising, the keywords are *purchased* by the advertiser (hence the practice also being known as *paid search*), with the ad that appears highest on the SERP's *sponsored* listings being the one that has had the highest bid made for it – although other criteria have an influence (these are covered in the next section). Having won the bidding, the advertiser – effectively – has won permission to have their ad feature on the relevant SERP. The amount of the bid is the fee payable to the search engine every time someone clicks on the ad (the pay per click model). Naturally, as in all business environments, keyword bidding is influenced by the level of competition in any given marketplace. So it is that some keywords in competitive markets cost far more than those in industries where competition is lower (note that less popular keywords within a market will be cheaper, too – consideration of such words is covered in the next section, see 'The long tail of keywords').

Whilst this section concentrates on advertising on search engine results pages, it is the case that similar technology and systems are used by ad networks in placing ads on other sites – indeed, the key players in ad networking are the three main search engines (Google, Yahoo! and Bing). Therefore, although network advertising is covered in the next section, it is necessary to read this section first in order to get to grips with the basics of the two models.

As we found in the previous chapter, search engine optimization is not an exact science – with its results being far from certain. Therefore, the key advantage to buying ads on SERPs is that whilst there is still no *certainty* that their ads will appear on the page, at least the advertiser maintains a degree of control over the situation. Whilst this element of being able to determine your own destiny is the prime reason for SERP keyword purchase, there are other advantages to using the system. These include:

> " *whilst there is still no certainty that their ads will appear on the page, at least the advertiser maintains a degree of control over the situation* "

- The text that searchers see can be determined by the advertiser – unlike the organic returns which present text taken (sometimes randomly) from the page which (a) may not be good sales copy, (b) may not be relevant to the search or worse still (c) is nonsensical. It is surprising, therefore, to see how many organizations pay for high listings and yet give no thought to the wording being used. In sales terms this is prime real estate – a chance to convert a browser to a buyer, or at least a chance to have them enter your sales funnel. As with all aspects of sales copy this is best left to an expert – hiring one will usually bring a return on any investment.

PRACTICAL INSIGHT

Use those characters with care

Although specifics vary between search engines, on Google SERP ads can use twenty-five characters for the title and thirty-five characters for each description line and the display URL (all of these including spaces). This does not give you much room to get your message across – and remember there will be several other listings all promoting the same product or service. Essentially, the message is a call to action – it must invoke something in the searcher that makes them click on your link. This will be something that meets the need of the searcher. Saying, 'we have sold grass seed for 50 years' doesn't mean anything: 'we guarantee a greener lawn' does.

- In the same way as much offline – and some online   advertising has brand building as an objective, so too can PPC be used for this purpose. Although they may not click on the sponsored ad, search engine users may perceive that the organization or product at the top of the list is the leader in its field. Repeated exposure in the sponsored ads can also help in brand recognition strategies. Note, however, that the clickthrough rate is significant, too, as is discussed in the next section.

RESEARCH SNAPSHOT

Being in the SERP top ten

Although the brand value of being at the top of natural searches (see Chapter 6) has long been recognized, SEO technology company Conductor (conductor.com) decided to test the value of appearing in the ads on the first page of search results. Their experiment measured brand awareness, perception of brand quality and purchase consideration – and found that they were up to 30 per cent higher than if a brand did not appear in the search results. Appearing in the top half of the search results and being featured in both natural and paid listing both gave the best results.

Source: Safran, 2012

- Potential customers might be aware of the brand or organization – perhaps as a result of offline marketing campaigns – but are unsure of the domain name, so they simply type the name into a search engine. If this is the case, the organization or brand *must* be listed on the first page of the results – and while brands like Nike will already have achieved number one spot in the organic listings, others might need to buy the top spot in the ad listings.

All is not positive, however. Achieving high *organic* listings is a long-term exercise that is difficult (if not impossible) for competitors to reproduce. A downside to PPC listing is that competitive advantage is difficult to sustain in that any successful keyword strategy can be copied – that is, if a competitor sees your site being listed for searches on certain keywords they too will bid on those keywords – though they might not have the other attributes described in the next section.

There is also the problem of matching the message on any ads to where on the buying cycle the user is. For example, if the potential customer is browsing around for general product information, then 'free shipping on all lawnmowers this month' is going to have little impact, whereas 'top ten tips for choosing the right lawnmower' would. And, of course, vice versa. Therefore, it may be worth considering multiple ads on similar keywords with regard to optimizing landing pages that are relevant to this practice.

PRACTICAL INSIGHT

Staying in the picture

In the first edition of this book I suggested that Google's AdWords would soon feature images. Well – with the exception of Google's Shopping facility – that never happened. So it is with some irony that as I write this book in 2013 it would seem that the search giant is beta testing images with its text ads. One significant issue related to this is that it means search engine advertising has the potential to achieve branding objectives. I'll keep the situation updated on the chapter's web page.

Keyword bidding

Before going into detail about how to bid for keywords on SERPs, it is worth emphasizing the importance of keyword selection – as we covered in Section 6.3. Any bids for keywords (and ads placed on them) that searchers are not using to find your product or service are a waste of time and resources. Similarly, not buying ads on the keywords your potential customers are using is akin to not advertising at all.

Although keyword bidding is the general term used for the exercise of buying keywords on a SERP, the actual practice includes more elements than simply making a bid, otherwise the organization with the biggest budget would always top the lists – and this is not necessarily what the search engines want. As with the organic listings, the search engines' primary concern is to satisfy searchers – and the same applies to their PPC ads. A searcher looking for a hotel in Las Vegas, for example, would not be happy if they clicked on an ad for 'Vegas hotel bargains' only to find they were on a website for 'adult entertainment' in that city. If the search engines listed ads were based only on the highest bid, then this is what would be likely to happen. This section, therefore, although titled 'Keyword bidding' considers all those elements that impact on getting your ad at the top of the 'sponsored ad' listings on the SERPs.

> " As with the organic listings, the search engines' primary concern is to satisfy searchers – and the same applies to their PPC ads. "

> ### GO ONLINE
>
> Follow the link on the chapter's web page to see an excellent video presented by Google's Hal Varian in which he explains – in basic terms – just now search ads rank and cost.

In addition to the monetary value of your bid, the strength – what Google refers to as the *quality score* – of your keyword bid might also be affected by:

- Clickthrough rate (CTR) history. Previous ads are considered to assess how successful they have been in attracting clicks from searchers – those with a good track record will gain credit. Naturally, this means that new advertisers are penalized as they have no history.

- Landing page quality. The search engine will look for relevance to the search keywords in headings and body copy as well as assessing the architecture and user experience of the destination site – including the landing page's download time. Part of this assessment is conducted by tracking post-click patterns – very short visits followed by the back button being clicked to go back to the SERP, for example, does not suggest a positive user experience on the advertiser's website.

- The business model of the advertiser. As this suggests, the search engines are not keen on sending 'their' customers to a site that might be some kind of scam or other dubious practice – so they check the validity of the advertiser's site.

- Although the search engines deny that variables such as length of advertiser tenure or total ad spend are part of their ranking agenda, many in the online advertising community feel this may well be the case. Therefore, all other things being equal – how much you spend on SERP advertising *might* influence your listings.

PRACTICAL INSIGHT

Levelling the playing field?

Google limits the number of listings each advertiser can have for each keyword. Unlike many – if not most – offline media, it attempts to maintain its integrity in its objective of satisfying the needs of the searcher, not the advertiser. On TV or radio, for example, a brand could buy up whole ad breaks to help launch a new product – or a magazine will sell an advertiser as many pages as they wish to pay for. But if every ad on a SERP were for the same brand, product or organization, this would restrict the options for the searcher, and so Google resists what would be a very lucrative practice to maintain its independence as the provider of search solutions.

DECISION TIME

Effective paid search is built around getting the highest number of conversions at a cost that still allows a realistic profit. As is the case with its offline relatives, search engine advertising relies on the marketer striking a balance between higher-cost ads that convert better and lower-cost ads that don't produce as many conversions.

The digital marketer can waste a lot of money or fail to win their share of the market in buying ads on search engine results pages if their keyword bidding is not considered carefully. As with the organic element of search, the search engines are keen to make the service they offer the public as effective as possible. As publishing ads on SERPs that also meet this criterion is important to the search engines they all offer advice to advertisers on how best to use their systems. Add to this advice the advertiser's knowledge of the market and the environment in which they are trading and you have a guide to search engine advertising. Worth a quick reminder at this point is that the actual keywords that are relevant to your ad campaign must be decided before this stage is reached – with all the elements discussed in Section 6.3 being relevant. Important keyword considerations in the bidding process include the following:

- Keyword matching options. The search engines offer a range of options, though many advertisers (often through ignorance) do not make a selection and so are given the default option – the *broad* match. Other options are the *phrase* match, the *exact* match and the *negative* match. Aspects of the four choices are addressed in Figure 7.2.

Type of match	Description	Advantages	Disadvantages
Broad	Ads are shown whenever the keywords appear in any order or combination with other keywords that might be search terms in their own right. For example, 'digital marketing' would appear under 'digital marketing training' and 'training courses for digital marketing' but not 'training courses for online marketing'.	As this is the default setting, it requires the least time to set up. The wide coverage might attract keyword matches you had not considered. Can be used for 'brand' advertising where appearing at the top of the ads for a search term is more important than direct sales.	As the keywords are not highly targeted, they may produce traffic that is not really in your target market and so is unlikely to convert. Generic keywords are usually more expensive as they have more competitors for the bids – in this example, 'digital marketing' could be targeted by any organization that offers any kind of online marketing service (including the publishers of this book!).

Phrase	The same as broad match, but the keywords must be searched in the order they are bid on. So 'digital marketing' would get no returns on 'marketing on the Internet', for example.	Can be useful if the phrase order is almost certain to match what you have on offer – i.e. it is the way your product is described. For example, 'football boots' is more likely to be searched on than 'boots for playing football in'.	As with the broad search, the costs can be higher and the traffic not specific.
Exact	The keywords used by searchers must exactly match those bid on. The purchased term 'digital marketing training', for example, would not appear on a search for 'Internet marketing'.	Produces the most relevant matches and so should result in a higher conversion rate from any clickthroughs. An organization offering Internet marketing training, for example, would be found by searchers looking for such a service rather than those seeking general information on digital marketing (students, for example).	Far more time-consuming to set up as a number of keyword bids may be needed to cover all aspects of the offering or terms the searcher might use. In the example, a user who searches on 'digital marketing courses' would not see an ad for 'Internet marketing training'.
Negative	This stops 'random' matches from a search phrase simply because it includes one of your keywords by making that word a *negative*. For example, a bid on 'digital marketing books' could add 'training' and 'courses' as negatives.	Makes targeting much more specific by preventing potential clickthroughs from users who do not want what you have to offer. Conversion rates should be improved with traffic better targeted.	As with the exact match, this requires more input by the marketer and so is more resource intensive.

Figure 7.2 Keyword matching options

Naturally, the selection of any of the above will depend on the product or service being advertised, the objectives of the ad campaign, the industry or market and the behaviour of buyers of that product. Some of these issues are addressed below.

- The long tail of keywords. This concept is built on the notion that the most popular keywords – those at the *head* of the list – are the most expensive because they should have the highest CTR. However, at the other end of the list – the *tail* – are the rarely used, and so inexpensive, keywords. It is also the case that such terms are so unusual that anyone using them should be considered as being better candidates for conversion. Continuing the example used in the Figure 7.2, I might extend 'digital marketing training' to 'digital marketing training Sunderland' or 'digital marketing training north east England'. Or I could add 'certified' or 'validated' to 'Internet marketing courses'. The more specific the keywords become the fewer competitors will bid for them – so they will come in at a minimum bid. That said, however, fewer – if any – users will include the keywords in their searches. But if anyone were to use the term 'certified digital marketing training north east England' and you offered such a service in that location then there is a very good chance that searcher will become a customer. And remember, if no one uses the term – and so no one clicks on your ad – then it costs you nothing other than the time it takes to develop the ad and bid on the term.

This concept can be extended to include the 'differentiators' that are common in offline marketing environments. If, for example, I offered a budget digital marketing service (rather than a certified), I could bid on 'cheap digital marketing training'. Similarly, if I ran courses that addressed different aspects of digital marketing, I might buy 'B2B digital marketing training'.

MINI CASE

Search engine advertising as a competitive advantage

The immediacy of search engine advertising can be used effectively by the alert marketer, such as reacting to the misfortunes of a competitor. For example if your main competitor has a widely reported problem with a product then you could bid on keywords that their customers might use to find out about the problem – and find themselves presented with your ad which offers a solution to that problem. The reverse is also true, of course. Faced with a problem with one of their products, the astute digital marketer could produce an ad that linked worried buyers to an information page that told them what the problem was, how it was being addressed and what they should do to seek a replacement product or refund. Such a message with a contact 'hot-line' might well help head off any loss of brand reputation caused by the original problem.

- Branded keywords. When purchasing keywords for search engine advertising, they are considered to be *branded* if they are associated with the names, trademarks or slogans of particular companies. Although it is legal to bid on branded terms the advertiser must comply with the search engines' trademark policy in their home country. The online advertiser should consider this issue from both sides. Using the branded terms of other organizations could be not only legally problematic but also expensive, because other advertisers might also wish to buy the term (several online retailers bidding on the brand name of a product stocked by them all, for example). Those marketers who have a brand of their own must also constantly be aware of it being used in the ads of others – particularly if the ads are competitive – 'our product lasts longer than brand X', for example.

- Ad scheduling. This facility allows you to automatically turn your ad campaigns on and off at specific times, so if your target audience surfs only on weekday evenings you can set your ads to show only at those times.

- Geographic considerations. If you trade only in Europe, then having ads seen by folk all over the world is a waste of resources. If you do trade globally, consider setting up ad campaigns on a country-by-country basis – with tailored keywords and ad copy to suit.

- Demographic targeting. Although this started with little more than the segmentation variables of male/female and a series of age ranges, technology has moved along at a pace. This is particularly the case with Google as it has expanded its empire to cover many kinds of website from which data can be drawn.

Not only do the search engines provide advertisers with tools to help in their online ad campaigns, but time-saving software is widely available. Examples of applications of 'bid management software or tools' include:

- Automatic optimization. This is where an individual advertiser might have a number of ads on similar keywords and the search engine identifies which ad is the best performer and then shows it ahead of others from the same advertiser.

- Dynamic keyword insertion (DKI). All other things being equal, a searcher is more likely to click on an ad whose text includes the search term they used rather than one that doesn't. Although this can be achieved manually by writing specific content for every keyword that is bid on, the search engine ad systems provide a facility whereby the text in the presented ad includes the actual keywords used in the search enquiry. The use of DKI simplifies the administration of any online advertising campaign.

Furthermore, led by the ubiquitous Google, the search engines now offer an abundance of online guides and manuals for the digital advertiser.

YOU DECIDE

Advise Milo Minderbinder on aspects of keyword bidding that might be particularly relevant to 22 Catches Fish Products (case study 7).

Alternatively, conduct the same exercise for your organization or that of your employer.

7.6 NETWORK ADVERTISING

In Section 7.2 we considered the role of the type of online advertising network that follows the *traditional* model of distributing ads to publishers. With the offline model, it has always been common practice for advertisers to appoint agencies to act as go-betweens in connecting those who wanted somewhere to place ads and the various media that could host them. For the major brands this is still the case. However, direct access to the networks means that it is comparatively easy for organizations – including micro businesses – to facilitate their own network ads.

PRACTICAL INSIGHT

How agency advertising works

Alan's Ad Agency (AAA) commits to buying a million ad impressions from an online publisher – let's say Yahoo! – at a fixed cost per impression (CPM). The agency then looks to make a profit by selling those ad spaces to advertisers. To do this, AAA's team has to ensure that ads delivered to each individual user match their wants and needs, so encouraging a higher clickthrough rate – and so more profit on AAA's business model.

Now, let's assume 'Jane' wakes up one morning and checks the email on her Yahoo! account. Yahoo!'s servers immediately alert AAA's system that Jane is online – though she is not known as an individual, only by her IP number or other unique identifier – and ask which ads AAA would like to show on 'Jane's' email page.

It is now time for the agency to take a look at its database to see what information it has on 'Jane'. Data specific to 'Jane' is normally gathered in-house, but other data relevant to her demographic can be purchased from other companies who specialize in gathering such statistics.

So what data might AAA hold on 'Jane'? Well, let's assume that last week she searched on the terms 'flights to Athens' and 'Athens hotels'. She has also had Facebook conversations with her friends about holidays in Greece and interesting places in and around Athens. She is also a Facebook 'friend' of the Hilton hotel group – where she has posted several good reviews. 'Jane' has also tweeted about her experiences on KLM, and has signed up to receive tweets from that airline. AAA will also look at the types of ad 'Jane' is most likely to click on. Static or dynamic? Plain or colourful? Serious or funny? Promoting discounts or advantages?

Then – and only micro seconds have passed since 'Jane' logged on to Yahoo! – AAA's system looks for advertisers on its account who match up with 'Jane's' data and shows those ads on the web page that 'Jane' sees. In this case, it might be discount flights on KLM, free extra nights at the Athens Hilton and a company that does island boat trips from the port of Athens.

Had any of these companies not been customers of AAA, the ads presented would have been less targeted – perhaps a budget airline that flies to Athens, or an online aggregator offering the best prices for hotels in the Greek capital.

The flip side to this, of course, is the question of privacy for the individual user. Don't forget that in this – and the majority of instances – 'Jane' is not a person but an anonymous number. However, she might be willing to give up more personal information to organizations that she trusts – in this case this would probably include KLM and Hilton Hotels. Ultimately, it comes down to how comfortable the individual is with having their personal data 'out there', and how willing they are to trade this off against the advantage of only seeing ads that are relevant to them.

Despite a dramatic increase in the number of networks that exist that will manage the placement of your ads, the term 'ad network' is predominantly reserved for those run by the three major search engines – with Google's AdSense being by far the biggest player, and so it is inevitable that – as with SEO – it is that application that becomes the most obvious example in this section. The concept is quite simple – and an obvious extension of the SERP-delivered ad programme. Where search-engine ads are *matched* with the keywords used by searchers on network sites the keywords chosen by the advertiser are *contextually* linked with the content of the hosting websites (it is the content aspect that has resulted in network ads being commonly referred to as *content* ads, as opposed to *search* ads.)

GO ONLINE

Ad men to math men

For an excellent introduction to network advertising, follow the link from the chapter's web page to Mediative's *This is Digital Marketing*. My only quibble is that the title suggests this excellent video covers every aspect of digital marketing, whereas I would argue it is about only online advertising.

A significant driver of the widespread adoption of content network ads by publishers is the way that Google and Yahoo! made it easy to include their ads on any web page. Figure 7.3 shows a page from my 'Athens guide' website. Having joined the Google AdSense network, I was able to include content ads on my site by simply cutting and pasting a section of code (supplied by Google) into the HTML of my pages. I even have some control over how the ads appear on my pages by selecting from a range offered by Google. Should anyone click on those ads I receive income through the pay per click model. Of course if no one visits the site (very few do!) then no one clicks on the links and I make no money. That no one might ever see them is not a significant problem for the advertiser – if there are no clicks it costs them nothing. On the plus side for the advertiser, notice how the ads are contextualized to the page's content – in my Athens Guide example, the ad from Google for taxi tours is, perhaps, a perfect example of effective contextual advertising.

home | Easter parade | eat & drink | football win | hotels | photos | places | traffic | transport | weather

Plaka

It is unashamedly tourist orientated, but manages to somehow avoid the seediness that many similar districts in cities around the world have. Perhaps this is because, with the exception of an odd few new buildings here and there, the place hasn't changed much for many a long year. Sure, there are some very narrow roads, derelict buildings and broken paving-stones [although the main streets were improved for the Olympics] but that's what gives it the character.

Typical Plaka street scenes

Think modern mall. Uniform walkways; matching shop fronts; unvarying unit sizes; planned layout with logical pedestrian flow. Now think of the absolute opposite - that's Plaka.

Athens Taxi Private Tours
www.athenstaxi-tours.gr
Transfers and Tours all around Athens and Greece.

AdChoices ▷

You can wander around Plaka every night for a month and never take the same route. Navigation is not helped by several streets seeming to be identical. The way to experience Plaka is not to use a map and try to follow a route - just head into the area and take turns as the mood takes you.

Figure 7.3 PPC network advertising in action – a Google ad on one of the author's web pages

Note that whilst Google and Yahoo! both encourage *all* website publishers to include their network ads, MSN Content is featured only on MSN 'properties', such as MSN.com, CNBC, the *Wall Street Journal* and Fox Sports. Whilst these premium sites offer high numbers of quality visitors, they are more expensive for the advertiser.

For the advertiser the process is almost as simple as it is for the publisher. There are two ways you can go about this – effectively, passively or proactively. The former means that you leave the network to choose the sites on which your ads appear by matching the ads' keywords with page content. However, this can be problematic. As in my example in Section 6.3 on keyword selection, if I were selling financial bonds then a keyword choice of 'bond' may see my income investment ads appearing on websites about Ian Fleming's secret agent, 007. For this reason, advertisers can be proactive in not only editing out places where they *do not* want their ads to be served, but choosing the types of sites on which they want the ads to appear. The ad network supplier will provide lists of content sites by (a) market or industry, (b) relevant sites by keywords used to find them, (c) specific named sites and (d) demographic information on site visitors. Although this is time-consuming in the first instance, it will bring better results in the long term.

> ### PRACTICAL INSIGHT
>
> #### Re-targeting
>
> Although many people in the digital marketing industry often confuse the two, this is a different concept to *re-marketing* (which was covered in Chapter 4). Re-targeting is a type of behavioural advertising whereby a consumer who has visited a site but not met the site's objective (usually a purchase) is shown relevant ads for that site in their subsequent surfing around the web. For example, you select a size and colour of a pair of shoes on the site of an online retailer, but do not make a purchase. As the network will have control of ads on other websites you might visit it can serve up ads for the retailer and those shoes. From the advertiser's point of view, this is an excellent use of behavioural data taken from their website and an effective way of delivering ads to a well-defined target audience. To the user, however, this form of advertising can be intimidating and uncomfortable – or even spooky if they are not aware of how the concept works, and so it should be used with caution.

A further advantage of using ad networks is that the text for specific ads within the network can be created. In the previous section mention was made of how paid ads on SERPs can be worthwhile for their definable text (as opposed to that which appears in the organic listings). In network ads this is taken a stage further in that marketers can create specific text advertising for each network campaign. This means that ads (for the same product) that are developed for a specific website, market or demographic can use copy that will best appeal to those customers. For example, an ad for the keywords 'car insurance' can present different text depending on whether the ad appears on a male- or female-oriented site – as selected in the demographics choice.

For more targeted advertising than the search engine-backed networks can offer, smaller contextual networks exist – using algorithms that more closely match page content with relevant ads. Whilst these do not have the breadth of hosting opportunities, they can produce better clickthrough rates and better leads.

An additional inducement for advertisers to use AdSense-type delivery is the metrics offered as part of the package. These are similar to website metrics (see Section 2.5) and any adoption will depend on your ad objectives. Easily available metrics include:

- How many people clicked through from the ad
- Where they were – geographically
- What page they were on when the ad was displayed
- Tracking the user through to a purchase – or rejection.

As with website analytics, more specific ad tracking than that provided as part of a package provided by an ad network can be completed in-house with resident programmers or outsourced to a service provider. The extent of your online advertising and the resources available will dictate which of the three routes you should follow.

Of course, whilst this process is fairly straightforward for just one or a small number of ads, for a retailer running hundreds or thousands of different ads for different products aimed at different target segments, the operation is far more complex – and that is where agencies, and the software they utilize (so-called dynamic ad technology), have a role to play.

GO ONLINE

The evolution of online display advertising

By its very nature, this book *introduces* students to the world of online advertising – but in reality its implementation is far more complex. In less than twenty years display advertising evolved from an advertiser contacting website publishers individually to the highly complex – and effective – system that now puts ad networks, ad exchanges, agency trading desks, demand-side platforms and sell-side platforms between the advertiser and the publisher. For an excellent three-minute video from the UK's Internet Advertising Bureau follow the link on the chapter's web page. This is a must-watch video if you want to get a basic understanding of how online advertising works.

DECISION TIME

Because *content* advertising is an extension of *search* advertising, essentially, the same decisions need to be made in this section as in the previous one on search engine advertising – indeed, an advertiser can extend their AdWords (search) campaign to Google's huge AdSense content network by doing little more than checking a box. For content ads to generate business, however, there are a number of considerations for the advertiser, not least that contextual (content) advertising is not like search in that the users haven't entered a search term to find your site – your ad is simply added to the page they are reading, making it closer to the *interruption* model so disliked offline. This means that tighter control of targeting will produce better results.

PRACTICAL INSIGHT

Ad – what?

Although there is a distinct possibility that it has changed again by the time you read this (check the chapter's web page for any updates), I find people are confused by Google's advertising provision. As I write this, what was once the Google Content Network is now called the Google Display Network. Google *AdWords* is part of the

Google Search Network – and refers to ads that appear on the Google SERP and are relative to the search term used in a search. *AdSense* is part of the Google Display Network – and refers to text, image, video and rich media adverts that are delivered on third-party sites and are relative to the site's content and audience. The Google *Network* is the 'parent' of AdWords/search and AdSense/display.

To develop an effective ad network campaign there are a number of steps to consider carefully – as Google is the biggest provider, the following pointers are specific to the search giant, but any decent ad network should offer similar facilities:

1. After joining AdWords, allow Google to distribute your ads around the AdSense network sites, and then

2. Study the 'placement performance' reports to identify the best-performing sites for your ads. The reports will include data that informs advertisers on such things as: which sites display their ads, how well the ads perform, the number of impressions and how many clicks were generated. Furthermore, Google even provides conversion rates and details of costs to evaluate ROI.

3. Use this data to target best-performing sites and exclude those that are failing to deliver acceptable results.

Note, however, that these issues are external to the organization – and any data derived from the placement performance reports must be used in conjunction with internal ad development and testing. For example, well-placed ads will not perform well if the linked landing pages are poorly designed – and they will not be effectively placed at all if the keyword decision-making procedure is inadequate.

GO ONLINE

AdWords advice

Far and away the most popular ad network is Google's AdWords, and in *The Maximum Effect* it offers advertisers advice direct from Google on how to use AdWords to its greatest effect. Follow the link on the chapter's web page to download the guide.

YOU DECIDE

Advise Frank and his management team at Hill Street Motorist Shop (case study 8) on relevant issues for any network advertising they might consider.

Alternatively, conduct the same exercise for your organization or that of your employer.

7.7 AFFILIATE PROGRAMMES

As is the case with several subjects in this book, affiliate programmes are a business model in their own right. However, as the book is about using the Internet as a medium for marketing, in this section we will only consider using affiliates (publishers) as a means of marketing a product – not how to make money by setting yourself up as an affiliate.

Affiliate programmes are a form of performance-based marketing where a commission is paid only if a sale is completed. Because multiple affiliate programmes can function on multiple websites, the notion of selling things through the practice has been dubbed *affiliate marketing*. Based on the offline practice of referrals – a tourist excursion company rewarding a hotel for any recommendations made by its staff, for example – affiliate marketing is where the website publisher is paid a fee for each user that clicks on an affiliate ad and ultimately makes a purchase (or whatever the affiliate conversion objective is). Because many affiliated sites simply use display or text ads to promote affiliated products, it is common for affiliate marketing to be associated with online advertising. As far as the user is concerned, an affiliate link is an *advert* and it is difficult for the uninitiated to tell the difference. However, just as the hotel owner will do more than simply display a leaflet for excursions, *effective* affiliates go further than simply posting ads. Although the description might be a little unkind to the former, affiliates can be divided into two camps: (1) the amateur and (2) the professional.

The amateur sees being an affiliate as a way of generating a little money from their website – which, although a money-making venture, is not a full-time job or sole source of income and any income often barely covers the cost of the site. It is this kind of member that originally made up many of Amazon's affiliates. This is not to undermine the online bookseller – it is said that much of its early success and brand development was through its affiliates and, if nothing else, was instrumental in developing the brand. However, having a significant number of affiliates is no use if they are not actively referring customers. It is also the case that sites like Amazon will retain the customer after their first referral from the affiliate site – which, as commission is paid only once, is good for the merchant but bad for the website publisher.

Professional affiliates, on the other hand, see the concept as a business model in itself. As Seda (2004) observed, 'with an affiliate network provider, you'll tap into thousands of commission-based sales people who are eager to deliver sales.' Although each *amateur* might deliver sales, they will be in limited numbers – and so a vast number are required to generate significant sales income. The professional affiliate networker, however, will deliver a much greater quantity of customers, but at increased cost per sale. The network will take a big commission and may include annual fees and software costs as well as transactional commissions. Furthermore, the professional affiliate is seeking to become rich from the practice and so they seek products that they can sell in large quantities – they are not interested in small-volume sales.

Such is the nature of the network affiliate that their sites can become brands themselves – indeed, a number of both review and shopping comparison-style sites generate affiliate income when shoppers clickthrough on their links and go on to make a purchase. In these cases, the affiliate is likely to generate its own brand loyalty – with users returning for their 'advice' or recommendations. Non-branded affiliates, on the other hand, act more like a referral service, with the user sticking with the *referred to* site for future transactions (as with my amateur/Amazon example earlier).

PRACTICAL INSIGHT

Affiliates are not just about books

Affiliate marketing is used in sectors ranging from financial services and gaming to health and beauty products. While sales are the usual objective, merchants do pay affiliate fees on other objectives – suitable leads, for example, are common affiliate objectives in the B2B environment. Although precise figures are hard to substantiate, it is estimated that around 10 per cent of all online sales are via affiliates.

DECISION TIME

Remember, in this text we are looking at using affiliates as a method of distributing our sales message around the web – and world – and not making a living by acting as an affiliate (in my previous example it is the small website owners who are acting as affiliates for Amazon, not the other way round). Essentially, we are considering *employing* affiliates as commission-based agents. As with the majority of marketing decisions, the nature of the product and the market will dictate the suitability of using affiliates or not.

Although the Amazon thousands-of-small-affiliates scenario is appealing, that example is unlikely to ever be repeated – it being a product of its time in the early development of the web. However, given the reasonably low cost of setting up an affiliate programme, it can still work for some firms. For the merchant who is looking to move significant amounts of product, though, it is the network affiliate that should be the chosen option – and even with *professionals* the number of affiliates can run into the thousands. For the business promoting goods through affiliate networks the major advantage is that not only is their reach into different markets increased, but the affiliated site effectively *sells* the product for them. If done well, affiliate marketing can provide a cost-effective and highly measurable way to acquire customers and grow sales (Gregoriadis, 2008). Indeed, some industry observers acknowledge the commission-only basis of the affiliates and point out that they can do a far better job of selling than the advertisers' own marketing team. Whilst this may send marketers reeling in indignant rage, it is case that in non-marketing-oriented organizations (a product-led firm, for example) employing affiliates is much the same as bringing in consultants to handle marketing and sales.

the major advantage is that . . . the affiliated site effectively *sells* the product

That not all companies opt to use affiliates is an indication that there are problems with the concept, however. Not least is that the firm can easily lose control of its marketing efforts. For example, affiliates are often criticized for over-aggressive tactics such as the heavy use of price and discount messaging. This can be a concern for marketers who feel affiliates are misrepresenting the brand or cheapening the product. Merchants can even find themselves competing against the advertising of affiliates for their own products. This is particularly the case with regard to search engine and network advertising where the merchant and a number of affiliates might all be bidding for the same keywords, so driving up the cost of that advertising. In a longer-term scenario, it might also be the case that an affiliate might be higher in the search engine's organic listings than the organization that makes the product.

Furthermore, as an affiliating merchant, it is your responsibility to put in place the systems that will track and record any activity so that sites hosting ads are paid their due rewards as and when they refer customers. Poor practice in this regard soon spreads around the affiliate community and you will find it hard to find high-quality sites to carry your affiliate ads. There are few companies that have the resources to manage their own affiliate programmes, however – but as with advertising, there are agencies (affiliate networks) that will handle your affiliate trading.

Gaining a good reputation as an affiliate merchant will depend on how you treat your affiliates and the service you offer – as well as your commission rates, of course. Issues that need to be addressed include:

- Make incentives realistic. Over and above a set commission, additional payments can be made for hitting predetermined sales targets – for example making a sales quota per month. This should be achievable so as to work as a motivation and not a cause for dissatisfaction.

- Offer affiliates a reasonable time-frame in which to generate commissions. Amazon, for example, has only a one-day window, so if a referred user purchases something after a couple of days or more the affiliate earns nothing. This is particularly pertinent for products that have a long buying cycle.

- Maintain good communications with affiliates so that they are aware of all news and events relating to the organization, products and the marketplace. Although they are unsalaried, the affiliates are part of your sales force – and should be treated as such.

- Provide superior display (banner) and text ads. Affiliates are not responsible for creating banners – and their quality will have an impact on clickthrough rates. Not only should there be a selection of type of message on the banners, but they should be offered in a range of sizes.

- Develop landing pages that are specific to ad messages. Sending leads to the product's or company's site front page will damage the chances of those visitors converting to customers (see next section for more on landing pages).

- Seek out the best performers and ensure they receive attention worthy of their status. Industry insiders reckon that the 80/20 rule applies in affiliate networks – that is, 80 per cent of sales come from 20 per cent of affiliate practitioners. Losing these 'super-affiliates' to a competing merchant could put a major hole in your business plan.

YOU DECIDE

Advise Robert Terwilliger on the suitability of affiliate marketing for the Modeller's Stand (case study 9).

Alternatively, conduct the same exercise for your organization or that of your employer.

7.8 LANDING PAGES

Imagine that you see an ad for a retailer on television that promotes a product in which you are interested. You then see a similar ad in your local newspaper. These ads include details of a local outlet where the product is available. You drive to the locale and as you near the retailer, billboards repeat the promotional offer. As you pull into the car park signs adorn the shop's windows. Then you enter the store. There is no signage or guides to where in the massive building your sought-after product is located. With the exception of a young checkout operator who knows little about the shop's merchandising, there are no sales staff to be found anywhere. After a few minutes of aimless wandering around you leave empty-handed. In this scenario, all the money spent on the various media advertising has been wasted because the point of sale activity was ignored.

> " the landing page is the web page to which the user is taken when they click on the link in an ad "

The online equivalent of this scenario is the landing page. Essentially, the landing page is the web page to which the user is taken when they click on the link in an ad. Although this subject is equally relevant in several other aspects of digital marketing – email marketing, for example – it is included here to emphasize the importance of landing pages in online advertising. Despite the recognized value of using landing pages, they are too frequently ignored by online marketers – even though substantial resources might have been invested in the adverts that drive potential customers to these pages.

In Section 1.6, in which we looked at online buyer behaviour, the concept of the sales, or conversion, funnel was considered – with the subject being revisited in Section 3.2, where the importance of good website navigation was addressed. It is this concept that underpins the importance of the landing page.

The issue is that if an advert motivates a potential customer to click on its link, it is essential that the impetus is maintained – hopefully through to the 'buy now' command. If, for example, a user clicks on an ad for a hotel in a specific resort in a specific region of a particular country, they should be taken to a landing page which features that hotel. They should not be taken to a hotel aggregator's 'home' page where they have to complete several elements of a search facility (e.g. 'which country do you want to go to?', 'which region?', 'which resort?') before they can see more details of the hotel featured in the ad.

Similarly, if I were to click on an ad that said '25% off selected colours of Ralph Lauren polo shirts' I would expect to be taken to a page that told me exactly which colours were available in the promotion. I would not want to arrive on the store's 'Ralph Lauren' section and have to navigate my way to the polo shirts section before finding out what colours were included in the offer.

In both of these examples, any *sales* momentum generated by the advert is lost. Indeed – and this is a key point – if the hotel (or any other) ad is just one of a number listed on a search engine results page then the searcher (the potential customer) is more likely to simply hit the 'return' button and go back to the SERP on which they saw the ad, continuing their hotel search from there by clicking on the next ad in the list.

GO ONLINE

Follow the link on the chapter's web page to see an example of how not using a landing page damages the chances of meeting the ad's objectives.

In Section 7.5 the issue of what stage of the buying cycle the potential customer is at was raised as a problem for advertisers. The landing page can help address this issue, with different landing pages being developed for each ad. I previously used the examples of 'free shipping on all lawnmowers this month' and 'top ten tips for choosing the right lawnmower' appealing only to buyers in the appropriate stages of the cycle. With the first, clicks are attracted from people who are ready to purchase, and so the landing page should swiftly move the customer into the selling environment. The latter, however, should have no 'hard sell' – instead, its content should adopt a softer, more advisory approach that might encourage the user to return to the site at a later date to make a purchase.

In an effort to give searchers relevant returns, the major search engines evaluate the landing pages that link from their SERP ads. This is mainly to prevent dubious advertisers from simply buying their way to the top of the (paid) listings. Essentially, a 'good' landing page gives you a better chance of topping the list than one the search engine feels is disingenuous. Whilst they don't declare all of the reasons a landing page might fall foul of their algorithms, Google warn against business models such as:

- data-collection sites that offer free items and so on in order to collect private information
- arbitrage sites that are designed simply for the purpose of showing ads and have little or no other content and
- malware sites that knowingly or unknowingly install software on a visitor's computer.

The search giant also 'treats with caution':

- ebooks that show frequent ads or install malware
- 'get rich quick' sites

- comparison shopping sites
- travel aggregators
- affiliates that don't comply with their affiliate guidelines.

GO ONLINE

For Google's guide to landing page and site quality, plus what business models to avoid, follow the link on the chapter's web page

---

DECISION TIME

As with so many aspects of advertising, both off- and online, the development of a landing page is best assigned to those skilled in its execution. Like ads, the design of the landing page can be handled by web designers, but it is the textual content that will determine whether or not the visitor moves down the sales funnel, or jumps back to the page on which the ad was displayed. It is this text that should be developed by an experienced copy-writer – in essence, it is an *extension* of the actual ad. Like all websites, landing pages should be developed with the user in mind, with any copy being written from the buyer's perspective. It is the landing page that is the medium used to communicate the value of whatever you are offering – and how it will meet the needs of the customer.

Given the objective of the landing page – to move customers down the buying funnel – each one requires a number of essential elements, including that the page should:

- most importantly – facilitate moving the customer on to the next step in making a purchase (or whatever the desired action of the original ad is)
- have content that is short and to the point
- represent the organization in colour, layout, tone, etc.
- be self-contained – it serves no other purpose than to act as an arrival page from an advert. This means that it must contain all relevant information, but at the same time it must focus the visitor on the product that is being promoted.

A final consideration for the landing page is how it is managed after the offer is finished. By their very definition, landing pages are created for a specific ad or campaign – which will have a limited life-span. It is normally the case that once the promotion is over, the landing page is removed. This can be a mistake for two reasons:

1. the page may have been indexed by search engines – and so the link to it remains live, and
2. the ads may still be available on forgotten or ghost websites, and customers may still click on them.

To remedy this, the landing page can be left live indefinitely, though obviously, if the promotion is time-specific, the actual content will need changing. This could be a simple message explaining that the original offer has now ended and a link to the site's home page. Better still, the link could go to any similar offers that are available at that time – though that course of action would require constant monitoring.

YOU DECIDE

Advise the board of the Matthew Humberstone Foundation Hospital (case study 6) on how specific landing pages will help convert 'lookers' into 'buyers'. What issues are particular to the hospital's products with regard to this issue?

Alternatively, conduct the same exercise for your organization or that of your employer.

CHAPTER EXERCISE

Giving justifications for all your decisions, advise the marketing team at the Gilded Truffle Hotel (case study 3) on all aspects of online advertising covered in this chapter.

Alternatively, conduct the same exercise for your own organization or that of your employer.

CHAPTER QUESTIONS

Follow the link from the chapter's web page to a series of multiple-choice, exam-type questions that will test your knowledge and understanding of the various elements of the chapter.

REFERENCES

Bly, R.W. (1985) *The Copywriter's Handbook*. Henry Holt & Company.

Charlesworth, A. (2007) *Key Concepts in e-Commerce*. Palgrave-Macmillan.

Goldman, A. (2011) *Everything I Know about Marketing I Learned from Google*. McGraw-Hill.

Gregoriadis, L. (2008) Affiliate marketing networks buyer's guide 2008. E-consultancy. Available on e-consultancy.com.

Nielsen (2013) The paid social media advertising report 2013. Available on nielsen.com.

Nielsen, J. (2007) Banner blindness: old and new findings. Available at www.nngroup.com/articles/banner-blindness-old-and-new-findings/.

Nielsen/NetRatings (2003). The state of online advertising. Available on nielsennetratings.com.

Safran, N. (2012) The branding value of search's page one. Conductor Research. Available on conductor.com.

Scott, D.M. (2007) *The New Rules of Marketing and PR*. Wiley.

Seda, C. (2004) *Search Engine Advertising*. New Riders.

Chapter **8**

Permission marketing

> *The secret of life is honesty and fair dealing. If you can fake that, you've got it made.*
> *Groucho Marx*

Chapter at a glance

8.1 Introduction
8.2 Personalization
8.3 Email as a medium for direct marketing
8.4 Email as a medium for marketing messages
8.5 Newsletters

8.1 INTRODUCTION

This chapter considers those elements of digital marketing that are deemed to be permission based – that is, the recipient of the marketing message has given explicit *permission* for that message to be sent. This is the opposite of interruption marketing, where the message interrupts whatever the recipient is doing to present itself – the obvious example is the advertising break in a TV programme.

As with so many elements of digital marketing, however, there is inconsistency in this definition. This comes about because – I, many others, argue – the Internet itself is permission based. This is built on the premise that every web page must be requested by the user – effectively, therefore, it is given *permission* to show itself on the user's computer screen. Indeed, this concept is key to web marketing in that because the user has requested your web page they are exhibiting an interest in your product, brand or organization, which is not the case when firing multi-media advertising at them. Note that it is possible to send web pages to users (when they close a browser tab, for example) but as this practice is so roundly derided by the web surfing community it is a practice that no legitimate digital marketer would ever consider. It is also the case that some websites will deliver ads *without* the express permission of the site's visitor. However, as such sites are using a content/advertising business model, any visitor accepts that ads are the price they pay for accessing the content for free, therefore their permission is implicit.

That said, in order to both study and practise the subject, we must differentiate elements of digital marketing into distinct sections – and so there is a chapter devoted to more specific permission-based digital marketing.

It is a common misconception in digital marketing that email can only be used in a direct marketing context – that is, the electronic delivery of a sales message. This is wrong because it ignores the value of *all* email communications as a medium for carrying a marketing message. Therefore, in this chapter we will consider these two aspects of email marketing separately, starting with direct marketing email and then looking at the use of email in non direct-sales communication.

Customer relationship management (CRM)

As with other elements of the discipline and practice we call *marketing* – the marketing mix and market research, for example – CRM is a subject in its own right and is not exclusive to the Internet. It is for this reason that I have elected to include it only as an element of this section and not address the subject as a whole. That Internet technology saw an advance – and a boom – in CRM practice is a cloud to the issue that it is not based, or dependent, on the Internet. Although the concept of CRM pre-dates the development of digital technology, the mid- to late 1990s gave light to the concept that intelligence on customers could be managed using that technology. Thus, the end of the twentieth century saw many organizations spending vast sums of money on CRM software and/or systems – many of which were sold as the panacea to all marketing ills. Not only is history littered with empirical evidence of the failings of these systems, but academic research supports the view that they did not achieve their objectives (see Ebnar *et al.* 2002, for example). The principal problem with CRM (at that time) was that it was perceived as being about IT, so it was predominantly IT-led. Systems were developed that gathered vast mountains of data simply because the software had the ability to gather it. That few (if any) organizations had staff with

> *managing relationships with customers is a better description of the objectives behind the concept*

the ability to (a) turn the data into information, (b) interpret that information and (c) use it in any kind of tactical or strategic planning was almost irrelevant because no one had the time to keep pace with the data being spewed forth on a daily basis.

CRM practice changed fundamentally when IT consulted other departments about their requirements of any system, and then developed the software to meet those needs. Contemporary CRM systems, when installed and implemented correctly, can be extremely effective. Badly considered and implemented poorly, they can alienate the very customers they seek to *manage*. As this book is about marketing, I am bound to say that CRM is a marketing discipline – indeed, I think that *managing relationships with customers is a better description of the objectives* behind the concept. This rewording shifts the emphasis to customers – as it should be – and away from customer relationship *management* where the title suggests the task of managing something that is a burden to the organization – like waste disposal, for example.

Experienced eCRM and social CRM strategist Andrew Campbell (2013) recognizes the way in which CRM should change for the online – and particularly, social media – customer, saying:

Companies need to move from managing customers, to facilitating collaborative experiences and on-going dialogue that customers value. By doing this companies will create the ability to monitor what consumers do and say to one another on social platforms accessing unbiased feedback and behavioural data on a huge scale. This insight should revolutionise the way marketers think and what they do.

However, this philosophy and the concept of 'managing' customers seem to be at odds – and yet the practice is (still) called 'customer relationship management', a situation that does not help anyone who has not lived through the development of relationship marketing and CRM over the last twenty-five years or so in understanding just what marketers are trying to achieve with such strategies.

Another key element to CRM is that it assumes there is a relationship between the organization or brand and the customer – and that the customer wants a relationship. Marketers, and particularly front-line sales staff, recognize this and adapt their actions accordingly. However, the all-encompassing CRM systems of the last century (designed by non-marketers) took no account of it and attempted to 'force' CRM where no relationship existed. The results were the exact opposite of what was intended.

It is also the case that CRM should be practised wherever there is a touch-point between organization and customer – hence it cannot be confined to the Internet only. It is for this reason that I have decided not to include a section in this book that is devoted to CRM. Pure-online CRM (eCRM?) does exist, but it is encompassed within the other elements of online marketing rather than being isolated as a separate subject. Much of this chapter, for example, is CRM-related in that actions are based on the information held on customers. Similarly, as consumers now expect a consistent and seamless shopping experience this requires the seller to provide personalized online content, service and special offers that can only be delivered if the organization is collecting data across all digital touch-points such as social media likes, purchases, browsed pages, product views, searched terms, redeemed offers, video views, ad clickthroughs and fulfilment, which all help in considering consumers' browsing behaviour, purchase behaviour, purchase history and customer attributes. I consider these to be a part of digital marketing, and not CRM. Important to add, however, is that any data – such as that above – gathered online can be included within any strategic CRM initiative.

MINI CASE

Seth Godin's rules on permission

Although he doesn't actually mention CRM, Seth Godin is critical of the concept in this rant against 'permission'. His rules reflect my view on customers not wanting to have a 'managed' relationship with sellers. They are taken from his book *Meatball Sundae*.

1. Permission doesn't exist to help you (the marketer). It exists to help **me**. The moment the messages you send me cease to be anticipated, personal and relevant, then you cease to exist in my world.

2. My permission can't be bought or sold. It's non-transferable.

3. I don't care about you. Not really. I care about me. If your message has something to do with my life, then perhaps I'll notice, but in general, don't expect much.

4. Privacy policies and fine print are meaningless to me. When I give you my permission to follow up, we're making a deal and you're making a promise. An overt and clear promise. If you break that promise, whether or not you are legally in the right, we're finished.

5. I demand your respect. I can get respect from plenty of organizations, so if you disrespect me (by mistreating me, by breaking your promise, by cheating or lying or by undervaluing our relationship), then sure, that's right, you're history.

Source: Godin, 2008

A final point is that *customer relationship management* and *relationship marketing* are most definitely not the same thing. Relationship marketing – as all marketing students should know – is a concept and ethos on which an organization's entire marketing – some might say business – strategy is based. A purist – like me – would argue that, in such a culture, building a relationship with customers does not need *managing*.

8.2 PERSONALIZATION

In this section there is yet another issue of how the subject is interpreted in an online scenario. The definitions to be addressed here are those of *personalization* and *customization* – and whether each applies to a tangible product or an intangible service. In an offline environment personalization of a product would normally refer to a bespoke product – a one-off, made-to-measure dress, for example. Using the same analogy, a customized dress might take a common pattern, but with additional features added to make it more individual. With regard to service, to a certain degree, it is always customized. As individuals will be involved in its performance, no matter how similar a task might be – fixing a leaking tap, for example – the interaction between the plumber and customer will never be exactly the same. So it is that when we move online we must consider the product and the service. For many products there is a direct correlation to the offline scenario. In customization, the optional accessories for a new car could, for example, be just as easily selected by checking boxes on a web page as face-to-face with a salesperson. That some buyers prefer to make such choices without any pressure – perceived or actual – from sales staff might be a good reason for making online purchase available. In essence, the product's customization is the same; it is simply made through a different sales medium. Online – like the personal shopper in an offline clothes shop – personalization refers to the service that is offered, not the product.

As all those who have worked in a sales environment will testify, one-to-one personal service is the most effective way to sell something. It is, however, extremely resource intensive – and so expensive. So it was that when the commercial Internet was gaining popularity in the mid-1990s some commentators predicted that the new medium would provide a platform where sellers could communicate with buyers on an individual basis – that is, each customer has their own personal web page interaction with the vendor – something that many consider to be the holy grail for marketers. Offline, the salesperson can ask pertinent questions of the customer and by listening to the answers can (if they are any good) provide a product that will meet the needs of that customer – resulting in satisfaction all round. Online, the idea is that by selecting elements of their own web page, the customer indicates their interests and buying preferences. In addition, the organization may have sales or surfing history on the customer indicating their possible buyer behaviour. Amazon provides an excellent example of this kind of personal service. In much the same way as the offline salesperson gleans information from the shopper, as they navigate around their site, the customer provides valuable information to Amazon's database – the online sales *facilitator*. Searching for, and visiting the pages of, books on horse riding, for example, will result in the ads featured on future Amazon pages that person downloads being related to the subject. In addition, by registering with the company the buyer gives permission for their sales data to be stored – so allowing *actual* purchases to be included in the recommendation algorithm. Personalization can then be taken a stage further by having promotions presented for authors or subjects that are related or similar to those purchased. Amazon's 'people who bought this product also bought . . .' facility is an example.

Whilst Amazon is the best-known example of this practice, this is because it operates in a B2C environment, which as well as attracting greater numbers of visitors, always attracts media coverage. However, many B2B sites operate similar systems, where sites are personalized to the most common requirements of the business buyer. This can include features such as on-page reminders when common reorder dates are approaching. For example, if a customer has a history of buying a box of paper every six weeks, the home page for week five will carry an 'are you running out of paper?' message. Commonly purchased goods can then be re-ordered on a 'one-click' basis on the home page. The same page might also be personalized to include links to industry-related third-party articles or stories – making the page a kind of *portal* that the buyer visits frequently and so increasing the chances of future purchases and enhancing their relationship with the vendor. Furthermore, technology can be used to supplement the *reactive* nature of tracking prior behaviour and responding to it. However, the rather simplistic product-recommendation type of personalization is considered by many to be standard fare on any ecommerce website.

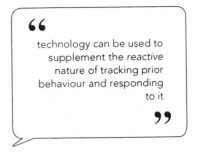

> technology can be used to supplement the *reactive* nature of tracking prior behaviour and responding to it

Long-time advocate of personalization Jack Aaronson, writing in his clickz.com column in 2013, argues that rather than being a tool, personalization is an aspect of the user's online experience. With this in mind, we have to consider that consumers now use multiple devices, in various places and at different times, to access an assortment of online presences owned or published by a single organization – and so personalization should cross over between all of these. Aaronson goes on to say that 'In multi-channel personalization, your actions in one channel (such as what movies you like to stream on your TV) affect your experience on other channels. Smart companies are backing multi-channel personalization into their multi-channel user experience strategy, whether they call it "personalization" or not.'

Furthermore, as we considered in Chapter 1, customers can visit the organization's online presence(s) at different stages of their buying cycle. Research by MyBuys (2013) suggests that customer-centric marketing – the ability of retailers to engage consumers in one-to-one conversations across the customer life cycle and all touch-points – increases buyer readiness, engagement and sales activity. Sellers should, therefore, be prepared to personalize the shopping experience across any and all of the various channels their customers might use.

Note: that the concept of multi-channel personalization will soon be *expected* by consumers (if it isn't already) is another reason for me to reject CRM as being an aspect of digital marketing. Certainly, multi-channel personalization might add to the organization's CRM data, but it is not part of CRM; it is about delivering the service that customers expect, when they expect it and how they expect it. It is not about *managing* their relationship during that process.

There is one aspect of digital marketing that has seen a significant advance in recent years that has impacted dramatically on personalization – the widespread adoption of smartphones. Part of this is due to users' relationship with their mobile device. As the Internet Advertising Bureau's Anna Bager stated (in an interview with ClickZ.com), 'mobile is a behaviour, not a technology. It's about accessing content wherever you are . . . It's really the use that is mobile, not the device.'

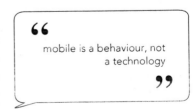

> mobile is a behaviour, not a technology

In this scenario, the user – that is, the customer – expects content to be on their device, and so the device itself becomes the *portal* of access to the web. To that end, organizations must ensure that their website works well on mobile appliances, or develop apps to present their content. Or both.

Other organizations have recognized the opportunity presented by the *mobile portal* concept and set themselves up as such. Perhaps the two dominant forces at this time in this concept are the ubiquitous Google and Apple, the former with its own smartphone operating systems and the latter with its iPhone. Swiping pages to one side to simply touch the screen over an icon is the way mobile users expect to connect to whatever they seek – be that search, maps, entertainment, videos, music, email, texting . . . or just making a good old phone call. If you are not on that screen, as far as these users are concerned, you do not exist. Personalization comes from the user making the choice of what apps their phone will include and what services they sign up for, as well as the providers using technology to personalize those services.

PRACTICAL INSIGHT

Google's app aims to know what you want before you do

The search giant's offering in the mobile portal stakes is Google Now. As well as finishing your search term for you, this app's predictive feature takes into account all of your activity on the various Google tools – including Gmail, Google+, Google Calendar – as well as the device's GPS to provide information without you asking for it. Links to local transport if you are away from home, exchange rates as soon as you land in a new country or synchronization with local traffic news to tell you how long it will take you to get to work – providing you have supplied your work's location, of course.

DECISION TIME

If your product has no scope for customization, then the Internet can do nothing to introduce that service. However, if you can in some way customize a product – no matter how minor that might be – the web allows a personalized service to be offered at a much lower price, and more conveniently, than it can be offline. If the nature of the product lends itself to being a gift, this gives an obvious opportunity for offering a personalized service in the fulfilment aspect of an online purchase. Instead of parcelling a book (for example) in plain brown card, it can be wrapped in gift paper with a personal message – supplied by the buyer – attached.

Personalization of a web page will first and foremost be dependent on how often a customer is likely to visit a site, with the width and depth of the range of products or services offered by a site having an obvious impact on visitor frequency. Tesco, for example, might expect a monthly, or even weekly, visit to their online store. Amazon would hope for multiple visits per year, but not on a regular basis – and so the visits-to-purchase ratio would be much lower. Both of these companies would look to develop a relationship with the customer – and personalization could have an intrinsic part to play in such a strategy. However, a car manufacturer might not expect people to visit its site on a regular basis – few people renew their car more often than every couple of years, and then they may not stick with the same manufacturer. Similarly, a *used* car sales operation would be best advised to maintain an offline relationship with customers rather than personalizing a website that people might never revisit after a purchase is made.

However, a car dealership (one franchised to a manufacturer) might not only look to get repeat sales for cars (they do – lifetime value of customers is an important metric to them), the same customers would be targeted for after-sales and service income. In this case, it might be the customer's car that is the key personalization criterion rather than the customer. Visits to the dealer's website would be personalized to include such content as service-due messages, promotions on accessories suitable to the car or seasonally related issues like winter safety checks.

Personalization features (widgets) should be considered with care – with frequency of visit being paramount. A flight-booking website, for example, could not be expected to include a permanent display of clocks showing times for all the world's cities. However, if I fly to a couple of time zones on a regular basis, perhaps being able to put clocks set at those times on my home page would be useful. Similarly, local weather forecasts for those places would add to my on-site satisfaction. Adding such facilities to company websites is not normally a good idea, however. Whilst these might have novelty value, they are unlikely to add to the customer experience – and could well detract from the validity of other content. If issues like the local weather are useful for a website (an airport, for example), then they should be permanent elements of the site, not optional add-ons.

However, this takes on a whole new perspective if the organization has more online touch-points than a single website. The contemporary customer expects to access the organization's Facebook page on their tablet during a coffee break at work, check out product information on their smartphone on the train on their way home and then have the company website on their home PC know all about their activities during the day and serve up a personalized service based on that. Just having a 'hello Alan' message simply does not cut it in that environment.

YOU DECIDE

Advise Frank at Hill Street Motorist Shop (case study 8) on how the use of personalized web content might better satisfy his customers.

Alternatively, conduct the same exercise for your organization or that of your employer.

8.3 EMAIL AS A MEDIUM FOR DIRECT MARKETING

Despite common assumptions – probably brought on by the media frenzy surrounding social media – the demise of email as a communication medium is far from absolute. Myriad surveys (see the Research Snapshot below for examples) have shown that no matter what device is used, checking email remains one of the most common reasons for going online. Furthermore, and with particular relevance to this book, the use of email as a direct marketing tool continues to be one of the most effective elements of digital marking. Twitter might be *sexy*, but email brings in the sales. It is – probably – an attempt to raise its profile as being contemporary that has seen direct marketing by email be commonly referred to as *digital direct marketing*.

RESEARCH SNAPSHOT

Email is dead – or is it?

Although the likes of social media and texting might gain the attention of the popular press, email still plays an important role in communicating on the Internet. Consider these stats:

- Email volume increased by 10 per cent from 2011 to 2012. And amongst adult Internet users, 92 per cent access email when they are on the web, and 69 per cent of consumers favour email as their first online activity of the day.
- Neither has the advent of smartphones and their multiple methods of communication diminished email's popularity, with 41 per cent of all email now opened on a mobile device and email being the top smartphone activity, ahead of both web browsing and Facebook.
- From a business perspective, email is still the most effective and inclusive channel for reaching consumers, with 77 per cent of consumers choosing it as their preferred method of receiving marketing messages (the second-placed online channel, Facebook, came in at just 4 per cent). Furthermore, it gets results: 66 per cent of us have made a purchase after receiving a promotional email.
- When asked where they first saw their most recent online purchase, the top answers were while surfing around online (29 per cent) and when looking to find something specific (25 per cent). However, emails from stores came in third (at 11 per cent). Trailing in behind were ads (6 per cent) and other web content sites (4 per cent).

Still think email marketing isn't worthwhile?

Sources: Experian Marketing Services (experian.co.uk);
PewInternet (pewinternet.org); ExactTarget (exacttarget.co.uk);
Knotice (knotice.com); IDC Research (idc.com); Shopzilla (shopzilla.co.uk)

Direct marketing email campaigns can be broken down into seven distinct elements. Chronologically, they are:

1. Determining objectives of the campaign
2. Development of a mailing list
3. Development of the content
4. Development of the landing page
5. Testing of content and technology
6. Sending
7. Measuring the results

Let's consider each of these in more detail.

Determining objectives of the campaign

A recurring theme of this book is that setting the objectives for any marketing exercise – off- or online – is essential, and email marketing is no exception. Without an objective (or objectives), none of the following tasks can be completed effectively – and so the campaign will not succeed (with no objectives, how would you know if you were successful anyway?) and will not give a return on any investment. For direct marketing emails, the objectives will normally be to elicit an action from the recipients. Although income generation is likely to be the ultimate aim of the email campaign, that can be too simplistic – not least because the email might start a recipient down the sales funnel, but some other element of marketing (price too high, for example) may stop them making a purchase. It is necessary, therefore, to consider the email campaign as (1) an element of an integrated marketing campaign where it dovetails with other elements of the strategy, or (2) a stand-alone operation. Where the email marketer's objective might be to drive customers to a web page or a bricks-and-mortar store – after that, it is the responsibility of the website or shop to convert those visitors into customers – effectively, their objectives.

Sales are not the only objectives, however. The email campaign might be looking to increase registrations to a newsletter, encourage membership of a club or promote donations to a charity. In Section 1.6 we considered how the AIDA concept can be applied to digital marketing – and it is also true of direct marketing by email. All of the elements – attention, interest, desire, action – can be achieved using email; indeed, a well-constructed message might accomplish all four in a single email. For example, a solicitor might be aware of a new law that will impact on a certain industry. Therefore, a mailing list made up of managers in that industry can be used to contact them. The same message would make them *aware* of the new law, develop *interest* by showing how it will impact on them, create *desire* by spelling out how the impending problem can be averted – and finally promote *action* by directing them to a web page or contact phone number for the solicitor.

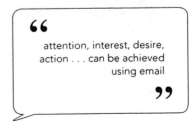

> attention, interest, desire, action . . . can be achieved using email

PRACTICAL INSIGHT

Spam – and legal attempts to stop it

Although an absolute definition is difficult, in legal terms spam is email that is sent to a recipient without them giving permission – explicit or implied – to receive it.

Both the European Union and the USA have introduced laws in an attempt to cut down email spam. The EU Directive on Privacy and Electronic Communications (introduced at the end of 2003) is Europe-wide, though how it is interpreted and implemented is up to each member country.

The CAN-SPAM Act of 2003 (Controlling the Assault of Non-Solicited Pornography and Marketing Act) – which has a much higher profile – set requirements for those who send commercial email and gave consumers the right to ask emailers to stop spamming them. The Act covers direct marketing email (where the primary purpose is to advertise or promote a commercial product or service) but not those emails that transmit a 'transactional or relationship message' (which update a customer in an existing business relationship, for example).

Whilst both laws were generally welcomed, they were criticized for not going far enough. The principal problem with each is that they apply only to emails sent from within the relevant countries and cannot be applied to entities operating outside those boundaries.

Rather than adding clarity, both of these pieces of legislation manage to further cloud the issue in their definitions of 'spam'. However, Chad White of the Email Experience Council offers a more down-to-earth interpretation. He says an email is spam if it is (1) unsolicited, (2) sent from spoofed addresses, (3) fraudulent, (4) full of objectionable content, (5) likely to contain viruses or malware – or all of the these.

For more details on both the Directive and the Act, follow the link on the chapter's web page.

Source: emailexperience.org

Development of a mailing list

If you are going to send emails, you need email addresses to send them to. However, simply to send an email to any email address you can find is both poor marketing and potentially illegal. Essentially, therefore, the digital marketer should be looking for the email addresses of (1) potential customers who are in the target market for whatever is being promoted, *and* (2) people in that segment that have given permission to receive promotional emails. These mailing lists – as they are called – can be built in two ways, internally or externally to the organization. Let's look at these two methods in more detail.

Internal

Lists that are developed in-house will always carry the most integrity – and so produce best results. Often an integral element of other marketing initiatives such as CRM or retailing, email addresses can be gathered both off- and online. Offline, practices used for decades to collect postal addresses can be applied to email addresses. These can range from free give-a-ways to competitions to win a free meal if you leave your email address at a restaurant. Online, technology can be used to save any email address that is gathered as part of the organization's online operations – a customer order or an online quotation form, for example.

No matter what methods of collecting email addresses are used, for reason of good practice and legal requirement, it is important for the online marketer to get permission from recipients to send them emails. There are two ways to get this permission:

1. Opt-out is where the receiver must take an action to opt out of receiving email messages. For example, the default setting for a message that says, 'do you wish to receive email messages?' is for there to be a tick in the 'yes' box. The visitor must, therefore, remove the tick if they do not wish to get emails.

2. Opt-in is where the receiver chooses to receive email by taking an action. With a *single* opt-in they could, for example, 'tick' a box in an off- or online form. This is open to abuse, however. Whether for a joke or more malicious purposes, someone might tick to receive email and enter the email address of someone else. Naturally, the receiver is not aware of what has happened and assumes any email from this source is spam. *Double* opt-in, however, requires confirmation by the recipient. After the initial opt-in is made, an email is sent to them giving details of the opt-in agreement. Only when the recipient replies to this email does the opt-in become active. Note that double opt-in reduces take-up rates but produces databases with the most integrity.

Note that a further use of the *opt-out* facility is that there should be such an option at the bottom of all emails sent to people as the result of them opting to receive emails – in other words, they must be able to change their mind. Although this is a legal requirement in the USA, it should also serve as a warning to keep any email contact relevant and interesting – or you will lose that customer when they elect to opt-out.

External

This option entails the buying-in of a list of email addresses from a third-party supplier – and can be effective if care is taken. There are legitimate brokers who, as a business model, collect email addresses from people who have given their permission – opted in – to receive emails from organizations with whom they have had no prior communication. These lists are then segmented and sold – or, to be more accurate, *rented* – to companies who wish to target specific groups of customers. The manufacturer of a new safety device for cars that are towing something might, for example, buy in a list of known caravan owners. For smaller organizations there is the added advantage that some of the brokers, particularly those who value their legitimacy, will also handle the sending of emails on behalf of their clients. Obviously, the purchase cost per email address will depend on how specific the list is, and therein lies the main problem – the validity of the list of email addresses. Some – less scrupulous – companies will simply gather email addresses from anywhere they can (often by harvesting them from websites) and sell them on for a few dollars per thousand. As these address owners have not given their permission to receive emails, any sent to them are spam. Such lists should be avoided by legitimate companies who value their reputation.

Unless you are conducting a one-off, never-to-be-repeated email campaign, it is important to treat the mailing list as a living thing that requires constant attention. Not only will new names be added, but addresses will need to be purged – whether by request (opt-out) or because the address has bounced a previous email. Simply conducting a periodic review just prior to a new campaign is not sufficient if the campaign is to be successful.

Development of the content

The development of the email itself – what the recipient will get in their inbox – has two distinct elements, (1) the technical aspect, and (2) the textual content. Let's now look at these in more detail.

Technical

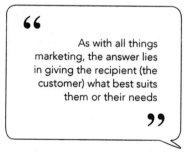

> As with all things marketing, the answer lies in giving the recipient (the customer) what best suits them or their needs

The problem with email is that it is not guaranteed to look the same when it is received as when it was sent. This is because different email clients *read* and present the message in a different way depending on both the default settings of each service provider and how each recipient has set up their own system. The problem is further compounded by the fact that users now use a variety of devices to access their email. A fabulously creative email message designed to be viewed on a seventeen-inch PC screen is not going to be effective on a smartphone screen – if it downloads at all. As with all things marketing, the answer lies in giving the recipient (the customer) what best suits them or their needs – even if they read their email on multiple devices.

Textual content

As with the development of website content (see Section 3.4), writing the words for a successful direct marketing email is a specialized task.

The sender has only a few words – and very little time – to impress upon the recipient that (a) the email is not spam, (b) it is relevant to them, and (c) they should take the action it promotes. Not only is the content important, but the subject line is essential in encouraging the receiver to even open the email – rather than simply click 'delete'. Get the subject line wrong and any resource spent on the rest of the email campaign is a waste of time, because the recipient simply won't open it. In essence, the textual content of the email is sales copy – it is there to elicit an immediate response – and very few people can write it effectively. The days of a subject line that says 'open this for a free gift' being effective have long since passed – if they ever existed in the first place. As with any sales or advertising, the subject line should seek to sell not the product – but the advantages gained by its purchase.

For example, a subject line that says 'shop for insurance' has no appeal for me – particularly if I have all the insurance I need. However, a subject of 'are you paying too much for insurance?' might well hit a nerve, particularly if I have an insurance policy due for renewal in the near future.

GO ONLINE

As mentioned earlier in this section (re spam) the legal aspects of email marketing are complex – in the UK, for example, each direct marketing email should include a company registration number, place of registration and the registered office address of the business in the email footer. For the sources of more information on this subject, follow the link from the chapter's web page.

Development of the landing page

In Chapter 7 great emphasis was placed on the importance of landing pages – so much so that I elected to devote a whole section to the subject. As direct marketing emails also seek to elicit a response from the receiver (as do ads), it is equally important to carefully consider the landing page for every email. Rather than covering all the details again here – I will simply advise you to take another look at Section 7.8.

Testing of content and technology

If there is an element of email marketing that is neglected – or even missed out altogether – testing is it. And yet the most successful practitioners will spend as much time testing as they will on all the other aspects of the campaign put together. As with development, testing of emails must consider technical issues and the content. Before reaching that stage, however, more 'traditional' direct marketing issues need to be tested – including such things as the target audience (market segment) and the promotion that is being transmitted (e.g. 20 per cent discount

> " A successful clickthrough rate can also be negated by a poor landing page "

or free shipping). You might be surprised how many email campaigns' failure is nothing to do with the medium of communication and everything to do with a promotion that does not appeal to the recipients. A successful clickthrough rate can also be negated by a poor landing page, therefore it too should be tested.

Technical issues will include the aforementioned browser issue – does the email configure in all browsers and email service provider client systems? If images are used, their size must be checked – many client systems (of universities, for example) will block emails that are above a certain file size. Anti-spam facilities – known as spam filters – will also look at elements of the email to assess its validity. Infringe any of their rules and not only will the email not be delivered, but your organization may be branded as a spammer, and have all subsequent emails from your domain blocked. A proactive approach is to have 'authentication tags' embedded into each email to identify the sending organization. These enable receiving ISPs to verify that senders are actually who they say they are, making it virtually impossible for spammers to hide their identities.

PRACTICAL INSIGHT

Guilty of spam by association

One of the issues with spam is that it is the offending email's Internet Protocol (IP) address that is 'blacklisted', not the organization committing the offence. This can be problematic in that most email service providers (ESPs) share IPs across a number of customers. This means that in a pooled IP environment the bad practices of one company can spoil the (innocent) reputations of everyone in that pool. The way around this potential problem is to pay the ESP for a dedicated IP address. That is, it is used for the emails of only one of their clients, therefore the email reputation belongs to that organization, rather than a group of clients. Further reputation security can be achieved by using a dedicated server that hosts only your IP (numerous dedicated IPs can be used on the same server). Naturally the cost increases accordingly, and so this option is only really for *serious* email marketers.

Testing of textual content – as well as images and presentation – most commonly uses A/B testing, where an equal number of test-users are exposed to an email that has been developed in two formats – hence A and B (using more than two options is known as multivariate testing). In the test, equal quantities of each variant are directed to recipients and results recorded to measure which works best. A basic – and obvious – test is to use different subject lines and see which results in more emails being opened. However, professional email marketers will also test everything from the headline through the colour of the text and different images to the size of the 'click here' button. Although this may seem excessive to some, it is very much a task of finding the best option in a numbers game. For example, if a million emails are to be sent and changing one element improves the open rate by a quarter of one per cent, that equates to a significant number of potential customers reading the marketing message. Make another three changes with a similar improvement and the open rate goes up by a full percentage point. Given that a click-through rate that is measured in single figures is the norm for many industries, an extra ten thousand emails being opened is a significant improvement.

Sending

This is the easiest part of the process, with technology requiring that all that is needed is to click on 'send'. However, consideration might need to be given to which day the emails should be sent, or even the time of day they are posted (note that there may also be an issue with time zones). It is also possible that they should be sent in batches to prevent an overload on whatever facility has been designated to handle the potential responses – for example, if recipients are encouraged to contact a freephone number they do not want to find it permanently engaged.

PRACTICAL INSIGHT

Today's the day

Over the years much research – and testing – has been conducted into what day is the best day to send out emails. And the answer, depending on who you ask is . . . Monday. Or Tuesday, or Wednesday, or Thursday, or Friday, or Saturday, or Sunday.

Essentially, unless your offer or message is day specific, then it doesn't really matter – not least because you have no control over when the recipient will actually read the email. It also stands to reason that *if* there were a universal best day to send emails, wouldn't our inboxes fill up on that day, and that day alone?

Measuring the results

One of the main advantages that email direct marketing has over its offline relation is that technology can be used to determine the success – or otherwise – of the campaign.

Like the metrics for websites, those for email campaigns should concur with the objectives of the campaign of which the emails are a part. It is also the case that the ultimate metric is how successful the campaign has been in its primary objective – sales generated, leads created or membership sign-ups, for example. However, there are metrics that can be tracked in order to assess the various stages required in meeting – or otherwise – those objectives. It is, therefore, necessary to identify those aspects of the campaign that can make or break the chances of success. These are commonly known as key performance indicators (KPIs).

Generic email KPIs include such things as:

- delivery rate – the percentage of sent emails that reach a 'live' inbox

- Open rate – the percentage of sent emails that are opened by the receiver
- Clickthrough rate – the percentage of sent emails that are opened and then have an embedded link 'clicked'
- Viral rate – the number of opened emails that are forwarded to another address.
- Campaign comparison – any of the above measured against metrics from similar previous campaigns.

These metrics – like all useful metrics – not only help measure success but help identify elements of the campaign's process that are not as effective as they should be. For example, if the open rate is low that might suggest that the subject line is not sufficiently attractive to the receiver that they feel compelled to open the email and read the full message. Note also that delivery, open and clickthrough rates are grouped as 'response rates' – valuable to branding campaigns because they suggest exposure to a brand message. KPIs for email campaigns with specific objectives might include:

- sales units
- sales' value
- orders
- average order value
- total profit
- downloads
- leads generated
- response rates – for both opening and clickthrough.

Note that all of the above can be calculated per total emails sent, total delivered, total opened or how many clickthroughs from the email.

Two other useful metrics represent the extremes of result. They are:

- The churn rate – the loss of addresses from an email list. This could be because the email is not delivered (e.g. the address no longer exists) or because the receiver decides to unsubscribe from the mailing list.
- List growth – how many people decide to join a mailing list as a result of an off- or online list-building campaign.

It is worthwhile for the email marketer to note that company CEOs, MDs, owners or finance officers prefer metrics that determine how the email campaign is benefiting the organization. For example, 'units sold' is a tangible metric that means something to them, whilst 'delivery rate' is an intangible that has no presence on the profit and loss sheet.

RESEARCH SNAPSHOT

Spam by any other name

A survey by online marketing services provider Q Interactive found that consumers' perceptions of what they consider to be spam does not match 'official' definitions. The report found that 56 per cent of consumers consider marketing messages from known senders to be spam if the message is 'not interesting to me'. Furthermore, 50 per cent think that 'too frequent emails from companies I know' also count as spam. This is problematic for online marketers as most ISPs make readily available a 'report as spam' button on their email browsers – this means that innocent companies can find themselves being reported as spammers for sending emails that the receivers have actually requested.

Source: Q Interactive and MarketingSherpa, 2008

DECISION TIME

After deciding whether or not direct email marketing might work for the organization (i.e. there are feasible objectives that will give an appropriate return on investment), the next key consideration is how will any objectives be translated into something that the receiver will value – in sales terms, what is the *offer*? The offer can take a number of guises, for example:

- A financial incentive – buy-one-get-one-free or free shipping
- Time specific – offer ends Saturday or one-day-only sale
- No direct monetary value – a quality upgrade or accumulated purchases rewards.

The next issue to address is how that campaign might be planned and implemented. At this stage, what denotes a *campaign* is open to interpretation. Certainly, for the major brands, a campaign will involve sending thousands, if not millions, of emails at one time. However, for the SME – or even a larger company that operates in a number of niche markets – the number of emails sent might not reach three figures. Obviously, the number being sent will impact on (a) whether any campaign is worthwhile, (b) what resources are required, and (c) are those resources are available in-house or is it necessary to outsource the operation?

Following the chronological order of the seven distinct elements of email marketing listed in the previous section, the next issue is the development – or acquisition – of a mailing list. This issue will depend on the nature of the objectives. If existing customers are to be targeted for increased business then it is likely that their email addresses will already be known. However, if gaining new customers – or generating sales leads – is the objective, then an email list will need to be bought in.

PRACTICAL INSIGHT

Whitelists prevent being blacklisted

Registered with an individual user's Internet service provider (ISP) and overriding any spam filters the ISP might operate, a whitelist is a list of email addresses that an Internet user is always willing to receive email from. Because the practice is seen as building a list of people that it is *safe* to receive email from, whitelists are also known as safelists. For the online marketer, the aim is to be included on the user's whitelist – which can be achieved by having a clear message on emails and subscription forms asking the subscriber to add the company's email address to their safelist (adding the sender to your address book normally serves the purpose).

Although guides are available, content development is usually best left to experts in the field. This will, however, cost money, something that should be taken into consideration when setting objectives. For example, a niche business's goal of identifying twenty new customers who might have an average spend of five pounds is not going to give a ROI if the development costs are over a couple of hundred pounds. This being the case, then a DIY approach – even if it is not as successful – will at least make a profit. As a budget campaign will have few resources for testing, sending the first draft to friends and family (and monitoring the results) is better than nothing. Results of the campaign should always be measured against its objectives – even if little is achieved, the experience can still be used in developing any future campaigns.

For the larger entity that has (or can obtain) a significant mailing list, using professionals or the appropriate software in-house is best practice. Sending direct marketing messages on the CC/BCC facility is bad practice – it gives an unprofessional image – and makes you look cheap.

YOU DECIDE

Advise the marketers at the Gilded Truffle Hotel (case study 3) on appropriate objectives for a direct marketing email campaign. What elements of the process might be particularly troublesome for this particular organization?

Alternatively, conduct the same exercise for your organization or that of your employer.

8.4 EMAIL AS A MEDIUM FOR MARKETING MESSAGES

In this section we look at the use of email for marketing purposes where the email is *not* a direct marketing message. The inclusion of this subject as a distinct section of this chapter might surprise some. However, it is an extremely important aspect of digital marketing and it is also one that is too often forgotten by even the most experienced marketers.

Offline, it is common practice that any contact with a customer – via any of the various touch-points – is carefully prepared, as even the smallest communiqué will play a part in any relationship building or CRM strategy. Online, however, it is common practice for emails – particularly those that are automated responses, sometimes called *triggered* emails – to be sent to customers with no consideration of how their content might impact on the marketing efforts of the organization. Worse still, many emails are written by non-marketing staff – who might write in such a way that a relationship can actually be damaged by the message's presentation. Furthermore, such emails do not need to be *customer*-oriented (i.e. serve a sales, service or marketing purpose, often dubbed *transactional* emails) – any email sent by human resources (to a prospective employee, for example), finance (an invoice reminder) or procurement (a purchase order) represents the organization and so should be seen as an element of brand building.

In these latter examples, it is likely that the staff can be trusted to write the content, but email design and presentation should always be managed for appearance and deliverability by email marketing experts – with best practice being the provision of email templates. It is also worth noting that communications do not need to be initiated by the organization. As with the examples above, the outgoing email might be in response to an enquiry from a customer or member of the public. Again, the content of the reply should be scripted by an appropriate member of staff and the design template (e.g. font, colour) and presentation (style of salutation and sign off) of the email should follow a corporate model.

PRACTICAL INSIGHT

Legalese or anti-relationship marketing?

It is now common for corporate emails to carry a disclaimer as a footer. The practice has sound *legal* foundations – it is to cover the organization in the event of an employee making libellous or inaccurate remarks that are not supported by the organization.

However, as a marketer, I find the practice questionable. Any relationship-oriented message should be written in a tone that helps build that relationship. To throw in a legal disclaimer at the end simply destroys the nature of the message. As an example, I recently made an email enquiry about the availability of a product. The reply was personal, informal (in response to my signing the original message 'Alan'), well presented and informative – and it prompted me to pursue a purchase. However, at the foot of the email was a legal message that had a word-count four times larger than that of the actual message. It also told me that I could not pass on the contents of the message to anyone else. This means that – *legally* – I could not pass on details of the product or its price and availability to any friends or colleagues who might also go out and buy it. I don't think that is what the product's marketers would have wished.

People who serve us in retail outlets do not start – or end – their sales pitch with us with a legal disclaimer about what they might say, or have said. If we don't do it offline – where it would be considered a sales-killer – why do we do it online?

Note: I have not named the organization in my example above – according to their legal message, I would be committing some kind of offence if I did so.

The list of types of email communications that have the potential to either impact on the brand or carry a marketing message include the following:

- Welcome message – if a user has registered with you for any reason – be that simply to access your site or make a purchase – an email can be sent to welcome them to your organization. This can be simply a polite 'hello', or it might include a generic marketing message or a promotion that is specifically aimed at new registrants.

- Order confirmation – the email that says your order has been received. It is essential in terms of credibility in that the customer needs to know the status of their order submission (i.e. did it work when I clicked on 'buy'?). It is also an opportunity to thank the customer for their business. Although there is little scope for a sales-related message on these (those suitable should have been delivered during the buying process), there is an opportunity for relationship-building with the use of a carefully composed pleasantry. For example, 'Santa thanks you for your order; it's less for him to carry down the chimney' on an order that is *obviously* a Christmas gift.

- Confirmation of shipping – very similar to the order confirmation, but on that reinforces the relationship by showing that the organization cares about its customers after the order is taken. It is now common practice for the shipper to provide an online tracking facility for parcels. In this case this email would include details and a link to the tracking page.

- Delivery confirmation – practised by few, this is an email sent several days after either delivery is confirmed (electronically, by the courier) or when the package *should* have been delivered. Though both of these cover the same details, in the former, the emphasis is on satisfaction with the product. In the latter, the tone should be one of checking the customer has actually received the goods. Both can have an element of market research to them. A spin-off with the latter is that if the delivery has not been made the organization is seen as being proactive and so complaints are minimized.

- Confirmation of registration – this could be for anything, including newsletters, clubs and forums. The importance of this is that the user has most likely registered to join some kind of community – and so they should be welcomed to that community.

- Quote confirmation – as comparison shopping engines have become more popular, people frequently complete forms for online quotes from multiple suppliers – car insurance, for example. Naturally, after the quote has been given online a confirmation email with the details will be sent – and it might be argued that this and any subsequent emails are *direct marketing* in nature. However, as the start date of the policy is known (from the application form), the company will know if it has not converted the quote into a sale. At this time a 'sorry we couldn't help you this time . . .' email could be sent – the tone of which might encourage the person to consider the company for their policy next year.

- Reservation reminders or status updates – particularly relevant in service industries, these can add to the product experience long before the customer samples it. How about the in-flight movie choice for a long-distance flight or the restaurant menu for the evening of a hotel booking, for example?

- Opt-out page – when someone decides to opt out of a mailing list, newsletter or whatever, this is possibly a last chance to convert them – or at least accept the decision gracefully – you never know, the customer might come back sometime in the future.

- After a first purchase – this should be after, or part of, any confirmation email. It is a personal welcome to the organization and might include details of any special deals or service they might now qualify for.

- After a frequent purchase – like all elements of this list, this is dependent on the organization's use of technology to store information – in this case, previous purchases. This email should help build on an existing relationship, and might include special offers that are only open to *regular* customers – free shipping on your next order, for example.

- After an infrequent purchase – this could be, (a) as with frequent purchase, though toned down, or (b) pertinent to products that are not bought on a regular basis. In the case of the latter, that a company remembers that you booked a hire car with them eighteen months ago is particularly impressive.

- Event related – if the data is held, a birthday greeting can be sent. Religious occasions can be problematic if the faith of the customer is not known, but 'holidays' are normally acceptable. Christmas is an obvious example here, where the greeting can be seasonal rather than religious, and also carry a commercial message – free shipping or savings in a post-Christmas sale, for example.

- Random – a simple 'thanks for your patronage' that – like the Christmas message – can be linked to a limited special offer and sent at random throughout the year – but don't overdo it.

Note that with all of these, the correct development of the content and their application is paramount. Nothing is more likely to kill a relationship than the email that says 'welcome to our new customer' when you have been a frequent purchaser for several years. Similarly, repeatedly sending the exact same email message thanking a regular customer for their business will look like an insincere automated communication. Essentially, this

> " repeatedly sending the exact same email message thanking a regular customer for their business will look like an insincere automated communication "

means that all of these emails should be part of a carefully planned, managed and implemented relationship or CRM strategy.

Also worth mentioning is that none of the above is likely to infringe on spam laws in that they are considered to be part of an already established relationship with the customer – though that is not an excuse to bombard the recipient with a mountain of irrelevant emails. Naturally, as well as the departmental emails mentioned earlier, there is also the email that is a reply to an enquiry – be it about products, the organization or the brand. Every one of these emails should not only be answered by a responsible person, but should follow corporate design criteria.

DECISION TIME

This is an aspect of digital marketing that is a necessity, so there should not be a question of 'do we do it or not?' The only real decision relates to who will be responsible for developing the templates on which all emails will be founded. First, however, there needs to be an audit of all emails that are sent from the company's email account. After removing direct marketing emails, the remainder can be divided into three main categories: (1) automated, (2) relationship-building, and (3) enquiry response. For the first two of these the template can include the exact text – meaning that the email can be carefully developed over a period of time. For others, content that responds to a specific question or situation will be required, and so preordained content cannot be used.

RESEARCH SNAPSHOT

Email: the poor relation?

The very idea of a customer-contact phone ringing for even a few minutes is something most organizations blanch at. Most will have a three- or five-ring maximum rule. Similarly, there will be a policy about leaving on-premises customers waiting for more than a few minutes.

So why is it common for email enquiry addresses or forms to have a message saying that the 'customer service team' – or whoever – will reply in twenty-four or forty-eight hours? Or even five working days? Surely, if you can pay someone to answer a ringing phone or greet a physical customer, you can pay someone to answer emails.

Follow the links on the chapter's web page for examples of this practice.

The development of all outgoing emails should consider two key issues:

1. Design and layout – as with direct marketing emails, these should have a corporate appearance and have technical criteria that ensure deliverability.

2. Writing style – as with websites, there should be a house style for all email content. This might be influenced by the culture of the organization (the salutation being 'Hi' rather than 'Dear', for example) or where the recipients are likely to be geographically (the use of British or US spelling, perhaps).

In the same way that one badly trained or poorly recruited member of front-line staff can destroy years of brand- or relationship-building – at untold cost – so too can one email message written by someone who does not appreciate the importance of what they are doing. Furthermore, it might be argued that the 'bad' email is even worse than a spoken incident in that it is preserved for ever as a computer file.

YOU DECIDE

For Phelps Online Department Store (case study 13), consider what types of email might be sent by the organization and advise Martha and her team on how those emails can be best used for marketing purposes.

Alternatively, conduct the same exercise for your organization or that of your employer.

8.5 NEWSLETTERS

Based on the traditional newsletter, the online version serves exactly the same purpose, but the e-newsletter has one distinct advantage over its printed forerunner – the hyperlink that can take the reader to a web page, image, video or audio link that enhances the original message. And it is this basic element of the Internet that is giving the *old-fashioned* concept of the newsletter its value in the age of social media. The electronically delivered periodic newsletter is a practice – like others in business environments – that seems to drift in and out of fashion. Indeed, it has been suggested by many that the increased popularity of social media in general and Twitter in particular in recent years would bring an end to newsletters, but in fact it has only served to confirm their value. This is because there are now so many sources of information on – it seems – every subject known to mankind for the casual follower to keep up with. And this is where the contemporary newsletter comes into its own. Distributing them on a daily, weekly or monthly basis, the editors of newsletters do the extensive tracking of events, stories and articles on behalf of the newsletter-recipient and list only that information they feel will be of interest. However, the newsletter cannot only play a vital role in maintaining a relationship between seller and buyer, but it can provide the in-bound links that will take customers back to the website – and so allows organizations – as online guru Jakob Nielsen (2008) puts it, to 'liberate themselves from being overly dependent on search engines'. In the same article, Nielsen makes the comment that the best loyalty mechanism is the email newsletter – and he goes on to say that it is important to design a website in such a way that it encourages newsletter sign-ups.

DECISION TIME

Although they can be a business model in their own right (income being generated by selling advertising space and/or registrant data), for the online marketer there are several ways in which a newsletter can be incorporated into a marketing strategy:

1. As part of any relationship marketing efforts – which may or may not be an element of the organization's CRM strategy.
2. Writing the articles that are featured in third-party newsletters – particularly useful for consultants.
3. Developing a newsletter that will be read by influential figures within an industry – so raising the profile of the organization in the marketplace.
4. Using newsletters as a medium for carrying company ads – which can be carefully targeted because the newsletter will be very subject-specific. Note that a newsletter developed by a practitioner (e.g. a consultant) risks having its validity diminished by carrying ads.
5. Newsletter content can be included on the organization's website, making it available as an archive – which can be attractive to search engines.

MINI CASE

Retail newsletters have ready-made content

Although some might argue that a list of special offers is not really a newsletter – the issue is actually decided by the consumer. If they perceive that an email with details of forthcoming promotions is worth receiving on a regular basis, then it meets the criterion of being a newsletter.

The massive advantage for retailers is that they will often run in-store promotions as part of their marketing strategy – and those offers are obvious content for a regular newsletter.

One issue is paramount in the use of newsletters. If content is king on websites, in newsletters it is the entire royal family. Whether the content is written for newsletters or is originally published on web pages, that content has to be *developed*. In much the same way as content for the organization's web presence should be developed *properly* (see Section 3.4), so too must that which is to be distributed to interested parties who have requested it. It is for this reason that many well-intentioned campaigns either fail to take off or simply wither on the vine of lack-of-content. For the organization that is sending its own 'our-company' newsletter to customers, developing content is problematic – not only finding interesting subjects, but writing about them. There are only so many 'new starters', 'promotions', 'new product developments' and 'CEO visits China' type stories that recipients will read before they cancel their subscription. Even if the newsletter is to be little more than a series of links to articles on other sites – with reviews or comments added – those articles must be sourced, read and the comments written, all of which takes time.

YOU DECIDE

Advise Milo and his marketing team at 22 Catches Fish Products (case study 7) on how a newsletter could be integrated into their online marketing. Comment on both advantages and disadvantages of undertaking either.

Alternatively, conduct the same exercise for your organization or that of your employer.

CHAPTER EXERCISE

Giving justifications for all your decisions, advise Howard Johnson and his marketers at the Rockridge Museum (case study 1) on all aspects of digital marketing covered in this chapter. This includes taking a look at the 'dummy' emails that can be found by following the link from the chapter's web page.

Alternatively, conduct the same exercise for your own organization or that of your employer.

CHAPTER QUESTIONS

Follow the link from this chapter's web page to a series of multiple-choice, exam-type questions that will test your knowledge and understanding of the various elements of the chapter.

REFERENCES

Campbell, A. (2013) *Customer Relationship Management in the Social Age: A Best Practice Guide*. Econsultancy.

Charlesworth, A. (2007) *Key Concepts in e-Commerce*. Palgrave-Macmillan.

Ebnar, M., Hu, A., Levitt, D. and McCrory, J. (2002) How to rescue CRM. *McKinsey Quarterly*. Volume 4 (special 'Technology' issue), pp. 49–57.

Godin, S. (2008) *Meatball Sundae*. Piatkus.

MyBuys (2013) How multi-channel personalization impacts shopper attitudes and buying behavior. Available on mybuys.com.

Nielsen, J. (2008) What SEO/SEM professionals should know about website usability. Available at http://searchengineland.com/080501-115858.php.

Q Interactive and MarketingSherpa (2008) Spam complainers survey. Available on qinteractive.com and marketingsherpa.com.

Chapter **9**

Social media marketing

Social circles spin too fast for me.

Sammy Davis Jnr

Chapter at a glance

9.1 Introduction

9.2 Consumer generated content

9.3 Social networks and online communities

9.4 Blogging

9.5 Viral marketing

9.6 Online public relations and reputation management

9.7 Strategic social media marketing

9.1 INTRODUCTION

In Chapter 1 of this book I made the assertion that not all businesses will benefit from having a presence on the Internet – if that is contentious, then stating that not all businesses will benefit from having a presence on social media (SM) is certainly not. Without doubt, for some brands, organizations and products, social media offers an efficient and cost-effective medium for two-way communication with customers. But for others, any

ROI is highly questionable. Indeed, such is the nature of SM that poor engagement is – in customers' perception – worse than no presence at all. Some industries or markets lend themselves to a SM involvement. Any brand leader in consumer packaged goods, for example – or retailer, restaurant, media company, charity or destination – should all be active in SM. However, there is little benefit to be had for the likes of highly specialized B2B traders or 'one-time client' services (replacement garage door suppliers in Sunderland, for example). Indeed, any business which requires significant personal involvement between the two parties is unlikely to profit from a SM presence.

Social media defined

As with a number of other elements of the online world, what is understood by the term *social media* is still open to debate. I have previously defined social media as 'a collective term for the various social network and community sites including such online applications as blogs, podcasts, reviews and wikis' (Charlesworth, 2007) and in more tangible terms as 'sites where users can add their own content but do not have control over the site in the same

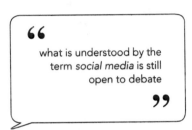

way as they would their own website' (Charlesworth, 2014). Both of these betray my conviction that social media existed long before the Internet made it so popular. Indeed, if you delete any reference to the Internet within any definition you might find for 'social media', that definition will still make sense simply by inserting any of the traditional media. For example, newspapers have always included 'readers' letters' sections, and radio has phone-in shows. Similarly, communities of like-minded people have always gathered to discuss, debate and disseminate their common interests, be that changes in political regimes, how to grow the best onions or anything in between. Before the digital revolution, however, those meetings were physical and so restricted by geography. For the digital generation, such limitations are gone. Like all things associated with it the Internet does things quicker and makes it easier for the *user* to participate. In 'The definitive guide to B2B social media', marketing management company Marketo (2010) defines social media as 'the production, consumption and exchange of information through online social interactions and platforms', whilst Kaplan and Haenlein (2010) also combine the concept of social media with digital media in describing the former as 'a group of Internet-based applications that build on the ideological and technological foundations of web 2.0 and that allow the creation and exchange of user generated content'. Whilst this directly associates social media with the Internet – it also adds to the debate by introducing another much-overused and misunderstood term: Web 2.0. The link between social media and Web 2.0 is highlighted by Tapscott and Williams (2007), who suggest that the *old* web was about websites, clicks and 'eyeballs', but the *new* web (Web 2.0) is about communities, participation and peering.

In order to help readers come to grips with what social media is – or includes – Figure 9.1 shows a matrix that should help. It is based on the original concept of David Bowen (bowencraggs.net), who used it as an attempt to describe how Web 2.0 fitted in to other online applications. Although Bowen developed this grid in 2007, little has changed to

	You control (home web)	Others control (extended web)
Two-way (horizontal web)	**HOME WEB 2** In this square communication is two-way from the organization to the customer – but is controlled by the organization. It is made up of the organization's own blogs and forums.	**EXTENDED WEB 2** Elements of this square are those most often associated with web 2.0. These are the sites over which organizations have no control and people talk to one another. It includes: individuals' blogs, social network sites, traditional forums or discussion areas, Q and A pages and sites such as Wikipedia.
One-way (vertical web)	**HOME WEB 1** In this quadrant, communication is one-way from the organization, mirroring traditional marketing where the marketing message is controllable. The organization's own web site(s) – including images, video, podcasts as well as textual content – makes up this section.	**EXTENDED WEB 1** This square represents the web sites on which the organization can place content, but they do not control. This includes consumer and review sites as well as (for example) videos on YouTube, photographs on Flickr and groups the organization has set up or sponsored on social network sites such as Facebook. It also includes ads hosted on other sites.

Figure 9.1 The four levels of content control on the web

Source: Charlesworth, 2014, based on an original idea by David Bowen (bowencraggs.net)

merit its being significantly updated. In essence, the four quadrants of the matrix describe web content that is controlled by the organization through to that over which it has no control.

So it is that for researchers, writers and practitioners of social media marketing the first problem is actually identifying what social media is – or at least what others perceive it to be. Ironically however, it is the flexible, dynamic and innovative nature of the medium which means that other than listing tactics in a SMM strategy or trying to write books on the subject *what it is* doesn't really matter. In many ways, social media is whatever it is perceived to be by an individual participating in it. Indeed, it is perhaps in an attempt to address this definition issue (or is it just a trend?) that social media marketing is now commonly referred to by digital marketers simply as 'social' – as in, 'our budget for *social* has increased by 50 per cent'.

In the subsequent sections of this chapter I have divided social media into different elements in order to address the various ways in which the web user can add their own content to a web presence. The first, consumer generated content, concentrates on reviews and ratings. Second is social networks and online communities, followed by blogging, the phenomenon of viral marketing, online public relations and reputation management. However, you should bear in mind that the distinctions between some of these categories are blurred – better that you try to consider the whole chapter as one big subject – which is why I finish with a section that looks at *strategic* social media marketing.

Also worth noting at this point is that in this chapter I have concentrated on the *social* aspect of social media. That is to say, content that is not written in a commercial context – that is, hobby or pastime, rather than work. This is not to say that social media has no commercial application – or else why would I have included the subject in this book? As the following sections will show, what the public writes is of great interest to many organizations. However, commercial communities do exist, where industry-related subjects – rather than *social* issues like your favourite rock band – are discussed. I have made the decision to include these in Section 5.5 on e-marketplaces – though I do appreciate that there can be a blurring of the lines where social and commercial networking sites meet.

In studying the subject, it is also worth considering the theory on which social media marketing hangs. With roots in psychology, sociology and economics (in which it is known as the theory of economic behaviour) *social exchange theory* suggests that social behaviour is the result of an exchange process where each party seeks to maximize benefits and minimize costs. In a commercial environment – where benefits and costs can be evaluated in financial terms – this is relatively straightforward to

> 66
>
> In a social environment . . . costs and benefits are far less tangible and will differ from person to person.
>
> 99

assess. In a social environment, however, the costs and benefits are far more intangible and will differ from person to person. Nevertheless, whatever the interpretation of costs and benefits, individuals weigh one against the other before deciding if what they will get out of any resulting relationship is offset by what they must put into it. If the risks outweigh the rewards, the relationship will be terminated or abandoned. It is the very nature of the online environment to make both the benefits and costs more easily gained or discarded than in the real world – a click of the mouse being all that is required. Perhaps it is this apparent ease in accepting or rejecting that makes social media so appealing to its predominantly young users and such a marketing minefield for those wishing to make commercial gain from it.

Also from offline sociology is reasoning for the success of viral marketing through social websites, in particular, Mark Granovetter's seminal paper on social networking, 'The strength of weak ties' (1973). In it he argues that while our acquaintances (weak ties) are less likely to be socially involved with one another than our close friends (strong ties), our acquaintances will have their own close friends – and our only link with those people is through our *weak ties* – hence, they are important to us. In social networking terms this means that if I have an idea that I pass on to my acquaintances (weak ties), I am reliant on *their* close friends (strong ties) to continue the spread of the idea. Pre Internet (a) it was difficult for me to make contact with weak ties, (b) it was easy for them to block any contact from me and (c) they had no motivation to pass on the idea, even if they received it. In the online world of social networking the click of a mouse on a 'friends' link means that my message (idea) goes out to all my friends and acquaintances (in an instant) – and not only do subsequent clicks from those people send the message to all of their friends and acquaintances, and so on and so on, but the flexibility of computer-mediated-communication (CMC) easily overcomes the offline communications hurdles of geography and time zones.

In terms of Granovetter's model, those people who are well down my 'friends' or mailing list (weak ties) all get my message, as do *their* weak ties – which means that in terms of networking of messages, as much (if not more) communication is conducted via weak ties than via strong ones – hence their strength.

PRACTICAL INSIGHT

AIDA moves into the digital age

In Sections 1.6 and 3.2 the AIDA model is used to demonstrate buyer behaviour and website development, respectively. In the original concept, the action – normally a purchase – is the end of a chain of events. However, when considering the impact of social networking on contemporary marketing, perhaps a further element should be added to make the social media version: Attention, Interest, Desire, Action and *Tell* (AIDAT), where the additional 'T' indicates that the customer should be encouraged to 'tell someone about it'.

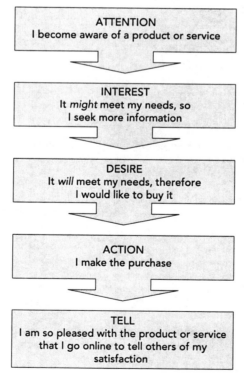

Figure 9.2 The AIDAT model – Attention, Interest, Desire, Action, *Tell*

When examining how the marketer can use social media in either strategic or operational planning, there are a couple of further issues to be addressed:

1. Digital marketing – and particularly social media – is a reflection of the time in which it developed. In the relationship between marketers and consumers, things were changing, and 'Internet marketing was simply the catalyst for a sea change that had been long coming' (Meadows-Klue, 2008).

2. Social media participants do not like to be lied to, or fooled. They don't even like to be *marketed at* – which makes using social media in marketing even more problematic.

These points lead us to what is the critical impact of social media on contemporary marketing – potentially the most significant change in marketing since the practice was recognized as a discipline in its own right. That impact is that the marketer no longer has control over the brand – a frightening thought for many who practise in the field.

Prior to the emergence of the commercial Internet, the marketer had control over any marketing message that reached the public. As US TV executive Don S. Hewitt once famously commented, 'The businessman only wants two things said about his company – what he pays his public relations people to say and what he pays his advertising people to say.' That age has now passed. Certainly, in the

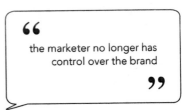

> the marketer no longer has control over the brand

past a dissatisfied customer could tell their friends and acquaintances of their experiences, they might even submit a letter to a newspaper or magazine (though the chances of any publication including a letter criticizing any potential advertiser was questionable), but their sphere of influence was limited. Now, the Internet – by way of social media – allows a single disgruntled customer to reach hundreds, thousands or even millions of people at the click of a mouse. And those recipients can then replicate that message to untold other masses of people.

Whether the marketer – or, more accurately, the organization – sees this loss of control as an opportunity or threat may well determine how well that organization will prosper in the new marketing environment. Social media marketing is, essentially, all about using the medium to encourage the dissemination of a positive brand, product or organization message. Marketing students – and practitioners – may also recognize that some elements of SMM could be viewed as part of a *relationship* approach to marketing, with the web being used as another conduit through which the organization can build and develop a relationship with its customers or public. One thing is certain, consumers are interacting with brands and participating in marketing on a scale that wasn't conceived by most marketers right up to the end of the last century.

PRACTICAL INSIGHT

SEO versus SMO

As with search engine optimization (SEO), social media optimization (SMO) is all about driving traffic to your site. However, whereas SEO traffic tends to be fairly steady, SMO traffic is likely to be a series of peaks and troughs. This is because it reacts to specific articles or events that can be optimized on a social network. This isn't to say that SMO results are instantaneous, like SEO some preparatory work is necessary. In the case of SMO a network of friends is necessary to pass on the message that will drive visitors to the website – and any network will take time to build. The main difference between SEO and SMO, however, lies in to whom they appeal. With SEO it is the search engine algorithms that are pandered to using code and content that help match keywords to searches. With SMO, the appeal is to humans, for it is humans who – albeit using technology – will pass on the message and so drive traffic to your site. It is essential, therefore, that the content appeals to people – including its visual presentation. Think of SMO as the onstage performance, with SEO the backstage support.

It is worth adding a footnote to this introduction that pervades subjects throughout the chapter – and it is this. Although marketers can use elements of social media in their marketing efforts, if the organization provides a quality product at an appropriate price, delivered by enthusiastic staff in places where customers expect to find it – then there is nothing for that organization to fear from what might be considered as negative aspects of social media. This notion is supported by research from Baird and Parasnis (2011), who found that more than 60 per cent of consumers believe that passion for a business or brand is a prerequisite for social media engagement.

9.2 CONSUMER GENERATED CONTENT

As is the case with other topics covered in this book, consumer generated content (CGC) is yet to have a finite definition. Indeed, in my own book *Key Concepts in e-Commerce* (Charlesworth, 2007), I favoured the term consumer generated *media* (CGM). I made the differentiation to represent the wider entity in which CGC is hosted (the media), rather than the content presented in that media. However, as the various elements of that media have now merged – and arguably the medium was always the Internet in its entirety – the emphasis is now more on the *content* than the media on which it sits.

A further complication comes from other popular terminology that is used in the same context as CGC and CGM – that being where, in both terms, the word *consumer* is replaced by *user* (i.e. user generated content). Whilst we could get pedantic and examine any possible differentiation of these terms, in reality there is little – with their application being down to individual preference or practice. This being the case, this section will always use the abbreviation CGC to cover the concept.

Although the issues surrounding the media/content and consumer/user issues can be considered one of semantics, another phrase that is often used in the same context has a distinctly different meaning. This is citizen journalism – or journalist – though *citizen* can be replaced by *civilian*. It is taken that this term refers to an amateur (i.e. not a trained journalist) who plays an active role in the collection, analysis, reporting and dissemination of news and information. Although the content may include statements, comments or stories about products, organizations or brands, it is not intended as some kind of review.

With CGC, on the other hand, the content suggests that the writer has experienced the product, organization or service and wishes to pass that experience on to others.

Another term that appears in social media is *citizen marketers*. In their book on the subject, McConnell and Huba (2007) comment that citizen marketers create what could be considered to be marketing and advertising content on behalf of people, brands, products or organizations. This differs from CGC in that the inference is that the content will be entirely positive (CGC having the potential to be indifferent or even worse, negative) and that the writer has actually set out to promote the subject of their writing.

MINI CASE

Citizen marketers help SoaP clean up

Although this example is now a few years old, it is worth reproducing here because it has become a benchmark for the concept of citizen marketing.

It is not unusual for films to generate cult followings – the Star Trek franchise springs readily to mind, as does the low-budget *Blair Witch Project*, which owed much to the Internet for its success – but the 2006 film *Snakes on a Plane* turned the concept on its head.

For some reason, the title itself created a spark with movie-goers and a *buzz* began to spread across the online community. Hundreds of images were posted on Flickr, whilst Technorati had over 20,000 blog entries about the movie – by this time abbreviated to *SoaP* by its fans. Those same fans created their own SoaP merchandise, with T-shirts being available featuring quotes from the film's star, Samuel L. Jackson. Trailers and posters also appeared for purchase on the web.

But there is a twist. This all happened *before* the film was ever released. The images, trailers and posters were all *invented* by the fans. They made up their own visions of what the film was about – and with that title, there was little room for doubt as to its storyline.

The film studio (New Line Cinema) played along with the viral community. No lawsuits about copyright infringement were issued – but most importantly, whilst endorsing the buzz they did not attempt to control, or even get involved in it. This was key. Had the SoaP-citizens perceived that they were being *used* by the movie-makers they would not only have abandoned their campaigns, but more than likely turned against the film and its makers. Furthermore, New Line – extending what is common practice in Hollywood – listened to what selected pre-release audiences had to say. And those audiences' comments were based on the buzz-fuelled perceptions they had before they saw the film. The result was the reshooting of some scenes in the movie with more violence, more nudity, more deaths, more snakes – and more swearing from the lead character played by Jackson. This only served to add more muscle to the film's pre-release buzz on two counts. Firstly, the makers had to up the parental guidance (PG) age rating – creating news in its own right – but secondly, one particular line of profanity spoken by Jackson's character became a catchphrase that appeared not only on T-shirts, but late-night TV chat shows.

On its eventual release, the film was a commercial success. Would it have been without the citizen marketing – who can tell? Will we ever see anything similar again? Doubtful – it was just the right title in the right place at the right time. Could a studio reproduce the effect? No, those people upon whom the viral buzz would depend would shun the commercialization of their medium. Lessons learned? Listen to your public. If a viral buzz is happening, let it happen – don't try to control or manipulate – then sit back and count the profits.

Note that I gathered details of this case study from various off- and online sources at the time that the events were taking place. However, Ben McConnell and Jackie Huba give an excellent narrative of the SoaP phenomenon in *Citizen Marketers* (2007: 162–169).

The proliferation of smartphones that come complete with high-quality video and still cameras as standard has served to increase the use of video clips and photographs as CGC rather than purely textual content. Although they can be a feature of reviews – a short video clip of a dirty hotel bedroom or unsafe swimming pool, for example – the majority of 'homemade' videos are not commercial *per se*; they are produced as a source of entertainment for both producer and watcher. Naturally, a publisher might sell advertising space around such content on a web page, but that is a business model rather than a marketing practice (YouTube, for example). If a home video includes the promotion of a brand, organization or product, then that is citizen marketing and beyond the control of the marketer – though they may benefit from it.

Before we go on to consider CGC in more detail it is worth reminding readers (again) that no aspect of online marketing sits in isolation from other elements. With respect to CGC, we have already considered a number of issues that relate to its use, not least online buyer behaviour in Chapter 1, website development in Chapter 3 and search engine optimization in Chapter 6.

MINI CASE

Say it with a song

If you have ever had bad service and wanted to get your own back, social media provides a perfect platform – and if you make your complaint into a song then millions of people might see it on YouTube.

That's just what Canadian musician Dave Carroll did when his guitar was broken during a trip on United Airlines. The song has become a classic social media hit – and a massive embarrassment for the airline.

Follow the link from the chapter's webpage to see, and sing along with, 'United Breaks Guitars' as well as reading the story as told by the man himself. Or you could buy his book: *United Breaks Guitars: The Power of One Voice in the Age of Social Media* (2012).

Reviews and ratings

The most significant impact that CGC has had on marketers is in the way that it encourages the general public to write their own comments about products and services that they have experienced. These comments are made public in online reviews – and whilst the concept has existed as long as there has been a print media, never before has it been possible to reach such a large audience.

Online review facilities come in a number of guises, the most significant being:

- Websites that publish review forums as a business model, generating income by selling on-site advertising and research data.
- Websites that use reviews as additional content that attracts visitors.
- Retail sites that offer feedback facilities for customers to leave comments on products that are available on that site.
- Manufacturer sites that encourage feedback on products.
- Service provider sites that use customer feedback as part of their product presentation.

It should be noted that some social networking and community sites (covered in the next section) also include customer reviews. These are, however conversational in nature, rather than being part of a more formal arrangement, and their use is sometimes dubbed either *social shopping* or *social searching*.

To simplify the issue for both reviewer and reader – notably, to reduce the time taken to write and read the content respectively – many sites provide a method of rating the product or service being assessed. This can be a simple image of a thumb up or down to signify recommend or not, an overall 'star' rating or more complex multi-element star ratings based on various aspects of the product. To personalize sites, stars are frequently replaced by images that are associated with the site – 'paws' on a pet-related site, for example. Based on the consumers' levels of approval, some sites aggregate the results so the rating becomes based on the average of responses.

User-submitted reviews are often well informed, articulate and, most important, trusted by others

Research from the Keller Fay Group (2007) suggests that review writers are predominantly motivated by goodwill and positive sentiment, with 90 per cent writing reviews in order to help others make better buying decisions, 70 per cent wanting to help companies improve their products and 79 per cent seeking to reward a company for good service. Furthermore, 84 per cent of reviewers also purchase products online – making them excellent targets for digital marketers. Offline marketers should also be aware, however, that over 65 per cent of reviewers have returned the retailer's website to leave an online review about an offline purchase. User-submitted reviews are often well informed, articulate and, most important, trusted by others – reflecting that reviewers are often experts in the subject area – a professional or serious hobby photographer commenting on camera lenses, for example.

RESEARCH SNAPSHOT

Who do you trust?

Although the exact figures might differ, research from a variety of sources suggests that consumers not only access reviews as part of their buying process but they favour CGC reviews more than they trust marketers. Statistics include:

- 78 per cent of online Americans aged 18–64 agree that online reviews help them decide whether or not to purchase a product.
- Searching for reviews online is the primary way consumer electronics buyers seek out product opinions – focusing more on consumer reviews than professional reviews in this all-important process.
- 98 per cent of respondents found user-generated reviews helpful when researching holiday shopping.
- Eight out of ten consumers trust online reviews as much as personal recommendations, and two out of three said that positive customer reviews make them more likely to use a local business.

Sources: Ipsos Open Thinking Exchange (theopenexchange.org);
Weber Shandwick, 2012; Expo (expotv.com); BrightLocal, 2013

But it is not for purely altruistic reasons that websites feature customer comments. As previously mentioned, for some sites they are a significant element of the publisher's business model. There are, however, other advantages. Luo (2002), for example, found that the availability of inter-consumer communications assists online consumers and helps to influence the perception of trustworthiness about a company. Freedman (2008) takes this a stage further by suggesting that unbiased reviews (where they are more transparent and trustworthy) engender customer trust and that trust translates into loyal, lifelong shoppers.

PRACTICAL INSIGHT

Testimony on testimonials

Although not strictly part of social media, testimonials are generated by consumers – and so can be considered in this section. Correctly worked customer testimonials on a website can help convert potential clients to customers – but badly thought out bland quips can do the reverse. Testimonials that work will:

- Be harvested continuously and not sought out retrospectively in order to update web content.
- Be found easily on the website – with prominent links guiding prospects to them.
- Appeal to the target audience – this is particularly the case in a B2B environment where business buyers need to be assured that the testimonial is from someone who has the same problems as them.
- Be from customers who are delighted with your service – 'happy' isn't enough.
- Describe how the organization helped the writer solve a particular problem and not simply be a generic 'I think they are wonderful' message.

However, doubts are beginning to creep in about the authenticity of some reviews. And as reports of organizations 'doctoring' reviews spread, web users may become even more sceptical. Worse still is another issue – the false review. Some industries are more susceptible to this than others, but the phenomenon is particularly problematic in the travel industry, where numerous websites invite customers to give feedback on hotels in which they have stayed. The problem is twofold: hotel owners and management leave (1) exceedingly positive reviews for their own establishments, or (2) negative comments about competitors' hotels.

GO ONLINE

To read stories on the problem of false reviews in the hotel industry, follow the links on the chapter's web page.

DECISION TIME

For the digital marketer, the dilemma is not only *how* to best utilize consumer, user or citizen input, but *can* they utilize it at all? In the case of the writings of a citizen marketer it is something that happens and it is doubtful if the marketer can influence it, but they can monitor and react to it. However, when considering consumer generated content, the online marketer has the choice of being passive or proactive. Most are passive, simply tracking comments made by consumers as they appear online. For many it is a case of using the reviews as market research and little more. However, in some circumstances it is feasible for an organization to be proactive by joining in with online comments or responding to them. Although some organizations choose to do this

> "For the digital marketer, the dilemma is not only *how* to best utilize consumer, user or citizen input, but *can* they utilize it at all?"

covertly – adding comments as another reviewer responding to previous comments – this is a risky practice. Not only would discovery result in lost credibility for the organization, brand or product, but under the Consumer Protection from Unfair Trading Regulations (2008), in Europe it is likely to be deemed an offence. Overt comments made in response to criticism, on the other hand, can have the opposite effect – with the public reacting positively to companies that are honest and upfront with regard to their failings.

There is a further consideration for the online marketer with regard to CGC that has its roots in traditional marketing. Marketers have long been aware that in order for a new product to be successfully launched they must win over those members of society that influence others in their purchase decision-making. These early adopters in the product life cycle were traditionally difficult to both identify and reach, but the advent of the Internet – social media in particular – has resulted in members of this influential segment actually identifying themselves. Not only that, but online marketers can actually assess their influence by monitoring the blogs, reviews and websites created by these online brand advocates, known as e-fluencers. Potential customers are most effectively persuaded by e-fluencers who carry some credibility in their online presence by becoming experts in a specific area of interest. Pre-Internet, such people were found only on TV, radio or in print – making them a kind of elite. In the digital era, however, anyone can go online and fulfil this role. As Chris Anderson points out in his influential book *The Long Tail* (2006), the new taste-makers aren't a super-elite of people cooler than us; they *are* us.

GO ONLINE

For an excellent article on the role and power of e-fluencers, follow the link on the chapter's web page to 'Is the tipping point toast?' by Duncan Watts.

However, although it is true that anyone *can* be an e-fluencer, few take up the opportunity.

Despite the phenomenon that is social media attracting hundreds of millions of people, research from Jacob Nielsen (2006) suggests that not too many actually contribute. He found that user participation often follows a 90-9-1 rule:

- 90 per cent are *lurkers* – that is, they read or observe, but don't contribute
- 9 per cent contribute occasionally
- 1 per cent participate a lot account for most contributions.

Nielsen goes on to say that blogs have even worse levels of participation – for them, the contribution rule is more like 95-4.9-0.1. Wiki sites perform even worse. Wikipedia's most active thousand contributors – 0.003 per cent of its users – contribute about two-thirds of the site's edits. Furthermore, Leetaru *et al.* (2013) found that the top 1 per cent of Twitter users accounted for 20 per cent of all tweets. Expanding that out a little, the top 5 per cent accounted for 48 per cent of all tweets and the top 15 per cent accounted for 85 per cent.

For digital marketers it is important to note that this small percentage of web users – particularly of review sites – who are contributors are the *e-fluencers* in the online marketplace – and so they wield an inordinate amount of power in that marketplace. However, the small percentage who 'contribute occasionally' can be encouraged to make those contributions. Methods will vary from industry to industry, and aggressive *encouragement* will produce results that are the opposite to the desired objective – and so they should be practised with care by staff who have been trained in their delivery. But here are some examples of how customers can be *persuaded* to submit reviews:

- Ask – it seems obvious, but even the most enthusiastic customers should not be expected to be proactive in seeking out methods of giving a review. Online, this would include having a clear *call to action* on every appropriate page. Offline, it means asking customers face-to-face.
- Make it easy – you are, in effect, asking the potential reviewer to do you a favour, so do not present barriers to that favour. Online forms should be quick and easy to complete – *less is more* being the key in these scenarios. Offline, easy access to an online device or a clear web address to be accessed at a later date could be part of an invoice or receipt.
- Use email – online bookings mean that you have the customer's email address – it can be used to contact them after the purchase.
- Offer an incentive – take care that this does not become a bribe, but a gesture toward rewarding a customer for their time might increase contributions.
- Formalize compliments – if you offer a great product or service, people may offer verbal compliments, so seek to turn those informal comments into reviews.

YOU DECIDE

Advise the consortium that owns the Gilded Truffle Hotel (case study 3) on how CGC might (a) impact on its marketing, or (b) be influenced by the organization's marketers.

Alternatively, conduct the same exercise for your organization or that of your employer.

9.3 SOCIAL NETWORKS AND ONLINE COMMUNITIES

If differentiating elements of social media is problematic, then splitting social networking and online communities borders on the impossible. Even where experts on the subject attempt differentiation, they blur the edges. In his excellent *Marketing to the Social Web*, for example, Larry Weber (2007) states that social networks are 'member-based communities that enable users to link to one another based on common interests and through invites', whilst e-communities are 'online sites where people aggregate around a common interest area with topical interest and often include professional content'. His point about 'professional content' on community sites is well made, but that ignores the fact that sites like YouTube thrive on clips from TV shows and videos of recognized music artists – all of which are very professional. Although it is possible to give definitions for both social networking and online communities (as I do in *Key Concepts of e-Commerce* (Charlesworth, 2007), where I include the notion that both concepts can be prefixed by *virtual*), such is the overlap between the two that for marketing purposes they can be considered as the same, and so rather than dwelling on labelling all of the elements, this section concentrates on how the marketer can use all such sites to their advantage.

It is also worth noting that in this book I fall into the same trap as many others by using the likes of Facebook, YouTube and Twitter as examples. This is because they are well known to the majority of, if not all, readers. However, whilst these might be the most popular sites with the press and TV, they are only part of the phenomenon that is social media. Using a variety of sources, I reckon that in the summer of 2013 the forty leading social networks were (in alphabetical order):

Ask.fm, Delicious, deNA, Entropia Universe, Facebook, FC2, Flixter, Foursquare, Google+, GREE, Groupon, Habbo, LinkedIn, LiveJournal, Meetup, Mixi, Mxit, MyLife, MySpace, Ning, Orkut, Pandora, Pinterest, Quirky, Reddit, Renren, Sina Weibo, Socl, Sonico, Spotify, Tagged, Tencent, Threadless, Tumblr, Twitter, Viadeo, VK, Yelp, YouTube and Zynga.

It is my guess that you have not heard of more than half of them – and yet their supporters will see them as infinitely preferable to the aforementioned Facebook, YouTube and Twitter.

> " That these communities effectively segment themselves for specific products and services provides an opportunity for the digital marketer. "

One thing that all social media sites share is that without content to maintain visitors' interest the sites soon lose any appeal they may have – even if that content is produced by the members themselves. Virtual communities depend on people visiting their sites, facilitating social interaction and, most significantly, enhancing the loyalty of community members. However, it is a perceived usefulness that is a significant antecedent of a member's sense of belonging to the virtual community. This might be an example of how social networking and online communities differ. Facebook, for example, is perceived more as a method of communicating (networking) with friends – be they virtual friends or the real-life versions. Communities, on the other hand, are more select groups of people who share an interest, but are not necessarily friends in the traditional sense – with any perceived usefulness of the community extending beyond mere bonding and togetherness. That these communities effectively segment themselves for specific products and services provides an opportunity for the digital marketer. Nelson and Otnes (2005) used wedding-planning discussion boards as an example of how users – the brides to be – solicit advice, opinions and information, as well as gaining emotional support, social comparison and camaraderie. However, alongside the personal chat and advice was marketing-related information, including links to websites that featured recommended products and services.

MINI CASE

In social media, look to the future

In the first edition of this book I suggested that 'MySpace, Bebo and Facebook are the giants of UK social media'. If you are reading this book then you will be only too aware how wrong that statement is less than five years later – so would anyone like to predict the state of affairs for social media in another five years? Certainly not me, though one thing that wouldn't surprise me would be Google+ becoming a much bigger player – if only because it has the might of the Google organization behind it.

Social media is, however, maturing. Bebo encouraged non-human members – Eric, your pet halibut could have its own page – and its own 'friends'. Facebook, on the other hand, is more formal – indeed, there is an argument that it is now an institution. Whilst that appeals to many – particularly those organizations that advertise on its pages – others see it as the antithesis of what social media is all about, and so are deserting what they perceive as a *corporate* Facebook and moving to smaller social media platforms which offer the informality they see as being essential in a *true* social media.

For the likes of YouTube and Facebook, social networking is the core of a business model whereby they host sites that facilitate social communication and sell advertising on those sites. While the public might love such sites, organizations and brands (other than the hosting firms) have struggled to find the best way of using them as a channel of communication with consumers. As we will see in the last section of this chapter, this is changing – but when social media analytics company Recommend.ly (2012) examined more than 5.7 million Facebook Pages with at least ten 'likes' they found that 70 per cent of them weren't actively posting – suggesting that the majority of organizations, brands or products have at best a half-hearted approach to social media marketing.

Relating to these statistics is an issue that is relevant to all and yet ignored by many – be they individual or corporation – and it is this. Whilst some elements of social media marketing can be tactical, to practise it effectively is a strategic decision in that it is long term in nature. A common reason for the failure of SMM initiatives is that they are incorrectly perceived as being both easy and a quick fit. Although a limited number of ad hoc campaigns have had some success – those which really help organizations meet their strategic online marketing objectives are well researched, planned and instigated. And so, expensive. Brands that have succeeded either offer something that meets the needs – physical or psychological – of users or have tapped into existing niche markets.

RESEARCH SNAPSHOT

Why consumers follow brands

Consumers use social networking sites to engage with brands for a variety of reasons:

- **Facebook** users 'like' brands to learn about products and services (56%), keep up with brand-related activities (52%), for promotions (48%), and to provide feedback (32%).
- **Twitter** users like to keep up with brand activities (57%) and learn about products and services (47%) – again, providing feedback has a role (27%).
- **YouTube** users engage with brands to learn about products and services (61%), keep up with brand-related activities (41%) and provide feedback (23%).
- **Pinterest** users follow brands primarily to learn about products and services (56%), keep up with brand activities (35%) and for promotions (20%).
- **Instagram** users keep up with brand-related activities (41%), learn more about products and services (39%) and make purchases (27%).

That significant numbers of consumers use these sites to provide feedback to brands is indicative of how the general public perceives the role of social media in a brand's communication mix.

Source: Technorati Media (2013)

That they have no control – or even influence – over social media content leaves the marketer with the problem of how to react to such networks. Even those sites that are supportive of the brand or product might react badly if the organization attempts to impose itself on the members.

More problematic, however, is how to react to *cyberbashing* or *gripe* sites. This is where disaffected customers develop social media presences – or websites – that have the single objective of criticizing a brand or organization.

These can range from fairly mild comments of frustration to actionable liable. More elaborate cyberbashing sites include forums to allow fellow disgruntled customers to add their comments. Whilst legal action can be taken against outright untruths, genuine accounts of actual events are far more difficult to censor. Proactive companies will monitor cyberbashing sites as part of their online reputation management and (1) use the criticism as customer feedback and act on it as such, and/or (2) move to diffuse potential situations by contacting the complaining individual, responding in the forums or setting up response sites. More defensive organizations, however, tend to react to the criticism – which only serves to fuel the criticism and make the site both newsworthy and, importantly, more attractive to search engine algorithms.

MINI CASE

Buying friends

In a digital world where credibility can be measured by the number of fans you might have, or it's embarrassing not to have an audience, it should come as no surprise that purchasing social media popularity is not only big business, but it's cheap and easy – and difficult for the average user to spot.

To find someone willing to increase your social media presence for a fee, just type something like 'buy fake followers' into a search engine – or to discover how to spot phoney friends, try 'fake followers'.

Readers should note that I have resisted the temptation to artificially inflate my Facebook, Google+ and Twitter followers – so why not reward that honesty by supporting me on those sites?

DECISION TIME

There are three models that the commercial organization can use in adopting online communities or the social media for strategic purposes. They are: facilitating, employing and joining. Let's consider each in more detail.

1. Facilitate

This is where the organization provides a system where users can create profiles and interact with other members of a community. A business model in its own right, it is expensive to develop and operate as a discrete income source. However, it can be an integral part of a wider online strategy – a 'club' as part of a web presence, perhaps.

2. Employ

This tactic uses social media as a channel for recognized promotional activities. There are two fundamental methods:

- Sponsorship – as with its offline application, online sponsorship is chiefly used as part of a wider branding exercise. The organization simply seeks to sponsor a community site where the majority of the participants are in the target market segment for the organization, brand or product. It is particularly useful for niche communities where the concentration of demographics is better, but still relatively inexpensive because overall member numbers are small.
- Advertising (for selling) aimed at the demographic represented by users, for example. As covered in detail in Chapter 7, social media and community sites provide excellent opportunities for targeted advertising – though, as noted in that chapter, clickthrough rates are poor.

Note that with both of these methods there may be a good opportunity to *join* the network – as described in the next element of this section. This is particularly the case if the members of the community use the advertised/sponsoring product or service in their activity subject.

3. Join

Perhaps the most common use of social media sites by marketers – because of its convenience (and perceived ease) – this is where the organization actively engages in publishing on social media sites by entering into exchanges and interacting with the community. Writing a blog would be included in this method. Note that any of these practices should be conducted with overt disclosure of the brand or organization being represented.

The key decision for organizations about this element of e-marketing not simply whether or not to be proactive in adopting it as part of your online activities, but also whether or not you are going to be reactive in response to any comments on social media sites that may be applicable to your organization.

Wider consideration of strategic social media marketing is covered in the last section of this chapter.

PRACTICAL INSIGHT

Students beware – in the digital world, there's no place to hide

Employers are now looking for job applicants online – so you've registered with the online jobs agency. Great – but what about social media pages?

Some SM sites are geared towards finding work – but not all of them. What about:

- That picture of you mooning/flashing passing cars – or just that risqué fancy-dress outfit you wore once?
- That story about you being so drunk/drugged-up after the party that you were too ill to go to work?
- Your blog that lists all the lectures you haven't been to?

Employers might think they are hilarious – but they are unlikely to offer you a job.

Furthermore, Facebook's Graph Search makes your 'likes' public – so it's easy for anyone to discover any ill-considered 'likes' you may have made without really thinking them through. A historic 'like' for that long-defunct boy band might be a bit embarrassing – others could scupper your chances with a potential employer.

So remember:

Make sure there's nothing on the web that you wouldn't want everyone to see, because online, there's no place to hide.

YOU DECIDE

Advise the marketing department at Huxley University (case study 10) on how they might best use social networks and/or online communities in their online marketing efforts.

Alternatively, conduct the same exercise for your organization or that of your employer.

9.4 BLOGGING

Although the term *weblog* was first used in 1997, with the *blog* being introduced in 1999, the practice dates back to the early 1990s, when individuals who surfed the web listed (or *logged*) websites they found interesting, often with their own reviews of the sites (Charlesworth, 2007). Since that time, blogs have developed through being online personal journals to mini websites based around the thoughts and interests of the writer. The advent of 'blogging' sites (e.g. blogger.com) that facilitate their easy development saw an explosion of blogs in 2006/7. However, since that time, the proliferation of alternative modes of social media has resulted in blogging becoming less popular – with both writers and publishers. However, it is reasonable to suggest that entries on Facebook and in particular tweets on Twitter, are themselves micro-blogs. Despite the medium's apparent decline in volume, blogs have an important role to play in digital marketing. Social media ad network Technorati Media's 'Digital influence report' (2013) found that although social networks are identified as playing a role in influencing purchases, it was blogs that led the way in social media (with 31.1%) lead the way – followed by Facebook (30.8%), YouTube (27%), LinkedIn (27%) and Google+ (20%).

> the majority of blogs have been created by individuals and are rarely read by anyone other than the writer's close friends

The same organization's 'State of the blogosphere' report (2011) identified that the majority of blogs have been created by individuals and are rarely read by anyone other than the writer's close friends – and untold millions are abandoned soon after their creators realize that it can be a chore thinking of content on a regular basis. Research from Jacob Nielsen published in 2006, but not contradicted since, suggests that only 0.1 per cent of bloggers contribute (to blogs) on a regular basis.

MINI CASE

Dell Hell demonstrates the power of the blogger

Although this case study is now several years old, it is worth including in that it is a seminal example of social media in action.

When Dell computers gave Jeff Jarvis poor-quality goods and even worse-quality after-sales service, they didn't realize the publicity that could be generated by someone who is (amongst other things) a former television critic, Sunday editor of the *New York Daily News*, journalism professor at City University, New York – and a keen blogger.

Jarvis's blog post – 'Dell lies. Dell sucks' – snowballed in size as readers added their own tales of 'Dell Hell' and dozens of bloggers added links to the page from their own sites. Despite Jarvis emailing Dell advising them to read his comments, and the blog appearing high in the search engine returns for searches on 'Dell', Jarvis only heard from the computer company when he sent an email to Dell's chief marketing officer. By this time, however, the story had been picked up by mainstream media around the globe, Jarvis had become a celebrity and 'Dell Hell' was synonymous with bad service. Not the sort of brand association any organization would seek.

The aforementioned 'State of the blogosphere' report also identified four different types of blogger:

1. Hobbyist: The backbone of the blogosphere, and representing 60 per cent of the respondents to Technorati's survey, hobbyists blog for fun and do not report any income. Half prefer to express their 'personal musings' when blogging.

2. Professionals – divided into part- and full-timers: These bloggers represent 18 per cent of the total. They are independent bloggers who either use blogging as a way to supplement their income or consider it their full-time job. Few professional bloggers consider blogging their primary source of income.

3. Corporate: Corporate bloggers make up 8 per cent of the blogosphere. They write as part of their full-time job or blog full-time for the company or organization they work for. The most popular subjects for these bloggers are technology and business.

4. Entrepreneurs: Thirteen per cent of the blogosphere is characterized as entrepreneurs, or individuals blogging for a company or organization they own, with the majority blogging about the industry they work in. Again, business and technology the top subjects.

Although the content of them all might be of interest to the digital marketer in that the writers can be influencers in their field, it is the final three that are written as a digital marketing activity.

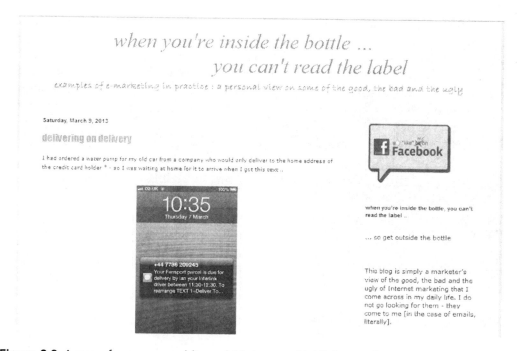

Figure 9.3 A page from my own blog, which I use to highlight good and bad practice in digital marketing; in this case, fulfilment

In commercial terms, blogs are normally used as a voice of an organization, an individual within an organization or as an outlet for people who are promoting themselves (e.g. their consulting services). With all of these, the writer is looking to exhibit their skills and experience within the topic on which they are writing and so develop an affinity between the brand and the reader. It is not surprising that many 'experts' in digital marketing have become recognized – or more extensively recognized – in their field by developing blog sites that are widely read. Similarly, the blog-commenter can also raise their profile by responding to comments in well-read blogs. Obviously this requires some knowledge in the subject area, and no little time – but my own limited experience shows that when I add a pertinent comment to a blog the visitor numbers to my website will rise for a day or so.

Bloggers are also a valuable tool in viral marketing – which is covered in more detail in the next section – in that they may comment in their blog on content from other sources, making their own observations on it. Such is the nature of the web that those observations may, in turn, be commented on in other blogs or aspects of social media – so extending the readership of the original content. Indeed, it is not unusual for individuals' blogs to become the debating chambers for online arguments.

PRACTICAL INSIGHT

Socially unacceptable

It is not uncommon for promotional companies to act as go-betweens for advertisers and bloggers – arranging fees for each time a blogger 'promotes' a product or brand. For example, within her daily content, a 'rewarded' female teen blogger might rave about a new movie she has just seen and suggest her online friends go and watch it. The practice becomes even more dubious if the blogger has a reputation as an expert within a certain subject area. Having an expert blogger tell of a website she finds useful – and why – is what social media is all about and so her being paid to do so raises moral questions about the blogger and betrays the concept that is social media. However, it is to the credit of social media and its users that 'phoney' bloggers are soon rumbled and so lose their appeal, readers and income. It is, however, acceptable for genuine bloggers to accept payments if they declare their interests. In the blogosphere, honesty goes a long way. Note that popular bloggers are often the e-fluencers I mentioned earlier in this chapter.

DECISION TIME

For many marketers – if not most – blogs are something that might cause a blip on their online radar occasionally, but in the main they simply ignore them as a medium for a marketing message. If you are to employ them, however, Scott (2007) suggests there are three ways to use blogs:

1. Monitor other blogs
2. Participate in conversations on others' blogs
3. Create and maintain your own blog.

I would add a fourth that falls between 2 and 3 – that is to respond only to comments made about your organization, product or brand.

Whilst the first of these can be completed by a software application that requires only monitoring, the key issues with the other two is that they are (1) enormously time-consuming, (2) not advertising, and (3) require skill and authority.

> **"** if . . . we accept that 'you are your website', then you are also your *blog* **"**

Considering the last of these first, if – as in Chapter 3 – we accept that 'you are your website', then you are also your *blog*. Any comments that go on the blog – or micro-blog – are effectively the opinions of the organization, even if the blogger is identified by name. For this reason, blogs in which individuals talk about themselves or their business are often more productive than those written by employees who have to answer to a higher authority. Also, where employees are responsible they should be aware of all of those issues that are relevant to website content development (see Section 3.4). For example, bad spelling or grammar will reflect badly on the organization or brand. The second point (advertising) is a difficult hurdle for the writer to overcome, and requires a mindset that often goes against the natural instincts of the corporate writer. However, even a hint of advertising copy within the blog will turn off those who might have been attracted to it in the first place. But it is the first of these points that is the key – blogging takes up an inordinate amount of time. Not only is it not something you simply tag onto a member of staff's workload to do 'when they have time', but someone has to be responsible for developing the subjects that are to be included. Essentially, having a 'corporate' blog is a strategic decision, not something to be decided by individuals or even individual departments.

If you do intend to participate in blogging as part of a digital communications strategy, there are a number of principles that you should honour if you are to be accepted into that *blogsphere*. These include:

- If you make your own observations about a subject published on another blog – more extensive than a simple comment on the blog site – acknowledge and link to the original blog. Note that offering constructive criticism is not a problem – it is the foundation of discussion and is making best use of the interactive nature of the Internet.

- If you are picking up on a response to an original blog, make sure that you link to the site where the argument originated, not just those blogs that have responded to the original blog (it's not unusual for the originator of the subject that has stirred up controversy to be left out of the links – and so its author gains no credit).

- If you use an article from another blog – or website – in your blog always seek permission and add a link to the original article.

- If you do relate to an original blog – make sure you (1) quote it correctly, and (2) get your facts right – that is, make sure you appreciate the point that is being made.

YOU DECIDE

Advise Lindsey Naegle (case study 12) on how she might use blogs as an element of the online marketing of her consulting service.

Alternatively, conduct the same exercise for your organization or that of your employer.

9.5 VIRAL MARKETING

It is worth starting this section by explaining why I have included it in a chapter on social media marketing. The reason is quite simple. Although it is an online marketing concept in its own right, if it is to be successful, any viral campaign relies heavily – perhaps totally – on people using the various elements of social media in order to forward the message. The concept of viral marketing is based on the centuries-old practice of word-of-mouth marketing – an oral, person-to-person communication between a receiver and a communicator (whom the receiver perceives as non-commercial) regarding a brand, a product or a service (Arndt, 1967). The term 'viral marketing' was originally penned in a newsletter by the venture capitalist behind Hotmail, Steve Jurvetson. He defined it as 'network-enhanced word of mouth'. Since then the term has become 'a buzz word that is used, misused, abused, and co-opted to cover whatever marketers are trying to push' (Wilson, 2012). Although the subject of the text is not strictly viral marketing, in his excellent book *Unleashing the Ideavirus* (2001), Seth Godin uses the phrase 'digitally-augmented word of mouth'. In essence, viral marketing describes any marketing strategy or tactic that encourages individuals to pass on a *marketing* – that is, promotional – message to others. Successful execution means the message's exposure grows exponentially – like a virus.

As with all online activities, this one is also based on a tried and tested offline business concept. Although Jurvetson used the phrase 'viral marketing' to describe an online phenomenon – Hotmail – the notion has been around much longer. 'Word-of-mouth', 'referral marketing' and 'network marketing' are descriptions given to offline viral marketing. 'Turn your customers into your sales force' is another phrase that has stood the test of time. It is interesting, however, that when seeking to describe 'viral marketing' some authors use offline examples that pre-date Jurvetson's creation of the phrase. It is not difficult to see why this has happened. Some of the best illustrations of viral marketing do actually precede the existence of not only the phrase – but the Internet as well.

The contribution made by digital media – as was the case with the printing press, the telephone, radio and television – is that once the word is out, it can get around faster than ever before. However, rather being used simply to describe online word-of-mouth the term, *viral marketing* has been somewhat hijacked by what social web expert Larry Weber (2007) describes as 'silly virals'. He uses Burger King's 'Subservient Chicken' (subservientchicken.com) promotion as an example of this phenomenon and goes on to suggest that true online word-of-mouth is about content-based *virality*. In other words, it is something about the product, brand or organization that the marketer wishes to be passed on by – hopefully satisfied – customers. To be employed successfully, it is the marketing message that should be communicated by the consumers. Seth Godin expands on the word-of-mouth origins of viral marketing by making the point that a viral message (his *ideavirus*) gains momentum by spreading across multiple media, so helping it reach more people. His point is well made – many online *virals* only move away from a niche audience when they are featured in offline media.

GO ONLINE

Walking the viral walk

Note that Seth Godin doesn't just talk the talk when he eulogizes viral marketing. *Unleashing the Ideavirus* can be purchased as a hardback book from a shop – but he also gives it away as an e-book. Follow the link on the chapter's web page for your free copy.

Indeed, the truly global virals – the ones that get featured in books like this one – depend on an aspect of both the off- and online exposure that is essential if the campaign is to be successful. Whilst viral marketing is built around consumers communicating with consumers (and the use of social media obviously enhances this), the main conduits for a successful viral campaign are often TV, radio and the printed press. Reporters pick up the viral message and release it through their own media – and for a short while this has the effect of a virtuous circle. People see the story on TV, hear it on the radio or read it in a newspaper (often as a news story, which means it meets the criteria of public relations when compared to advertising) and so seek out the viral message online. They then forward it to their friends and colleagues and so the virus spreads even faster.

Effective viral campaigns depend either on something that can be transmitted online – a joke, image or game, for example – or they are in response to an event or happening – Canadian Space Agency's astronaut Commander Chris Hadfield's Twitter and Facebook entries and videos on YouTube of him singing in space, for example (follow the link on the chapter's web page if you are unaware of this story). There is, however, a third option – the *manufactured* event. In this case the viral elements will need a kickstart from (1) the event being in some way amusing or interesting, and (2) there being offline coverage through news and/or PR.

Viral marketing does not have to be a complex undertaking, however. As with Weber's comment (re 'silly virals') the custom-made event, video clip or campaign that – ultimately

– promotes the organization is often perceived as what viral marketing is all about. This is not the case – and many would argue that the 'manufactured' viral is more like *advertising*, and betrays the basic ethos of the concept, which is to encourage, aid or prompt satisfied customers to spread a good word about – or recommendation for – the product, service, brand or organization. An email signature line that encourages users click through the link to a web page, for example, would be considered as viral. Similarly, a website, email link or Facebook comment that prompts readers to 'tell a friend' helps transmit the message beyond the original recipient. Indeed, Twitter is built around the concept that users are encouraged to 're-tweet' stories to their own friends and contacts. Perhaps the classic example of online viral marketing is Hotmail (hotmail.com), which went from launch to twelve million users whilst spending less than $500K on marketing, advertising and promotion. The Hotmail concept was simple – develop a quality product, then give it away, but on every 'product' (email) include a message advising readers on how to sign up for the same free service. The users did the rest (Gay *et al.*, 2007).

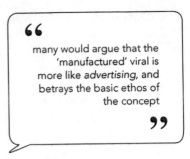

"
many would argue that the 'manufactured' viral is more like *advertising*, and betrays the basic ethos of the concept
"

Essentially, the success of any viral marketing depends on three fundamental issues, which are that:

1. The originator of the message must benefit from its propagation – therefore there should be a specific objective behind any viral campaign.
2. The sender – that is, anyone who passes the message on to others – is actively seeking, or at least willing to receive, any kudos that comes from forwarding the message.
3. The receiver must perceive value in the message. For example if it is a joke they should find it funny.

A fourth element might be added here – one that relates to the time that the viral is in the public domain and is consistent with another offline model – the product life cycle (PLC). In its early days, the viral message will be worth more kudos to the sender in that it is new – these people are the early adopters in the PLC. They are proactive in seeking new virals and are seen as influencers in the marketplace. As time goes by – the life cycle of the viral, if you will – the early adopters will distance themselves from the campaign as the mainstream and (eventually) laggards take up the viral. In the longer time-frame this notion becomes detrimental to the campaign itself. If anyone has already received the message when the media-fed user sends it out, then:

- The esteem in which the sender is held is reduced – and so they are unwilling to risk their reputation by forwarding 'old news'
- If they have seen it before, the receiver perceives no value in the communication, and so
- The originator receives no benefit – and because some campaigns need to be seen as 'leading edge' they may experience an 'unfashionable' backlash if they go on for too long.

PRACTICAL INSIGHT

YouTube's top 10 Global Trending Videos of 2013 was:

1. Ylvis : The Fox (What Does the Fox Say?) – a spoof video made to promote a TV talk show.
2. Harlem Shake (original army edition) – In 2012 it was Gangnam Style, in 2013, the most widely parodied dance craze was the Harlem Shake.
3. How Animals Eat Their Food – slapstick humour at the dinner table.
4. Miley Cyrus – Wrecking Ball – controversial pop music video.
5. Baby&Me – Evian Babies are back after six years.
6. Volvo Trucks – The Epic Split – Jean-Claude Van Damme doing the splits between a pair of moving Volvo trucks.
7. YOLO (feat. Adam Levine & Kendrick Lamar) – comedy group The Lonely Island's spoof pop video.
8. Telekinetic Coffee Shop Surprise – video promoting a remake of the horror film 'Carrie'.
9. THE NFL : A Bad Lip Reading – ridiculous comments dubbed into the mouths of athletes, coaches and managers.
10. Mozart vs Skrillex – one of a series of spoof vocal battles from the Epic Rap Battles of History Season 2 by ERB.

This year only two videos feature in both the US list and that for the UK & Ireland – reflecting, perhaps, a local bias in viewers' tastes.

1. How Animals Eat Their Food
2. My Wedding Speech
3. Attraction perform their stunning shadow act – Britain's Got Talent audition
4. Will & Jaden Smith, DJ Jazzy Jeff and Alfonso Ribeiro Rap!
5. asdfmovie6 – a collection of animated comics composed into a video
6. Harlem Shake (original army edition)
7. Tom Daley: Something I want to say
8. Francine Lewis with her many impressions – Britain's Got Talent audition
9. PEOPLE ARE AWESOME 2013 (Hadouken! – Levitate)
10 Learn the Alphabet with Peppa Pig!

Note that in 2013 around half of most popular videos are clearly promotional in nature i.e. made as adverts. This is up on 2012 when most were more 'novelty' in nature and were not part of a strategic marketing campaign.

DECISION TIME

With the exception of the basic aspects of what is recognized as viral marketing ('forward this to a friend', for example), the concept is not for all – indeed, some would argue that it is suitable for very few organizations. Even those basic elements should be considered carefully. It is not unknown for organizations to have the IT department set up a 'footer' that is appended to every email sent by every member of staff. Such messages are marketing-related, but sadly they are not suitable for all communications. Something like 'see the special offers on our website' (with an associated link) might be OK for new customers – but not so for email messages to suppliers, potential employees or even dissatisfied customers. Even the excellent concept of a 'forward to a friend' facility should be carefully considered before being put into practice. I have come across such services that required me to complete a form with my name, address, phone number (and more) before I could forward the page. The email address of the sender and the recipient plus either a fixed message (your friend at this email address thought you would find this useful) or space for a personalized message should be enough.

If viral is to be used beyond these basic elements, however, there are a number of criteria that any successful viral campaign requires, not least that:

- The message is worth forwarding – peer status rises or falls depending on the quality of the messages forwarded. Good news, or that which makes the receiver feel happy, is more likely to be forwarded repeatedly (Lin *et al.*, 2006). Adding something tangible – a quiz, video or joke, for example – adds to the chances of a message being passed on.

- It must be easy to forward – good usability techniques should make it simple for the receiver to pass the message on to others. A prominent, easy to use (e.g. no detailed form to complete) 'forward to a friend' button is essential. Advances in social media have made this issue almost redundant in that the likes of Facebook's and Twitter's very existence depends on users passing messages on – and so forwarding is an intrinsic part of those platforms' user experience.

- The right audience is targeted – though, by the very nature of viral marketing, this is problematic. The difficulty is that although the targeting of the original message is controlled by the organization – that control is lost once the message is released. The original recipients cannot be relied on to forward the message to those who will appreciate it, particularly if 'group' or 'all friends' lists are used to pass it on.

- The message is placed where it can be seen – rather than targeting a mailing list, for example, the original message can be placed on an appropriate website, message board, blog, micro-blog or social media site.

As with so many elements of digital marketing, specialist help is best engaged in instigating a viral marketing campaign. Although the original idea of – for example – a spoof video can come from in-house, the technical aspects of developing both the video and the way in which it will be communicated is not something the staff (marketing and technical) of most organizations will be able to do themselves. And do not be fooled by those 'amateur' viral videos that are often successful; though very rare

> As with so many elements of digital marketing, specialist help is best engaged in instigating a viral marketing campaign.

exceptions exist, they too are the result of skilled craftspeople who recognize that the façade of amateurism serves the objective better than a more 'professional' appearance.

It is worth noting here that the online marketer must have appropriate objectives for any viral campaign they instigate. As with the online presence, where few businesses can expect thousands of visitors every day, *success* for a campaign does not necessarily mean it has been featured on CNN and the BBC and has become a catchphrase for comedians. For a small B2B organization, having your industry-related viral game played by most of your customers and a few of their social contacts is as much as you can expect. And as with all marketing – off- and online – there must be a return on any investment made, so paying out £10,000 for a personalized game for twenty customers who have an annual invoice value of a few hundred pounds each is simply not going to pay dues. Similarly, as with some TV adverts, in any viral form should not take priority over substance – it is no good having a novelty video that everyone is talking about if no one can remember the brand behind the promotion.

A final point to raise is one that is addressed in detail in Section 9.2, but warrants reinforcement for viral marketing – and it is that the most successful viral campaigns are strategically planned and executed, they do not 'just happen'. With a very few exceptions (and industry insiders will argue that there are none), commercial – that is, planned, marketing – videos (for example) are not simply put on YouTube and suddenly thousands of people choose to watch them. That the video becomes 'most watched' is all part of a co-ordinated effort to publicize that video. Commmmenting in a controversial exposé of viral marketing practice, Dan Greenberg (2007) opined: 'How the hell did that video get so many views? Chances are pretty good that this didn't happen naturally, but rather that some company worked hard to make it happen.'

PRACTICAL INSIGHT

Viral tricks of the trade

For some of the secrets behind successful social media marketing, follow the link from the chapter's web page to the controversial articles 'The secret strategies behind many "viral" videos' and 'You didn't make the Harlem Shake go viral – corporations did'. The first article in particular caused quite a furore (make sure you take a look at some of the folks commenting on it).

My view? Did you really believe that the video that launched a new pop career (or whatever) was made by some girly on her mobile phone in her bedroom and then she put it on YouTube and millions of people just happened to see it? Yeah right – of course it was. Hello, welcome to social media marketing. The conclusion to Greenberg's article sums it up: 'You simply can't expect to post great videos on YouTube and have them go viral on their own, even if you think you have the best videos ever. These days, achieving true virality takes serious creativity, some luck, and a lot of hard work.'

9.6 ONLINE PUBLIC RELATIONS AND REPUTATION MANAGEMENT

Before getting into the detail of this section, it is worth pointing out why I decided to include it in this chapter. The *Collins English Dictionary* describes 'public relations' as 'the practice of creating, promoting or maintaining goodwill and a favourable image among the public towards an institution, public body etc.' – the same term being used for 'the methods and techniques employed' in that practice. As you will see in the following pages – with the exception of the content of the organization's own website – online those 'methods and techniques' invariably use social media sites. The examples I use in the section on viral marketing are evidence of this. It is also the case that in the twenty-first century, public relations (PR) goes beyond promoting goodwill and has responsibility for responding to – or defending that goodwill from – events, actions or stories that might damage its reputation or brand. It is also worth mentioning that I do appreciate that *public* and *press* relations are not the same thing. However, such is the nature of public relations that any relationship with the press is an important element of its practice – therefore an element of press relations is integral to this section.

Also significant is the increase in the number of media outlets brought about during the digital age. Up until the last decade of the last century newspapers and TV and radio channels were limited in number. This meant that the journalists held positions of some power in that they were the gatekeepers to a limited number of media outlets. With the proliferation of media outlets, however, the power has switched somewhat. Now, rather than the PR operative seeking out a small number of influential journalists, it is becoming the case that it is the reporter who is the one seeking the information – and in a very competitive

> " It has also diluted PR's role as the 'gatekeepers of access' that representatives of offline media had over the dissemination of information. "

marketplace. Digital technology and its use have led to PR being made available to marketers beyond the close-knit society that is (was?) offline public and press relations. It has also diluted PR's role as the 'gatekeepers of access' that representatives of offline media had over the dissemination of information. Prior to the Internet, an organization's PR staff or agents would have a list of journalists to whom they would pass (by post, fax or 'wire') their carefully prepared releases. If the journalist (a) received the release, (b) read it, (c) liked the content, and (d) had space in their column or publication, then the release was published in a place where the general public might read it. Nowadays, however, the release can be made immediately available to the general public – which includes citizen journalists. Obviously, having any press release featured on a popular or influential website will undoubtedly help spread the message further and faster. To this end, the online PR team should get the attention of those publishers and bloggers that are prominent in the marketplace or environment relevant to the story being propagated.

MINI-CASE

Ye olde versus the new

In his best-selling book, *The New Rules of Marketing and PR (2007)*, influential author and practitioner David Meerman Scott suggests that 'the web has transformed the rules and you must transform [your press] releases to make the most of the web-enabled marketplace of ideas.' His old and new rules are:

Ye Olde Press Release Rules

- Nobody saw the actual press release except a handful of reporters and editors.
- You had to have significant news before you were allowed to write a press release.
- A release had to include quotes from third parties, such as customers, analysts and experts.
- The only way your buyers would learn about the press release's content was if the media wrote a story about it.
- The only way to measure the effectiveness of press releases was through 'clip books' which were collected every time the media deigned to pick up your release.

The new rules of press releases

- Don't just send press releases when 'big news' is happening; find good reasons to send them all the time.
- Instead of just targeting a handful of journalists, create press releases that appeal directly to your buyers.
- Write releases replete with keyword-rich copy.
- Create links in releases to deliver potential customers to landing pages on your website.
- Optimize press release delivery for searching and browsing.
- Drive people into the sales process with press releases.

Source: Scott, 2007

Link development and public relations

As we discovered in Section 6.5, having links into your website can increase its search engine ranking – and it didn't take search engine optimizers long to realize that all online press releases should include a (legitimate) link to the organization's website. This meant that if any reputable online news sites featured the story, a *quality* link would be a by-product.

However, for some organizations, this *by-product* soon became equally important – and for many, the primary motive for extensive PR campaigns. Indeed, there is a reasonable argument that to a certain degree the *traditional* purposes of a press release have been hijacked by SEOs and are now used simply as a means of creating in-bound links. Consider, for example, PRWeb (prweb.com), the leading online distributor of press releases – on its website, at the top of a list of benefits to their service, is that 'PRWeb gets your news straight to the search engines that everyone uses'. Supporting this argument is research conducted in 2008 by non-profit think-tank the Society for New Communications Research. According to the study, less than a third of press releases have their primary objective as conveying information to the press – their traditional purpose. Their value in search engine optimization is the chief objective.

Purists argue that it is this practice that has diluted both the reputation and the quality of the press release. An example would be the 'manufactured event'. Whilst traditional PR is normally concerned with getting the best leverage from events that take place as part of an organization's operations, for link development – as with some aspects of viral marketing, with which online PR has a strong relationship – events are staged with no other objective than to create a newsworthy story. But then, 'publicity *stunts*' have been a staple of some industries for as long as there have been media to report them in – as I alluded to at the beginning of this section, *public relations* can mean different things to different people.

Whatever the primary objective of the press release, however, it is still the case that in the majority of cases it is the standing of the releasing organization that dictates its proliferation. Whilst a story about a factory extension that will create twenty new jobs might make the local news, it carries little or no interest outside the region in which the factory is located. Similarly, the announcement of a new product in a specific industry will interest only those who will benefit from that product's development. Although both of these examples will generate limited publicity – and so in-bound links – they cannot compete with the PR of major organizations or brands.

In some countries it is a disclosure provision of publicly listed companies that they 'release' any and all information about the organization and its operations. A decision – in July 2008 – by the US Securities and Exchange Commission to (under certain circumstances) accept websites and blogs as meeting public disclosure requirements has increased the use of digital media as the medium for press releases. Naturally, such releases will appear on a variety of websites – all of which will link to the corporate site. A Google press release, for example, *might* be of interest to (1) anyone who uses search engines, (2) those who work in that industry, and (3) the financial institutions that monitor the value of Google's stock. Ultimately, as with all marketing, effective press-release practice requires the targeting of segments that are receptive to the message you are sending. Get that right, and you will benefit from both the PR exercise and in-coming links to your website.

Reputation management

Although the issue of reputation management is an element in every on- or offline strategy, it would normally fall under the remit of the public relations department. It has long been common practice for an organization to keep track of how it – and its brands or products – are depicted in the media. Prior to the Internet, this would amount to perusing national or significant local newspapers and tracking TV and radio news and current affairs programmes. However, as we have seen in earlier sections of this chapter, there are now more media channels and even more websites or social media platforms that are accessible for the 'person in the street' to comment on products, brands and organizations. Negative reputation issues might arise online in a number ways, including:

- Detrimental feedback on forums or review sites
- Cyberbashing sites
- Negative blog posts – or damaging comments added to posts that originally took a neutral or positive stance
- Logo infringement – bids on trademarked terms in pay per click advertising, for example
- Negative social network groups – not all groups set out to support products or organizations
- Comments made on social network or micro-blog sites – increasingly, the ease with which comments can be repeated on these platforms has made them the main focus of reputation management teams.

Fortunately, software is available to help the PR professional to track what is being said online. As with many aspects of marketing – both off- and online – the process can be carried out in-house or outsourced to a specialist firm. Either way, an effective reputation management process, such as that shown in Figure 9.4, is necessary.

A final consideration for those responsible for online reputation management is that of disaster recovery. Although any contingency planning to address potential disasters that might strike the organization is a strategic business decision – it is the PR department that will be the public face of that plan – and online has a part to play. No matter what the size of the organization, or its dependency on the Internet for its income, any contingency plan should include pre-prepared web content, be that in the form of PR releases, blog content, micro-blog messages, social media pages, email messages, or mini-sites complete with contact details, FAQ pages and a media newsroom. Not that it ever was, but particularly in the digital age, burying your head in the sand when something goes wrong is not an option.

DATA COLLECTION
This could be from such online presences as: blogs, forums, review sites and message boards for user-generated content, plus news and magazine sites as well as PR news wires for that of professional journalists.

↓

PROCESSING
Useless data (duplicated content that is common in blogs, for example) or irrelevant data (perhaps a similar brand or organizational name) is discarded. Useful data is then processed into logical groups for analysis.

↓

DATA ANALYSIS
This phase normally sees the first human action, where staff can review that data deemed important by the digital investigation. Such analysis would grade each article or comment based on criteria that might include: its relevance (potential effect on sales or marketing) and spread (how popular is the website on which it appears?) as well as the influence of its author and/or the web presence that hosts it. Reports are then developed that can be made available to decision-makers.

↓

ACTION
It is at this stage that many reputation-management programmes fail as, by their very nature, online problems need to be addressed immediately. Preferably, the reputation-management team will have the authority to react themselves (a good reason for it to be part of PR) or have immediate access to decision-makers if the issue is more serious. Having the report sit in an in-tray or inbox of a senior manager is not the way to manage your reputation online.

Figure 9.4 The reputation management process

MINI CASE

Shell's integrated online response

When Shell's Arctic-class drillship, the *Kulluk*, grounded in heavy seas on the coast of Alaska in the final hours of 2012, the Anglo-Dutch company's co-ordinated risk-management response was as efficient as its efforts to make safe the *Kulluk*, its crew and the environment in which the accident occurred.

With no fatalities, serious injuries or environmental damage resulting from the incident, the outcome was favourable for all concerned – so its news value was limited. Nevertheless, Shell's online response really is a textbook example of excellent practice.

Not only was the incident covered on the corporate website (shell.com), but an incident website was quickly established on its own domain name (kullukresponse. com) – with official Shell statements and several of the Unified Command news releases included links to this site. Shell also established a dedicated Twitter feed and Flickr gallery along with 'page tools' enabling users to share a link with their followers in various social media or add it to their blog account.

DECISION TIME

Although this section includes the term 'online public relations' in its title, it is unlikely that any organization will conduct purely online PR – even online-only traders need to address PR offline. It is the case, therefore, that the online element will be just part of the overall PR strategy. This being so, as with other aspects of marketing covered in this book, the online ingredients of the PR mix will take their lead from the offline strategy and so I will not spend time attempting to cover the entire subject of PR (a book in its own right) – I will simply address the web-based aspects.

The first issue to address is: what do we tell folk about? I'll ignore the manufactured events covered earlier as features of other aspects of online marketing (SEO and viral, for example) and concentrate on *natural* events. David Meerman Scott (2007) suggests that news releases should be a frequent occurrence and not just for 'big news' – and he is right, although too many minor stories may overload recipients and cause major events to pass without notice within the volume. Careful consideration over segmentation can help here. The appointment of a new sales director might interest industry insiders, for example, but be of little interest to a product-oriented blogger.

The second issue to address is: where can releases be published online? Possibilities include:

- Your own website – preferably on a dedicated press or news page.
- Social media platforms or micro-blogs – though these would serve only as promotions for the release, with a link to the relevant page of the corporate website.
- Trade associations – spreading news about their members' activities is normally part of any association's objectives.
- Local business networks – as with trade associations, these networks, many of them government sponsored, actively seek to promote releases from local businesses as part of their remit.
- Online magazines and journals.
- Newspapers – particularly those local to your organization – they all have an online edition.
- Blogs – always do your research on the relevant blogs to see how, or if, they accept releases. Attempting to sneak them in as comments or feedback is not good practice.

- Online press services – websites where you can upload press releases so that they are available to be searched by a global audience.
- Press release distributors – who, for a fee, will handle the online distribution of your release. For those organizations that lack in-house resources this might be the best option.
- PR agencies – the full-service option, these undertake your entire PR requirements from research through writing to publishing and distribution of releases.

Note that for all except your own website, time should be spent in identifying which person or department you need to send your release to before its submission. It is also the case that a release can be tweaked to best suit a particular publication's readers. Both of these time-consuming exercises would be part of a PR agency's commission – usually making the fee worth paying. It should go without saying that any release – press or public – should be professionally written. Like any corporate communication, the message and its presentation is a portrayal of the sending organization – and as with all web content, cost-cutting in this regard is an error. Two important issues to note with regard to content the development are that (1) releases can benefit the SEO of the organization, therefore they should also be written with keyword inclusion as a priority, and (2), as highlighted by Scott (2007), because the public is just as likely to read the publications in which the releases appear, they should appeal to buyers, not just journalists.

> the message and its presentation represent the sending organization – and as with all web content, cost-cutting in this regard is an error

PRACTICAL INSIGHT

Online timing isn't the same as offline timing

Press releases delivered in traditional media are immediate, and, by tomorrow – they are history. Therefore, when putting a release online – where it may sit for years – it is worth 'doctoring' it for an online audience. For example, the prose of the release will be that it is breaking news – it will use 'today' in its description of events, not something that makes sense if read on a website several months later. Similarly, it will include a description of the key players and even the organization itself – none of which is necessary if the release is being read on that organization's website.

It is also the cast that the contemporary journalist will expect certain information to be easily available in digital format from the organization and so 'electronic press rooms' have evolved from their early days as simply PR page on the website. The best now include 'virtual press kits'. Designed to facilitate the journalists' thirst for easily accessible information, as well as the press releases, a kit will include such content as:

- An up-to-date list of individual press contacts within the organization
- A frequently asked questions section
- Downloadable company logos – different sizes to suit all publications
- Details of the company, including a concise history
- Details of company locations
- Descriptions of the products or services offered by the organization. If a press release is about a product, a 'background' to that product would be included
- Short biographies of significant staff
- A photo library – all relevant staff, products, head office, manufacturing centres, distribution centres, etc.
- If the press release has been communicated verbally, audio and video clips of the event can be included. A transcript of what was said should also be available.

Furthermore the organization should take advantage of social media disseminating information. As well as the more traditional items listed above, the 'social media newsroom' might include:

- The facility for journalists to add their own comments in blog style to news releases
- In addition to 'stock' pictures that might be suitable for the print media, an online album hosted on a photo-sharing site (Flickr, for example) could feature photos that are 'cool' enough for social media sites
- Videos in a library hosted on YouTube
- Links to facilitate all news releases being saved or shared via social media sites
- Content that is represented by a keyword cloud – allowing visitors to organize the content for their own purposes.

With regard to reputation management, the key decisions are:

1. Is it worthwhile – that is, will the cost outweigh any potential damage?
2. To what extent do we need to monitor the web?
3. In-house or outsource – do we have the resources within the organization, or do we use a specialist company?

Let's consider these issues in turn. Although this chapter (and others) cover in detail the role of the web in buying decisions, there are still markets and industries that are not Internet-dependent. Someone commenting on an obscure blog that they think a certain employee in a local restaurant somewhere in downtown Smallsville is bad at their job is not going to cause that business to close down. The truth of the matter is that no one except the blogger's friends will ever read the comments – and the blogger will already have told them about the restaurant anyway. However, if you are a global entity or you trade in a market that is greatly influenced by the web then ignoring negative comments – whether they are valid or not – could lead to lost sales.

These two extremes can be carried over into the consideration of what depth you go to in monitoring what is being said about you. For the one-off restaurant, simply tracking the use of your trading name using basic software (blog-monitoring tools, for example) will normally be sufficient. Even cheaper is to simply get into the habit of putting your business name into a search engine on a regular basis – if you don't find any adverse comments neither will anyone else. As with other aspects of Internet marketing, the medium's technology can actually come to your aid here. Outside agencies will set up and host reputation management systems that meet your requirements and simply send you the reports – though you will need to facilitate the appropriate action being taken when necessary. A good rule of thumb would be that if your organization is big enough to have a dedicated PR department then its duties should include in-house reputation management. If you outsource your PR operations, go external for reputation management also.

MINI CASE

Threatening more than a SLAPP on the wrist

A weapon used by some US organizations to defend their reputation is the *strategic lawsuit against public participation* (SLAPP). This is intended to censor, intimidate and silence critics by threatening them with a legal action that will be expensive to defend – and so they recant their criticism or abandon their opposition. In reality, no such action will ever take place, but the writer of the critical hotel review or forum complaint is unlikely to know that – or even take the chance that it is not the case. This is, however, a heavy-handed response that is associated with organizations that have something to hide, and it is against the ethos of social media – a result of which being that the 'SLAPPing' company will normally suffer further at the hands of other SM writers. That many states in the US have outlawed SLAPP actions reflects their being something to be rejected by reputable organizations.

A final point worth mentioning is that it is not only your own brand or organization's online reputation that is worth tracking – what people are saying about your competitors' reputations is worth watching, too. It may not be very sporting, but if one of your competitors does something to damage its public standing, if you are on the ball – and creative with your marketing – you might be able to take advantage of their slip.

MINI CASE

Managing away bad reputations on the SERPs

As part of their job, reputation managers will aim to keep websites that have anything negative to say about their clients away from the top of the search engine results pages. They know, however, that it is impossible to close down these sites – some of them may be reputable publications reporting true stories. What the reputation manager does, therefore, is make sure the SERP has plenty of *positive* sites ahead of those with damaging content. Using SEO tactics (see Chapter 6), alternative sites – some of which the client may have influence over – are optimized to appear at the top of the rankings. If none exist then sites with suitable content are developed to serve the purpose. For obvious reasons such search engine management is not made public, but a little time spent searching for famous – or infamous – celebrities can produce some interesting results.

For an example, follow the link on the chapter's web page.

YOU DECIDE

Advise the marketing team at Hill Street Motorist Shop (case study 8) on whether or not they should undertake a strategy of online reputation management – and what might be the consequences of not doing so.

Alternatively, conduct the same exercise for your organization or that of your employer.

9.7 STRATEGIC SOCIAL MEDIA MARKETING

As the commercial Internet developed through the final years of the last century, it was common to hear owners and managers respond to the question of why they had a website by saying *'because everyone else has one.'* Hardly a sound objective, but at least they were going online – even if their websites lacked purpose, and so achieved little. Fast forward a decade or so and once again a spate of 'me-too' online marketing began to appear – this time it was organizations jumping on the social media bandwagon. Sadly few succeeded in accomplishing anything by these ill-judged and poorly considered ventures – with some doing more damage than if they had left this 'latest big thing' alone.

This last section addresses all of the issues that are relevant to strategic social media marketing – effectively asking all the questions to make those strategic decisions.

MINI CASE

Coca-Cola's SMM objectives

Given that it has 61.5 million fans on Facebook (more than any other brand), it came as something of an eye-opener when Coca-Cola's Senior Manager – Marketing Strategy and Insights, Eric Schmidt, announced (in 2013) that, following research, 'We didn't see any statistically significant relationship between our buzz and our short-term sales.'

Social media – naturally – was awash with comments on the statement, many using it to support the theory that SMM was an ineffective medium for generating sales. However, such comments were – in my opinion – erroneous, with many of the commentators referring to a Facebook presence as 'advertising'.

In response to her colleague's comments, Wendy Clark, Senior VP – Integrated Marketing Communications and Capabilities at Coca-Cola, wrote that the research finding was true in isolation but should not obscure the role that social media plays. She said on the company's website:

None of our plans are simply social, or TV, or mobile or experiential. On the contrary, it's the combination of owned, earned, shared and paid media connections – with social playing a crucial role at the heart of our activations – that creates marketplace impact, consumer engagement, brand love and brand value.

In line with the objectives for digital marketing that are presented in Section 1.8, I think that means that Facebook is part of the organization's branding efforts, and not income generation.

Soure: coca-cola.com

DECISION TIME

Objectives

In Section 1.8, potential online objectives are identified as being (1) brand development, (2) income generation, and (3) service – or any combination of these – and they are equally valid for any social media marketing efforts. Within these three strategic online objectives, there are a number of key considerations before determining any strategic social media marketing objectives, namely:

1. **Is it what our customers expect from us?**

    In pure marketing terms, if the answer to this question is 'yes', then the organization should be active in social media. Indeed, if the organization is market-oriented, this question should not need asking – and the subsequent questions asked in this section become superfluous.

2. **Is social media worth the effort?**

    If we engage in SMM, even if its costs might never be recovered in financial terms, what are we trying to *accomplish*? Indeed, as subsequent sections might suggest, perhaps social media is not one on which direct income can be generated, but as Levine *et al.* suggested – with commendable foresight – in 1999, 'engagement in these open free-wheeling exchanges isn't optional. It's a prerequisite to having a future. Silence is fatal.'

3. **Is it right for us?**

    If the nature of your product, brand or organization doesn't generate passion, then the very culture of the organization might disqualify it from participation in SMM.

4. **Does it fit in with our other marketing efforts?**

    Given that this book is about digital marketing, the subject of *offline* strategic marketing is beyond its remit. Nevertheless, it is a frequent failing of online marketing initiatives – including SMM – that they are not in sync with the organization's wider strategic efforts. No marketing effort exists in a vacuum, and like all other elements, to be effective SMM must be part of a larger marketing – and integrated communications – strategy.

5. **What elements of social media are suitable for our objectives?**

    As with other aspects of the organization's marketing (both off- and online), the choice of media is established by the objectives of that marketing. These will determine the characteristics of the type of social media on which you need to have a presence.

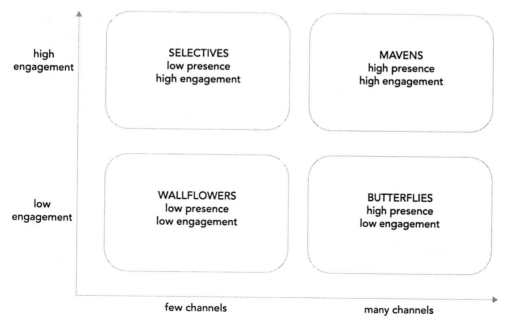

Figure 9.5 Four types of engagement profile
Source: Adapted from Engagementdb, 2009

Management and implementation

As already suggested in this chapter – where contemporary marketing can be controlled by the *marketer*, social media marketing is controlled by the *market* that is the target of the marketing message. In the previous section the point was made that social media marketing is not suitable for every brand, product or organization. The issue of the organization needing to have a culture that suits social media continues into the practice of marketing in social environments where it is advisable – if not essential – that engagement must be embraced by the entire organization and it cannot be the sole province of

> 66
> there has been something of a 'land-grab' for ownership of social media within the various constituents of marketing
> 99

a few social media experts. However, even though the entire organization should buy into the concept, it is important to manage that involvement. In Chapter 2 the issue of who has 'ownership' of the organization's website is addressed – and as social media marketing is accepted as part of strategic marketing the same question is raised for this latest addition to the online marketing mix. For the smaller entity, it is likely that all marketing is managed within one department. However, larger enterprises will have a number of subdivisions within their marketing division, and so there has been something of a 'land-grab' for ownership of social media within the various constituents of marketing.

Whether any SMM undertaken is tactical or strategic, it is certain that any participation takes a lot of work. At the lower end – in an offline small business, for example – it has to be someone's job. Similarly, at strategic level, continuing resources must be budgeted for – effective SMM on the cheap is simply not possible. Addressing the question of whether the organization has the resources to keep up a SMM strategy is essential before any commitment is undertaken. SMM must be considered as an ongoing process, not a campaign that has an end date – as does a TV advertising promotion, for example. Breaking off from a SMM initiative is likely to have a negative impact that is inversely proportional to any objectives it might have been launched with. Furthermore, TV ads can be budgeted in advance – for an effective social media presence financial commitment must go beyond the fiscal year in which it is launched. In Chapter 3 the point is made that website development is not a project that comes to an end, and for SMM the message is accentuated. In that it is always ongoing, social media should be considered as a journey, not a destination.

MINI CASE

Job vacancy: blogging for the leader of the free world

Whilst this vacancy – posted in February 2010 – is to work for the president of the United States, the requirements should be no less for any organization. The vacancy said:

The Social Networks Manager is responsible for maintaining the Democratic Party and Organizing for America accounts on all social networks (such as Facebook, Twitter and MySpace accounts, etc.). The Social Networks Manager works closely with the rest of the New Media department to execute grassroots campaigns to advance the President's agenda for change.

And the required qualifications included:

- Excellent writing and editing skills with strong attention to detail; your writing is strong, sharp, and personable

- Strong organizing and campaigning instincts; you can craft messages that move people to act, and you know what actions will achieve the right impact at the right time
- Strong familiarity with social networks such as Facebook, Twitter, MySpace, etc.
- Ready to work hard; this isn't a 9–5 sort of job
- Ability to work under deadline pressure
- Ability to manage multiple complex projects.

Source: www.barackobama.com

As with all aspects of marketing, effective SMM practice is a result of careful selection of the *right* aspects of the available mix of tools available at a given moment in time.

Note that significant parts of this chapter – particularly the last section – are taken from my book *Social Media Marketing* (Charlesworth, 2014).

GO ONLINE

For some excellent examples of how leading brands use social media strategically, follow the link from the chapter's website.

CHAPTER EXERCISE

Giving justifications for all your decisions, advise the board of the Matthew Humberstone Foundation Hospital (case study 6) on all aspects of social media marketing covered in this chapter. This includes taking a look at the 'dummy' blog that can be found by following the link from the chapter's web page.

Alternatively, conduct the same exercise for your organization or that of your employer.

CHAPTER QUESTIONS

Follow the link from this chapter's web page to a series of multiple-choice, exam-type questions that will test your knowledge and understanding of the various elements of the chapter.

REFERENCES

Anderson, C. (2006) *The Long Tail*. Hyperion Books.

Arndt, J. (1967) *Word of Mouth Advertising: A Review of the Literature*. Advertising Research Foundation.

Baird, C.H. and Parasnis, G. (2011) *From Social Media to Social CRM*. IBM Global Business Services.

BrightLocal (2013) Local consumer review survey. Available on brightlocal.com.

Carroll, D. (2012) *United Breaks Guitars: The Power of One Voice in the Age of Social Media*. Hay House.

Charlesworth, A. (2007) *Key Concepts in e-Commerce*. Palgrave-Macmillan.

Charlesworth, A. (2014) *Social Media Marketing*. Routledge.

Engagementdb (2009) Ranking the top 100 global brands. Available at www.slideshare.net/PingElizabeth/engagementdb-social-media-engagement-study-of- the-top-100-global-brands.

Freedman, L. (2008) *Merchant and Customer Perspectives on Customer Reviews and User-Generated Content*. PowerReviews/the e-tailing Group.

Gay, R., Charlesworth, A. and Esen, R. (2007) *Online Marketing: A Customer-Led Approach*. Oxford University Press.

Godin, S. (2001) *Unleashing the Ideavirus*. Do You Zoom.

Granovetter, M. (1973) The strength of weak ties. *American Journal of Sociology*. Volume 78, number 6, pp. 1360–1380.

Greenberg, D. (2007) The secret strategies behind many 'viral' videos'. Available at http://techcrunch.com/2007/11/22/the-secret-strategies-behind-many-viral-videos.

Kaplan, A.M. and Haenlein, M. (2010) Users of the world, unite! The challenges and opportunities of social media. *Business Horizons*. Volume 53, number 1, pp. 59–68.

Keller Fay Group (2007) WOM marketing. Available on kellerfay.com.

Leetaru, K., Wang, S., Cao, G., Padmanabhan, A. and Shook, E. (2013) Mapping the global Twitter heartbeat: the geography of Twitter. *First Monday* (online journal). Volume 18, number 5/6.

Levine, R., Locke, C., Searls, D. and Weinberger, D. (1999) *The Cluetrain Manifesto: The End of Business as Usual*. Basic Books.

Lin, T.M.Y., Wu, H.-H., Liao C.-W. and Liu, T.-H. (2006) Why are some e-mails forwarded and others not? *Internet Research*. Volume 16, number 1, pp. 81–93.

Luo, X. (2002) Trust production and privacy concerns on the Internet: a framework based on relationship marketing and social exchange theory. *Industrial Marketing Management*. Volume 31, pp. 111–118.

Marketo (2010) The definitive guide to B2B social media. Available on marketo.com.

McConnell, B. and Huba, J. (2007) *Citizen Marketers*. Kaplan.

Meadows-Klue, D. (2008) Falling in love 2.0: relationship marketing for the Facebook generation. *Journal of Direct, Data and Digital Marketing Practice*. Volume 9, number 3, pp. 245–250.

Nelson, M.R. and Otnes, C.C. (2005) Exploring cross-cultural ambivalence: a netnography of intercultural wedding boards. *Journal of Business Research*. Volume 58, number 1, pp. 89–95.

Nielsen, J. (2006) Participation equality: encouraging more users to contribute. Available at www.useit.com/alertbox/participation_inequality.html.

Recommend.ly (2012) Facebook pages usage patterns. Available at blog.recommend.ly/facebook-pages-usage-patterns.

Scott, D.M. (2007) *The New Rules of Marketing and PR*. Wiley.

Tapscott, D. (1996) *The Digital Economy*. McGraw-Hill.

Tapscott, D. and Williams, A.D. (2007) *Wikinonics*. Atlantic Books.

Technorati Media (2011) State of the blogosphere. Available at technorati.com/state-of-the-blogosphere.

Technorati Media (2013) Digital influence report. Available at technoratimedia.com/technorati-medias-2013-digital-influence-report.

Weber, L. (2007) *Marketing to the Social Web*. Wiley.

Weber Shandwick (2012) Buy it, try it, rate it. Available at www.webershandwick.com/uploads/news/files/ReviewsSurveyReportFINAL.pdf.

Wilson, R.F. (2012) Demystifying viral marketing. Available at www.webmarketingtoday.com/articles/viral-deploy/.

Chapter 10

Epilogue

> *The essence of strategy is choosing what not to do.*
>
> *Michael Porter*

This is the shortest chapter of the book, and yet it is – perhaps – the most important. If you fail to read and appreciate this chapter, then you have wasted your time with the nine that went before it.

Sadly, too many organizations do just that. They practise a number of digital functions, but have no digital strategy. Worse still, different departments of organizations practise elements of digital marketing in isolation from other departments that are also practising elements of digital marketing. Furthermore, different marketing departments practise elements of digital marketing without considering the impact on, or of, any offline marketing practised by the organization.

It is also the case that some colleges and universities teach elements of digital marketing as independent modules. Whilst I appreciate the educational practicalities of this, I am uncomfortable with it. Students who do not realize that subjects covered within each chapter of this book are just parts of marketing will never become truly effective in practising them. As I say in my classes, you do not want to call out a breakdown mechanic only for them to stare at your car and say, 'sorry, looks like it's a problem with the engine and I have only trained in repairing brakes.' It's no good having good brakes on a car that won't move because the engine is broken. So, if you are a student who has used this book to study one or some of the elements of it, make sure you ask your lecturer how those elements fit within a wider marketing – and business – perspective.

In some ways then, this chapter is also a paradox of not only what has gone before it – but of the book's subtitle. A *practical approach* suggests that the content is about getting things done at the sharp end of business, whereas *strategy* is about the overall planning of those tactics. OK, so that is a somewhat basic definition of strategy, but there are books with the title *What is Strategy?* – and so I do not intend to debate the issue any further here. Sufficient to say that if you have used this book as part of a Business and/or Marketing programme, then you should be well aware of just what strategy is, and its role in the management of organizations, be they businesses or not-for-profit.

What I want to do in this epilogue is to remind you that *effective* marketing is holistic in nature. The concept of the marketing mix reinforces this, where each element is dependent on the others.

There are, therefore, two aspects of strategic integration to consider – let's consider them in turn.

STRATEGIC DIGITAL MARKETING

I would hope that a marketing student would have come to appreciate this as they worked through the book – indeed, many chapters allude to the subject's relationship with other aspects of digital marketing – but effective digital marketing is holistic in nature. In some instances, one element requires another also to be practised, whilst in other cases one practice negates another.

For example, it is a waste of time committing time and resources (or paying an agency) to develop an effective network advertising campaign if the shopping website customers are driven to has poor usability and a checkout process that would baffle a NASA scientist. Similarly, marketers will always be working to a budget, so do you really need to spend a lot on search engine advertising if your SEO is so good that your site tops the SERP for all of the pertinent keywords in your marketplace? Or switch that round and consider what is the best solution for a new business that is struggling to establish its website with the search engines?

The aforementioned issue of different departments being responsible for different aspects of digital marketing is also an issue – most commonly where social networking is involved. Is, for example, your Facebook presence in sync with the website – or do consumers get a different message about your brand?

THE ROLE OF *DIGITAL* IN MARKETING STRATEGY

This is, obviously, more complex – and realistically is beyond the scope of this book. To ignore it, however, would be a mistake. My reading and experience tell me that it is not yet the norm for *digital* to be considered an integral element of a marketing strategy. I'll go further: it is still the norm for *digital* to be considered to be an 'add-on' to most marketing strategies.

It is my belief – and I was a marketer before I was a *digital* marketer – that *digital* is now an integral part of the marketing mix. As with all aspects of that concept, not all elements are appropriate to every organization, brand or product in every situation – that is the essence of the marketing mix. However, *digital* should be there on the table along with the rest of the elements. Indeed, perhaps there is a *digital* 4Ps: *digital* product, *digital* promotion, *digital* place and *digital* price – however, I would argue that this suggests an add-on to the traditional 4Ps, and that this is wrong. *Digital* is a part of marketing, not something to be tagged on to it. For example, promotion must include consideration of both off- and online advertising. And yet, I still read examples of current books on marketing strategy and/or planning where *digital* is just that – an additional chapter or section of a chapter added to the conventional elements of marketing. Wake up marketers: *digital* is not only here to stay – it is replacing *some* of the practices deemed sacrosanct less than a decade ago, and it is doing them in a more effective and efficient way. In some circumstances, *digital* marketing *is* marketing – and it is only just getting started.

Index

Above the fold, 93, 240
Affiliate Programmes, 258
After-sales services, 33, 60, 175
Agency advertising, 252
AIDA, 23–5, 102, 295
Amazon, 15, 43, 53, 87, 103, 149, 164, 166, 258, 260, 269
American Life Project, 10, 29, 30, 91
Anderson, Chris, 117, 137, 303
Apple Computer Human Interface Group, 123
Application service provider (ASP), 52
App, 31, 139, 217, 271
Argos, 138
ARPANet (Advanced Research Projects Agency Network), 2
Aaronson, Jack, 270
AT&T, 3

B2B (B to B), 14, 18, 169; Buying cycle, 173; Buying practices, 170; Marketplace, 180; Website, 174–6
B2C (B to C), 132
Bacon, Sir Francis, 7
Bank of America, 44
Banner ads, 226; Sizes and types, 238
Banner fatigue, 231
BBC, 4, 10
Bebo, 306
Beckham, David, 205
Berners-Lee, Sir Tim, 2, 80
Bezos, Jeff, 149
Blair Witch Project, 298
Blogger.com, 310

Blogs / blogging, 216, 232, 292, 303, 310–14, 325
Bly, Bob, 115, 242
Bond, James, 200, 254
Bowen, David, 99, 292
Brand development, 32, 59, 133, 258
Bricks and clicks, 133, 197
Burger King, 315
Buying cycle, 23–4, 102, 112, 142–3, 246, 262

Call to action, 102, 110, 146, 177–9, 239–41, 304
CAN-SPAM Act, the, 275
Carlton, John, 115
Cascading style sheets (CSS), 77, 206
Chat rooms, 210, 232
Checkout process / facility, 150–3
Children's Online Privacy Protection Act (COPPA), 38
Chrome, 103
Citizen marketers, 298
Click fraud, 228–9
Click stream, 60
Clicks and mortar, 34
Clickthrough rate, 103, 209, 212, 245, 247, 252, 255, 260, 279–81, 308
CNBC, 254
CNN, 319
Coca Cola, 75, 177, 330
Cohen, Jared, 3
Community website, 232
Comparison shopping engines, 162–5, 286

comScore, 11, 30, 143, 228
Consumer generated content, 297–304
Consumer Protection (Distance Selling)
    Regulations, the (2000), 38
Conversion rates, 60, 249, 257
CPM (cost per thousand impressions),
    227, 243, 252
Cross selling, 60, 145–6
Customer Relationship management
    (CRM), 266–8
Cutts, Matt, 190
Cyberbashing, 307, 323

Data Protection Act, the (1998), 37
Decision making unit (DMU), 112, 171
Dell, 310
Department for Business, Enterprise and
    Regulatory Reform (BERR), 67
Department for Trade and Industry, 67
Dictionary.com, 44
Digg, 214
Digital divide, the, 12, 21
Direct Line, 136
Directories, 218–19
Disney, 112
Display ads, 226–8, 238
Domain names, 41–51
Download time, 90, 247
D'Souza, Sean, 118

eBay, 34, 75, 137, 139, 149, 153, 156, 159,
    164–7, 193
Eisenberg, Bryan, 23, 102
Eisenberg, Jeffrey, 102
Elliance, 196, 201
Email, 273–83
Email Experience Council, the, 275
e-Marketplaces, 162–5, 180–3
e-Metrics, 57–66
Enquiro, 171
EU Directive on Privacy and Electronic
    Communications, the, 275
ExactTarget, 273
Expedia, 163
Experian, 273

Facebook, 6, 8, 14, 26, 36, 43, 68, 75, 106,
    147, 164, 189, 211, 217, 231–2, 252,
    273, 305–33
Firefox, 77, 103
Flash, 77, 87, 89, 91–2, 95, 206, 241
Fleming, Ian, 254
Flickr, 298, 325, 327
Fonts, 96
Forrester Research, 6, 14, 26, 90, 133,
    143, 156,
Forums, 124, 181, 213, 216, 232, 285,
    300, 307, 323
Four Seasons Hotels and Resorts, 86
Fox Sports, 254
Fulfilment, 154–62

Gobbledygook manifesto, the, 112
Godin, Seth, 213, 268, 314–15
Goldman, Aaron, 191, 228
Google, 46, 54, 63, 67, 69, 76, 90, 93, 101,
    104, 147, 164, 189–96, 202, 204, 207,
    226–8, 243–63, 271
Google+, 211, 306, 310
Google AdSense, 224, 253–7
Google AdWords, 243, 256, 257
Google Display Network, 226, 256
Google Search Network, 257
Gore, Al, 5
GoTo.com, 242
Granovetter, Mark, 294–5
Green Bay Packers, 191
Gross, Bill, 242–3

Hampel, Alvin, 89, 241–2
Hedonic browsing, 142
Hewlett Packard, 45
Hits, 59
Hotmail, 47, 71, 233, 314, 316
Hyperlinks – see 'links'

Infographics, 121
Information Superhighway, 5
In–game advertising, 243
In–site search, 100–1, 146–7
Integrated retailing, 136

Interactive Advertising Bureau, the, 30
Internet Advertising Bureau (IAB), 223, 227, 256, 270
Internet Corporation for Assigned Names and Numbers (ICANN), 44
Internet Protocol (IP) address, 279
Internet service provider (ISP), 4, 52, 103, 283
IPhone, 92, 241, 271

Jackson, Samuel L., 298
Jarvis, Jeff, 310
Jurvetson, Steve, 314

Kelkoo, 163
Keller Fay Group, the, 300
Key Concepts in e-Commerce, 59, 104, 150, 218, 243, 297
Keynote, 67
Key performance indicator (KPI), 59, 280
Keyword, 198–202
Kranz, Jonathan, 107
Krugg, Steve, 90

Landing pages, 247, 260, 261–4, 278
Lead generation, 60, 82, 133, 177–9, 216, 226
Lewis, St Elmo, 23
Linkedin, 68, 305, 310
Linking strategy, 213–14
Links / linking, 80–1, 95, 102, 117, 143, 206–17, 243, 288–9, 321–2
Loans.com, 44
Logistics, 154–81
Long Tail, the, 117, 137, 303

Mailing list, 276–7, 281–3
Market research, 66–72, 302
Marketing Evolution, 15
MarketingProfs, 55, 107
MarketingSherpa, 282
Marx, Groucho, 106
McGovern, Gerry, 17, 26, 32, 33, 55, 79, 82, 83, 88, 99, 100, 108, 124, 215

Meerman Scott, David, 55, 109, 112, 321, 325
Message boards, 232
Microsoft, 9, 47, 50, 53, 83
Miniwatts Marketing Group, 10, 11
Mintel, 67
Mobile marketing, 31
Mosaic, 3
MSN Live, 243
MySpace, 305, 306, 333

Netnography, 70
Netscape, 77, 103
Network advertising, 252–7
Newgistics, 160
Newsletters, 233, 288–9
Niche markets, 135, 197, 200
Nielsen Company, the, 133
Nielsen, Jacob, 89, 102, 115, 303, 310
Nielsen/NetRatings, 231
Nielsen Norman Group, 97
Nike, 43, 47, 112, 241, 245
Nokia, 177
Nottingham Forest, 113

O2, 45
Online auctions, 183–6
Online tendering, 183–6
Opodo, 51
Opt-in/out, 276
Orvis, 161
Oxfam, 20

PayPal, 137, 152, 159
Pay Per Call, 227
Pay Per Click (PPC), 68, 165, 227, 243–4, 253, 323
Personalization, 268–72
Persuasion architecture, 178
PEW Internet, 11
Phones4U, 51
Podcasts, 21, 123, 216, 232, 292
Portal, 163, 180, 231, 232, 236, 271
Product life cycle, 303, 316
Product pages, 145

PRWeb, 322
Pure–play, 51, 79, 113, 133, 136, 141, 197

QR codes, 140

Ralph Lauren, 262
Rappa's online trading business models, 35, 36
Rate card, advertising, 223, 226
Reference.com, 44
Re-marketing, 151
Reputation management, 320–9

Safari, 103
Sales funnel, 23, 25, 103, 146–7, 178, 263, 274
Save the Children, 20
Schmidt, Eric, 3, 195, 330
Search engine marketing (SEM), 188–9, 192, 198, 242
Search engine optimization (SEO), 188–214
Search engine results page (SERP), 61, 103, 189, 196, 226, 244, 329
Segmentation, 224, 225
Shell, 324–5
Shipping, 154–6
Showrooming, 30
Snakes on a Plane, 298
Social media, 33, 113, 189, 231; Definition, 292; Marketing, 291–333
Social networks, 304–9
Society for New Communications Research, 322
Spam, 194, 203, 210–14, 242, 275–9, 282, 283
Stakeholders, 20
Stanford University; Persuasive Technology Lab's, 106–7
Star Trek, 298
Stock control, 154, 161
Strategic lawsuit against public participation (SLAPP), 328.
Strong, E K, 23

Sunday Times Magazine, 97
SurveyMonkey, 72

Targeting, ads, 224
Task Performance Indicators, 61
Technorati, 26, 298, 307, 310, 311
Tesco, 87, 105, 271
Testimonials, 118, 122, 301
Testing, 103–5, 278–80
Thesaurus.com, 44
Third-party websites, 165–6
TNS, 15
Travelocity, 163
TRU, 15
Twitter, 43, 68, 273, 303, 305, 307, 310, 316, 318

United Airlines, 299
URL (Uniform Resource Locator), 4, 19, 45, 52, 61, 80, 94, 153, 205, 244
User generated content (UGC), 68, 292, 297

Viral marketing, 314–9
Virtual worlds, 232
Wall Street Journal, the, 254

Wanamaker, John, 224–5
Website; Analytics, 57–65; Content, 110, 116, 118, 119, 123, 178; Copy, 115, 176, 241; Global, 126; History, 209; Hosting, 52–4; Management, 79–80; Metrics, 63, 227; Responsive design, 94; Source code, 63, 77, 203, 204
Web 2.0, 292–3
Weber, Larry, 304, 315
Whitelist, 283
Widgets, 123
Wikipedia, 303
Wilson, Dr R F, 87, 314
Wired magazine, 3

Yahoo!, 164, 191, 202, 231, 243, 252, 254
YouTube, 5, 59, 75, 121, 232–3, 299, 305–7, 317, 319

CPSIA information can be obtained
at www.ICGtesting.com
Printed in the USA
FFOW02n1925250117
31717FF

9 780415 834834